Reformed
Theology
in America

Reformed Theology in America

A History of Its
Modern Development

Edited by
David F. Wells

Baker Books

A Division of Baker Book House Co.
Grand Rapids, Michigan 49516

Published by Baker Books
a division of Baker Book House Company
P.O. Box 6287, Grand Rapids, MI 49516-6287

Second printing, April 1998

The material in this volume originally comprised part of a book titled *Reformed Theology in America: A History of Its Modern Development*, copyright 1985 by Wm. B. Eerdmans Publishing Company.

The material in this volume was also previously published in three volumes titled *The Princeton Theology: Reformed Theology in America*, *Dutch Reformed Theology: Reformed Theology in America*, and *Southern Reformed Theology: Reformed Theology in America*, copyright 1989 by Baker Book House Company.

Printed in the United States of America

ISBN: 0-8010-2148-0

For information about academic books, resources for Christian leaders, and all new releases available from Baker Book House, visit our web site:
http://www.bakerbooks.com

To Roger Nicole
A man of God

CONTENTS

CONTRIBUTORS

James D. Bratt is assistant professor of history, Calvin College, and author of *Dutch Calvinism in Modern America: A History of a Conservative Subculture* (Grand Rapids: Eerdmans, 1984).

W. Andrew Hoffecker, professor of religion at Grove City College has penned *Piety and the Princeton Theologians* (Phillipsburg, NJ: Presbyterian and Reformed, 1981) and coedited (with Gary Scott Smith) *Building a Christian World View,* 2 vols. (Phillipsburg, NJ: Presbyterian and Reformed, 1986–1988).

Douglas Floyd Kelly, former editor of the *Journal of Christian Reconstruction,* ministered at the First Presbyterian Church, Dillon, SC, and the First Presbyterian Church, Raeford, NC. Currently he is associate professor of systematic theology, Reformed Theological Seminary, and cotranslator and coeditor of *The Westminster Confession of Faith: A New Edition* (Greenwood, SC: Attic, 1979)

George M. Marsden, professor of the history of Christianity in America at The Divinity School, Duke University, is the author of *Reforming Fundamentalism: Fuller Seminary and the New Evangelicalism* (Grand Rapids: Eerdmans, 1987), *Fundamentalism and American Culture* (New York: Oxford University Press, 1980), and *The Evangelical Mind and the New School Presbyterian Experience* (New Haven: Yale University Press, 1970); coauthor (with Mark Noll and Nathan Hatch) of *The Search for Christian America* (Westchester, IL: Crossway, 1983); and editor of *Evangelicalism and Modern America* (Grand Rapids: Eerdmans, 1984).

C. T. McIntire, associate professor of history, Trinity College, University of Toronto, has edited *God, History, and Historians* (New York: Oxford University Press, 1977), *Herbert Butterfield: Writings on Christianity and History* (New York: Oxford University Press, 1979), and *History and Historical Understanding* (Grand Rapids: Eerdmans, 1984). He also is the author of *England Against the Papacy, 1858–1861* (Cambridge: Cambridge University Press, 1983).

Mark A. Noll, professor of history at Wheaton College, has coauthored (with George Marsden and Nathan Hatch) *The Search for Christian America* (Westchester, IL: Crossway, 1983), and has edited *The Princeton Theology, 1812–1921: Scripture, Science, and Theological Method from Alexander to Warfield* (Grand Rapids: Baker, 1983), *The Bible in America* (New York: Oxford University Press, 1982), and *Eerdmans' Handbook to Christianity in America* (Grand Rapids: Eerdmans, 1983).

W. Stanford Reid is professor emeritus of history, University of Guelph (Guelph, Ontario), formerly lecturer and professor of history at McGill University (Montreal, Quebec, 1941–1965), and founder and chairperson of the Department of History, University of Guelph, 1965–1970. He is the author of *The Church of Scotland in Lower Canada: Its Struggle for Establishment* (Toronto: Thorn, 1936), *Skipper from Leith: The Life of Robert Barton of Over Barnton* (Philadelphia: University of Pennsylvania Press, 1964), *Christianity and Scholarship* (Nutley, NJ: Presbyterian and Reformed, 1966), and *Trumpeter of God: A Biography of John Knox* (New York: Charles Scribner's Sons, 1974; Grand Rapids: Baker, 1980).

Wesley A. Roberts, formerly professor of church history at Gordon-Conwell Theological Seminary, is now pastor of Peoples Baptist Church of Boston.

Morton Smith has been stated clerk of the General Assembly of the Presbyterian Church in America from 1973 to the present. Formerly professor of systematic theology at Reformed Theological Seminary (Jackson, MS), he is now a faculty member at Greenville (NC) Seminary. He is the author of *Studies in Southern Presbyterian Theology* (Amsterdam: Kampen, 1962) and *How Is the Gold Become Dim* (Jackson, MS: Continuing Presbyterian Church, 1973).

David F. Wells, Andrew Mutch Professor of Historical and Systematic Theology at Gordon-Conwell Theological Seminary, has authored *Revolution in Rome* (London: Tyndale, 1973), *The Search for Salvation* (Downers Grove, IL: InterVarsity, 1978), *The Prophetic Theology of George Tyrrell* (Chico, CA: Scholars Press, 1981), *The Person of Christ: A Biblical and Historical Analysis of the Incarnation* (Westchester, IL: Crossway, 1984), *God the Evangelist: How the Holy Spirit Works to Bring Men and Women to Faith* (Grand Rapids: Eerdmans, 1987), and *Turning to God: Biblical Conversion in the Modern World* (Grand Rapids: Baker, 1989).

Luder G. Whitlock, Jr., is president of Reformed Theological Seminary (Jackson, MS) and formerly its associate professor of Christian missions.

Henry Zwaanstra is professor of historical theology at Calvin Theological Seminary and the author of *Reformed Thought and Experience in a New World: A Study of the Christian Reformed Church and Its American Environment, 1890–1918* (Kampen: J. H. Kok B.V., 1973).

PREFACE

One of the quirks of American theology is that it is frequently unaware of being American. German theology, of course, is the result of the ponderous and enormously thorough German academic machinery from which it has emerged. British theology, with its keen interest in historical accuracy, fair play, and civility, obviously reflects the virtues of the middle- and upper-middle classes in which it is largely nurtured. South American theology makes no bones about being South American. It wears its heart on its sleeve. North of the border, however, this is not so. Here, we simply do theology!

If that were really true, then we should expect to find in the various expressions of Reformed theology a striking conformity, for they are all disciplined by the Reformation principles of *sola Scriptura, sola gratia, in solo Christo,* and *sola fide.* What we actually encounter is a most astonishing variety of expression, despite the common ownership of these principles. Immigrants who have come to these shores, nurturing within themselves the Reformed faith on which they were reared, did not melt into the national pot as they were supposed to. Ethnic interests, in fact, were often preserved through language and custom even as a diffuse sense of what it meant to be American also grew in importance. And, along the way, Reformed theologies have struck up alliances with the habits of mind that have prevailed in this or that age as well as being shaped by the towering figures who, from time to time, have arisen above the tradition and given it new cogency, new direction, and sometimes new horizons. American Reformed theology, as a result, is a complex tradition made up of strands and tributaries that are not only diverse but also sometimes quite oblivious to one another.

In 1985, *Reformed Theology in America: A History of Its Modern Development* appeared. To those with eyes to see, it was a thinly disguised festschrift for Roger Nicole, who was celebrating his seventieth birthday that year. But it was also a serious accounting of the Reformed tradition in all of its diversity. I chose what I saw to be the five major streams of Reformed thought: the Princeton theology, the Westminster school, the Dutch schools, the Southern tradition, and neoorthodoxy. Within each of these sections I followed the same pattern of providing readers with a general essay on the school and essays on its two most prominent theologians.

The success that attended the publication of this study was nowhere better attested than in the dozens of letters I received, as well as in the reviews that were published, which complained about this or that group which had been excluded from consideration! All of a sudden I was beset with the knowledge of numerous groups, streams, traditions, and movements that would have liked to have been recognized and felt a little aggrieved that I had not seen fit to include them! It was then that I knew that I had to seek a new publisher for this work once the Eerdmans edition had run its course.

In 1989, Baker Book House proved willing to do this. They divided the original study into three smaller books, representing the sections originally published as the Princeton theology, the Dutch schools, and the Southern tradition (two essays from the Westminster section on Machen and Van Til were included with Princeton theology and Dutch schools, respectively). Each volume included an introduction by George Marsden and a bibliography. James Bratt (the Dutch schools), William Yount (the Southern tradition), and Mark Noll are to be commended for their excellent work. In 1997, due to continuing interest in these studies, Baker reissued the three volumes in a single tome.

This study will be of particular interest to those who identify with these traditions. I hope, however, that in addition to this anticipated readership, there will be many others who look with fresh interest on this work. Those who care about the church, who treat their faith with seriousness, and who long that God's greatness, his sufficiency, and his glory would be more widely owned and celebrated, can only watch the current developments in the evangelical world with growing disquiet. Evangelical faith is showing too many signs of having become secularized, of fragmenting, of regressing to a stage of immaturity that surely raises the question of how long it can survive as recognizably evangelical in the midst of the furnace of modernity. In the Reformation traditions there is a strength, a virility, a power of correction that needs to be heard again in today's evangelical world, and it is my prayer that in some small way this volume may contribute to that end.

D.F.W.

INTRODUCTION: REFORMED AND AMERICAN

GEORGE M. MARSDEN

WHAT sense does it make in late twentieth-century America to talk about being "Reformed"? For most Americans the word conveys no clear meaning. Very few would think of it as a religious designation at all, and most of those would think it referred to Judaism. Even if, as in the present work, we limit the audience to those who have some notion of "Reformed theology," we are left with the problem that even among such a select group, "Reformed" has numerous differing connotations. In the United States alone there are about a dozen Reformed denominations and perhaps another half-dozen with a Reformed heritage. Within each of the Reformed denominations varieties of meanings are given to being "Reformed." These may reflect European traditions, such as Scottish or Dutch, or continental neoorthodox, as well as a variety of American developments. Each such type includes differing subtypes. For instance, within the Reformed Church in America alone, ten distinct approaches to the Reformed faith have been identified.[1] Differences across denominational lines may be sharper. A strictly confessional member of the Reformed Presbyterian Church in North America (Covenanters) might be most unhappy with the preaching at Robert Schuller's Crystal Cathedral. A fundamentalist Bible Presbyterian would refuse fellowship with almost any member of the United Church of Christ. And within most of the larger Reformed denominations, conservatives and progressives are locked in intense struggles over the true meaning of the faith.

A major purpose of this essay is to cut through the bewildering confusion of the many meanings of "Reformed" by reducing the categories to the three major Reformed emphases that have flourished in the American cultural setting. Not every Reformed heritage can be subsumed under these categories and the categories are ideal types or models rather than fully nuanced representations of the growth of each type. Nonetheless, these are the major subgroups that have been prominent among the Reformed throughout American history. So if we understand some-

1

thing of these three developments and emphases we can gain a fairly good picture of the main varieties of being "Reformed" in the American cultural setting.

Perhaps an illustration from my own experience can make clear the characters of the differences among these major American Reformed traditions. Most of my life I have lived in one or the other of two communities that placed great merit on being Reformed. The central meaning of "Reformed," however, has differed greatly in these two communions. The Orthodox Presbyterians, among whom I was reared, meant by "Reformed" strict adherence to Christian doctrine as contained in the infallible Scriptures and defined by the standards of the Westminster Assembly. Only Christians whose creeds were fully compatible with Westminster's and who viewed subscription to them as paramount were fully within the pale. Other factors were important to Christian life, especially a proper emphasis on the law of God as the central organizing principle in the Westminster formulations. But the operative test for "Reformed" was, with this important practical proviso, always doctrinal.

In the other community in which I have spent many years, the progressive wing of the conservative Christian Reformed Church, being "Reformed" is also taken seriously, but with very different meaning. There, a "Reformed" Christian is one who has a certain view of the relationship of Christianity to culture. She or he must affirm the lordship of Christ over all reality, see Christian principles as applicable to all areas of life, and view every calling as sacred. Although subscription to the authority of the Bible and classic Reformed creeds is significant in this community, the stronger operative test for admission is support for separate Christian schools at all levels (except, oddly, the graduate university), where the "Reformed" world-and-life view can be exemplified and taught.

I have also spent some time at institutions of mainstream American evangelicalism, such as Trinity Evangelical Divinity School and Fuller Theological Seminary, where one finds still another meaning to being "Reformed." In this context being "Reformed" must be understood in the framework of being "evangelical." "Evangelical" is a word with a more elusive meaning than "Reformed." Basically it refers to anyone who promotes proclamation of the gospel of salvation through the atoning work of Christ and has a traditional high view of Scripture alone as authority. Evangelicalism is thus much larger than just the Reformed tradition. Within American evangelicalism, however, there is an important subgroup that might be called "card-carrying" evangelicals.[2] These are persons who think of themselves primarily as "evangelicals" and who, as such, identify at least as much with evangelicalism as a movement as with their own formal denomination. Billy Graham, *Christianity*

Today, Eternity, Inter-Varsity Christian Fellowship, Wheaton College and its imitators, and seminaries such as Trinity, Fuller, and Gordon-Conwell have been prototypes of this influential interdenominational evangelicalism.

In this evangelical fellowship the dominant theological tradition is Reformed. It is by no means, however, the only tradition. One trait of this type of being "Reformed," unlike the other two, is that it is tolerant of diversity to the point of keeping close fellowship with persons of other traditions. The operative tests for fellowship among the Reformed in such communities are those of the broader American evangelical-pietist tradition—a certain style of emphasis on evangelism, personal devotions, Methodist mores, and openness in expressing one's evangelical commitment. To be "Reformed" in this setting means to find in Reformed theology the most biblical and healthiest expression of evangelical piety.

The differing emphases of these three communities suggest that in America there are at least three major meanings to being "Reformed." There are, of course, also a number of other Reformed traditions and styles in America. These include the southern, ethnically and racially defined groups, smaller denominations, progressive Reformed in mainline denominations, and some neoorthodox. Nonetheless, the three we have begun with suggest classically distinct types of emphasis that give us some working categories. Many of the developments of America's Reformed groups can be understood as variations on these typical themes.

For convenience' sake, we shall designate these three types as doctrinalist, culturalist, and pietist.[3] In doing so, it is important to remark again that the terminology refers to "ideal types" or descriptive models emphasizing one dominant trait. In reality all three groups typically embody the traits dominant among the other two. Thus a "pietist" is not typically a person who is lax in doctrine or lacking in cultural concern. Similarly, to call people doctrinalists or culturalists does not imply lack of the other two traits.

The Puritan Stock

The oldest major Reformed community in America was the Puritan, which combined strong elements of each of these emphases. Stress on strict Calvinism helped distinguish these early American settlers from their Arminian Anglican opponents. And Reformed orthodoxy was retained in most New England pulpits for at least a century and a half, to the time of the Revolution.[4] Puritans were also characterized by intense piety, often keeping close records of their spiritual health. Moreover, New England's Puritans were America's most successful Reformed culture builders. Virtually free from outside control during their formative first half-century, they built the closest thing humanly possible to their conception of a biblical kingdom. This impressive effort had a lasting impact on the ideals of American civilization. It is ironic that "Reformed" has so little meaning in America today when in fact the culture has been so shaped by that heritage.

The lasting culture-shaping impact of seventeenth-century Puritanism is rivaled by the long-term influence of its eighteenth-century style of piety, epitomized by the Great Awakening. The eighteenth century was generally an era of widespread resurgent pietism, emphasizing personal commitment to the Savior more than Christian culture building. The Great Awakening in New England was part of a wider Protestant pietist awakening that had begun in Germany and spread to most of the Protestant world. In England its largest manifestation was in Methodism. In America it appeared first primarily as pietist revivalism in Reformed churches.

At the height of the first surge of the Great Awakening in America, around 1740, the classic patterns of American Reformed divisions began to emerge. By this time the other major Reformed group, the Scotch-Irish and Scottish Presbyterian, was on the scene. The often changing relations of the Scottish churches to the state, and the sometimes troubled colonial experiences of the Scotch-Irish in the north of Ireland, fostered among Presbyterians in America varieties of views, or perhaps an ambivalence, concerning culture shaping. They inherited the Calvinist impulse to establish a Christian commonwealth; but they also had enough experience of religious oppression to be suspicious of religious establishments, especially when they were living, as in America, under British rule. The Christian commonwealth would be built by persuasion and education.[5]

The symbol of Presbyterian distinctiveness and unity was thus not a social-political program (except that they were militantly anti-British during the Revolution) but doctrinal orthodoxy. Strict confessionalism was a major trait of the largest party of Scotch-Irish and Scottish Presbyterians from their first appearance in the colonies. Presbyterianism in America, however, was from the outset fed by some other streams, not of Scottish but of English origin. English Presbyterianism itself had become tolerant of doctrinal diversity by the early eighteenth century. More importantly, New England Puritans, especially those in Connecticut, viewed themselves as close allies of Presbyterianism in the Middle Colonies and in the early eighteenth century were providing the newly formed (ca. 1706) Presbyterian Church with personnel and leaders. By the time of the Great Awakening, the New England party was closely linked with the more pietistic revivalist group of the Presbyterians. In

1741 this revivalist "New Side" group split from the antirevivalist Scotch-Irish or Scottish "Old Side."

Remarkably, these two Presbyterian "sides" reunited in 1758, thus suggesting that pietist revivalism and doctrinalist confessionalism were compatible. But the tension between these two emphases repeatedly reemerged. The classic instance was in the Old School/New School schism of 1837-38, in many ways a repetition of the Old Side/New Side conflict. The Old School was clearly the stronghold of Scotch-Irish and Scottish elements and found its unity in strict confessionalism. The New School, on the other hand, represented an alliance of more strongly pietist or prorevivalist Presbyterians with New England Congregationalists.

The Growth of Reformed Branches

By this time, however, a number of other issues surrounded this renewed confrontation between confessionalist and pietist axes. The New School was the more typically American of the two groups, its distinctive characteristics reflecting the tendencies of the ethos of the dominant American evangelicalism. This meant that they were more tolerant of theological innovation and variety than had been their predecessors in the seventeenth- and eighteenth-century American Reformed camps. This doctrinal latitude, however, was not a liberalism that involved intentional concessions to secularism (as in later modernism). Rather, it was an outgrowth of pietist zeal for revivalism. In politically liberal America, such zeal translated into some mildly anti-Calvinist (or semi-Pelagian) doctrines emphasizing an unaided human ability voluntarily to accept the revivalists' gospel message with its culminating summons of "choose ye this day." Such doctrinal innovations were held more closely in check by the New School Presbyterians than by their revivalist Congregationalist allies, such as Charles G. Finney. Moreover, they propounded these innovations in the name of greater faithfulness to Scripture alone, as opposed to what some saw as an unhealthly traditionalism of the Old School.

Openness to practical innovation also characterized the New School pietist strand of the heritage. Finney's "New Measures" for promoting revival in the manner of the high-pressure salesman were only the most prominent examples of evangelicalism's openness to departures from tradition. The spread of gospel music perhaps best exemplified the new evangelical style. Especially notable was a new emphasis on personal experience. Controversial also among the Presbyterians was the New School enthusiasm for working through ecclesiastically independent societies (what are now called parachurch agencies) for missions, evangelism, publication, education, and social reform.

This latter issue of social reform was creating a new source of controversy concerning what it meant to be "Reformed," a debate over what we are calling its culturalist heritage. Prior to the nineteenth century, questions concerning social reform had not been conspicuous, divisive issues. Until that time almost all the Reformed groups seem to have been working on the basis of a vaguely formulated, but deeply entrenched, tradition that, ideally, the religion of a nation should be exclusively Reformed. So they assumed that being Reformed accordingly involved transforming the moral ethos and legal system of a people so that it should comport with God's law. The Puritans, as we have seen, worked these principles out most fully in practice. By the early nineteenth century, however, these Reformed principles had to be translated to fit a pluralistic and democratic situation. The question therefore became that of how much emphasis the Reformed Churches should put on shaping the legal structures of a society they did not otherwise control. Was it not the case that the true mission of the church was to proclaim a pure gospel and be a model moral subcommunity within the larger community, leavening it rather than attempting to legislate morality for all?

Finding answers to these questions was complicated by the fact that sometimes the resolution to moral issues could have as much to do with where one stood politically as it did what theological principles one held. Thus, whereas regarding Sabbath observance most nineteenth-century Reformed groups could unite in supporting legislation, on the issue of slavery they were sharply divided. Moreover, opinions on the slavery issue varied strikingly with geography. In the deep South, Reformed people were adamantly opposed to any interference with the practice of black slavery and emphasized aspects of the tradition that favored confining the activities of the church to strictly "spiritual" issues. In New England, by contrast, Reformed Christians often took the lead in insisting that the churches should unrelentingly urge the state to enact immediate emancipation. In the upper South and the lower North, opinions were more varied and often more nuanced. New School Presbyterian leaders, having New England connections, were typically moderate antislavery types, while the Old School sided with the theologically conservative South in wanting to sidestep this and other social reform issues.

"Old School" and "New School" outlooks had thus emerged as the two leading American patterns of being Reformed. The Old School was most characteristically doctrinalist, while the more innovative New School combined pietist revivalism with a culturalist emphasis, inherited from the Puritans, looking for a Christianization of American life. These divisions were not confined to Presbyterians, although they took their clearest shape among them. A number of smaller denominations, including some Baptists, were strictly Reformed doctrinalist groups. Other groups, among whom were some Baptists, the Reformed Church in America, and especially the majority of New England's Congregationalists, were clearly in the New School camp and part of the Reformed wing of the formidable American evangelical coalition that stressed pietism and culturalism. Through the Civil War era, these two schools of Reformed were not irreconcilable, especially once the slavery issue was removed. Most notably, after the war, in 1869 the New School and Old School Presbyterians in the North reunited.

The South, on the other hand, remained separate, holding on to its predominantly Old School tradition and urging the church to stay out of politics. Ironically this apolitical stance of the southern church was deeply mixed with defense of the southern way of life. Accordingly, during the next century the Old School doctrinalism of the Southern Presbyterians was associated with (at least local) cultural influence. In the North, on the other hand, confessionalism lost much of its social base and became more and more associated with a remnant mentality.

The New School heritage, on the other hand, emerged by the end of the century as the stronger of the two traditions in the North. The New School, however, was a combination of two emphases, pietist and culturalist, and these were separable. The divorce between them occurred under the pressures associated with the rapid modernization and secularization of American life between 1870 and 1930. Industrialization, urbanization, immigration, and pluralization undermined the social basis for the old evangelical (and often Reformed) religious quasi-establishment. Moreover, liberal democratic ideology, emphasizing human freedom, ability, and essential goodness, undermined the distinctly Calvinist doctrines. Even more basically, the new naturalistic science and history of the day challenged the authority of the Bible.

Broadly considered, evangelical Christians who responded to these crises moved in one of two directions. One group adjusted to modern times by toning down the supernaturalistic aspects of the gospel and stressing rather those parts of the Christian message that could be realized by developing natural (although God-given) human individual or cultural potentials. On the other side, conservatives reemphasized the fundamentals of the faith, which stressed God's supernatural interventions into history. Thus in the Reformed communities, as in many other areas of American life, a new division was superimposed on existing patterns.

The modernist accommodations to prevailing ideas and ideals fit least well with doctrinalist emphases and best with culturalist. Such theological liberalism was in principle compatible with some pietist emphases (as in a romantic religion of the heart), but in the long run piety proved difficult to sustain from generation to generation without a strong sense of radical divine intervention.

In the New School traditions (including Presbyterian, Congregationalist, Reformed Church in America, Baptist, and other heirs of the nineteenth-century evangelical mainstream), where doctrinalism was not especially strong, the new liberalism flourished, at least among some of the denominational leadership. It grew first, in the late Victorian era, as a version of evangelical romantic piety. In the progressive era, following the turn of the century, it also blossomed as part of the theological basis for the social gospel movement. By this time liberal Protestantism was moving away from crucial parts of traditional evangelical doctrine, repudiating emphases on personal salvation through trust in Christ's work of substitutionary atonement and rejecting the infallibility and reliability of Scripture. These liberal notions alarmed some of the heirs to revivalist pietism. Ecclesiastical warfare broke out and eventually brought a long series of splits between the two camps. Since the social gospel was associated with the modernist tendencies, the "fundamentalist" opponents tended to reject all "social gospels," or culturalist emphases. Such rejections, however, were seldom consistently sustained. New School revivalists also had a heritage of aspiring to Christianize America on a voluntary basis. Thus even when, especially after about 1920, fundamentalists decried the social gospel, they typically still endorsed a politically conservative culturalism that involved efforts to return America to nineteenth-century evangelical standards, as was seen in the anti-evolution and prohibition movements.

The supernaturalist or fundamentalist party among the Reformed included major elements of Old School or doctrinalist heritage as well as the successors to New School evangelicalism. The Old School party, centered first at Princeton Theological Seminary and after 1929 at Westminster Theological Seminary, provided intellectual foundations for defending the traditional faith. The common enemy, modernism, brought these strict confessionalists into close alliance with Reformed people of more New School or pietist-revivalist heritage for a time. Thus by the early 1930s the strictly confessionalist Presbyterians who followed New Testament scholar and apologist J. Gresham Machen were closely allied with Presbyterians among the more strictly revivalist fundamentalists, such as those at Wheaton College or Moody Bible Institute.

The groupings among these theologically Reformed fundamentalists were complicated by the presence of still another major new camp— the dispensationalists. Dispensationalism was essentially Reformed in its nineteenth-century origins and had in later nineteenth-century America spread most among revival-oriented Calvinists. Strict Old School confessionalists were, however, uneasy with dispensationalists' separation of the Old Testament dispensation of Law from the era of Grace in the church age. Dispensationalism, accordingly, was accepted most readily by Reformed Christians who had a more New School, or revivalist-evangelical, emphasis than among the various Old School, or doctrinalist, groups. During the fundamentalist controversies, however, these two groups were thrown into each other's arms.

The union, however, did not last. In 1937 the followers of Machen who had just left the Presbyterian Church in the U.S.A. split roughly into Old School and New School camps, with the more revivalist group, led by Carl McIntire, favoring dispensationalism and total abstinence from alcoholic beverages. About the same time, doctrinalist Southern Presbyerians took a stand against dispensationalism in their denomination.

Another, less separatist branch of the New School evangelical party survived well in the "new evangelicalism" that grew out of fundamentalism after World War II. The new evangelicals were largely Reformed in leadership and had moved away from strict dispensationalism. Institutionally they gained strength at centers such as Wheaton College, Fuller Theological Seminary, Trinity Evangelical Divinity School, and Gordon-Conwell Theological Seminary. *Christianity Today*, founded in 1956 under the editorship of Carl F. H. Henry, gave them wide visibility and influence. Inter-Varsity Christian Fellowship, InterVarsity Press, and the ministry of Francis Schaeffer also added substantially to the outreach of this Reformed evangelicalism. Keeping cordial relations with many individuals and groups not Reformed and with evangelicals both within and outside mainline denominations, this New School tradition has emerged as one of the most influential expressions of evangelicalism today.

The Old School, though smaller, also remains active. It has wide influence through Westminster Theological Seminary and similar conservative schools. Denominationally, it is especially strong in the Presbyterian Church of America and in the conservative wing of the Christian Reformed Church. It is also found among Reformed Baptists and in other smaller Reformed denominations.

Of the three strands of the heritage, the culturalist emphasis is the least unified today. Nonetheless, it is perhaps as prominent as it ever has been. This continuing emphasis, that Calvinists should be transforming culture and bringing all of creation back to its proper relationship to God's law, has been resurgent due to the convergence of a number of developments. Most clearly articulating these views have been the North American Kuyperians, followers of the turn-of-the-century Dutch theologian and politician, Abraham Kuyper. Kuyperianism was brought to America largely by the Dutch-American Christian Reformed Church, where a hard-line Kuyperianism also developed among the admirers of

Dutch philosopher Herman Dooyeweerd. Dooyeweerdianism has enlisted non-Dutch disciples, but the widest influence of Kuyperianism spread in a mild form through the neoevangelical movement after World War II. The fundamentalist tradition, said neoevangelical spokespersons such as Carl F. H. Henry, had not sufficiently recognized that the Christian task involves relating a Christian "World-and-life view" to all of culture and politics.[6]

By the 1970s such moderately conservative emphases were converging with the resurgence of conservative politics among American fundamentalists and fundamentalistic evangelicals. Fundamentalists had their own, vaguely Reformed, traditions of wanting to Christianize America. Versions of Kuyperian Calvinism such as those suggested by Francis Schaeffer in the influential political ministry of his later years helped articulate the new fundamentalist conservative political emphases of the Moral Majority. Schaeffer drew many of his political ideas from the work of the politically conservative Dooyeweerdian thinker, Rousas J. Rushdoony. Rushdoony also contributed to the emergence of the hyper-Reformed "theonomist" movement, which insists that Old Testament law should be the basis of American civil law.

The irony in this resurgence of Reformed culturalism is that the culturalists, who are often united in theological theory, are so deeply divided in practice. Cutting across the culturalist movement is a seemingly insurmountable divide between those who are politically conservative and those who are politically liberal. Many of the American followers of Kuyper have been politically liberal and these had an impact on the politically progressive evangelicalism that emerged during the 1960s and early 1970s.[7] Moreover, the politically liberal Reformed culturalist camp includes Reformed Christians in mainline denominations whose traditions still reflect the political progressivism of the social gospel days. In addition, the neoorthodox heritage in such denominations has contributed, especially via the work of H. Richard Niebuhr and Reinhold Niebuhr, to generally Reformed culturalist sensibilities tempered by a Lutheran sense of the ambiguities inherent in relating Christianity to an essentially pagan culture.

The American Reformed community today, then, still includes substantial representation of the three classic emphases, doctrinalism, pietism, and culturalism. These three are, of course, not incompatible and the unity of Reformed Christians in America would be much greater were this compatibility recognized and emphasized.

The question of unity, however, is complicated by the twentieth-century divisions of modernists and fundamentalists that have cut across the traditional divisions. Neoorthodox and dispensationalist variations add further complications. Moreover, among those who are primarily culturalists, conflicting political allegiances subvert Reformed unity. Nonetheless, there remain a substantial number of Reformed Christians whose faith reflects a balance, or potential balance, of the three traditional emphases. It is these Christians who need to find each other and who might benefit from reflecting on what it should mean to be Reformed.

They can also learn from considering the characteristic weaknesses, as well as the strengths, of their tradition. Perhaps the greatest fault of American Reformed communities since Puritan times is that they have cultivated an elitism. Ironically, the doctrine of election has been unwittingly construed as meaning that Reformed people have been endowed with superior theological, spiritual, or moral merit by God himself. The great irony of this is that the genius of the Reformed faith has been its uncompromising emphasis on God's grace, with the corollary that our own feeble efforts are accepted, not because of any merit, but solely due to God's grace and Christ's work. The doctrine of grace, then, ought to cultivate humility as a conspicuous trait of Reformed spirituality. A strong sense of our own inadequacies is an important asset for giving us positive appreciation of those who differ from us.

Yet too often Reformed people have been so totally confident of their own spiritual insights that they have been unable to accept or work with fellow Reformed Christians whose emphases may vary slightly. Perhaps some review of the rich varieties of theological views among the Reformed in America today will contribute to bringing tolerance and search for balance. Moreover, the unmistakable minority status of the "Reformed" in America today should help foster the need for mutual understanding and respect. Above all, however, a revival of the central Reformed distinctive—the sense of our own unworthiness and of total dependence on God's grace, as revealed especially through Christ's sacrificial work—should bring together many who in late twentieth-century America still find it meaningful to say "I am Reformed."

Notes: Reformed and American

1. I. John Hesselink, *On Being Reformed: Distinctive Characteristics and Common Misunderstandings* (Ann Arbor: Servant Books, 1983), 2 and 113.

2. This concept is elaborated in *Evangelicalism and Modern America*, ed. George M. Marsden (Grand Rapids: Wm. B. Eerdmans Publishing Company, 1984).

3. These categories are roughly those suggested by Nicholas Wolterstorff, "The AACS in the CRC," *The Reformed Journal* 24 (December 1974): 9-16.

4. Harry S. Stout, *The New England Soul: Preaching and Religious Culture in Colonial New England* (New York: Oxford University Press, forthcoming).

5. The Reformed efforts to build a Christian culture are well described in Fred J. Hood, *Reformed America: The Middle and Southern States, 1783-1837* (University, AL: University of Alabama Press, 1980).

6. Carl F. H. Henry, *The Uneasy Conscience of Modern Fundamentalism* (Grand Rapids: Wm. B. Eerdmans Publishing Company, 1947), 10.

7. See Robert Booth Fowler, *A New Engagement: Evangelical Political Thought, 1966-1976* (Grand Rapids: Wm. B. Eerdmans Publishing Company, 1982), for an account of this relationship and other developments in evangelical political thought.

1

THE PRINCETON THEOLOGY

MARK A. NOLL

Archibald Alexander

A. A. Hodge

THE Princeton Theology was a distinctly American and a distinctly nineteenth-century expression of classical Reformed faith. Misunderstanding results if we regard it either as a simple restatement of Augustinian Calvinism, untouched by its surroundings, or as a simple product of American culture, haphazardly garnished with traditional Reformed words. During the nineteenth century—which in America may be regarded as that period stretching from the inspiring moments of the Revolution to the disillusionments of World War I—the Princeton theologians functioned as a loyal opposition. On the basis of their Calvinism, they questioned American myths about the power of the self, the American trust in consciousness, the American rejection of the past, and the American idolization of democracy. Yet they also took their stand as cultural insiders. They spoke Calvinism with an unmistakable American accent. With most other intellectuals of their day, they relied on a Common Sense approach to truth, they assumed the value-free character of scientific investigation, they were suspicious of high-flown ideas from the continent, and they took economic and political self-reliance for granted. The men who articulated the Princeton Theology, the convictions that constituted it, and the institutions in which it took shape were much more than functions of nineteenth-century American culture. But neither were they ever less than that. This paper attempts to place these men, convictions, and institutions in proper context before making an assessment of this important theological school, both in comparison to other varieties of Reformed faith and with regard to its relevance today.[1]

Men

Of the many individuals who contributed to the Princeton Theology during its long life from the founding of a Presbyterian seminary at Princeton, New Jersey, in 1812, to the reorganization of that institution

15

in 1929, three were clearly most important: Archibald Alexander, founding professor; his pupil, Charles Hodge; and Benjamin Breckinridge Warfield, who in his turn had studied under Hodge.

Archibald Alexander's experience before coming to Princeton and his initial leadership of the seminary set the course that his successors followed.[2] Alexander (1772-1851) arrived at Princeton in 1812 after a full career as revivalist, educator, pastor, and theologian. During the 1780s and 1790s he witnessed and led revivals in his native Virginia. As a result he remained more disposed to value "enthusiastic" religion than was normally the case at Princeton. Yet even as he took part in the practical renewal of the church, he was also putting his mind to use. Alexander studied privately with the Rev. William Graham, one of the most ardent disciples of John Witherspoon, then president of Princeton College. What Graham taught Alexander especially was to think for himself, to distrust learned authorities in favor of the testimony of his own experience. Alexander, however, soon went beyond Graham's instruction to embrace as well major expressions of historic Calvinism. Early in his ministry he eagerly read Jonathan Edwards, especially Edwards's treatment of the will. Alexander later worked through several seventeenth-century Reformed dogmaticians for his own benefit. When he came to Princeton, after service as a pastor in Virginia and Philadelphia and a stint as president of Hampden-Sydney College, he carried the intellectual resources and the practical concerns that would mark that seminary long after his passing.

Charles Hodge (1797-1878) and B. B. Warfield (1851-1921) receive separate treatment in this book, so it is not necessary to outline their careers here.[3] Suffice it to say that Hodge fleshed out the framework Alexander had established in a wide-ranging collection of works: exegetical commentaries, popular exhortation, denominational history, lectures, and eventually a massive textbook in systematic theology, but above all polemical periodical essays. Although not as comfortable with revivalistic piety as Alexander nor as technically brilliant as Warfield, Hodge was the most complex of the major Princeton theologians. He succeeded in bringing together more elements from the Reformed heritage, American culture, and pastoral concern than anyone in the tradition. Warfield, for his part, faced a different range of challenges than his predecessors, including wholesale intellectual defalcation from the evangelical Protestantism that was a cultural given in the America of Alexander and Hodge. Warfield set himself to expose the fallacies of modern alternatives to historic Christianity, a task that he carried out in hundreds of essays and thousands of reviews. His mind was discriminating, and his heart was faithful to historic Calvinism. Warfield did not have the same pastoral or ecclesiastical instincts as Alexander or Hodge, but he was no less a warrior for the convictions that they held dear.

A. A. Hodge (1823-1886), who taught at Princeton for ten years between the old age of his father and his own death, heads the second rank of Princeton theologians. He was a master of summation and popular presentation, rather than of the polemics that Charles Hodge and Warfield mastered. In this regard his service resembled that of many other Princetonians who augmented and expanded the major insights of Alexander, Hodge, and Warfield, including especially James Waddel Alexander (1804-1859) and Joseph Addison Alexander (1809-1860), sons of the founder who carried out a myriad of intellectual and practical services to the Presbyterian Church, Princeton College, and the seminary; Lyman Atwater (1813-1883), a transplanted New Englander who shouldered the major burden in replying to the theological errors that Princetonians perceived in his native region; William Henry Green (1825-1900), a professor of Old Testament who held firmly to traditional ideas about the Bible even while he appreciated new scholarship on the Middle East; and J. Gresham Machen (1881-1937), a New Testament scholar who led a remnant of the Princeton Theology out into the wilderness after the directors of the seminary altered its course in 1929.[4]

The leaders who formulated the Princeton Theology were men of intelligence, theological insight, pastoral concern, and practical wisdom. Yet what set them apart in their day, and what makes them intriguing objects of inquiry after their passing, is the beliefs they held, the methods they used to propagate those beliefs, and their efforts to preserve them for later generations.

Convictions

The Princeton Theology was not as simple as either proponents or opponents liked to make it. Princetonians sometimes spoke of themselves as Francis Landy Patton did in 1912 at the seminary's centennial: they "simply taught the old Calvinistic theology without modification." Those who doubt the wisdom of Old Princeton sometimes perceive an equally simple, if contrasting picture. One of these was Frank Hugh Foster who, writing of Charles Hodge as representative of the school, suggested in 1907 that Hodge "may be safely left by the historian of a progressive school of theology to the natural consequence of his own remark that during the many years of his predominance at Princeton that institution had never brought forward a single original thought."[5]

The reality was something different. Princeton did maintain a Reformed position in continuity with previous generations of Calvinistic theologians. But the Princetonians did not always organize their efforts, or emphasize the same relationships, as their Reformed predecessors had. Old Princeton often took procedural and methodological questions for granted, even when these exerted considerable influence on the shape of its thought. In these and other ways the theology that developed at Princeton was as complex as that of any of the other major bodies of Christian thought in nineteenth-century America. The strengths and complexity of Princeton stand out more clearly in an examination of those convictions that were most important to the school.

1. *Reformed Confessionalism.* "Calvinism," wrote Warfield in 1904, "is just religion in its purity. We have only, therefore, to conceive of religion in its purity, and that is Calvinism."[6] The Princetonians would no doubt have been distressed had they known that theologians in the late twentieth century would study them primarily in regard to their technical views on the Bible or for their use of the Scottish Philosophy of Common Sense. While they certainly held firm views on Scripture and philosophy, these matters were parts of a larger enterprise, to proclaim the dignity, necessity, and cogency of the Reformed faith. Warfield's words spoke for them all.

Princeton theologians freely employed the riches of the Calvinist heritage in setting out their own faith, although they did not draw equally from all varieties of Reformed tradition. Charles Hodge, for example, admired both the Thirty-Nine Articles of the Church of England and the Heidelberg Catechism, but seems to have made slight use in his *Systematic Theology* either of these documents or of the theological traditions they represent. Yet their wide-ranging use of Augustine on salvation, of Calvin, of several major Puritans, of Luther and orthodox Lutherans, of the Westminster standards, and of Swiss dogmaticians after Calvin suggests the breadth of their Reformed commitments.

The winsome proclamation of this Calvinism was the heart of their concern. Nowhere was Charles Hodge more eloquent than when defending Reformed views of human nature or of divine sovereignty in salvation—as, for example, in polemics directed at Charles Finney or the New Haven Theology of Nathaniel W. Taylor. Warfield was constrained to write scores of articles upholding a broadly orthodox view of the Bible's inspiration, but he wrote even more on specifically Reformed concerns: defending Calvinistic views of revelation (against evangelical perfectionists as well as against Catholics and modernists), offering the views of Calvin and Augustine for modern inspection, and detailing the intended purposes of the Westminster divines.

Princeton Calvinism shared the main emphases of the Reformed tradition: The Fall perverted a perfect creation, led to divine condemnation, and established human guilt. Adam's sin was imputed to all humans, who properly deserve the condemnation which that sinfulness entails. The same process of imputation that rendered humanity doomed in Adam justified the elect through faith in Christ. God expressed his saving purposes in covenanting to offer salvation through Christ. Sinners, turned from God by rebellious natures, were "bound" to their own sinful desires until God changed their hearts through Scripture, Christian nurture, preaching, and the sacraments. Redeemed sinners, though hamstrung by the lingering effects of the Fall, yet were fitted by the Holy Spirit for fruitful service in the Kingdom of God. These principles made up the solid core of Princeton belief to which all other major concerns were attendant.

Questions do remain, however, about the nature of Princeton's Reformed faith. The school tended to assume that positions drawn from various Reformed sources, shaped by the questions of the nineteenth century, and applied in modern polemics were simple restatements of an undifferentiated Reformed orthodoxy. In other words, Princetonians regarded theology as a static entity not affected to any appreciable degree by historical development. Arguments first made by Augustine against Pelagius, by Calvin against the Council of Trent, or by Francis Turretin against his opponents in the late seventeenth century were, to them, parts of one dogmatic whole. They did not consider the possibility that previous Reformed theologians may have individualized aspects of the biblical revelation even as they put the Scriptures to use in their respective eras.

This relative lack of sensitivity to historical conditioning, much more than a supposedly servile use of Turretin, is the most important question concerning the place of Princeton in the history of Reformed thought.[7] No doubt can exist that they were important spokesmen for that tradition. Some doubt may arise as to whether they always represented the tradition to its best advantage. The Princeton assumption that it was possible simply to restate tested and true positions for the present arose from both their confidence in the truth-telling character of Scripture and their particular beliefs in philosophy and science, convictions that deserve individual attention in any overview of their theology.

2. *Scripture.* From first to last the Princeton theologians held to a high view of the Bible's inspiration and authority. At his inaugural in 1812, Alexander preached on John 5:39, "Search the Scriptures," in order to establish the Bible as the foundation for the seminary's existence.[8] In 1915 Warfield summed up a lifetime's work on the same subject by contending in a magisterial interpretation of "Inspiration" that "the Scriptures are throughout a Divine book, created by the Divine energy and speaking in their every part with Divine authority directly to the heart

of the readers."[9] This conviction undergirded the long history of the theology.

Charles Hodge was called upon to make the first major restatements of Alexander's views on Scripture as the claims of Higher Criticism began to enter the United States at mid-century. Yet even in his *Systematic Theology*, which was finally published in 1872-73, Hodge offered his teaching on Scripture mostly as a corrective to deficient positions that he had encountered early in the century, especially those of Roman Catholics and subjectivist pietists. It fell to his son and Warfield to scrutinize the new criticism more thoroughly. They did this most completely in a memorable essay published in 1881, entitled simply "Inspiration," in which they upheld the church's historic confidence in the letter as well as the spirit of the Scriptures, described presuppositions on both sides of the contemporary discussion, and contended for the traditional view on the basis of the Bible's own testimony concerning itself.[10] In later essays Warfield explored numerous facets of the issue, laying especially heavy emphasis on the way in which the Bible's inspiration did not detract from its character as a thoroughly human (though errorless) book. Princeton's fidelity to the plenary inspiration of the Bible was consistent; each generation refined the position that it had received. The effort throughout was painstaking, careful, scholarly, and learned.

The Princeton adherence to strict views of inspiration does not, however, answer every important question one can ask about Scripture. Why, for instance, should we believe the Bible and a biblical faith? Charles Hodge sometimes said, as in quoting a German source in 1840: "Faith is no work of reason, and therefore cannot be overthrown by it, since believing no more arises from arguments than tasting or seeing."[11] Alexander and Warfield were more likely to suggest that irrefragable testimony and close logic can demonstrate that the Bible is God's word and that we should base our faith on that reasonable certainty.[12] Or again, why do the Princeton theologians usually act as if the Bible existed primarily for the formulation of dogma? As George Marsden points out in this book, other Reformed communities, though not despising dogma, have used the Scriptures as much to inspire piety or guide cultural reformation. For their part, the Princeton theologians usually considered biblical piety a strict product of correct biblical dogma. And they were largely silent about the Bible's potential for cultural reformation.[13] Yet rarely did Princetonians reflect directly on their preference for a dogmatic approach to Scripture.[14] A further question concerns relationships between the "book of God" and the "book of nature." Charles Hodge felt that ideas of design, which he found in Scripture, negated Darwinism. A. A. Hodge and Warfield, on the other hand, both felt that the Bible could be read in such a way as to make peace with Darwinism.[15]

To summarize, the Princeton teaching on the nature of Scripture was consistent and very clear: the Bible was God's written word; it was a genuine product of human activity that could be studied historically; yet the Bible was also the presentation of the most perfect truth in all that its human authors (under the inspiration of the Holy Spirit) meant to affirm; it was effective in doing the converting and sanctifying work of the Spirit. On questions about the place of the Bible in apologetics, its place in the church's life more generally, and its interpretation in relationship to general revelation (as in science), the Princeton testimony on Scripture was less unified. Such unanswered questions do not detract from their positive testimony on Scripture, but rather suggest that the many good words from Princeton on the Bible did not include the last word.

3. *Scottish Common Sense Philosophy*. Although it had long been recognized that the Scottish Philosophy of Common Sense played a leading role at Princeton, it was not until the publication of Sydney Ahlstrom's seminal essay on the general subject in 1955 that this dimension of the theology began to receive careful attention.[16] Since then it has become a commonplace to hold that Old Princeton was heavily, even uniquely, indebted to this philosophy. There are several plausible reasons for doing so.

John Witherspoon (1723-1794), the instructor of Alexander's mentor William Graham (1746-1799) at Princeton College, had trained his students in the convictions of the Scottish philosophy. And Graham was among its most ardent exponents.[17] From study with Graham, Alexander adopted many of the principles that Witherspoon brought with him to America from Scottish thinkers like Francis Hutcheson (1694-1746) and Thomas Reid (1710-1796). These philosophers were attempting to rescue the English "moderate" Enlightenment of Isaac Newton and John Locke from the skepticism of David Hume and the idealism of George Berkeley.[18] As Alexander came to express these positions, they included an affirmation that the "common sense" of humankind could verify the deliverances of the physical senses and of intuitive consciousness (i.e., the "moral sense"). It was second nature for him to think, as illustrated in his earliest lectures at the seminary and in his last, posthumously published book, that this "common sense" provided the basis for an irrefutable apologetic concerning the existence of God and the reality of biblical revelation.[19] Along with Witherspoon, Graham, and their Scottish mentors, Alexander was an enthusiast for empiricism and induction. Scrupulous investigation imitating methods of the "natural philosophers" would lead to the same kind of success in ethics and theology as the great Newton had enjoyed in studying the physical world.[20]

Charles Hodge imbibed the Scottish Philosophy from Alexander, as well as from the pastor of his youth, Ashbel Green, who became president of Princeton College in 1812, the year that Hodge began his studies there. (Green's major educational change at the college was to restore Witherspoon's lectures in moral philosophy as the integrating text for the undergraduates.) Hodge's debt to the Scottish Philosophy appears most clearly in the opening pages of his *Systematic Theology* where, in oft-quoted lines, he likened the construction of dogmatic systems to scientific exploration: "The Bible is to the theologian what nature is to the man of science. It is his store-house of facts; and his method of ascertaining what the Bible teaches is the same as that which the natural philosopher adopts to ascertain what nature teaches."[21] Warfield learned the Scottish Philosophy from James McCosh, the last prominent defender of the system, who in 1868 came from Scotland to Princeton College as Witherspoon had a century before. That was also the year in which Warfield began his undergraduate studies. Other spokesmen for the Princeton Theology asserted Common Sense convictions aggressively or, like A. A. Hodge, simply accepted them as the natural axioms for theological inquiry.

When this eighteenth-century philosophical position was added to Princeton's Reformed convictions, the result was not always propitious. Princetonians could be overconfident in assuming that the deliverances of their own consciousness equaled the common intuitions of all humanity. They were naive in thinking that chains of apologetical reasoning could begin with no moral preconditions in the seeker and no predetermined assumptions about the end of inquiry. And although their Calvinism pointed in an opposite direction, their philosophical allegiance could at times leave them sounding like scientistic positivists.

Yet this is not the whole story. Princeton's accommodation to Scottish Common Sense Philosophy was neither total nor comprehensive. While harboring few reservations about epistemological and methodological aspects of the Scottish position, they regularly resisted its ethical implications, at least on major doctrines.[22] They were not like their theological contemporaries in New England who substantially altered traditional Reformed views of human nature and divine sovereignty on the basis, in E. A. Park's words, of "the fundamental laws of human belief," those "ethical axioms, which so many fathers in the church have undervalued," which are derived from *"the philosophy of common sense."*[23] By contrast, the Princeton theologians never allowed the deliverances of refined Victorian conscience to overwhelm basic Calvinistic beliefs in human moral incapacity or to replace supreme confidence in the sometimes "unenlightened" pronouncements of the Bible.

Thus, the Princeton investment in Common Sense Philosophy did not lead to a comprehensive reordering of traditional Reformed theology as it did for N. W. Taylor. Rather Princetonians merely added Common Sense to their more traditional theological convictions. The result was a system with more internal stress and less methodological rigor than Taylor's New Haven Theology; and it was a system that did not come to terms with religious experience as forthrightly as did Horace Bushnell.[24] Yet for all these weaknesses, the very naiveté of Princeton's Common Sense convictions was a disguised blessing. Acting intuitively, Princeton made profitable conjunctions where Common Sense really did support traditional Reformed positions (as in the impossibility of living as if there were no God who maintained the physical and moral worlds). To be sure, they muddied the waters when discussing the first principles of ethics by clumsily intermingling Scottish beliefs about universal human capacities with Reformed convictions about the moral effects of the Fall.[25] But Common Sense intuitionism was never the last word, especially when it came to teachings on the sovereignty of God over human consciousness and the superiority of divine revelation to the inner voice of the self. And these were convictions that were fading during the nineteenth century almost as fast among American evangelicals at large as among the champions of the new theologies.[26]

4. *Religious Experience, The Work of the Spirit.* In spite of their reputation as scholastics or rationalists, and in spite of their fidelity to the objective works of God, the Princeton theologians constantly stressed the importance of religious experience and the need for the work of the Holy Spirit. The Sunday afternoon "conferences" with seminary students that lasted from generation to generation throughout most of the century, their occasional sermons, and especially the commentaries and selected polemical essays of Charles Hodge testify to consistent efforts at giving the supernatural work of the Spirit its proper place in the life of the individual believer and of the church as a whole.[27] As Reformed theologians, the Princetonians always insisted that the Spirit worked through "means."[28] Yet none of them neglected the importance of religious experience, even if they insisted that such experience not be opposed to the propositional testimony of Scripture and the intellectual structure of the confessions.

The pertinent question for the Princeton theologians is not whether they had a place for religious experience and the work of the Holy Spirit. As Professor Andrew Hoffecker's fine recent book makes clear beyond cavil, they certainly did.[29] The question is rather where this religious experience, where the work of the Holy Spirit, fit into their theology. It is hard to escape the conclusion that on this score, as in the Princeton appropriation of Common Sense Philosophy, no entirely satisfactory integration occurred. The Charles Hodge who laid such great store by "facts" and "scientific method" could also argue for the priority of inner convictions over external argument in the reception of religious truth. And as David Kelsey has pointed out, even Warfield, the most carefully logical of the Princeton theologians, often described his belief in Scripture as arising more from the internal power of the written word than from conclusions out of a neutral chain of argument.[30] At issue is not their seriousness about religious experience, but the incorporation of that seriousness in their theology as a whole.

The quickening power of the Holy Spirit, manifest through divinely ordained means, was a principal feature of Princeton religion. That this element of the Princeton Theology seems to stay in the background is the responsibility first of these men themselves, since they seemed less clear about the place of the Spirit's work in their theology than in their lives. But it is also a result of a historical failure to realize that occasional Princeton statements that ignore or play down the importance of religious experience were not necessarily the foundational axioms of the theology as a whole.

Institutions

The convictions of the Princeton theologians are the main reasons for their continuing importance. Yet historically considered, the institutions that embodied those beliefs were nearly as impressive as the doctrines themselves. The ideas gave the theology its direction, but the institutions made it influential in America.

Princeton Seminary, the second major American school devoted to postgraduate theological education, was, quite naturally, the place where the Princeton Theology received its fullest institutional expression. The way the seminary came into existence had more than a little influence on the course that the Princeton Theology would take.[31] The seminary was founded in 1812, five years after the establishment of Andover Seminary, in response to a feeling that America was undergoing a cultural crisis of unprecedented seriousness. Its founders—Ashbel Green and Samuel Miller as well as Alexander—had several related purposes for the school: to fit clergymen to meet the cultural crisis, to roll back what they perceived as tides of irreligion sweeping the country, and to provide a learned defense of Christianity generally and the Bible specifically. The conserving character of the institution did not change during the life of the Princeton Theology. As its centennial in 1912, the seminary had enrolled over 1,000 more students than any other theological school in the United States. A total of 6,386 students studied at Princeton from Alexander's inauguration to Warfield's death. Some of them became famous theologians, educators, and ministers in their own right (by 1912 the alumni included fifty-six moderators of General Assemblies and five bishops of the Protestant Episcopal Church). Even more impressive was the steady infusion of ministers into the ongoing congregational life of the nation, ministers exposed to a powerful expression of American Calvinism and, much more often than not, its advocates as well.

The Princeton Theology spread outward through seminary graduates, but even more visibly through the printed page. A vast cornucopia of essays, commentaries, treatises, reviews, and pamphlets—on an incredibly diverse range of topics—tumbled from the presses of Philadelphia, New York, and Princeton itself to present this theology to the public. Many of these books, like Charles Hodge's *Way of Life* and his *Systematic Theology*, or the theological compendia of A. A. Hodge, reached wide audiences throughout the nineteenth century. A remarkably large number of Princeton books remain in print to this day.

Significant as the books undoubtedly were, the Princeton Theology received its fullest expression in periodicals.[32] Their learned and extensive reviews contained the fullest exposition of Princeton positions, the most vigorous attacks on rivals, and the most thoughtful reflections on great national events and significant intellectual milestones. The greatest of these journals was Charles Hodge's *Biblical Repertory and Princeton Review*, begun in 1825 in an effort mostly to transmit European theological scholarship to America, but changed over the years, and under a series of titles, to a mighty instrument of theological instruction. Although he had assistance in editing its pages, as indicated by the long lists of articles contributed by the Alexanders, Lyman Atwater, Albert Baldwin Dod, and other stalwarts, this was the supreme vehicle for Charles Hodge's convictions.[33] After managing the review for nearly forty years, he called his labor "a ball-and-chain" borne "with scarcely any other compensation than the high privilege and honour of making it an organ for upholding sound Presbyterianism, the cause of the country, and the honour of our common Redeemer."[34] Yet even foes recognized the power of the work in the journal, like the editor of Lyman Beecher's autobiography who said it was "the most powerful organ in the land." Friendly voices were even more extravagant, like the *British Quarterly Review*, which in 1871 called Hodge's journal "beyond all question the greatest purely theological Review that has ever been published in the English tongue."[35]

What made the *Princeton Review* so powerful, and what also contributed to the influence of the journals that A. A. Hodge and B. B. Warfield managed, was the Princeton ability to enlarge a parochial controversy into a full-blown defense of Reformed doctrines. For depth of treatment, clarity of argumentation, and seriousness of purpose, there is simply nothing in twentieth-century American religious life to match the theological discussions in nineteenth-century periodicals. And the

Princeton Review took a leading role in many of these. Whether Hodge was debating the relationship between intellect and feeling with E. A. Park (7 articles, 265 pages, over 18 months, in the *Princeton Review* and Park's *Bibliotheca Sacra* during 1850-52), tilting with Horace Bushnell (three lengthy articles over a twenty-year span), or addressing more particular issues of interest only to Presbyterians, the journal demanded reading.

After Hodge's day, changes in the American academy reduced the influence of the theological journals. Still, A. A. Hodge in *The Presbyterian Review* (1880-1889) and Warfield in *The Presbyterian and Reformed Review* (1890-1902) and *The Princeton Theological Review* (1903-1921) reached nearly the same degree of seriousness and comprehension.

The final institution of the Princeton Theology was the Presbyterian Church. Although the seminary never enjoyed the confidence of the entire denomination, its influence made it a power to be reckoned with. It maintained consistent Old School views in the schism of 1837, urged caution in the reunion of the northern Old and New School denominations in 1867, arrayed itself at the turn of the twentieth century against innovation on the Confession and theological inclusiveness as a denominational strategy, and in general sought to keep the denomination close to its confessional Calvinist roots.[36] From 1835 through 1867, with but one exception, Charles Hodge reported on the year's General Assembly in the *Princeton Review.* This quickly established Hodge as one of the most visible arbiters of Presbyterian opinion in the century. "There is no inducement," one of Hodge's allies once wrote, "to prepare a good article for the July number, because every one turns at once to that on the General Assembly which absorbs all interest."[37]

The expression of Princeton convictions in these institutions—the seminary, their books and journals, the Presbyterian Church—was *the* Princeton Theology. Many convictions of Old Princeton deserve a place among the church's perpetual beliefs. But a judicious definition of this theology as a concrete historical entity must always come back to the institutions in which the Princeton beliefs took shape during the nineteenth century. To say this, however, raises the question of the Princeton Theology in relation to its times.

The Nineteenth-Century Context

Many of the supposed defects of the Princeton theologians, and some of their vaunted triumphs as well, become less striking if the work of the school is placed in its historical context. To study Princeton only in relationship to twentieth-century theological developments, or, from a different perspective, to ignore the centuries between Calvin's activity in Geneva and Alexander's in Princeton, is to short-circuit sympathetic understanding of these theologians. It may even be that the genuine contribution of the Princeton Theology will only be apparent when it is placed against the background of its times.

To do this shows immediately that much of the Princeton Theology was simply a singular expression of the ordinary affirmations of their day. For example, the Princetonians used Scottish Common Sense Philosophy mostly because it was America's common intellectual coinage of the nineteenth century. Early in the period orthodox Congregationalists at Yale as well as Unitarians at Harvard embraced this perspective nearly as enthusiastically as did Presbyterian Princeton. Common Sense assumptions later became commonplace in the theological pronouncements of an incredibly broad range of American theologians: revisionist Calvinists like N. W. Taylor, more consistent Calvinists like E. A. Park, New School Presbyterians like Albert Barnes, Disciples of Christ spokesmen like Alexander Campbell, Unitarians like Andrews Norton, and so on. At least for much of the nineteenth century, the Princetonians' Scottish Realism shows us more how they moved with their culture than against it.[38]

Once again, Princeton defended the authority of the Bible because for most of the century almost all evangelical Protestants took this for granted. In the last third of the century, the Princetonians came to stress more the cognitive than the affective veracity of Scripture. But even here the fact that these later Princeton proposals received such wide support from non-Calvinist groups would suggest that there was nothing peculiarly distinctive about the positions. And for the first two-thirds of the century, as essays by Randall Balmer and John Woodbridge have shown, it is hard to distinguish the Princeton views on the Bible from those of the American evangelical world at large.[39]

Similarly, Princetonians advocated a naive empiricism in the construction of theology because most American intellectuals approached theory-formation like this. During the nineteenth century historians, public servants, social scientists, and even artists, geniuses, and crackpots, all looked to simple scientific generalizations as the path to truth.[40] In this climate the Princeton methodological naiveté was part and parcel of a more general epistemological innocence in America.

For most of the nineteenth century, then, the Princeton theologians merely shared widespread cultural values in their convictions about the Bible, Scottish Common Sense Philosophy, and scientific empiricism. The distinctive Princeton achievement was to absorb these cultural assumptions into their Calvinism without losing that Calvinism. To be heard in the nineteenth century, it was necessary for Princeton to adopt the intellectual conventions of the day. Schools of theology that did not do this, like the Mercersberg theology of J. W. Nevin, are of considerable interest to twentieth-century scholars, but they were close to nullities in their own day. The truly remarkable thing about the work of the Princetonians was that so much historic Calvinism remained even as they adjusted their thought to accommodate American intellectual conventions.

Perspective: Princeton, Jonathan Edwards, and the Dutch

To assess the accomplishments of the Princetonians as well as their deficiencies, it is helpful to compare them with other representatives of Reformed theology. Two obvious candidates for such a task are Jonathan Edwards, who forged the most powerful engine of American Calvinism during the eighteenth century, and the Dutch followers of Abraham Kuyper, who through immigrant communities had established a presence in America by the end of the nineteenth century.

The many striking contrasts among these Reformed theologians can loom larger than their commonalities, even if their agreements were far more extensive than their disagreements. Though later theologians and historians have belabored their differences, the compliments that Princeton and the Dutch paid to Edwards and to each other were sincere.[41] The three represented different geographic regions and ethnic origins— New England from English stock, middle American from largely Scotch-Irish background, and immigrants from Holland—and they possessed very different temperaments, but the three shared a remarkable resemblance in efforts to do theology and approach life in a Calvinistic way.

Yet the differences were major. Edwards and the Dutch, first, showed much more concern for the intellectual framework of theology than did Old Princeton. The former wrestled with these questions as full-scale theological issues in their own right. Opinions differ concerning the success of these efforts, but they still resulted in a great deal of insight concerning method and a more obviously Christian grasp of procedural problems than the Princetonians displayed. By way of compensation, Princeton's relative lack of sophistication on such matters left its theology more accessible to a wide audience—at least so long as their assumptions about method corresponded roughly with those of the general populace, and that was for nearly one hundred years.

Second, the three differed in how their approach to Scripture affected their picture of the Christian's task in society. Princeton used the Bible to construct dogma, while it was content to accept the cultural conventions of the merchant-yeoman middle class without question. To Edwards the Bible was a resource for reflective piety, for discovering the divine and supernatural light that graciously converts the darkened heart; his absorption was so thorough on this theme that he seems to have given little thought to the late-Puritan society in which he lived. The Dutch, by contrast, almost defined themselves by their capacity to find scriptural principles for cultural formation, whether in education, politics, voluntary organizations, or economics. These varied uses of Scripture have appeared complementary in some circumstances and competitive in others.

Finally, the three differed in their ability to adapt to America. In spite of the combination of his genius and his piety, Edwards's Calvinism did not long survive his death. Within seventy years of his passing, "Edwardseans," though following his lead in some methodological and ethical matters, had stood on their head most of Edwards's basic affirmations about human nature, the process of salvation, and the relationship between Christ and the elect. Dutch Calvinism has sustained itself better in America, but at a price. The precepts of Kuyper and Bavinck remain a beacon for their theological descendants. Yet these descendants are still largely isolated, still relatively unconcerned about the wider American scene and only just beginning to exert an influence in that larger arena.

The Princeton Theology, by contrast, proved both consistent and influential. Of major American seminaries besides Princeton, only the Harvard Divinity School could claim that its teaching remained relatively stable over the first century of its existence. But unlike Princeton, the Harvard Divinity School was not a national force. The Calvinism of Princeton, on the other hand, was remarkably powerful for more than a century from 1812 on. This is a major achievement when viewed as a chapter in Reformed history, not for the trivial reason that lack of change somehow implies virtue, but for the much more important reason that the undeviating Princeton convictions were largely Reformed. Everything in the nineteenth century conspired against Calvinist views of humanity and of divine sovereignty. In holding to these positions, the Princeton theologians may have uncritically imbibed a good bit of the American self-determination, especially on matters epistemological, that they professed to repudiate. They may have responded woodenly to a changing philosophical situation. Nonetheless, the constancy of the Princetonians in steadily proclaiming the weakness of human nature and the divinely originated path of salvation, not to speak of their success at shaping institutions to embody this message, testifies to a Reformed vigor the like of which has never been seen in America.

Perhaps it is sufficient to conclude this comparison by saying that Edwards, the Dutch, and Old Princeton each faced cultural-theological crises of considerable magnitude, that each chose somewhat different ways of responding, and that these choices lent each school its distinctive character. Edwards chose to give himself unstintingly to intellectual toil of the most fundamental sort. As a result he left few genuine successors, for those who followed in Edwards's train lacked his powers of insight and his unreserved dependence upon a sovereign God. His books, which have remained to inspire a theologically promiscuous host, constituted his enduring legacy. The Dutch chose the path of cultural formation on a European model. The result was great internal strength, but only slight impact in America at large. Princetonians chose to pour their energies into a seminary devoted to dogmatic inquiry. The result was considerable ambiguity in relationship to American thought and social conditions, but also extraordinary influence within the American milieu.

The Princeton Theology Today

The steady reprinting of books from Old Princeton as well as a continuing, if not overwhelming, flow of critical attention testifies to the vitality of this school among Reformed and evangelical Americans at the end of the twentieth century. Nonetheless, it is no revelation to say that the unique blend of concerns and institutions that constituted the Princeton Theology has passed away. A brief survey of the conservative Reformed denominations, where one might naturally expect to find a continuing Princeton Theology, testifies instead to its absence. Within the Orthodox Presbyterian Church and at Westminster Theological Seminary, great respect remains for the Princeton Theology, but the presuppositional apologetics of Cornelius Van Til has largely replaced Old Princeton's commitment to the Scottish Philosophy of Common Sense, and so unhinged one of its crucial elements. In the Christian Reformed Church, which lacked organic historical connections to Old Princeton to begin with, other varieties of Dutch epistemology—from Kuyper, Bavinck, or Dooyeweerd—take the place of Princeton beliefs about apologetics and religious knowledge. Theologians in the Presbyterian Church of America (PCA) speak kindly of Old Princeton, but here again, philosophical, apologetic, or intellectual tendencies exist that distance members of this body from the Princetonians. The ecclesiology of Thornwell and Dabney, the prospects of Christian Reconstruction, or even a spirit disinclined to sophisticated academic endeavor provide alternative theological foundations in the PCA to those that Old Princeton affirmed. Only a scattering of individuals today combine Augustinian Calvinism, empirical realism, evidentialist apologetics, and piety based on propositions in the manner of the Princeton theologians.

This is not to say that individual parts of their theology do not remain influential. The historical work of Ernest Sandeen, as well as the ongoing efforts of the International Council on Biblical Inerrancy, shows how important the Princeton views on Scripture, especially as refined by Warfield, still are.[42] In addition, the apologetic strategies of the school enjoy considerable currency; some evidentialists who emphasize the reliability of consciousness, logic, and history in demonstrating the truthfulness of the faith make their debt to Old Princeton explicit.[43]

In all this, however, a historian may be pardoned for wondering if the burden of the Princetonians, the critical position that made them a great force for the faith in the nineteenth century, has not been overlooked in our day. Helpful or harmful as their particular views on inspiration and apologetics may be, the Princeton theologians looked upon these matters as subordinate constituents of a more general theology whose end was to glorify God in his greatness and rejoice in the mercies of his salvation. As with so many things in our century, the tendency is to concentrate on means and slight the end. During the nineteenth century the Princeton Theology stood for divine grace, it stood against human pretense in self-salvation and self-revelation, it proclaimed the moral weakness of humanity, and it championed a salvation won for us by God himself. These are the themes that the latter-day friends of the Princeton Theology too often neglect and its latter-day critics too often avoid. But these are also the themes that, if they could be revived, might constitute the greatest gift of Old Princeton to the contemporary world.

During his great debate with E. A. Park in 1850 over the intellectual apprehension of Christianity and the role of the feelings, Charles Hodge paused to summarize the foundation stones of his faith, for which he was prepared to battle without ceasing: "That a sentence of condemnation passed on all men for the sin of one man; that men are by nature the children of wrath; that without Christ we can do nothing; that he hath redeemed us from the curse of the law by being made a curse for us; that men are not merely pardoned but justified." Hodge continued that, by dividing the mind and the heart, Park was preparing "a weapon" against these beliefs. He then closed with a word of hope that Hodge applied to the doctrines themselves but that an admirer can apply to the Princeton version of these convictions as well: "Our consolation is that however keen may be the edge or bright the polish of that weapon, it has so little substance, it must be shivered into atoms with the first blow it strikes against those sturdy trees which have stood for ages in the garden of the Lord and whose leaves have been for the healing of the nations."[44]

Notes: The Princeton Theology

1. Some of the themes developed in this essay are similar to those that introduce the anthology *The Princeton Theology 1812-1921: Scripture, Science, and*

Theological Method from Archibald Alexander to Benjamin Warfield, ed. Mark A. Noll (Grand Rapids: Baker Book House, 1983). This anthology also contains a detailed bibliography and fuller notes than are possible here.

2. See James Waddel Alexander, *The Life of Archibald Alexander* (New York: Charles Scribner's Sons, 1854); and Lefferts A. Loetscher, *Facing the Enlightenment and Pietism: Archibald Alexander and the Founding of Princeton Theological Seminary* (Westport, CT: Greenwood Press, 1983).

3. The basic biography for Charles Hodge is the life by his son, A. A. Hodge, published by Charles Scribner's Sons in 1880. In the absence of a good biography for Warfield, John E. Meeter and Roger Nicole, *A Bibliography of Benjamin Breckinridge Warfield 1851-1921* (Nutley, NJ: Presbyterian and Reformed Publishing Company, 1974), is invaluable.

4. On these individuals, see *The Princeton Theology 1812-1921,* 14-16.

5. Francis Landy Patton, "Princeton Seminary and the Faith," in *The Centennial Celebration of the Theological Seminary of the Presbyterian Church in the United States of America at Princeton, New Jersey* (Princeton: Princeton Theological Seminary, 1910), 349-50. Frank Hugh Foster, *A Genetic History of the New England Theology* (Chicago: University of Chicago Press, 1907), 432.

6. B. B. Warfield, "What is Calvinism?" in *Selected Shorter Writings of Benjamin B. Warfield,* ed. John E. Meeter, 2 vols. (Nutley, NJ: Presbyterian and Reformed Publishing Company, 1970, 1973), 1:389.

7. On Turretin's role at Princeton, see *The Princeton Theology 1812-1921,* 28-30, 116. On the Old Princeton understanding of history, see George Marsden, "J. Gresham Machen, History, and Truth," *Westminster Theological Journal* 42 (Fall 1979): 157-75.

8. Archibald Alexander, *The Sermon, Delivered at the Inauguration of the Rev. Archibald Alexander* (New York: J. Seymour, 1812).

9. B. B. Warfield, "Inspiration," in *International Standard Bible Encyclopedia* (Chicago: Howard-Severance, 1915), as reprinted in *The Works of Benjamin B. Warfield,* vol. 1, *Revelation and Inspiration* (Grand Rapids: Baker Book House, 1981), 96.

10. A. A. Hodge and Warfield, *Inspiration,* introduction by Roger R. Nicole (Grand Rapids: Baker Book House, 1979).

11. Hodge, "The Latest Form of Infidelity," *Biblical Repertory and Princeton Review* 12 (January 1840), as reprinted in Hodge's *Essays and Reviews* (New York: Robert Carter & Brothers, 1857), 90.

12. For example, Alexander, *Inaugural Address;* Warfield, review of Herman Bavinck's *De Zekerheid des Geloofs* in *Princeton Theological Review* 1 (January 1903): 138-43, reprinted in *Selected Shorter Writings of Warfield,* 2:117-22.

13. See William S. Barker, "The Social Views of Charles Hodge: A Study in 19th-Century Calvinism and Conservatism," *Presbyterian: Covenant Seminary Review* 1 (Spring 1975): 1-22.

14. A good discussion of these different approaches is Richard J. Mouw, "The Bible in Twentieth-Century Protestantism: A Preliminary Taxonomy," in *The Bible in America: Essays in Cultural History,* eds. Nathan O. Hatch and Mark A. Noll (New York: Oxford University Press, 1982), 139-62, with 143-44 on the doctrinal emphases of Old Princeton.

15. See, in general, James R. Moore, *The Post-Darwinian Controversies: A Study of the Protestant Struggle to Come to Terms with Darwin in Great Britain and America, 1870-1900* (Cambridge: Cambridge University Press, 1979); and, more specifically, David N. Livingstone, "The Idea of Design: The Vicissitudes of a

Key Concept in the Princeton Response to Darwin," *Scottish Journal of Theology* 37 (1984): 329-57.

16. Sydney E. Ahlstrom, "The Scottish Philosophy and American Theology," *Church History* 24 (1955): 257-72. An early work commenting on Princeton's use of the Scottish Philosophy was Ralph J. Danhof, *Charles Hodge as Dogmatician* (Goes, The Netherlands: Oosterbaan and le Cointre, 1929). The fullest consideration of this subject is now John C. Vander Stelt, *Philosophy and Scripture: A Study in Old Princeton and Westminster Theology* (Marlton, NJ: Mack Publishing Company, 1978).

17. See Wesley Frank Craven, "William Graham," in *Princetonians 1769-1775: A Biographical Dictionary*, ed. Richard A. Harrison (Princeton: Princeton University Press, 1980), 289-94.

18. For an excellent general picture, see Henry F. May, *The Enlightenment in America* (New York: Oxford University Press, 1976).

19. Alexander, "The Nature and Evidence of Truth," in *The Princeton Theology 1812-1921*, 61-71; Alexander, *Outlines of Moral Science* (New York: Charles Scribner's Sons, 1852).

20. The best study of this enthusiasm for the new science among theologians is Theodore Dwight Bozeman, *Protestantism in an Age of Science: The Baconian Ideal and Antebellum American Religious Thought* (Chapel Hill: University of North Carolina Press, 1977).

21. Hodge, *Systematic Theology*, 3 vols. (Grand Rapids: Wm. B. Eerdmans Publishing Company, 1946), 1:10.

22. The different uses of this philosophy by evangelicals is discussed in Mark A. Noll, "Common Sense Traditions and American Evangelical Thought," *American Quarterly* 37 (Summer 1985): 216-38.

23. Park, "New England Theology," *Bibliotheca Sacra* 9 (January 1852): 191-92.

24. For comparison, see, on the power of the New England Theology, Bruce Kuklick, *Churchmen and Philosophers: From Jonathan Edwards to John Dewey* (New Haven: Yale University Press, 1985); and on Bushnell, Daniel Walker Howe, "The Social Science of Horace Bushnell," *Journal of American History* 70 (September 1983): 305-22.

25. See especially the discussion of Alexander's ethics in D. H. Meyer, *The Instructed Conscience: The Shaping of the American National Ethic* (Philadelphia: University of Pennsylvania Press, 1972), 55-58.

26. On the more general trends, see Nathan O. Hatch, "The Christian Movement and the Demand for a Theology of the People," *Journal of American History* 67 (December 1980): 545-67; and Hatch, "Evangelicalism as a Democratic Movement," in *Evangelicalism and Modern America*, ed. George M. Marsden (Grand Rapids: Wm. B. Eerdmans Publishing Company, 1984).

27. A thorough recent discussion of these emphases is Steven L. Martin, "The Doctrines of Man, Reason and the Holy Spirit in the Epistemology of Charles Hodge" (M.A. Thesis, Trinity Evangelical Divinity School, 1984).

28. Warfield's discussions of the human elements in biblical inspiration and of natural processes in the creation of the natural world illustrate the sophistication of this useful theological construction. See *The Princeton Theology 1812-1921*, 268-79, 293-98.

29. Hoffecker, *Piety and the Princetonians: Archibald Alexander, Charles Hodge, and Benjamin Warfield* (Phillipsburg, NJ: Presbyterian and Reformed Publishing Company, 1981).

30. Kelsey, *The Uses of Scripture in Recent Theology* (Philadelphia: Fortress Press, 1975), 17-24.

31. See Mark A. Noll, "The Founding of Princeton Seminary," *Westminster Theological Journal* 42 (Fall 1979): 72-110; and *The Princeton Theology 1812-1921*, 18-20, 51-58.

32. See *The Princeton Theology 1812-1921*, 22-24, for a discussion of the various Princeton journals from 1825 to 1929.

33. To obtain an overview of the work of this journal, see *Biblical Repertory and Princeton Review. Index Volume from 1825 to 1868*, 3 vols. (Philadelphia: Peter Walker, 1870-71).

34. Charles Hodge, "The *Princeton Review* on the State of the Country and of the Church," *Biblical Repertory and Princeton Review* 37 (October 1865): 687.

35. Cited in A. A. Hodge, *Life of Charles Hodge*, 257, 259-60.

36. A good modern treatment of Old Princeton positions is to be found, emphasis of the title notwithstanding, in George M. Marsden, *The Evangelical Mind and the New School Presbyterian Experience* (New Haven: Yale University Press, 1970).

37. *Biblical Repertory and Princeton Review. Index Volume*, 2:206.

38. See Noll, "Common Sense Traditions and American Evangelical Thought," *American Quarterly*.

39. Randall H. Balmer, "The Princetonians and Scripture: A Reconsideration," *Westminster Theological Journal* 44 (1982): 352-65; Balmer and John D. Woodbridge, "The Princetonians' Viewpoint of Biblical Authority: An Evaluation of Ernest Sandeen," in *Scripture and Truth*, eds. Woodbridge and D. A. Carson (Grand Rapids: Zondervan Publishing House, 1983). Woodbridge and Balmer rightly criticize Sandeen for suggesting that Old Princeton invented the concept of biblical inerrancy (see Sandeen, *The Roots of Fundamentalism: British and American Millenarianism 1800-1930* [Chicago: University of Chicago Press, 1970]; and "The Princeton Theology: One Source of Biblical Literalism in American Protestantism," *Church History* 31 [September 1962]: 307-21). Still, a modified version of Sandeen's argument—that Princeton refined, clarified, and emphasized certain aspects of the common evangelical heritage concerning Scripture—is quite defensible. Sandeen's work on fundamentalism, as well as other standard treatments of the subject that document the eager fundamentalist use of Princeton's views on Scripture (e.g., George W. Dollar, *A History of Fundamentalism in America* [Greenville, SC: Bob Jones University Press, 1973]; George M. Marsden, *Fundamentalism and American Culture* [New York: Oxford University Press, 1980]), suggests two things: (1) that fundamentalists recognized the Princeton formulation as a powerful statement of their sometimes inarticulate convictions, but also (2) that A. A. Hodge and Warfield were in fact highlighting in a new, effective way elements of an earlier, more amorphous confidence in Scripture.

40. On this widespread trust in a simple scientific epistemology, see, among many others, Bozeman, *Protestants in an Age of Science*; Henry Warner Bowden, *Church History in the Age of Science: Historiographical Patterns in the United States 1876-1918* (Chapel Hill: University of North Carolina Press, 1971); Foster, *New England Theology*; E. Brooks Holifield, *The Gentlemen Theologians: American Theology in Southern Culture, 1795-1860* (Durham, NC: Duke University Press, 1978); Herbert Hovenkamp, *Science and Religion in America, 1800-1860* (Philadelphia: University of Pennsylvania Press, 1978); Daniel Walker Howe, *The Unitarian Conscience: Harvard Moral Philosophy, 1805-1861* (Cambridge: Harvard University Press, 1970); May, *The Enlightenment in America*; Meyer, *The Instructed Conscience*;

Alexandra Oleson and Sanborn C. Brown, eds., *The Pursuit of Knowledge in the Early American Republic: American Scientific and Learned Societies from Colonial Times to the Civil War* (Baltimore: Johns Hopkins University Press, 1976); Douglas Sloan, *The Scottish Enlightenment and the American College Ideal* (New York: Teachers College Press, 1961); and Laurence R. Veysey, *The Emergence of the American University* (Chicago: University of Chicago Press, 1965).

41. The best work I have seen in comparing Princeton and the Dutch is by Stephen R. Spencer of Grand Rapids Baptist Seminary, "A Comparison and Evaluation of the Old Princeton and Amsterdam Apologetics" (Th.M. Thesis, Grand Rapids Baptist Seminary, n.d.). On connections between Edwards and the Princetonians, see Mark A. Noll, "Jonathan Edwards and Nineteenth-Century Theology," in *Jonathan Edwards and the American Experience*, eds. Nathan O. Hatch and Harry S. Stout (forthcoming); and on relations between Warfield and Kuyper and Bavinck, *The Princeton Theology 1812-1921*, 302-07.

42. Sandeen, *The Roots of Fundamentalism*; at least two recent books by the Inerrancy Council feature consideration of Old Princeton: see John Gerstner, "The Contributions of Charles Hodge, B. B. Warfield, and J. Gresham Machen to the Doctrine of Inspiration," in *Challenges to Inerrancy: A Theological Response*, eds. Gordon R. Lewis and Bruce Demarest (Chicago: Moody Press, 1984); and D. Clair Davis, "Princeton and Inerrancy: The Nineteenth-Century Theological Background of Contemporary Concerns," in *Inerrancy and the Church*, ed. John D. Hannah (Chicago: Moody Press, 1984).

43. For example, R. C. Sproul, John Gerstner, and Arthur Lindsley, *Classical Apologetics: A Rational Defense of the Christian Faith and a Critique of Presuppositional Apologetics* (Grand Rapids: Zondervan Publishing House, 1984).

44. Hodge, "The Theology of the Intellect and That of the Feelings," *Biblical Repertory and Princeton Review* 22 (October 1850): 674; reprinted in *Essays and Reviews*, 569.

2

CHARLES HODGE

DAVID F. WELLS

Charles Hodge

THE mainstay of Protestant orthodoxy in the nineteenth century, both within Presbyterianism and the wider evangelical movement, was Princeton Theological Seminary. And Princeton, during most of these years, was identified substantially with the work of its most formidable representative, Charles Hodge. Hodge taught there from 1822, ten years after the founding of the Seminary, almost to his death in 1878, except for two years of study abroad in Germany. The celebration of the fiftieth year of his professorship in 1872 was without precedent in American academic life. Even the shops in Princeton closed on this day to honor a patriarch, a theologian, and a teacher of more than three thousand ministerial students.[1]

Hodge's theological views were formed remarkably early, and in the long and unremitting struggle with the New School thinkers, a struggle that occupied him for much of his life, he defended his convictions unflinchingly and unswervingly. It is true that his *Systematic Theology*, written late in his life as a replacement for the Latin text that had been used at Princeton—Turretin's *Institutio theologiae elencticae*—does evidence a mellower tone than his essays published earlier in *The Biblical Repertory and Princeton Review*, but changes in his theology were few and far between. It was the stout consistency of Hodge's theology and the rigorous defense he gave of it that earned him an almost oracular standing among Old Schoolers. And, with the passing of the years, it created an identity between Hodge's outlook and that of the Seminary. "Princeton theology" in the early years was really Charles Hodge's theology.

Posterity, however, has not always dealt kindly with Hodge, and certainly the perspective in which we now view his theological accomplishments is quite different from that in which his contemporaries viewed them. This is particularly evident at three points. First, we usually identify Hodge's theology with his three-volume *Systematic Theol-*

ogy; his contemporaries for the most part did not. They knew him principally as an essayist and polemicist. Long before the thick volumes of his *Systematic* appeared in 1872 and 1873, he had forged his place in American church life with his incisive and rigorous excursions in the *Biblical Repertory* and its successors. There is a passion and liveliness in these essays that is sometimes absent from his systematic theology.

Second, the cultural and ecclesiastical context in which Hodge was writing has today largely been forgotten. In part, of course, Hodge is himself responsible for this. The fact that he was living in a time of dramatic social and intellectual change within the country is not always evident in the pages of his *Theology*; indeed, he often ignored the world around him much as Jane Austen's novels did the Napoleonic Wars. Yet it is this context that actually engaged Hodge all of his life. He and his colleagues at Princeton worked within the lengthening shadow of the country's "infidelity," against those who were perceived to have been tainted by it theologically, and alongside those through whom revival was occurring but whose means and methods were creating ecclesiastical chaos. Hodge cannot be understood adequately if he is divorced from this context and yet, paradoxically, his *Systematic Theology* gives us insufficient help in understanding it.

Third, the argument that biblical inerrancy was a Princetonian creation has resulted in an obsessive interest in the formulation of this tenet and it has skewered our assessment of Hodge. A contemporary of Hodge would have noticed that while he affirmed his belief in the integrity of Scripture, he spent relatively little time formulating and defending it. Hodge's theological interests lay elsewhere. They were interests foisted upon him by his religious and cultural context. The hotly contested issues, the questions that called forth his great polemical powers, were, as Earl Kennedy has noted, "the doctrines of the imputation of Adam's sin, original sin, inability, and regeneration."[2] These were the issues on which Hodge forged a distinctive position as he stated his opposition to New Schoolers like Nathaniel William Taylor, revivalists like Charles Finney, the "progressive orthodox" like Horace Bushnell, the Unitarians, and, beyond them, a culture turned self-confident in its post-Enlightenment rationalism.

It is this obscured Hodge, the forgotten Hodge, the polemical Hodge, upon which this essay is focused, not the Hodge of later years who is reflected—and, some say buried—in the stout volumes of his *Systematic Theology*. First, then, I want to develop the Princetonians' perceptions of the religious state of the country and consider some of the consequences of these perceptions. Second, I will elaborate upon the contest between the Old School and New School theologies but especially as this was focused in the contest between the faculties at Yale and Princeton.

Third, I want to examine Hodge's view of the atonement, which, with its closely related issues, was at the center of his debate with Nathaniel Taylor of Yale.

Declension and Infidelity

At the beginning of the nineteenth century much of American Christianity was at the nadir of its fortunes. This, at least, was the view of many of the influential orthodox clergymen. The 1730s and 1740s, when the whole eastern seaboard had glowed with the incandescent light of the Great Awakening, were followed, as they saw it, by five decades of lethargy and declension. In these years, the Church was graced with few great divines and even fewer reports of revival. The scenes of uproar, repentance, transformation, and exultation that had marked the days of Edwards and Whitefield were not repeated; they passed into the faded corridors of Christian memory where they quietly expired.

At the same time, Enlightenment ideas were flooding into the country. Colonial militia found themselves in the company of British and French troops whose Christian views were at best uncertain and whose morals were invariably loose. The Revolution opened the door still wider to various forms of rationalism, for the French, many of whom according to Timothy Dwight were possessed "of ardent minds and daring speculations," sided with the aggrieved colonists. "No knight errant ever offered himself to an affrighted damsel with more generosity as her protector," Dwight complained, "than they to the human race."[3] The Revolution, he claimed, brought with it "a long train of immoral doctrines and practices which spread into every corner of the country."[4]

This became the common perception among ministers at the turn of the century and provided the impetus for many a sermonic foray on a Sunday morning. In a typical analysis, Joseph Lathrop reminded his congregation in 1798 that:

> In these American States, there has, for many years, and more especially since our late revolution, been a visible tendency to infidelity, and an observable growth in impiety and immorality. Family religion is falling into disuse; the ancient strict observance of the Sabbath is mightily relaxed, social worship in the church, as well as in the family, is sinking into neglect, not to say contempt. . . . In this state of general indifference, the barriers against infidelity are fallen down, and the way is open for its swift and easy progress.[5]

Lathrop went on to speak of how swiftly and easily infidelity was actually progressing. Licentious books were multiplying and circulating "without modesty," even finding their way into the stacks of "social libraries." Other people, trafficking in "indecent ridicule and malignant satire," had attacked the Bible itself. Ministers spoke of the corruption of justice that had resulted, of the growth of taverns and of tippling, of sabbath desecration, of the abuse of children, and of riots and licentiousness.[6]

The alarm thus sounded, the faithful rose as one to defend the land against further intrusion of infidelity. But what was quickly discovered was that there was no single enemy. Infidelity was a synonym for the whole range of departures from Christian faith, be they small or large.

The most flagrant expression of infidelity was found among the devotees of irreligion who followed in Thomas Paine's footsteps, although they never posed a serious challenge to more orthodox faith. In 1825 the Free Press Association was formed with its literary outlet, *The Correspondent*. A freethinkers' society that deliberately profaned the sabbath by sponsoring lectures on that day sprang up in New York. By 1830 it was rumored that twenty thousand people had been attracted to these lectures. Although this figure appears to be an exaggeration, it is undoubtedly true that anti-Christian sentiment was gaining popular support. Similar societies began to appear in other cities. In 1831 Boston saw the creation of the First Society of Free Thinkers, which was dedicated to the pursuit of "useful knowledge" such as the education of children "without regard to religious opinions." In 1835 these and other societies were linked together in a national network through the creation of the United States Moral and Philosophical Society.

The specter of unbelief, organizing itself, capitalizing on the economic disorders to enlist support for its socialism, and breeding communes and subversive ideas, greatly alarmed Christian leaders, who exaggerated its importance. Horace Bushnell, who did not panic easily, wrote in 1835 of the "considerable number" of societies of freethinkers, which were growing with "fearful rapidity." He thought he discerned why the movement was gaining ground. By opposing religion, private property, and marriage, he asserted, "they unite irreligion, rapacity and lust."[7] Therein lay their power. However, just as the movement began to gather momentum it began to disintegrate from within. By the early 1840s it had expired, the victim of apathy, inertia, penury, a bad reputation, and the devastation of the Second Great Awakening. Those who might have lent a hand to freethinking now called themselves "liberals" and abandoned the movement to its own failing devices.

The transition from "liberalism" to Unitarianism took place between 1805 and 1819. In 1805 Henry Ware was elected to the Hollis chair of theology at Harvard. In reaction to this appointment, Andover Theological Seminary was founded in 1807 to preserve and defend Christian orthodoxy, its two most distinguished faculty recruits being Moses Stuart and Leonard Woods. Orthodoxy and Christian "infidelity" were thus becoming entrenched on opposing sides of the battle.

The controversy with the emerging Unitarianism was sparked in 1815. A book inspired by Jedediah Morse was published and reviewed by the orthodox journal, *Panoplist*.[8] This drew a response from William Channing, the Unitarian luminary, that was answered by Noah Worcester. Channing then wrote two additional letters and Worcester wrote three.[9] In 1819, the controversy was suspended, but not before the orthodox had achieved their aim. "Unitarianism," observed Wisner, "which had before operated and spread in secret, was brought to light."[10] The entire subject was illumined still further by Channing himself in that same year, 1819, when in the course of an ordination sermon he systematically defended Unitarianism.[11] For the first time, responded Taylor, the world was informed about what Unitarians *did* believe rather than what they *did not* believe! Instead of "sneers and insinuations," the orthodox had some solid arguments to oppose. And oppose them they did. Channing's defense precipitated several rather complex literary duels between himself and Stuart, between Leonard Woods and Henry Ware,[12] and, in 1821, between Samuel Miller, Charles Hodge's colleague at Princeton, and the Unitarian movement as a whole.[13]

From 1821 to 1827 the New School Connecticut Calvinists spearheaded the assault on this, the latest form of Bostonian liberalism, but two new elements were added to the controversy. First, the battle was taken to Boston itself by Lyman Beecher. The object was to deprive Unitarianism of its popular support by bringing the city under the sound of revival preaching. Second, Nathaniel Taylor, professor of theology at Yale, who was most dissatisfied with the approach of the Andover theologians and offered the opinion that they had set the cause of orthodoxy back by fifty years, developed a new apologetic by softening the doctrine of human depravity, which was the most important bone of contention. Taylor was also changing direction, it needs to be noted, because he accepted the estimate made of human nature by the Scottish Common Sense realism.

Beecher's responsibility in checking Unitarianism was to advance to Boston with the Christian gospel, but when he arrived he came as a man of peace; he had honey on his tongue. Not one "knocking down" sermon was preached, he informed a friend. "I have not felt *once* the spirit of rebuke; have not uttered an ironical or sarcastic expression; have not struck one stroke at an antagonist."[14] What was needed, he said, was "luminous exposition" that wooed rather than battered, because ordinary Unitarians were not so much opposed to Christian orthodoxy as ignorant of it. They had never really had a chance to reject it. The strategy was most effective. "New cases of inquiry and of hope appear every week," he wrote, "and an impression is made among the Unitarian population too deep and solemn in favor of the revival to allow their ministers to preach against it."[15] A little less irenically, he later exulted that "orthodoxy in Massachusetts is becoming a phalanx terrible as an army with banners, and that our adversaries shall no more be able to frame iniquity by law, and draw sin as with a cart-rope."[16] Thus were his opponents left to splutter feebly as their congregations were wooed away and the ground was cut from beneath their feet. Here was Beecher, by his own admission "a man of war" from his youth upward, melting impenitent infidels with his soft words while from afar his friend, Nathaniel Taylor, was drawing their blood with his sharp treatises. It is an arresting picture.

This context deeply affected the form and direction that Hodge's theology took. First, the debate with Unitarianism, in which the Princetonians also participated, set up a deep cleavage between the New School and Old School divines. New Schoolers like Beecher and Taylor were embarrassed by the defense of Old School Calvinism made by Hodge, Woods, and Stuart. Hodge, in turn, was scandalized by the defense offered by Taylor. What the Yale divine was advocating seemed to be indistinguishable from Pelagianism. Thus were the battle lines drawn within Presbyterian and Congregational circles.

Second, the alarming situation in the country awakened the Princetonians to the need for a defense of Christianity as a whole. This was present incipiently in Hodge, although it was not to come into full bloom until a little later when Francis Patton and B. B. Warfield began their work. The emergence of apologetics as a fundamental and central concern, not merely as a peripheral exercise, was a nineteenth-century interest; more precisely, it was Princeton's innovation. It was born in a deep commitment to defend biblical faith in all of its essentials. It was this commitment that really explains Charles Hodge.

The New Theology and the Old

A reviewer of E. A. Park's *The Atonement*, a volume of considerable importance for New England theology, declared optimistically in 1854 that "there is general agreement in these views by Evangelical Christians—certainly here in New England."[17] There was, as a matter of fact, general agreement on Park's collected essays neither in New England nor anywhere else. A century earlier, there had been unanimity but for those of a more traditional bent all of this had changed when Taylor had been appointed at Yale and, according to Ebenezer Porter of Andover, had volunteered to shed darkness on the world. It was not long before the "old paths began to be called in question," another dissatisfied author said, "and the ardor of youth began to be enlisted in making new discoveries in the polar regions of speculation," especially, he noted, with respect to finding "a channel of communication between Calvinism and Pelagianism."[18] Likewise an anonymous Presbyterian speaking for the Old School charged that the New Haven divines, philosophizing to faith rather than from faith and trafficking in Scholasticism's "subtle questions," "endless logomachies," and "absurd barbarisms," had unfortunately drifted into "Arminian, Socinian, Arian and Pelagian errors."[19] This was a new turn of events, for as late as 1755 President Clap had claimed that all tutors at Yale were, as a matter of course, examined theologically and, if found guilty of Arminian or "Prelatical principles," were summarily suspended. The "New Scheme of Divinity," which Clap himself had assembled from various New England divines, was not, to judge from Hodge's review of Clap,[20] altogether above suspicion, but certainly Taylor had taken prevailing tendencies to an extreme. And when the Yale divine made his coy retreats into doubt—"it may be no one can prove" or "how do you know?"—it seemed to many Old Schoolers that he was using phrases that, "like a magic wand, have made truth and error appear alike."[21] Consequently, Charles Hodge argued that the bearers of the authentic Edwardsean mantle were the Princetonians, despite the fact that Edwards's Idealism made them a little nervous. The tradition of Dwight, Emmons, and Hopkins was being substantially preserved at Princeton and substantially subverted at Yale.

Hodge took the long view as to why this conflict had arisen. He argued that from its inception Christianity had been plagued by the conflict between two competing doctrinal systems. The one, he said, "has for its object the vindication of the Divine supremacy and sovereignty in the salvation of men; the other has for its characteristic aim the assertion of the rights of human nature. It is specially solicitous that nothing should be held to be true, which cannot be philosophically reconciled with the liberty and ability of man."[22] These competing outlooks, Hodge believed, were again at war in the nineteenth century, each claiming to be the true representative of biblical faith and both asking for the allegiance of the church. Subsequently, of course, historians have come to see that there were many other factors involved in this growing bifurcation, yet it is undeniable that at its center was a contest between two types of Reformed theology and two different estimates of the degree and consequences of human corruption.

In 1820 Taylor judged that the moment was ripe to attack the Unitarians. His objective, however, was only partly that of exposing them for the infidels he judged them to be; his other aim was to hoist to the flagpole of orthodoxy a different kind of Calvinism from the one that the Unitarians had so confidently been mocking.

The point at which Taylor entered the fray was after the ground had been cleared by the debate between Woods of Andover and Henry Ware of Harvard. Taylor now took on another Harvard divine, Andrews Norton.[23] What Taylor sought to show was that the opponents of Calvinism "never fairly attack its doctrines, as they are stated by Calvin himself, or exhibited in the creeds of the churches, or in the writings of the authors which bear his name";[24] these opponents attacked straw men! Specifically, they held up to ridicule a doctrine of human nature that even the sects would consider to be injurious and false. Calvinists in fact believed, said Taylor, that "mankind come [sic] into the world in such a state, that without the interposition of divine grace, all as soon as they became moral agents, sin in every accountable act."[25] This belief in depravity, he said, must be distinguished from "theories" about it. Among these theories was the notion of "the imputation of Adam's sin to his posterity."[26] Sin is not imputed; at least, it is not imputed in the way that Old Schoolers like Hodge imagined. All are born with a corrupted nature, Taylor affirmed, but this is not in and of itself sinful. This corrupted nature only provides the occasion for our sinning when the agent is of a morally accountable age. Furthermore, people sin inevitably, said Taylor, but not necessarily. This was a subtle distinction that the Yale professor would be called upon to defend more than once in the ensuing controversy. But it allowed Taylor to argue that his Calvinism, which he believed to be historic Calvinism, differed from that espoused at Princeton.

Posing the issue in this way appeared to Beecher to be a stroke of brilliance, and it is undeniable that it did relieve the Connecticut Calvinists of some hard apologetic tasks. Unitarians, for example, had been able to expose the harshness of Calvinistic doctrine by picturing hell as paved with the remains of innocent babies.[27] This could now be denied *fortissimo*. To Beecher Nettleton wrote: "I believe it to be a matter of fact that you and I are *really* a different kind of Calvinist from what the Unitarians have imagined or been accustomed to imagine."[28] He suggested that the New Haveners should argue that they had no interest in defending "old Calvinism"; their sole concern was with the "evangelical system." Beecher apparently accepted this as sound advice. Late in 1829, he went up to Boston to deliver a series of discourses on political atheism. On that subject, as he said, he "opened the ground tier; and let out, without let or hindrance, all the caustics in the locker."[29] He also let out a few caustics on "old Calvinism." Referring to the old view of Adam's solidarity with the human race and the imputation of his sin to all people, he said: "It is my deliberate opinion that the false philosophy which has been employed for the exposition of the Calvinistic system has done more to obstruct the march of Christianity, and to paralyze the saving power of the Gospel . . . than all other causes beside."[30] By an unnatural collusion, the Connecticut Calvinists seemed to be uniting in part with the Unitarians against the more traditional Calvinists like Hodge. This was a maneuver fraught with danger, as they were soon to discover. For while the emancipation from "old Calvinism" might be used to discomfort Unitarians by denying them their best arguments, it could also be used against those Calvinists who were thus emancipated. Unitarians seemed to grasp that the sword had two edges far more rapidly than did Taylor and his friends.

Initially, the new twist that Taylor was trying to put into Calvinism was hailed by the Unitarians as a sign that Taylor was in full flight. Realizing that "old Calvinism" was indefensible, Taylor had moved on to new ground. Then the full implication of what was taking place seemed to dawn on them even more fully. In the same year that Taylor was concluding his debate with Norton, the *Christian Examiner* decided to review a sermon of Beecher's. The reviewer spoke of "its decidedly *anti*-Calvinistic leaning." What he meant, the reviewer went on to say, was that Beecher had denied some of the "peculiarities" of Calvinism and had distinctly asserted none of them. As to particulars, the author argued that Beecher had asserted "in as strong and unqualified language as was ever used by an Arminian or Unitarian, the doctrine of man's actual *ability* and *free agency*. . . . On the doctrine of *original sin* and *native depravity*, our author is hardly less unsound in his orthodoxy." Even the doctrine of atonement, he added, "might also be adopted by all Unitarians of whom we have any knowledge."[31]

The new apologetic must have appeared almost heaven sent to the Unitarians and they were quick to exploit it. Yale was played off against Andover, then against Princeton. In the meantime, Taylor's own Calvinism had clarified further in the new direction. The 1828 *Concio ad Clerum* that he delivered to the Congregational clergy of Connecticut was a manifesto for, even an explication of, the new position. With flamboyance and subtlety, he spelled out in some detail what Calvinism meant vis-à-vis the issues raised in the debates. The Unitarians hailed the address as "able and satisfactory." They saw sure signs everywhere that Calvinists were "silently but surely advancing towards the very opinions they so eagerly condemn."[32] More embarrassing accolades could not have been heard. Disquieted and anxious about Taylor's views, many Calvinists began to have second thoughts about New Haven theology. In the following year, 1829, the Unitarians were given a break that was not altogether unexpected. The orthodox divided against themselves.

Taylor's address, *Concio ad Clerum*, had served as a call to arms for the Princetonians. Alexander fired off a broadside against Pelagianism. This was followed by a heated exchange between Hodge and Goodrich,

who had earlier purchased *The Quarterly Christian Spectator* as a literary
outlet for the Yale divines and as a voice for the New Theology. The
debate was over what, from a historical point of view, constitutes historic
Calvinism. Goodrich was simply taking Taylor's defense against the Unitarians and turning it into an aggressive offense against the Princetonians. In this he was modestly successful, for he was able to show that
Hodge was not as competent historically as he was in other ways. Hodge
had participated in an evolution within Calvinism without being fully
aware of the reasons for or results of that change. Goodrich's success,
however, had only a little to do with the theological issues at stake, and
on these matters Hodge was unmovable.

The inevitable parting of the ways came in 1837. In that year, the
General Assembly, at the instigation of the Princetonians, and especially
of Hodge, abrogated the Plan of Union of 1801, thereby excising approximately sixty thousand church members and ministers from four
synods, most of whom were predominantly under New School influence.[33] Sympathizers of the New Schoolers like Leonard Bacon expressed
their outrage, complaining that "their titles to all their church property
[were] put at hazard without the form of a trial, without the citation of
a witness, without the opportunity of defence, after having been re-
proached in mass, as disorganizers and heretics, and after measures had
been commenced leading to a judicial investigation of the charges preferred against them."[34]

Technically, this was correct. Nevertheless, it needs to be remembered that the grounds for the excision were largely theological and these
theological issues had been extensively debated in the church during the
two decades that preceded this event. It is doubtful whether further
debate in 1837 would have provided new light or changed very many
opinions. In a roundabout way this was conceded by the New Schoolers
who were Congregationalists. They decided in 1852 that Congregationalism should go its own way without any further alliances with the
Presbyterians, a preponderance of whom were Old Schoolers. It is this
context, of painful theological debate and wrenching ecclesiastical schism,
which must be allowed to form the backdrop for Hodge's theological life.

Polemics and Convictions

In the first half of the nineteenth century, down the eastern seaboard at least, ecclesiastical life was much affected by the Second Awakening. What dominated discussion, consequently, were the practical
issues that evangelists had to confront. How should conversion be presented? What is a legitimate use of persuasion? What about the Anxious
Bench? Can all accept the gospel? Should it be offered indiscriminately

to all? These were, of course, the questions provoked in particular by
Charles Finney and his "New Measures," and the answers Finney developed had an uncanny resemblance to many of the things that Taylor
had been elucidating at Yale.

Hodge was deeply concerned with this development because he
saw in its resurgent Pelagianism the supposition that conversion is a
merely human work. That being the case, Christ's work on the cross was
being emptied of any serious significance. He explained his concern in
this way:

> The constant exhortation is, to make choice of God as the portion
> of the soul, to change the governing purpose of the life, to submit
> to the moral Governor of the universe the specific act to which the
> sinner is urged as immediately connected with salvation, is an act
> which has no reference to Christ. The soul is brought immediately
> in contact with God, the Mediator is left out of view. We maintain
> that this is another Gospel. It is practically another system, and a
> legal system of religion. We do not intend that the doctrine of the
> mediation of Christ is rejected, but that it is neglected; that the
> sinner is led to God directly; that he is not urged, under the pres-
> sure of the sense of guilt, to go to Christ for pardon, and through
> him to God, but the general idea of submission (not the specific
> idea of submission to the plan of salvation through Jesus Christ)
> is urged as the making a right choice. Conviction of sin is made of
> little account, Christ and his atonement are kept out of view, so
> that the matter of salvation is not distinctly presented to the minds
> of the people.[35]

Hodge saw clearly that soteriological conclusions arise from anthropo-
logical premises, that a deficient view of the atonement could not be
corrected until the inadequate doctrine of sin had been attacked. It was
this that was at the root of the problem and it was this that was attacked
with a devotion to principle that was unswerving.

The debate now centered on whether people can be held accountable for what Adam had done. The reverse side of this coin, of course,
was whether people could be acquitted by what Christ had done. In
each case responsibility was being interpreted corporately, for in each
case there was representation of the many by the one. But there were
complexities in this that needed to be resolved.[36] In Scripture, condemnation and justification are sentential acts. We are not made unrighteous
by being pronounced so any more than we are made holy by being
declared justified. We are declared righteous when Christ's righteousness
is forensically imputed to us, but does this similarly mean that we are
unrighteous only by the judicial reckoning of Adam's sin to us? To allow
that this might be so would be to allow a Unitarian conception that we

are all natively innocent, that unrighteousness is a matter merely of divine decree and not of human constitution. The idea of condemnation as judicial pronouncement therefore had to be given underpinning in a doctrine of the actual transmission of sin from parent to child. This, however, disturbed the symmetry between the two Adams and their representative roles, for in the one case we are declared righteous without ever actually being so whereas in the other case we are declared unrighteous and we are actually so.

Hodge's solution was forged in direct opposition to the idea of mediate imputation favored by the New School divines. They argued that Adam's posterity was not involved in his sin either because they were in his loins, philosophically speaking (as the Edwardseans believed), or because this sin was simply reckoned to them as the Princetonians said. Imputation, rather, is the transmission of the consequences of that Adamic sin in the legacy of tainted human nature. Sin is, Nathaniel Taylor said, in the sinning. No one sinned in Adam but we do sin because of Adam. We are therefore pronounced guilty when we become culpable for our own sinning and never because we have a connection with Adam's sin. But as this solution was developed both in respect to conversion and in relation to Christ's work, its tendency to become a form of works-salvation, dependent ultimately not on what Christ did and does but upon what we do, became unmistakable. Hodge rejected it unconditionally.

In developing his own view of Adam's federal representation, Hodge was aware that he was taking an unpopular and unfashionable stand. The Old School doctrine, which he only belatedly discovered was not entirely identical with his own, was subjected, he said, to "execration and contempt" from the New School men and a little earlier Alexander had said that they treated it as "so absurd" that they did not condescend to discuss it. This was a provocative statement, for the New School divines were seldom reticent to discuss Old School absurdities!

Hodge dismissed the Idealist's notion of a universal humanity, a generic life common to all people, as "a mere hypothesis,"[37] perhaps not so much out of theological considerations as from philosophical. He was also dissatisfied with the consequent notion of imputation. Edwards's theology used the old word but it had none of the old doctrinal content. But what Edwards had that Nathaniel Taylor lacked was a doctrine of "native depravity"; it was Hodge's agreement with Edwards on this point that he felt entitled him to be called an Edwardsean. It was the deviation from this point by the New Haven theologians that made them usurpers of the Edwardsean heritage. Hodge nevertheless found himself at odds even with the more traditional Edwardseans in explaining how we are culpable for Adam's sin. People have a common nature, Hodge countered, only in the sense that they have a common origin, belong to the same species, have generically identical rational and moral faculties, and are commonly alienated from God at birth. Adam "was an individual man, with no more of the generic life of the race than any other man."[38] Thus Hodge might loudly claim his Edwardsean heritage when in debate with New Haven theologians, but his claim became a good deal more muted when he was in discussion with more conservative followers of Edwards! Indeed, with them Hodge saw his differences with Edwards as more important than his similarities, whereas with Taylor Hodge accentuated his similarities and passed over his differences in silence.

The Protestant Reformers, but in particular John Calvin, included under the single term original sin both the imputed guilt of Adam's sin and the inherent depravity consequent upon it. Hodge believed, however, that it was the latter aspect that the Reformers emphasized. He suggested that this was partly because Roman Catholic theologians at the time held an inadequate view of human corruption and partly because Calvin wanted to affirm that we are not innocent creatures condemned merely because Adam sinned. Hodge himself was to assume Calvin's perspective but only as a result of being embroiled in this extended debate on the subject. Initially he stressed the former aspect, the imputed guilt of Adam's sin, and declared that evangelical religion would survive only if this emphasis was maintained.

The idea of imputation, that one person suffers the penalty for another's sin, he saw to be the working principle of the universe. This principle would still be part of the warp and woof of life even if the Fall, the Bible, and God were to be denied. No man is an island. No one lives out his or her life in a vacuum. The individual acts of one person always touch and affect others. It was the perception of this truth that redeemed Bushnell's study *Christian Nurture*, and it was the failure to see this by the late followers of Edwards that was subverting "the whole evangelical system." For they contended that God could not justly condemn a person for sins other than his or her own. How then, Hodge asked, could he justify a person for righteousness other than that person's own?

The notion of federal representation came into its own when the idea of covenants began to be important.[39] The notion of a probationary period in which the human race was on trial through its representative, Adam, was then advanced. Because of this covenant, only Adam's first sin was imputed to his posterity, for at this point the covenant was abrogated. This was the basis of Hodge's view that, he said, was also stated with "extraordinary unanimity" by both Lutheran and Calvinistic confessions and could be summarized thus:

1. That Adam, as the common father of all men, was by divine appointment constituted not only the natural, but the federal head or representative of his posterity. The race stood its probation in him. His sin was the sin of the race, because the sin of its divinely and righteously constituted representative. We therefore sinned in Adam in the same sense that we died in Christ. 2. The penalty of death threatened against Adam in the event of his transgression was not merely the dissolution of the body, but spiritual death, the loss of the divine favor and of original righteousness; and the consequent corruption of his whole nature. 3. This penalty came upon his race. His sin was the judicial ground on which the favor and fellowship of God were withdrawn or withheld from the apostate family of man. 4. Since the fall, therefore, men are by nature, or as they are born, the children of wrath. They are not only under condemnation, but destitute of original righteousness, and corrupted in their whole nature. According to this view of the subject, the ground of the imputation of Adam's sin is the federal union between him and his posterity, in such sense that it would not have been imputed had he not been constituted their representative. It is imputed to them not because it was antecedently to that imputation, and irrespective of the covenant on which the imputation is founded, already theirs; but because they were appointed to stand their probation in him.[40]

We all, therefore, sustain a twofold relationship to Adam. He is both our natural head and our federal representative. In all of his writings prior to the publication of the *Systematic Theology* in 1872 and 1873, Hodge insisted that it was on the grounds of the latter relationship, federal headship, that we are made liable to the penalty for Adam's sin, a penalty that consisted in the deprivation of righteousness, the suffering of inner corruption, and exposure to God's wrath. Hodge was forced to take this position because of his creationist views—namely, that the soul was not derived from the parents as the body is, but was given individually by divine fiat. The soul comes fresh from the hand of God and at the moment of birth becomes liable to punishment for Adam's sin. Some of Hodge's critics believed that this was a curious position for a Reformed divine to take, but it should be noted that Hodge could claim some company among the Reformed. It seems to court the idea that there is perhaps a moment of innocence in the life of each person before the sentence of guilt begins to be implemented. Furthermore, it reduces the idea of original sin to something less than Protestant theology has usually held out for; original sin, it seems, is not really an inherent corruption transmitted from parent to child, but a corruption inflicted upon people by God. The link is not a common nature, nor yet a universalized humanity, but a decree of God. To deny that we were in some sense acting in Adam through a common nature was to make the same denial that the Remonstrants had uttered. The belated concession by Hodge, then, that we are condemned not only because of federal representation but also because of natural relationship may have been an indication that the Princeton theologian realized some of the difficulties to which his theory was leading, but it is doubtful whether the concession alone, without any serious modifications to the entire doctrine, could save him from the charge, ironical as it was, that he had inadvertently espoused Arminian tenets.[41]

In view of this, it is necessary to examine in some detail the exegetical grounds on which Hodge's views of representation were built. The principal writing in which this is made plain is his *Commentary on the Epistle to the Romans*. It was no accident that Hodge chose to write on this letter. Both Moses Stuart and Albert Barnes produced commentaries on it and in the process slighted the view of immediate imputation espoused by Hodge.

In Romans 5:12-21, the central argument according to Hodge is contained in verses 12, 18, and 19, verses 13-17 being a parenthesis. This in itself cut across the grain of Barnes's and Stuart's argument, for it suggested that the passage did not intend to dwell on the disproportionate blessings of Christ's righteousness compared with the evils occasioned by the Fall. The apostle, rather, was arguing for the similarities between Adam's representative and Christ, not for their dissimilarities. The crux is verse 12, "As by the offence of one all are condemned, so by the righteousness of one are all justified," verses 18 and 19 being its amplification. The apostle sets out to show, however "contrary to the common mode of thinking among men," that God dealt with mankind in this representative. For if a penalty has been inflicted on men, a law must have been transgressed. Sin is not imputed where there is no transgressed law. The law in question, however, could not have been Moses' Law, since there were many who died before it was given (v. 14); it could not be nature's law written on the heart. Therefore, "as neither of these laws is sufficiently extensive to embrace *all* the subjects of the penalty, we must conclude that men are subject to death on account of Adam; that is, it is for the offence of one that many die, vs. 13, 14."[42] Thus is Adam a type of Christ.

The key to understanding the critical words in verse 12 is to understand the word *death* not in a physiological sense, but a penal one. In that case, the verse could be paraphrased thus: "All men are subject to penal evils on account of one man; this is the position to be proved, (v. 12) that such is the case is evident, because the infliction of a penalty supposes the violation of a law. But such evil was inflicted before the

giving of the Mosaic law, it comes on men before the transgression of
the law of nature, or even the existence of inherent depravity, it must,
therefore, be for the offence of one man that judgment has come upon
all them to condemnation."[43] Hodge maintained this causal link between
Adam's sin and our condemnation without using the Augustinian device
of translating the *eph' hō* as *in whom (in quo)*, in which case it would
read: By one man all men became sinners, and hence death passed upon
all men, *through that one man*, in whom all sinned. He settled for the
simple statement "All die for that, or because that, all have sinned." He
insisted, however, that the last phrase is to be interpreted as meaning
that "all men are regarded and treated as sinners" on account of Adam's
act. Interpretations that sever the causal link between Adam's act and
God's subsequent treatment of mankind under conditions of condemnation are to be rejected. Thus Stuart suggested that the verse be rendered "As Adam sinned and died, so in like manner death has passed
on all men, because all have sinned," and others proposed: "As by
Adam, sin (corruption of nature) was introduced into the world, and
death as its consequence, and so death passed on all men, because all
have become corrupt." The point of this verse, Hodge countered, is not
to contrast Adam and Christ, showing that corruption sprang from the
one and holiness from the other, nor to show that Adam was the reason
for our condemnation as Christ is for our justification. It is true that
inner corruption comes from Adam, but this is neither the truth that is
in view nor the basis on which God pronounces his judgment on us.
Unless this is granted, the biblical doctrine of justification falls away.[44]
Union with "Adam is the cause of death; union with Christ is the cause
of life,"[45] and in both cases the principles of representation, of imputation, of federal union, are identical. In the one case human beings are
treated as judicially guilty without respect to their actual condition, and
in the other case Christians are treated as judicially innocent without
respect to their actual condition.

That the ground of imputation of sin was man's federal relationship
to Adam, rather than natural union, is clear from the fact that Jesus was
part of Adam's natural posterity yet Adam's sin was not imputed to him.
The fact that Jesus was regarded as sinless "supposes that the federal,
and not the natural union is the essential ground of the imputation; that
the sense in which Adam's sin is ours is a legal and not a moral sense
and that the sense in which we sinned in him is that in which we act
as a representative and not a literal sense."[46] Inner pollution was not
transmitted to Christ, not because the Virgin Birth interrupted its transmission, but because Adam had not represented him and therefore God
did not inflict him with this depravity.

The symmetry between the two Adams is almost perfect in Hodge's theology. We are justified and declared free from penal sanction not for what we do, but for what Christ did for us, just as we are declared liable to punishment not for what we have done, but for what Adam did as our representative. Hodge summarized his doctrine thus:

> 1. That Christ, in the covenant of redemption, is constituted the head and representative of his people, and that, in virtue of this federal union, and agreeably to the terms of the eternal covenant, they are regarded and treated as having done what he did and suffered what he suffered in their name and in their behalf. They died in him. They rose in him; not literally, so that his acts were their acts, but representatively. 2. That the reward promised to Christ in the covenant of redemption, was the justification, sanctification, and eternal salvation of his people. 3. That the judicial ground, therefore, of the justification of the believers is not their own personal righteousness, nor the holy nature which they derive from Christ, but his obedience and sufferings, performed and endured in their name, and which became theirs in virtue of the covenant and by gracious imputation of God. 4. That the believer is not only justified by the righteousness of Christ, but sanctified by his Spirit.[47]

The work of Christ, then, was centrally that of satisfying the demands of justice, thereby enabling God to be just when justifying sinners. To do this, Christ represented us in our sin, as a priest offering himself sacrificially in our stead. He bore our sin, propitiating the divine wrath that it called forth.

The atonement led naturally into considerations of theodicy, for Hodge believed that the justice of God required an atonement and the atonement made possible the preservation of the moral structure of the world. The character of God was on trial and remains on trial, for his justice demands that he treat his creatures as they deserve. If he is moral, he will favor what is good and show his disapprobation for what is wrong. This disapprobation, Hodge believed, is administered not merely as a deterrent to society, nor as a form of rehabilitation of the sinner, but because it is deserved. And because it is deserved, only Christ's interposition could preserve us from that calamity which the vindication of God's character would produce.

Here lay the crux, so to speak, of Hodge's differences with the New School thinkers. For they believed, in most cases, that in God's government of the world punishment was used but the purpose was to prevent sin and to correct the sinner. This attitude led naturally to the assumption that the chief goal of existence is happiness, and holiness is simply the best way to get there. But, countered Hodge, "we know that holiness is something more than a means; that to be happy is not the end and reason for being holy; that enjoyment is not the highest end of being." This results in our viewing ethical choices in commercial terms. A choice is made, not because it is the inherently right thing to do, but because it produces profit of some kind and avoids loss. Virtue becomes expediency. The end justifies the means. And human beings are degraded because their moral capacities are reduced to being merely the instruments of happiness.

The debate between Hodge and Taylor represented the collision between two entire theological systems. At the center of one was the representative view of the atonement, of which Hodge was the chief proponent, and at the center of the other was the governmental theory whose most articulate advocate was Taylor. And related to each view were different understandings of human nature and of God's moral relationship to the world.

Hodge's view was obviously constructed around a symmetry between the two Adams. This had the twofold advantage of providing a cutting edge in the debate over human nature and placing justification at the center of Christ's work, for both doctrines—that of sin and that of justification—depended upon the idea of imputation. In the one, Adam represents us covenantally, being the federal head of the race, and in the other Christ represents us in his righteousness and through that righteousness redeems us from the law's sanction, bearing it in himself in our stead.

The parallel was not of course precise in every detail. The sin of Adam, as Hodge came to stress, was not only imputed to us by means of a sentence or declaration, it was also transmitted to us by nature. We are sinners both by what we are and by what we did in Adam our head. On the other hand, we are justified not by what we are—that is the Roman Catholic view—but by what we are declared to be in Christ. The chronology of these aspects, in other words, is not paralleled on the two sides of the equation. The declaration of human sin followed after it, whereas the declaration of the Christian's righteousness in Christ precedes its actual existence. In Hodge's thought, however, this parallelism was greatly complicated by the fact that he was a creationist. This meant, then, that the depravity of Adam was handed on to succeeding generations as much by divine decree as anything. This is quite unlike the manner in which our actual righteousness is transmitted to us by Christ, which occurs, not by divine decree, but by union with him.

Taylor's view was, of course, quite different. He opposed the view of depravity as believed by Hodge and though he on occasion used the word *imputation*, it was never in a Hodgean sense. The atonement was for Taylor the ground upon which God could forgive sin. What, then, was this ground? Was it that Christ bore the sin of those whom he represented, suffering vicariously for them? Not at all. Rather, he held as had Grotius before him that an equivalent manifestation of God's justice is made in Christ's death. This means that the Cross was the occasion upon which God showed his general displeasure about sin. Having done so and thereby sustained his own moral government of the world, he had secured for himself, as it were, a free hand to forgive all or any without requiring of them a strict equivalent of punishment in Christ for sins committed.

This principle was taken a step further in Bushnell, who articulated a view held more or less in common with Auguste Sabatier, A. Ritschl, A. Harnack, Hastings Rashdall, and R. S. Franks. The essence of the idea, originally stated by Abelard, was that through the incarnation, God illumined the world by his wisdom and aimed to excite in us a love for him. The atonement is important, not for what was done objectively on the Cross, but for the *effect* that it has on us subsequently and subjectively; the atonement, in other words, takes place in and with the human response that it evokes. It is this principle that Bushnell clarified. Love, he said, provided the identity between God and sin; we do not look to the vinegar and gall and the writhing body of Jesus as the grounds for forgiveness, but to that divine love in the depths of which our sin is borne and absorbed. The Cross, therefore, is a declaration, not of the satisfaction of our sins in Christ, but of their cancellation within the being of God so that, having expressed his displeasure over sin and painfully accepted the consequences, his moral government of the world is still intact. But such a solution does mean that by grounding the principle of sacrifice solely in love, even if the character of God is magnified in the process, Bushnell leaves his readers with the impression that the work of Christ is not unique. There is, he says, a Gethsemane and a Calvary in *all* love, the mother who tearfully suffers over her child, the husband who mourns the premature death of his wife, those in the nation who sorrowfully bear in their spirits the weight of collective calamities and follies. Love, he declares, suffers the adversities and pains of others, taking on itself the burden of their evils. This is true not only of divine love, but also of human.

Nathaniel Taylor, therefore, represents a halfway house between Hodge and Bushnell. In Hodge the work of Christ, even if it has to be appropriated subjectively, is nevertheless firmly objective; in Bushnell it is largely subjective. In Hodge the law in accordance with which the universe runs is an expression of what God is; in Taylor and Bushnell there is more than a hint that this law is outside of God, and hence of itself arbitrary. In Hodge the work of Christ, relative to the expressed character of God, is unique; in Bushnell it is not.

Conclusion

It was Hodge's calling to live in a time of extraordinary intellectual transformation in the nation, a time when many of its structures and institutions were in disarray, and when the church itself was in some disorder and perplexity. The church stood at a crossroads, and Hodge pulled mightily in one direction while Taylor, aided by the changing climate in the country, pulled equally insistently in the other. They were both victorious. Hodge succeeded in excising the New School cancer from Presbyterian church life, but Taylor succeeded in opening the door to theological views that would soon spread far and wide and be the ruin of evangelical faith, Reformed and Arminian. Taylor was the stepping stone to the next generation's Liberalism, and that in turn would produce the countermovement of Fundamentalism. How very different subsequent American church life might have been if Hodge had prevailed in expunging Taylorism not only from Presbyterian circles but also from Protestantism in general! As it was, he slowed the inevitable march toward a theology resonant with human self-confidence, as was the culture, but he could not halt it.

It is not difficult to see Hodge's weaknesses. He was not a great historian; only when he was stiffly debated about his claims to historic Calvinism did he grudgingly allow that he believed many things Calvin never taught. He did not recognize as matters for serious theological reflection what was going on in the culture. His *Systematic Theology*, as a result, reads like a piece of eternal wisdom, albeit gathered from European divines, which could be deposited in any age or place with equal ease. He was more astute philosophically than his readers may realize, but he was prone to treat philosophy with the back of his hand. At the same time, he drew heavily off philosophical writers. He also imbibed the interests of Common Sense realism, which was, after all, an Enlightenment philosophy. This occurred almost without recognition on his part.

All of these things are true. But these weaknesses occurred within a man who at times almost alone held back the floodwaters of a sickly cultural theology and who, as a result, must be accorded a place in the annals of church history that cannot be erased. He was a man of very great integrity who followed single-mindedly his calling to obey the teaching of the biblical Word, and through this to live his life to God's glory. And in this he succeeded.

Notes: Charles Hodge

1. The creation of Princeton Theological Seminary had originally met with considerable resistance among ministers. Philip Lindsley spoke of the "popular

clamour [sic] so extensively raised against our school" because of the fear it would become "an engine of political power" and undercut the role of practicing ministers in training future ministers (Philip Lindsley, *A Plea for the Theological Seminary at Princeton, N.J.* [Trenton, 1821], 19, 18). Despite its successful establishment, as well as that of other seminaries, the preparation of ministers lagged far behind the need. Timothy Dwight, who was appointed President of Yale College in 1795, noted that between 1700 and 1801 the population had doubled every twenty-three years. In 1801, however, of 1,008 active churches in Massachusetts and Connecticut, only 749 had ministers. This pattern persisted through the nineteenth century. In 1828, the *Journal of the American Education Society* reported that among 960 Congregational churches, 240 had pastoral vacancies; among 3,723 Calvinistic Baptist churches, 1,146 were vacant; among the Protestant Episcopal churches 112 of the 598 churches were vacant. The next year Hodge reported that between 600 and 700 Presbyterian congregations out of 1,880 were "destitute of regular pastors," and he went on to note that "the proportion of ministers, to the population of the United States, is every year rapidly diminishing" (Anon. [Charles Hodge], *Articles on the American Education Society* [Philadelphia, 1928], 7). In 1846 the American Home Missionary Society issued a "loud call" for men for the West and South; Ohio needed 11, Indiana 14, Michigan 13, Wisconsin 11, Illinois 16, Missouri 9, Iowa 10, Georgia 2, Kentucky 4, Tennessee 2 (*Thirtieth Annual Report of the Directors of the American Education Society* [Boston, 1846], 47). The fear that Hodge expressed, that the proportion of ministers relative to the population was declining, was paralleled in some figures Ebenezer Porter published in 1821. In his survey of college graduates, he had found that between 1620 and 1720, approximately 1 in 2 became ministers; between 1720 and 1770, the proportion dropped to 1 in 3; between 1770 and 1810 to 1 in 5; and between 1800 and 1810 to 1 in 6 (Ebenezer Porter, *A Sermon Delivered in Boston, on the Anniversary of the American Education Society* [Andover, 1921], 5).

2. Earl William Kennedy, "An Historical Analysis of Charles Hodge's Doctrines of Sin and Particular Grace" (Ph.D. diss., Princeton Theological Seminary, 1968), 17.

3. Timothy Dwight, *A Discourse on Some Events of the Last Century, Delivered in the Brick Church in New Haven, on Wednesday, January 7, 1801* (New Haven, 1801), 23. Cf. Dwight's attitude to·vard the French Revolution in his *The Major Poems of Timothy Dwight (1752-1817), With a Dissertation on the History, Eloquence, and Poetry of the Bible* (Gainesville, FL: Scholars' Facsimiles and Reprints, 1969), 384.

4. Dwight, *A Discourse,* 19.

5. Joseph Lathrop, *A Sermon, on the Dangers of the Times, from Infidelity and Immorality; and Especially from a Lately Discovered Conspiracy Against Religion and Government, Delivered at West Springfield and afterward at Springfield* (Springfield, 1798), 12.

6. Characteristic assessments are found in Lyman Beecher, *A Sermon, Delivered in the North Presbyterian Church in Hartford, May 20, 1813, On the Evening Subsequent to the Formation of the "Connecticut Society for the Promotion of Good Morals"* (Hartford, 1813); R. D. Mussey, *An Address on Ardent Spirit, Read Before the New Hampshire Medical Society at their Annual Meeting, June 5, 1827 and Published at their Request* (Boston, 1929); Leonard Bacon, *Total Abstinence from Ardent Spirits, An Address Delivered by Request of the Young Men's Temperance Society of New-Haven, in the North Church, June 24, 1829* (New-Haven, 1829); James Dana,

The Folly of Practical Atheism. A Discourse Delivered in the Chapel of Yale College, on Lord's Day, November 23, 1794 (New-Haven, 1794).

7. Horace Bushnell, *Crisis in the Church* (Hartford, 1835).

8. Thomas Belsham, *American Unitarianism; or a Brief History of "the Progress and Present State of the Unitarian Churches in America," Compiled from Documents, and Information Communicated by the Rev. James Freeman, D. D. and William Wells Jun. Esq. of Boston, and From Other Unitarian Gentlemen in this Country, by Rev. Thomas Belsham. Extracted from His "Memories of the Life of the Reverend Theophilus Lindsey," Printed in London, 1812, and Now Published for the Benefit of the Christian Churches in this Country, without Note or Alteration* (Boston, 1815). Jedediah Morse and Jeremiah Evarts, "Review of American Unitarianism," *Panoplist* 11 (June 1815): 241-72.

9. William E. Channing, *A Letter to the Rev. Samuel C. Thatcher, on the Aspersions Contained in a Late Number of the Panoplist on the Ministers of Boston and the Vicinity* (Boston, 1815); Noah Worcester, *A Letter to the Rev. William E. Channing on the Subject of His Letter to the Rev. Samuel Thatcher* (Boston, 1815); William E. Channing, *Remarks on the Rev. Dr. Worcester's Letter to Mr. Channing, on the "Review of American Unitarianism"* (Boston, 1815); Noah Worcester, *A Second Letter to the Rev. William E. Channing on the Subject of Unitarianism* (Boston, 1815); William E. Channing, *Remarks on the Rev. Dr. Worcester's Second Letter to Mr. Channing on American Unitarianism* (Boston, 1815); Noah Worcester, *A Third Letter to the Rev. William E. Channing on the Subject of Unitarianism* (Boston, 1815).

10. [B. B. Wisner], *A Review of the Rev. Dr. Channing's Discourse, Preached at the Dedication of the Second Congregational Unitarian Church, New York, December 7, 1826* (Boston, 1827), 4.

11. William E. Channing, *A Sermon Delivered at the Ordination of the Rev. Jared Sparks, to the Pastoral Care of the First Independent Church in Baltimore, May 5, 1819* (Baltimore, 1819).

12. Moses Stuart, *Letters to the Rev. Wm. E. Channing, Containing Remarks on his Sermon, Recently Preached and Published at Baltimore* (Andover, 1819); [Andrews Norton], *A Statement of Reasons For Not Believing the Doctrines of Trinitarians Respecting the Nature of God, and the Person of Christ. Occasioned By Professor Stuart's Letters to Mr. Channing* (Boston, 1819); Leonard Woods, *Letters to Unitarians Occasioned by the Sermon of the Reverend William E. Channing at the Ordination of the Rev. J. Sparks* (Andover, 1820); Henry Ware, *Letters Addressed to Trinitarians and Calvinists, Occasioned by Dr. Woods' Letters to Unitarians* (Cambridge, 1820); Leonard Woods, *A Reply to Dr. Ware's Letters to Trinitarians and Calvinists* (Andover, 1821); Henry Ware, *Answer to Dr. Woods' Reply, In a Second Series of Letters Addressed to Trinitarians and Calvinists* (Cambridge, 1822); Leonard Woods, *Remarks on Dr. Ware's Answer* (Andover, 1822); Henry Ware, *A Postscript to the Second Series of Letters Addressed to Trinitarians and Calvinists, In Reply to the Remarks of Dr. Woods on those Letters* (Cambridge, 1823).

13. Samuel Miller, *Letters on Unitarianism; Addressed to the Members of the First Presbyterian Church, in the City of Baltimore* (Trenton, 1821). Cf. Moses Stuart, *Letters on the Eternal Generation of the Son of God, addressed to the Rev. Samuel Miller, D. D.* (Andover, 1822); Samuel Miller, *Letters on the Eternal Sonship of Christ: addressed to the Rev. Prof. Stuart, of Andover* (Philadelphia, 1823). Archibald Alexander, "Remarks on Correspondence between Prof. Stuart and Doc. Miller," MS, File D, Speer Memorial Library, Princeton Theological Seminary.

14. Lyman Beecher, *The Autobiography of Lyman Beecher*, ed. Barbara M. Cross, 2 vols. (Cambridge, 1961), 1:430.

15. Ibid., 1:400.

16. Ibid., 2:11.

17. Anon., Review of *The Atonement: Discourses and Treatises by Edwards, Smalley, Maxy, Emmons, Griffin, Burge, and Weeks. With an Introductory Essay by Edwards A. Park, The Congregational Quarterly* 1 (July 1859): 309.

18. An Edwardsean [Joseph Harvey?], *Letters, On the Present State and Probable Results of Theological Speculations in Connecticut* (no publication information), 27-28.

19. A Presbyterian, *A Critical, Philosophical, and Theological Review of A Dissertation on Native Depravity, by Gardiner Spring, D. D.* (New York, 1833), 9.

20. Charles Hodge, Review of *A Brief History and Vindication of the Doctrines received and established in the Churches of New England*, by Thomas Clap, *The Biblical Repertory and Princeton Review* 11 (July 1839): 369-404.

21. An Observer [N. Hewit?], *An Address, to the Congregational Churches in Connecticut, on the Present State of Their Religious Concerns* (Hartford, 1933), 17.

22. Charles Hodge, "Remarks on the Princeton Review," *The Biblical Repertory and Princeton Review* 23 (1851): 309.

23. Andrews Norton, "Thoughts on True and False Religion," *Christian Disciple* 2, new series (1820): 337-65; [Nathaniel Taylor], "Review of Eskine's Evidences, and Norton on True and False Religion," *The Quarterly Christian Spectator* 4 (1822): 249-64, 299-318, 445-48, 667-68; Andrews Norton, "Views of Calvinism," *Christian Disciple* 4, new series (1822): 244-80; [Nathaniel Taylor], "Review of Norton's Views of Calvinism," *The Quarterly Christian Spectator* 5 (1823): 196-224; Anon., "The State of the Calvinistic Controversy," *Christian Disciple* 5, new series (May and June 1823): 212-35; Anon. [Nathaniel Taylor], "Review Renewed," *The Quarterly Christian Spectator* 6 (1824): 310-37, 360-74.

24. Anon. [Nathaniel Taylor], "Review Renewed," 301.

25. Anon. [Nathaniel Taylor], "Review of Norton's . . . ," 217.

26. Ibid.

27. Leonard Bacon, "Future Punishment of Infants Not a Doctrine of Calvinism," *Spirit of the Pilgrims* 1 (January 1828): 45-52; "Future Punishment of Infants Not a Doctrine of Calvinism," *Spirit of the Pilgrims* 1 (February 1828): 78-95; and "Future State of Infants," *Spirit of the Pilgrims* 1 (March 1828): 149-64. Lyman Beecher, "To the Editor of the Christian Examiner and Theological Review," *Spirit of the Pilgrims* 3 (January 1830): 17-24; "To the Editor of the Christian Examiner and Theological Review," *Spirit of the Pilgrims* 3 (February 1830): 72-86; "To the Editor of the Christian Examiner and Theological Review," *Spirit of the Pilgrims* 3 (April 1830): 181-95. Cf. "Examination of a Note by Dr. Beecher," *The Christian Examiner* 4 (September and October 1827): 431-48; 5 (May and June 1828): 229-63.

28. Beecher, *Autobiography*, 1:410.

29. Ibid., 2:158.

30. Ibid., 2:159.

31. Anon., "Beecher's Sermon at Worcester," *The Christian Examiner* 1 (January and February 1824): 49-50.

32. Anon., "On the State of the Question Between the Orthodox and Liberal Parties in This Country," *The Christian Examiner* 5 (January and February 1828): 1.

33. Charles Hodge, "General Assembly of 1837," *The Biblical Repertory and Princeton Review* 9 (July 1837): 407-85. Cf. Charles Hodge, "Reunion of Old and

New-School Presbyterians," *The Biblical Repertory and Princeton Review* 37 (April 1865): 271-313.

34. Leonard Bacon, *Seven Letters to the Rev. George A. Calhoun, Concerning the Pastoral Union of Connecticut, and its Charges Against the Ministers and Churches* (New Haven, 1840), 20.

35. Charles Hodge, "The New Divinity Tried," in *Theological Essays: Reprinted from the Princeton Review* (New York, 1846), 12.

36. See Elwyn A. Smith, "The Doctrine of Imputation and the Presbyterian Schism of 1837-38," *Journal of the Presbyterian Historical Society* 38 (September 1960): 129-51.

37. Charles Hodge, "What is Christianity?" *The Biblical Repertory and Princeton Review* 32 (January 1860): 137.

38. Ibid.

39. See Peter Y. DeJong, *The Covenant Idea in New England Theology 1620-1847* (Grand Rapids, 1945).

40. Charles Hodge, "The First and Second Adam," *The Biblical Repertory and Princeton Review* 32 (April 1860): 340.

41. The Reformers included under the term *original sin* both what was inherited and what was imputed. The distinction between original sin and original damnation was to come later. Hodge's opponents saw in his position such a stress on imputation, hence on original damnation, that current corruption was not adequately affirmed. This objection took several forms. Goodrich in his debate with Hodge, carried in *The Christian Quarterly Spectator*, sought to embarrass Hodge on this point, arguing that "by insisting that *reatus* denotes mere *liability to punishment* rather than ill-desert (true guilt), [Hodge] has unwittingly espoused the position which Turretin ascribes to the Remonstrants, and which he attacks as really a denial of imputation" (Kennedy, "Charles Hodge's Doctrines of Sin and Particular Grace," 73). Later, Robert Dabney charged that Hodge's insistence on parallels in every detail between the representation of the two Adams led naturally to Arminianism and Romanism. On the latter point, justification would have to be seen as an infused righteousness to correspond to the infused corruption, and on the former point, faith must precede and not follow regeneration: "Every one who has a *modicum* of theological knowledge knows that this is precisely Arminianism" (Robert L. Dabney, "Hodge's Systematic Theology," *The Southern Presbyterian Review* 24 [1873]: 209). Along a slightly different line, Landis argued that Hodge undercut, with his insistence on this parallel between the Adams, an actual participation in Adam's sin. For Hodge, he thought, there was only imputed sin and not actual participation in Adam in his sinning (R. L. Landis, " 'Unthinkable' Propositions and Original Sin," *The Southern Presbyterian Review* 26 [April 1875]: 313-15). This charge was developed fully in his book *The Doctrine of Original Sin, as Received and Taught by the Churches of the Reformation, Stated and Defended, and the Error of Dr. Hodge in Claiming that this Doctrine Recognizes the Gratuitous Imputation of Sin, Pointed Out and Refuted* (Richmond, 1884).

42. Charles Hodge, *Commentary on the Epistle to the Romans* (Philadelphia, 1864), 176.

43. Ibid., 190.

44. Ibid., 185.

45. Charles Hodge, *Systematic Theology*, 3 vols. (New York, 1872), 2:203.

46. Hodge, "The First and Second Adam," 367.

47. Ibid., 340-41.

3

BENJAMIN B. WARFIELD

W. ANDREW HOFFECKER

Benjamin B. Warfield

WHEN Benjamin B. Warfield was called from Western Seminary in Pittsburgh to Princeton Seminary in 1887, the Seminary had been an established and dominant force for over seventy years. He joined a succession of professors that included Archibald Alexander, Charles Hodge, and his son A. A. Hodge, who were influential in training over six thousand students in Christian theology.[1] Warfield occupied the chair of Didactic and Polemical Theology. His task at Princeton, like his predecessors', was to produce ministers who were so thoroughly trained in Reformed theology that they could effectively proclaim the gospel and refute any teaching that did not conform to the high standard of Calvinistic orthodoxy.

Warfield's legacy at Princeton was a proud tradition. As Archibald Alexander, Princeton's first president, approached death, he summoned Charles Hodge to his bedside and gave him a walking stick. This stick, explained Alexander, was handed down to Hodge "as a symbol of orthodoxy."[2] The elder Hodge fulfilled that theological mission by his dedicated leadership of Old School Presbyterians, his voluminous publications, and his diligent seminary teaching. Charles's son, A. A. Hodge, filled the chair of theology for only seven years after his father's death in 1878. Although the younger Hodge's premature death prevented him from attaining the stature of his father, his *Outlines of Theology* has been recognized by some followers of Princeton as a model of theological precision. Also, in his *Popular Lectures on Theological Themes*, published posthumously in 1887, Hodge articulated as forcefully as any of the other Princeton men a Calvinistic basis for the integration of Christianity with cultural activity. And when nineteenth-century secularists mounted campaigns for religious activity in American public life, Hodge urgently insisted that Calvinism was the only theological worldview from which Christians could defend traditional American values and institutions such as family, law, education, and economics.

Of course, in many academic circles today, theological wags would sarcastically whisper that Warfield's appointment perpetuated an already ingrown theological atmosphere. Their criticism would be that instead of adding diversity of opinion, the party line simply gained yet another advocate. But the Princetonians considered their tradition a sacred trust; they gloried in their Reformed heritage. And Warfield's appointment certainly enhanced their efforts through writing and lecturing to maintain orthodoxy's influence in American religious life. In a remark long remembered and often berated by Princeton's detractors, Charles Hodge twice publicly claimed that "a new idea never originated" at Princeton. Those sympathetic to Reformed theology echoed his words, interpreting them to mean that although scholarly research went forward, no modification of belief resulted. Not only did Princetonians deny adjusting their message to suit their times, but they also staunchly resisted any attempt to move Presbyterianism from its Calvinist moorings.

In fact, at the seminary's 1912 centennial celebration, Francis L. Patton proudly claimed that Princeton theology "is exactly the same as it was a hundred years ago." He added that while there has been a New Haven Theology and an Andover Theology, "there never was a distinctively Princeton Theology; Princeton's boast, if she has any reason to boast at all, is in her unwavering fidelity to the theology of the Reformation."[3] Hodge's and Patton's claims have been the object of much debate between old Princeton's friends and critics alike. Ned B. Stonehouse, as a sympathetic biographer of one of Princeton's revered professors, J. Gresham Machen, pointedly argues that Hodge's and Warfield's theologies were not "at every point as completely free of philosophical and speculative influences as they wanted to be and supposed they were—or as lacking in originality as they seemed to claim." Yet he qualified his remarks by saying that any noticeable change in emphasis was due to a "new note of militancy as the issues were drawn . . . in America and Europe."[4]

The purpose of this chapter is to evaluate several of Warfield's major contributions to the Princeton theology in light of discussions about continuity and discontinuity in thought among the various men. Even though Warfield produced no *magnum opus*, he wrote hundreds of articles and reviews that provide ample material by which both the broad outlines and the details of his views may be judged. This chapter will examine three areas that reflect concerns not only prominent in Warfield's work but stressed by his Princeton predecessors as well: religious experience, scholarly criticism in academic journals, and the use of Scottish Common Sense Philosophy. Warfield's predecessors had already articulated clear positions on each of these subjects. A commitment to preserve an established tradition was foremost in each of their minds, yet a changing historical context brought radical changes in the late nineteenth and early twentieth centuries. Liberal theological trends from Europe were threatening to dislodge not only Princeton's Reformed theology but evangelical theology as a whole.[5] Therefore, Warfield's views of the religious life, the theologian's academic task, and rational defense of the faith will be seen against the backdrop of a changing intellectual and cultural milieu.

Religious Experience: Private Piety and Cultural Transformation

Mark A. Noll has provided a revealing account of what concerns motivated Presbyterians to found a seminary in the opening years of the nineteenth century. In "The Founding of Princeton Seminary,"[6] he points out that Christian experience joined with sound theology was stressed at Princeton Seminary from its very inception in 1812. In fact, when Ashbel Green drafted his plan for the Seminary, he not only included a "plan of governance," but he also stipulated that academic study and spiritual nurture together were to form the foundation of ministerial training. Students were expected to explain and defend the Bible and to cultivate vital Christian piety. Princeton's founders wanted a learned clergy who could answer speculations posed by deism and unbelief and a respectable clergy who could bring stability to a newly formed and restless political order. But these founders also demanded a "pious clergy" whose spiritual influence could combat religion's loss of influence, which was threatening to engulf American society. In previous works I have attempted to show the Princetonians' desire and labors to fulfill this charge.[7] Not wanting merely to repeat conclusions of these studies, I believe that further clarification of what Warfield attempted is in order.

Writing in a popular journal, *The Presbyterian Messenger*, in 1896, Warfield explicitly stated his conception of how religious experience was to be related to theology. The conservative view that religion was the product of theology was being radically eclipsed among theological writers by liberals who reversed this relationship. By positing truth prior to both theology and experience, Warfield successfully sidestepped this recurring debate in which conservatives charged that liberals had subjectivized theology and liberals claimed that conservatives intellectualized religious experience. To Warfield, such disputation was fruitless. "Neither," he claimed, "is the product of the other, but both are products of religious truth, operative in the two spheres of life and thought."[8] Warfield's intention, however, was not to probe a dichotomous phenomenon—head versus heart, intellect versus feeling—as he was most wont to do in discussions of theology and religious experience. Instead he enumerated *three* "media" or "channels of communication"—authority, intellect, and heart—all three of which must relate harmoniously as the bases of both religion and theology. Each of these channels may plausibly be argued as the basis for the religious life and theological formulation. For example, he stated that by authority one knows "only what and as God tells." God's truth is also clearly "addressed to the intellect." Yet someone might contend that "our upward strivings, our feeling of dependence and responsibility supply the points of contact between us and God."[9]

But any simplified reduction of religion and theology ends in distortion. Exaggeration of authority yields traditionalistic dogmatism that renders mute the heart and intellect. Stressing intellect, on the other hand, results in rationalistic system building based on "*a priori* fancies" which system in turn precludes any authoritative claims of God's Word or of human conscience.[10] Finally, following only the heart renders one susceptible to mysticism that will bow to no authoritative word or rational thought, but only to "currents of feeling which flow up and down in our souls," giving birth to "competing revelations" and worshiping "the most morbid of human imaginations."[11] True to his Augustinian heritage, Warfield proposed that dangers can be avoided by following another great trinity similar to those enumerated by the famous early church father. Authority, intellect, and heart are the three sides of "the triangle of truth," which can be diagrammed as follows:

God's authoritative Word initiates both the religious life and theology.

Christian experience converts the soul and produces power for an obedient life.

CHRISTIAN THEOLOGY

Christian theology converts the soul and leads the renewed mind to receive spiritual things from the Spirit of God.

The unified triangle represents Warfield's belief that authority, intellect, and heart are unified under God's truth. He contended that Scripture is not, therefore, merely grist for the theologians' systematizing mill. It is also life-producing nourishment for the soul. To change the metaphor, it both "enlightens" the mind and "beautifies" the heart. God's truth reaches its final end not merely by being assembled and organized into a theological system. Scripture is only fully "understood," Warfield claimed, when it is "lived." Fittingly, he concluded with the Augustinian motto "Believe that you may understand," which is taken from Isaiah 9:7: "Unless you believe, you will not understand." An individual has intellectually apprehended the truth only when he displays a corresponding power in his religious experience. True theology, shaped by a sanctified intellect, is always inextricably united with vital religion motivated by an instructed heart.[12]

If this triangle of truth was the model for Reformed religion and theology, how consistently were religion and theology integrated by Warfield at Princeton Seminary? From its earliest days until its reorganization in 1929, weekly conferences were held on Sunday afternoons to discuss practical religion. In two of Warfield's most memorable conference talks, he spoke on seminarians' cultivation of the religious life.[13] Two points stand out in both addresses. First, Warfield admitted that at Princeton students could easily feel compelled to emphasize academics over piety. He cited an interesting story, however, related by the famous Episcopal clergyman Phillips Brooks of Trinity Church, Boston, that illustrated the opposite emphasis at another seminary. Because he had never attended a prayer meeting before, Brooks almost despaired during his first evening devotions at seminary when he could not pray with the fervent spirit of his peers. Yet the next day he was amazed that the same students who had prayed so piously the previous evening displayed a woeful lack of preparation for their first Greek class recitation. Warfield candidly commented: "Well, it was not at Princeton Seminary that Dr. Brooks saw these evils!"[14]

Since the Princeton ideal had always been scholarship accompanied by piety, the greatest danger confronting theological students was not the lack of religion or theology but the tendency to view the two as antithetical.[15] With the same deliberation used in discussing the "triangle of truth" (i.e., by refusing to give priority to authority, intellect, or heart) in "Spiritual Culture in the Seminary" Warfield ascribed equal importance to devotion, intellectual training, and practical experience. "If intellectual acuteness will not of itself make a man an acceptable minister of Christ, neither will facility and energy in practical affairs by themselves, nor yet piety and devotion alone. The three must be twisted together into a single three-ply cord."[16]

Second, Warfield exhorted students to cultivate both corporate and individual piety. By temperament Warfield was more inclined to stress the latter over the former;[17] therefore, his inclusion of an extended discussion on "public means of grace" is all the more significant. He emphasized that the seminary provided several opportunities for formal gatherings: weekly worship on Sunday, conferences on practical religion, and daily prayer at the conclusion of each day. In addition classes were opened by prayer and monthly prayer meetings were organized for missions.[18]

A second part of Warfield's emphasis on corporate religious life was his challenge for students to be motivated by a theology of organic church life while they were still students. Every group of seminarians, he explained:

> bound in as close and intimate association as we are, must have an organic life; and if the bonds that bind them together are funda-mentally of a religious character, this organic life must be funda-mentally a religious one. . . . No richness of private religious life, no abundance of voluntary religious services [i.e., in "voluntary" movements in society] on the part of members of the organism, can take the place of or supersede the necessity for the fullest, richest, and most fervent expression of this organic religious life through its appropriate channels. I exhort you, therefore, brethren . . . to utilize the public means of grace afforded by the seminary and to make them instruments for the cultivation and expression of the organic religious life of the institution.[19]

So important is participation in the seminary's public means of grace that Warfield said, "The entire work of the seminary deserves to be classed in the category of the means of grace,"[20] and he attributed to it the power of penetrating much more deeply into the foundation of their religious natures than activity in voluntary societies and other forms of public service. He also asked students quite pointedly: "Shall you have everything also [i.e., dormitory life, classroom studies, etc.] in common except worship?" If they had been separated from their normal family and church life, should they not form a "religious community, with its own organic religious life and religious expression?"[21] One might expect a proposal for a "religious order" to follow!

Using these probing questions, Warfield attempted to broaden the focus of Princeton piety, since its adherents usually viewed religon as a private, individualistic walk with God. In these two conference talks Warfield challenged seminarians to appreciate the significance of the visible church and participate in its life. Unfortunately, Warfield never explained in greater detail how to implement his vision of seminary corporate religion. How should students integrate community and pri-vate life beyond attending formal worship and maintaining individual devotions? What biblical materials as well as writings in church history stress public worship as a means of grace? And what role should the sacraments play in both corporate and private life? Of course these ques-tions might be addressed by other seminary departments that dealt di-rectly with practical theology, but Warfield's lack of attention to them is regrettable. Perhaps his own predisposition to private piety was too strong, and he could not ever fully overcome it. Nevertheless, the fact that Warfield mentioned these matters is significant in light of his prescient remarks about the future character of religious institutions: "Without at least this much common worship [i.e., common prayer in morning and evening and formal gatherings twice on every Sabbath] I do not think the institution can preserve its character as a distinctively religious institution."[22] Today Warfield's words are an appropriate warning for seminary trustees and administrators since one of their most difficult challenges at the end of the twentieth century is the recovery of spirituality. "Spiritual formation" has become a priority at many seminaries where leaders now perceive a danger in viewing ministerial training solely as an academic discipline.

Warfield's view of the religious life also affected how he viewed the believer's relation to the broader culture. But not all his predecessors agreed with his emphasis. Although Princeton Seminary was founded largely to stem the rising tide of unbelief in American culture, its founders and early leaders sought to combat these evils primarily through constructing and defending sound theology. Little stress was placed on cultural reformation.[23] Such a generalization was defensible in Princeton's founders and early leaders. However, it was least true of Warfield's immediate predecessor, A. A. Hodge. Among Princeton's theologians, the younger Hodge articulated most compellingly the Christian responsibility to implement cultural change. In one of his popular lectures Hodge took umbrage at secularists' campaigns to introduce religious neutrality into American public life and uttered a solemn pronouncement that intellectual and spiritual integrity requires Christians "to bring all the action of the political society to which they belong obedient to the revealed will of Christ the supreme King, the Ruler among the nations."[24] Hodge ended his lecture by surveying civilization from the Flood to his own day and concluding not only that America completes Christianity's westward expansion, but also that Christianity's phenomenal growth confirms its destiny to exercise moral and religious leadership in the world. God's challenge to this generation is to use its vantage point at "the pyramid top of opportunity on which God has set us [to view] forty centuries!" Christianity's commission is to "stretch our hand into the future with power to mould the destinies of millions."[25]

Despite the fact that Warfield succeeded Hodge at a time when secularization had infiltrated much of American life,[26] he did not emphasize Christian commitment to cultural renewal as strongly as the younger Hodge. But neither did he exclude it altogether. In fact, Christians' cultural responsibility appears more frequently in his writings than might be expected. His review of Herman Bavinck's *De Zekerheid des*

Geloofs recounts in some detail Bavinck's criticism of "pietistic legalism," Moravianism, and Methodism for their failure to acknowledge God's sovereign purpose in public as well as private life. Warfield quotes approvingly an extended passage that bears remarkable resemblance to Hodge's view of Christ's Kingdom:

> The earthly spheres of art and science, of literature and politics, of domestic and social economy are underestimated in value and significance by them, and are consequently not reformed and regenerated by the Christian principle. To "rest in the wounds of Jesus" or "to be converted and then go forth to convert others" seems to constitute the entire content of the Christian life.[27]

By limiting piety to "sentimentality and unhealthy emotion" and "excitement and zeal without knowledge" Moravians and Methodists avoid discharging their Christian vocation in everyday life. "The open eye, the wide outlook, the expanded heart—these things do not come to their rights."[28] In a word, he emphasized, Christianity so considered has lost its "leaven."[29] Warfield was not merely mouthing Bavinck's emphasis. His deep personal conviction is evident from his challenge reminiscent of Hodge's decades earlier: Reformed Christians call for "the reformation of the world after the plan of God and its gradual transmutation into his Kingdom in which his will shall be done even as in heaven."[30]

Warfield's advocacy of Christian cultural responsibility developed from his admiration of Calvin's broad influence in the Reformation. Frequently he linked Calvin's name to the growth of free institutions in the West. In *The Methodist Review* Warfield claims that by freeing the Genevan church Calvin created the Protestant Church and instilled a spirit in his followers "to the efflourescence of which this modern world of ours owes its free institutions."[31] But Calvin's foremost contribution to Western culture was education. Due to Calvin's influence three theological schools opened in France. Peasants in Scotland rose higher in their economic status than their counterparts in other countries. But the prime example of Calvinists' pervasive use of education to raise the general cultural level is Puritanism in America. The Puritan educational system "is opening up a new era of human history."[32] He also defends the Genevan Reformer against oft-repeated charges that Calvin depreciated art. Rather than condemning art, Warfield answered, Calvin argued for a "pure and reverent employment of art as a high gift of God, to be used like all others of God's gifts so as to profit man and glorify the Great Giver."[33]

Finally, he contrasted Calvin's holistic perspective on the Christian life with Martin Luther's tendency to limit the Christian vision to an individual sense of sin and justification. Calvin's interests were broader, resulting in a religious worldview encompassing all of life, public and private. Besides the redemption of individuals, Calvin envisioned in Geneva a redeemed social life. He summarizes the Reformed worldview as one that "begins . . . centers . . . and ends with the vision of God in His glory; and it sets itself before all things to render to God His rights in every sphere of life-activity."[34]

How seriously Warfield took the Reformed vision by attempting in his own calling as a Christian scholar to influence American culture is indicated by two essays published in 1888 and 1889. Because he was born and raised in Kentucky he wrote self-consciously as a southern Christian addressing the church's responsibility to recently freed American blacks. His proposals are quite striking considering Warfield's reputation as a conservative. Since Christians know "that God has made of one blood all the nations of the earth" and has invested them with "the missionary spirit," their task is to "serve as the hand of the Most High in elevating the lowly and rescuing the oppressed."[35] Warfield even asked whether it is "good public policy" to compact a lower class and thus continue a social system that allows a class to have heaped on it "year after year, petty injustices and insults."[36]

Convinced that secular training alone was insufficient to the task and that merely preaching a spiritual gospel that does not motivate concrete action in the public life is ineffectual, Warfield called for Christian schools staffed by teachers with missionary zeal to educate believers on how to heal this social evil. He closed with a question directed not at individuals but at his denomination: "Can the Presbyterian Church safely neglect to do her part in this great work?"[37]

His second essay, "Drawing the Color Line," challenged America's churches even more directly. In this essay he complains that so little has been accomplished for the blacks since the Civil War[38] and that even ecclesiastical bodies had succumbed to the political suggestion that only racial segregation would prevent future racial antipathy. He criticized denominations for debating about "drawing the color line" and creating separate white and black groups within their ecclesiastical bodies. Warfield argued against a proposal in the Presbyterian Church by which the General Assembly is "willing to buy reunion with its Southern brethren at the fearful cost of affixing an unjust stigma" on the blacks.[39] The results, he predicted, would only be future racial conflict. Although Warfield's unpopular proposals went unheeded, they clearly reflected his contention that Christian piety definitely should result both in changed individual attitudes toward blacks and in active efforts to integrate public life. Obviously some might argue that his support of blacks was out of character with his traditional private and individualistic piety. But Warfield's prophetic public rebuke of American Christians exemplified his own desire to use biblical principles to challenge trends in the culture and improve it by concerted Christian action.[40]

Conservative Reaction to Nineteenth-Century Scholarship

Contemporary historians of American religion have not recognized Warfield's substantial contributions in their surveys. Typically Hodge has received more attention than any of the other Princeton theologians. Sydney Ahlstrom in *A Religious History of the American People* mentions Hodge four times[41] and Warfield but once. In Ahlstrom's words, Warfield brought "great theological and historical prowess to the defense of the Reformed tradition." His interests in "Reformed doctrine and Biblical inerrancy provided a major theme in the 'Fundamentalist Controversy' that raged within Northern Presbyterianism."[42]

Summarizing Warfield's contribution simply in terms of defense and advocacy of Reformed theology and biblical authority has much in its favor. But those who notice only these two categories ignore the breadth of his interests and the sheer volume of his writings. Most scholars overlook his extensive reviews in various journals, primarily the *Princeton Theological Review*. No major movement or writer in Europe or in America escaped his notice. From the 1830s to the 1870s Old School Presbyterians faithfully read Charles Hodge's views of Charles Finney's revivalism and the theologies of New Haven and Mercersburg, and eagerly awaited the July issue of the *Biblical Repertory and Theological Review* to devour his carefully prepared assessment of business and debate at the General Assembly. Because Warfield was unable to leave the Princeton area due to his caring for his invalid wife, he could not continue Hodge's reportage of denominational affairs. Instead, he kept Americans abreast of contemporary liberal scholarship through his indefatigable writing of reviews in journals.[43]

Content to allow Hodge's voluminous *Systematic Theology* to remain as the fundamental statement of Princeton's views,[44] Warfield focused his energies on writing articles and reviews for periodicals, journals, dictionaries, and the popular press.[45] Warfield's numerous reviews testify to the tremendous pressure conservatives felt to respond to the flood of scholarly works written by liberals who advocated radical change in the study of religion and Christianity. His review articles show Warfield the scholar "in the trenches" fighting not only to fend off foes of his beloved Reformed theology but also to defend doctrines dear to conservatives of every theological stripe. Supernaturalism itself was being repudiated by scholars who believed that the academic study of religion should be treated just as "objectively" as any other academic discipline; that is, it should be subjected to accepted scholarly canons of "neutral" judgment. Radical critics denied the Western tradition of treating Christianity as the uniquely revealed religion. Instead it was just one religion among others, and scholars were to study its origins, doctrines, history, and influence with the same detached scientific method they used in examining the world's other major faiths.

Thus Warfield's struggles were with several factions: radical scholars who denied the supernatural and wanted to reinterpret Christianity on naturalistic terms, and liberals who wanted to alter basic Christian doctrines in less varying degrees. Since the former were making significant inroads in Germany, Warfield most frequently devoted his exceptional powers of analysis and erudition to prevent their ideas from gaining acceptance in America.

What immediately strikes the reader is Warfield's candid assessment of each work he reviewed. When confronting the most capable radical critics, he genuinely praised their intellectual gifts and scholarly acumen while he scorchingly derided the paucity of their radical presuppositions. For example, Warfield expressed sincere appreciation for the scholarship of the Tübingen School:

> There is no student of the New Testament who will not confess deep indebtedness to the work of [Ferdinand Christian] Baur, for example, both for facts in abundance and for generalizations and points of view of the most stimulating character.[46]

Critiquing the famous German church historian Adolf Harnack's *History of Dogma*, he said that it was "a great book, full not only of learning, but of genius and stimulus." Even though Harnack possessed "powers and learning second to no man's of our generation," his defective presuppositions made him "one of the most destructive forces" in Christendom.[47]

Warfield's candid respect for radical critics reflects that he was sufficiently secure in his own position that he could admire the talents and self-confidence of his opponents without fear that such admission might be interpreted as a concession. Warfield believed his own position was unassailable despite his opponents' assaults upon it. His predecessors also were confident that their theology could withstand all attacks. In the 1820s Charles Hodge had fearlessly gone to Europe to prepare himself more adequately in biblical languages and criticism for his teaching responsibilities at the seminary. In his journal and his correspondence with Archibald Alexander, Hodge reveals challenges to his faith posed by exposure to Friedrich Schleiermacher's pantheism and his liberal synthesis of Christianity and romanticism. But despite the threats of new criticism and Schleiermacher's innovations, Hodge returned with his faith intact.[48] At the end of the century Warfield, firmly grounded in the same self-assured tradition, believed that he could successfully meet whatever Europe could send in written form to America.

During the last decade of the nineteenth century Warfield penned several articles surveying the current theological scene—its trends, recent developments, net gains and losses for conservatism. His most positive assessment of nineteenth-century scholarship was "The Century's Progress in Biblical Knowledge" (1900), while other articles such as "The Rights of Criticism and of the Church" (1892), "Evading the Supernatural" (1894), "Heresy and Concession" (1896), and "Recent Reconstructions of Theology" (1898) indicate by their titles the battles that the Princetonians were fighting.

Warfield was pleased that the century's scholars had greatly expanded the store of biblical knowledge. They had advanced the fruits of preceding centuries' biblical study to a greater degree of completion than had been accomplished in any previous era.[49] And as biblical knowledge grew, conservatives successfully blunted critical attacks. Although the century had been filled with controversy, he believed the Bible emerged "without so much as the smell of smoke upon its very garments."[50] While these remarks suggest that orthodoxy remained victorious in the academic arena, Warfield had to concede that his opponents' ranks had increased in number. In "Evading the Supernatural" he admitted that at the thought of Strauss's and Baur's popularity in Europe "American cheeks used to burn in indignation. But now [in 1894] "we have grown used to something like them at home."[51]

In order to appreciate why Warfield claimed victory despite the increasing number of opponents, we must examine the claims of radical critics as well as Warfield's response to them. Warfield's most lasting contribution to late nineteenth- and early twentieth-century scholarship was his analysis and criticism of its worldview. In responding to one theologian's statement that "theologies change as doth a garment," Warfield said this represents the contemporary "despair of dogmatics,"[52] which must have motivated him all the more to show the inadequacies of their presuppositions, methods, and conclusions. He disarmed the radical critics' claim that Christianity was merely another natural religion by demonstrating that such assertions arose not from an examination of the Bible itself, but from the naturalistic presuppositions that critics brought to their study of Scripture. Under such rubrics as "modernizing the faith" or "thinking through Christianity in modern terms" biblical critics and theologians justified refashioning Christianity to suit their own philosophies. Warfield's most telling rejoinder was that because demands for updating the faith are based on the obvious truth that every age "has a language of its own and can speak no other," too frequently critics invert the relation between Christianity and its contextual expression: "Instead of stating Christian belief in terms of modern thought, an effort is made, rather, to state modern thought in terms of Christian belief."[53] Warfield had occasion to use this criticism in the opening paragraphs of his reviews more than any other single point.

Typical of Warfield's approach is his review of Wilhelm Bousset's *What is Religion?* (1907). Warfield first establishes that Bousset is not simply an advocate of "comparative religion" nor of the "history of religion" but of the "comparative" or "history-of-religion [*Religionsgeschichte*] *school*" (my emphasis). Warfield's careful distinction alerts the reader that Bousset's method of studying religion was based on a carefully developed school of thought. His method was an outgrowth of an underlying philosophy or worldview that explains Christianity "in its entirety, as a religion among religions, the product like other religions of the religious nature of man." Warfield argues convincingly that Bousset adopts naturalistic assumptions "practically as a postulate" in his introduction.[54] By presupposing historical evolution, the author considered "impossible, . . . irreligious, and Godless" any claim that Old and New Testament religions are revealed and that all others are the product of human imagination.[55]

In the remainder of his review Warfield shows how at every point Bousset's interpretation of Christianity is a function of his philosophical perspective. Christianity is presented as a product of "the universal evolution of civilization," a development that began with animism and continued as a function of social organization through a series of increasingly complex stages until universal religions developed. Bousset claimed that Christianity emerged out of "the soil of its own time," and Jesus' singular innovation was his simplification of Judaism. But Jesus' religion was not Christianity's final form, because Christianity continued to evolve up to the modern period. Liberal scholars now jettison Paul's, Augustine's, and Luther's ideas of redemption, Christ's deity and atoning sacrifice, and a revealed Bible by contending they are not compatible with modern thought. Bousset finally reduces Christianity's content to the parable of the Lost Son, the forgiveness of sins, obedience to God's will, and eternal hope. Warfield pointedly remarks that whenever Christianity is "reduced to a 'natural religion' in its origin, it is reduced also to a 'natural religion' in its contents: it shrinks at once to the meager contents of the familiar trilogy, of God, morality, and immortality."[56]

In addition to exposing Bousset's worldview Warfield demonstrated that his "primal assumption" of naturalism was then buttressed by a biblical critical method involving another "immense assumption, or rather a whole series of immense assumptions" that included the Graf-Wellhausen critical reconstruction of Old Testament religion and history and the results of the "history-of-religions" reconstruction of New Testament religion. And behind these is the assumption of the traditional view's invalidity.[57] In the final analysis, Bousset's and other recastings of Christianity are merely a thoroughly consistent hypothetical construction: Bousset says, in effect, "See, if this be conceived to be the way religion has come into existence and developed itself in the course of the ages, then Christianity may be conceived to be a growth of nature. The 'if' here is, however, a mighty one. . . ." In Warfield's opinion, Bousset's radical criticism has no "argumentative value" whatsoever. He has not demonstrated that Christianity is what he claims it to be. Bousset has merely shown "that a self-consistent scheme of the origins of Christianity as a natural religion can be constructed."[58]

In a similar manner Warfield evaluated Dr. William Mackintosh's denial of miracles in *The Natural History of the Christian Religion*. Mackintosh's refutation appears to succeed only because a "more or less clearly formulated assumption of the impossibility of miracles underlies the strenuous opposition to the admission of their reality."[59] A direct outcome of the critics' claim that Christianity is a natural religion is their reinterpretation of its central doctrines beginning with biblical revelation. Warfield's most frequent assertion was that critical scholars were preoccupied with separating the "kernel from the husk." He charged that a scheme which presupposes that divine revelation in Scripture is separable from the "husk" of its historical expression inevitably led to the weakening of biblical authority. Warfield stressed two tendencies in liberal views of Scripture: critics redefine revelation and question the Bible's reliability.

Warfield's review of Reinhold Seeberg's *Revelation and Inspiration* (1909) begins with a reminder that Seeberg's goal is to "modernize" these doctrines. Warfield characteristically takes great pains to explain—several pages containing many citations from the text—Seeberg's view of *Heilsgeschichte*, God's redemptive history, narrated in Scripture. Significantly, Seeberg contended that even though Scripture is a record of God's redemptive history, the Bible is not always trustworthy in what it affirms. It includes some statements that are "notoriously false," outdated cosmologies, and errors in both worldview and interpretation of prophecy.[60] Yet in contrast to naturalists such as Mackintosh and Bousset, who contend that errors only confirm Scripture's natural origins, Seeberg attempts to salvage Scripture's value as a record of revelation despite its errors. His purpose, states Warfield, is "Pragmatistic" because the redemptive record's purpose in Scripture is to work in us "a remarkable inward experience, in which we find ourselves in the presence of God."[61] Warfield's assessment is very astute. Seeberg's introduction of a distinction between historical facts and ideas of revelation—the husk that is irrelevant and sometimes wrong and the kernel that produces our experience of redemption—substantially changes our conception of the Bible's authority.

> The basis of confidence is shifted from the Bible to Christian experience, or to what we used to call "the Christian consciousness," and the Bible is made to play the role only of vehicle of transmission. The whole conception of an authoritative book is set aside and we are to accept in the Bible only what Christian experience validates.[62]

Warfield terms Seeberg's interpretation an example of "Modern-positive Theology," which in his opinion is not really new. It is merely the latest expression of subjectivism, which can be traced back to Schleiermacher.

A final emphasis in Warfield's reviews was his criticism of liberal Christologies. His efforts not only to expose what he believed to be false christological thinking but also to articulate the Reformed viewpoint were untiring.[63] The Princeton apologist was especially skillful in confronting christological studies constructed on naturalistic premises. In 1911 he reviewed a series of Johannes Weiss's works on Christ. Warfield declared Weiss to be "[Wilhelm] Wrede's successor as the *enfant terrible* of the 'liberal school.'"[64] His opening remarks conform to his usual pattern of establishing that the author's worldview is the most significant factor shaping his Christology. Weiss's works, though destructive to the faith, have this "virtue," that they disclose in no uncertain terms "the violence of the assumptions on which alone the naturalization of the origins of the Christian religion can be accomplished."[65]

Weiss discusses the doctrine of Christ through the New Testament from the history-of-religions perspective. He admits that his view of Jesus is not the same as the New Testament's—that Jesus was a "resurrected and exalted Christ." Instead of what he called "primitive Christianity," Weiss espouses a theology that "has its full satisfaction in permitting itself to be led to the Father by Jesus of Nazareth."[66] Warfield explained that basic to liberals' distinguishing various views of Christ even within the New Testament was their tendency to reject Pauls' view, which Weiss called "not a development but a transmutation of the religion of Jesus."[67]

What astounded Warfield, however, is that Weiss, against all reasonable expectation considering his radical bias, refuses to take the liberal critical method to its absurd conclusion and join the most radical scholars who denied that Jesus even existed. Instead, Weiss assumes the improbable mantle of a conservative apologist by arguing in favor of the historical Jesus.[68] But he retains his mediating position between orthodox affirmations of Jesus' true historical existence only by abandoning his usual naturalistic critical method. Warfield revels in Weiss's being caught between two worldviews:

> Either he must continue to use the methods common to him and his more radical opponents, and then he can scarcely escape their extremities of negation. Or else he must allow the sounder methods he tells them they ought to follow, and then he can surely not fail ultimately to reach "conservative" conclusions. It appears to be only a new instance of the old difficulty: "I see the good; the evil I pursue."[69]

Warfield frequently mentioned Ernst Troeltsch's assertion that even though many scholars in Germany were turning to "reduced Christianity" advocated by the most radical critics, the radical school was manifesting no productive power in German culture and showed little future promise. Warfield took great comfort in Troeltsch's judgment that "almost all the religiousness of today draws its life from modifications of the strong religious treasures propagated in the churches and in them alone." Interestingly, Warfield's warmest endorsement of Troeltsch was that his usually consistent naturalism did not prevent him from affirming that Jesus' historicity was essential for Christianity. Warfield never tired of citing passage after passage in which Troeltsch either affirms the historical Jesus or rails against those who made Jesus merely a symbol expressing their peculiar faith in God.[70]

Our survey of Warfield's reviews demonstrates that although he never constructed his own systematic theology, conservatives ever since have been greatly in his debt. While some may argue that conservatives could have rallied around a fresh restatement of orthodoxy to stem the liberal tide, others could justly counter that Warfield discharged his stewardship in forms most suited both to his gifts and to current needs. Through his reviews, Warfield not only kept his followers abreast of liberal scholarship, but he also disarmed the critics by disclosing how dependent their ideas were on their naturalistic philosophy.

Of course, Warfield did more than analyze critical scholarship. He carefully honed an apologetic system by which he believed the conservative position could be defended. Having discussed his evaluation of naturalistic criticism, we now turn our attention to how Warfield showed that positive use of reason can establish Christian truth.

Common Sense Philosophy and Its Appropriateness to Reformed Theology

Warfield was convinced that simply because radical critics misused criticism, that fact certainly did not negate conservatives' responsibility to carry out its proper function. Contrary to widespread belief that conservatives oppose criticism, Warfield answered in "The Rights of Criticism and of the Church" (1892) that the existence of truth demands criticisms for its vindication. Biblical scholars are just as obligated to test the claims of the Bible as classical scholars are to examine Aristotle's works.[71]

Crucial to any critical scrutiny is establishing what Warfield called "the pure facts."

> Everyone of us exercises all the faculties God has given him and exhausts all the tests at his command to assure himself of the facts. . . . [Careful scrutiny of the facts] is good or bad in proportion to the accuracy and completeness with which the facts are apprehended and collected and the skill and soundness with which they are marshalled and their meaning read.[72]

A crisis has arisen, claims Warfield, not because of criticism itself but because of an "ineradicable tendency of man to confound the right of criticism with the rightness of his own criticism."[73] The Presbyterian Church must address modernism's proud claim to autonomy if it is to stand for the truth. Preserving revealed truth through apologetics has been vouchsafed to the church in the modern age just as it has been throughout history. Fundamental to Warfield's description of apologetics and his confidence that it would succeed in its task was his belief in Scottish Common Sense Philosophy (CSP). Philosophers in Scotland established commonsense principles in the eighteenth century to answer the skepticism of David Hume. Thomas Reid (1710-1796) argued that man's mind is so constituted by God as to know reality (not only the external world but also cause and effect and basic moral principles) directly by "common sense." John Witherspoon introduced Scottish philosophy in America when he became president of Princeton College in 1768. All the Princetonians learned it as the philosophical perspective by which they could not only achieve certainty in knowledge but also demonstrate fundamental apologetic truths. Princeton's dependence on this philosophy and particularly the question whether its use is consistent with Princeton's Reformed theology or whether it distorts their theology have stimulated heated debate between contemporary students and critics.[74] John Vander Stelt has written the most comprehensive, and critical, study of Scottish influence at Princeton in *Philosophy and Scripture: A Study of Old Princeton and Westminster Theology* (1978).[75] He explains how each of the Princeton thinkers was trained in Scottish philosophy and used its epistemological principles to ground his faith in rational certainty. Alexander used it to certify Scripture, Hodge developed it to construct an inductive method in theology, and Warfield carefully refined it into a rational apologetic system. Each development reflected the nature and intensity of opposition mounted against Princeton's position.

While he disagrees with all conservatives' use of Common Sense Philosophy, Vander Stelt is especially critical of Warfield's. Vander Stelt concedes that philosophical attacks increased after the Civil War and that Warfield believed that only a full-scale defense was capable of preserving Reformed thinking from crumbling. Nevertheless, he finds that Warfield's "entire framework of thought in his apologetics and Scripture is unmistakably intellectualistic" and has as its foundation a "dualism," an "ontological and religious distinction between the supernatural and the natural."[76] In one of his summary paragraphs on Warfield's thought, Vander Stelt explains this dualism:

> As to the structure of the natural world, Warfield found the basic assumptions of a philosophy of reality and truth that was greatly indebted to Scottish CSP acceptable and helpful in curtailing any threats upon certainty and security. By placing all of this within the larger context of the supernatural, Warfield tried to reinsure the former with the latter. Through a curious fusion of two basically conflicting worlds of thought, Warfield struggled to obtain theoretical and practical certainty for knowledge and faith by linking this certainty up with a *supra*-naturally qualified notion of infallibility and inerrancy that is supposed to be—but, in fact is not as the original autographs of the Bible are lost—within the reach of all rational men in this natural world.[77]

Thus Warfield took the Princeton faith in Common Sense to its furthest extreme without recognizing the vast internal tension it created within his system.[78]

In my previous work on Warfield I attempted to qualify some of the criticisms of Warfield's intellectualism and lack of emphasis on subjectivity that Vander Stelt has chosen to ignore.[79] While I agree with the central point of Warfield's critics, a defense can be made for his dependence on Common Sense principles. In a recent article Darryl Hart has defended Warfield's successor, J. Gresham Machen, on this point. His arguments apply with similar force to Warfield. Hart believes that Machen's continued adherence to Common Sense principles was a virtue despite its significant weaknesses. Without some of Common Sense Philosophy's principles epistemological skepticism might well have proven unavoidable. Its emphasis on universality, language, and history were not simply basic to knowledge but were also used in the defense of Christianity. All people are so constituted that they can know reality and communicate about it truthfully. Our knowledge of the past is something objective because memory is not just of an idea, but of the reality itself. These principles appeared fundamental as well to the biblical worldview, which holds man to be made in the image of God, recipient of a written revelation, and dependent on knowing certain objective redemptive historical events.[80] Long before Machen, Warfield used these principles repeatedly in his confrontations with liberal theology.

But an even more important factor in Warfield's retention of Scottish philosophy was his recognition of the bankruptcy in perspective of various philosophical systems that had replaced Common Sense. As we noted in the previous section, Warfield's skepticism of modern method was equally the match of modern thinkers' skepticism of traditional views of knowledge. Although he did not always refer to various philosophical systems, when he did, he barely concealed his contempt for them. Kantian epistemology, for example, in which the categories of the human mind take the place of God as the basis for knowing and in which God is reduced to a postulate of practical reason instead of its determining ground, represented "a veritable revolution by which God is dethroned and man elevated to His place as the center of the universe."[81] Kant's subjectivism was succeeded by Schleiermacher's, which ultimately gave way to Ritschlian thought. Frequently he attacked Albrecht Ritschl and his followers for their repudiation of metaphysics. Because the Ritschlites viewed revelation in purely personal terms and granted no place for propositions, they are unable to bequeath to the church anything more than "individualistic dogmatics."[82] In another summary for *The New York Observer* Warfield claimed that Ritschl's theology "was merely the old Socinianism in a new garment, cut from the cloth of Neo-Kantian speculation."[83] What Ritschl was attempting to do, Warfield continues, was to reduce Christianity's content to a nondogmatic faith. Thereby he hoped to save it from being ravaged by naturalistic philosophers, unbelieving scientists, and skeptical historians. While his motives may have been good, Ritschl made a common nineteenth-century error of gutting the Christian faith of its contents.[84]

Warfield's answer to modernist skepticism was that certainty is still achievable despite denials by contemporary philosophers and theologians. All that is required is a careful scrutiny of rational evidence. In an article written early in his career at Princeton, "Christian Evidences and Recent Criticism" (1888), Warfield claimed for rational apologetics virtually what he was to claim in 1900 about the Bible and criticism, that each had escaped from controversy without even the "smell of smoke" to suggest the battle. As we might expect, the method of proof for both was the same, examination of rational evidence—the facts.

Warfield's most memorable statement of Christianity's apologetic task was militant: "It is the distinction of Christianity that it has come into the world clothed with the mission to reason its way to dominion."[85]

The context of Warfield's remark is his rebuke of Abraham Kuyper's subordination of apologetics to the "narrow task of defending developed Christianity against philosophy, falsely so called."[86] One can sense Warfield's perplexity if not disdain as he claims that Kuyper's method of defending Christianity as only "the great assumption" bears all too much similarity to the hypothetical constructions of Bousset and Mackintosh. If Kuyper is correct, Christian scholars have been robbed of their incentives to validate Christian truth. The combined labors of exegetes, historians, and systematic theologians has "all hung, so to speak, in the air; not until all their labor is accomplished do they pause to wipe their streaming brows and ask whether they have been dealing with realities or perchance with fancies only."[87]

Several themes that we have examined so far coalesce in Warfield's repudiation of Kuyper's apologetics. Even more than he eschewed fancies in religious experience, Warfield despised them in theology and its preparatory discipline, apologetics. Conservatives, especially Reformed Christians in keeping with their holistic redemptive view, had a mandate not only to recapture Christian scholarship but also to regain the cultural mind.[88] These tasks in Warfield's opinion could never be accomplished by the Dutch apologetics of Kuyper and Bavinck. In his review of Bavinck's *De Zekerheid des Geloofs*, Warfield restates his commitment to evidentialist apologetics, which has the task among others of demonstrating God's existence and authenticating Scripture as God's Word. Christian faith, therefore, is a reasonable faith based on good and sufficient evidence, not a "blind and ungrounded faith."[89]

Warfield's frequent critique was that his opponents' theology was "Modern-Positive," as we saw above in his criticism of Seeburg. However, his own view of using "facts"—both rational facts to demonstrate God's existence and the authority of God's Word and biblical facts to arrive at a sound theology—sounds even more modern. His demand that critics ought to pay attention to facts carried the implication that liberals could be corrected if they would recognize the naturalism of their own position and scrutinize the evidence by virtually suspending their belief in naturalism just as phenomenologists advocate an epistemological epoche, "bracketing of existence," or suspension of belief in order to achieve greater accuracy in description of an object.[90]

Fortunately, in at least one significant writing, "The Right of Systematic Theology," Warfield discusses the influence of doctrine on facts. In the article Warfield challenged theologians and biblical scholars who were hostile to theology and saw in doctrine and propositional truth obstacles to religion. Some feared that doctrine would quench religious life and therefore they summarized Christianity as life, not doctrine. But the other group invented the watchword "Christianity consists of facts, not dogmas."[91]

Considering Warfield's predisposition to stress the objective or the factual basis of Christianity, we are not surprised that if given a choice between doctrine and facts, he would choose the facts. Nevertheless, consistent with many other instances in his writing he demands that neither can be relinquished; no antithesis is ever to be proposed which separates these two elements.

> What Christianity consists in is facts that are doctrines, and doc-
> trines that are facts. Just because it is a true religion, which offers
> to man a real redemption that was really wrought out in history,
> its facts and doctrines entirely coalesce.[92]

All this we might have expected. But when Warfield discusses its implications he makes some strong statements that differ from his usually strict objective emphasis on facts.

> What is a fact that is wholly separated from what is here called
> "dogma"? If doctrines which stand entirely out of relation to facts
> are myths, lies [then] facts which have no connection with what we
> call doctrine could have no meaning to us whatsoever. It is what
> we call doctrine which gives all their significance to facts. A fact
> without doctrine is simply a fact not understood. That intellectual
> element brought by the mind to the contemplation of facts, which
> we call "doctrine," "theory," is the condition of any proper com-
> prehension of facts.[93]

A few lines later, after quoting Dr. James Denney's statement that a fact without theory is a "blank unintelligibility, a rock in the sky, a mere irrelevance in the mind of man," Warfield adds that

> so closely welded are these intellectual elements—those elements
> of previous knowledge, or of knowledge derived from other sources
> —to facts as taken up into our minds in the complex act of apper-
> ception, that possibly we have ordinarily failed to separate them,
> and consequently, in our worship of what we call so fluently "the
> naked facts," have very little considered what a bare fact is, and
> what little meaning it could have for us.[94]

Certainly these few words do not make Warfield a presuppositionalist, just as Hart asserted that some of Machen's phrases did not make him one either. But Warfield never subjected facts to such searching criticism as he did in these words.

If the heirs of Warfield's evidentialist view and the advocates of Dr. Van Til's presuppositionalism are to make any progress in their internecine struggles, surely an item high on the agenda is a discussion of what constitutes a fact and how facts are to be used in both apologetic and theological disciplines. Was Warfield inconsistent in his apologetics, if only a few times? How are we to understand his use of Augustine's motto when we would have expected him to cite Thomas Aquinas' credo, "I understand in order that I might believe"? What is the significance of his basically presuppositionalist attack of his opponents in his reviews? What did he mean when he said that an "ineradicable tendency" in people makes them assert their own autonomy in critical studies? Has this any significance for discussions concerning the noetic effect of sin? How much effect, if any, do historical or contextual factors as well as individual subjective bias have on knowing, and can their effects be reduced or eliminated? Warfield's apologetic as a whole provides a vast storehouse of information for one side of the debate. But he was aware of other sides and established a precedent of interaction with them.

Conclusion

Benjamin B. Warfield's contributions to contemporary scholarship are more varied and complex than is immediately apparent. His scholarly production was voluminous and his range of interests spanned several theological disciplines. Even though his writing was often formal and his appeal was primarily to the scholarly community, he wrote on more than simply Reformed theology and the authority of Scripture where he left his considerable mark.

In the three areas that we have examined in this chapter we have noticed nuances and emphases that broaden our appreciation for Warfield's accomplishments. His piety was not exhausted by appeals to personal holiness and application of scriptural truth to one's private life. Even though his vision for a transformed American culture was cast in terms of his postmillennial faith, he challenges all followers of the Reformed tradition to rethink views of the visible church and of the leavening effect of the gospel in public life in order to extend what Warfield himself left unfinished.

Warfield's example in scholarly writing and particularly in the area of reviewing contemporary theology could hardly be more pertinent today. Reformed theologians need not only to continue to develop their theologies carefully in light of the Word of God but also to show how many contemporary theologians continue in the lines of their nineteenth-century counterparts by espousing twentieth-century presuppositions and proposals for action cloaked in terms borrowed from the Christian worldview.

Finally, Reformed theologians must continue to discuss how Christian truth can best be defended. The secularism that was building in

Warfield's day has become a dominant and established force at the end of the nineteenth century. Even though Warfield based his apologetic method on presuppositions that were more consistent with Scottish philosophy, he still possessed an essentially biblical vision of recapturing not only his church but also the wider culture with the gospel message.

Notes: Benjamin B. Warfield

1. Mark A. Noll, *Princeton Theology 1812-1921* (Grand Rapids: Baker Book House, 1983), 19.
2. A. A. Hodge, *Life of Charles Hodge* (New York: Charles Scribner's Sons, 1880), 382.
3. Ned B. Stonehouse, *J. Gresham Machen* (Grand Rapids: Wm. B. Eerdmans Publishing Company, 1954), 62.
4. Ibid., 63.
5. See Gary S. Smith, *The Seeds of Secularization* (Grand Rapids: Wm. B. Eerdmans Publishing Company, 1985), ch. 2.
6. Mark A. Noll, "The Founding of Princeton Seminary," *Westminster Theological Journal* 42 (1979): 72-110.
7. "The Relation between the Objective and Subjective Elements in Christian Religious Experience. A Study in the Systematic and Devotional Writings of Archibald Alexander, Charles Hodge, and Benjamin B. Warfield" (Ph.D. diss., Brown University, 1970) and *Piety and the Princeton Theologians* (Phillipsburg, NJ: Presbyterian and Reformed Publishing Company, 1981).
8. B. B. Warfield, "Authority, Intellect, Heart," in *Selected Shorter Writings of Benjamin B. Warfield*, ed. John E. Meeter, 2 vols. (Nutley, NJ: Presbyterian and Reformed Publishing Company, 1970), 1:668.
9. Ibid., 669.
10. Ibid.
11. Ibid., 670.
12. Ibid., 671.
13. "Spiritual Culture in the Theological Seminary," (1904), in ibid., 2:468-96 and "The Religious Life of Theological Students" (1911), in ibid., 1:411-22.
14. Ibid., 2:474.
15. Ibid., 412.
16. Ibid., 472.
17. He devoted more time to encouraging private piety, which he called "the center of our subject" (ibid., 481) and "the foundation stone of piety" (ibid., 1:422).
18. Ibid., 2:476.
19. Ibid., 477.
20. Ibid., 478.
21. Ibid., 1:418.
22. Ibid., 419.
23. In his excellent treatment of these issues Mark A. Noll probes Green's, Alexander's, and others' tendency to disparage active involvement in culture. They considered theological education to be the primary function of both the seminary and the college. Unfortunately, Princeton scholars were not devoted to

developing the Christian liberal arts. Noll also astutely argues that a symbiotic relationship should have existed between Princeton College and the seminary. The seminary should have provided the college "with the fruits of its labors from biblical study, theological reflection, and interaction with the Christian past," while on the other hand the college should have provided the seminary "with interpretations of modern learning and creative ventures of its own into the developing fields of nineteenth century thought." And both should have reflected "together on the foundational theological stances and philosophical presuppositions which shaped the inquiries of both bodies" (Noll, "Founding of Princeton Seminary," 105).

24. Hodge cited a list of corruptions in American society (divorce laws, desecration of the Sabbath, corrupt trade and commerce practices, and secularization of education) that needed to be redeemed by instituting Christian principles in public life. A series of impassioned questions revealed his concern over the dilution and elimination of Christian principles from American political, economic, and social institutions: "Whence come these portentous upheavals of the ancient primitive rock [Christianity] upon which society has always rested? Whence comes this socialistic earthquake, arraying capital and labor in irreconcilable conflict like oxygen and fire? Whence come these mad prehistoric anarchical ravings, the wild passages of a universal deluge which will blot out at once the family, the school, the church, the home, all civilization and religion in one sea of ruin?" (A. A. Hodge, *Popular Lectures on Theological Themes* [Philadelphia: Presbyterian Board of Publication and Sabbath School Work, 1887], 256).

25. Ibid., 334.

26. For a detailed view of the growth of secularization in American culture from the end of the Civil War to the beginning of World War I, see Smith, *Secularization*, ch. 2.

27. Warfield, *Shorter Writings*, 2:108.

28. Ibid., 108-09.

29. Ibid., 109.

30. Ibid., 110.

31. "John Calvin, the Man and His Word," in *Calvin and Calvinism* (New York: Oxford University Press, 1931), 20. In "Calvinism," an encyclopedia article originally written by Hodge but revised by Warfield, he narrates Calvin's effort to establish ecclesiastical freedom in Geneva. (See Warfield, *Shorter Writings*, 2:411.)

32. Warfield, *Shorter Writings*, 2:445.

33. Ibid., 184. He referred readers to Kuyper's Stone Lectures of 1898 at Princeton and to Emil Doumergue's "L'Art et le Sentiment dans l'oeuvre de Calvin" (1902) as correctives to the view that Calvin opposed artistic expression.

34. Ibid., 355.

35. "A Calm View of the Freedmen's Case," in ibid., 740. In words that might be labeled paternalistic today, Warfield calls on Christians to raise the blacks in their moral education. "The task before the American people in dealing with the blacks is nothing less . . . than the uprooting and expulsion of a settled and ingrained system of morality [which is the result of slavery itself] in order that a true morality may be substituted for it" (p. 737). Their social standing can only be compared to the caste system of India: "The harm that caste does toward those whom we would elevate cannot be overestimated. It kills hope; it paralyzes effort" (p. 741).

36. Ibid.

37. Ibid., 742.

38. Warfield quotes another commentator approvingly: "Emancipation has abolished only private but not public subjugation; has made the ex-slave not a free man but only a free Negro" (ibid., 744).

39. Ibid., 749.

40. Warfield's lack of comment on social issues is probably based on two factors: his temperament and his relatively secluded life. Unlike the Hodges who played significant roles in Presbyterianism, Warfield was confined to Princeton to care for his invalid wife. In his biography of Machen, Stonehouse said that Warfield rarely spent more than two hours away from her at a time and did not leave the town of Princeton between 1905 and 1915 (see Stonehouse, *Machen*, 220).

41. S. Ahlstrom, *A Religious History of the American People* (New Haven: Yale University Press, 1972). In each instance his discussion is inadequate considering Princeton's contribution to nineteenth- and twentieth-century theology and the depth of analysis Ahlstrom devoted to other movements such as Mormonism and Christian Science.

42. Ibid., 18. Winthrop Hudson in *Religion in America* (New York: Charles Scribner's Sons, 1965) discusses Warfield only briefly as a defender of the Westminster Confession and as instrumental with A. A. Hodge in forging the "Princeton doctrine of inspiration." Charles Hodge is discussed much more extensively. (Cf. pp. 167, 171, 180-81, 269, 284.)

43. For a cataloging of Warfield's articles and reviews see John E. Meeter and Roger Nicole, comps., *A Bibliography of Benjamin Breckinridge Warfield 1851-1921* (Nutley, NJ: Presbyterian and Reformed Publishing Company, 1974).

44. Cf. Patton's summary in his "Memorial Address," *Princeton Theological Review* 19 (1921): 387, explaining why Warfield never wrote his own systematics.

45. Due to limitations of space I will limit my remarks primarily to reviews collected in Vol. 10 of the Oxford series, *Critical Reviews* (New York: Oxford University Press, 1932), and to Warfield's *Shorter Writings*.

46. He credited Baur and his followers with pressing conservatives to increase their effort "to explore more deeply its record and to draw from them even more purely their treasures of truth" (Warfield, *Shorter Writings*, 2:9). In the very opening lines of one review of Ernst Troeltsch, Warfield said his "chief merit as a writer on theological themes lies in his straightforward downrightness" (*Critical Reviews*, 287).

47. Warfield, *Shorter Writings*, 2:451.

48. See my treatment of Hodge's trip in *Piety*, 48-52.

49. Throughout the article Warfield lists in detail major movements and publications in various areas of biblical scholarship, e.g., Old and New Testament, commentaries, textual aids, archeology, etc. Warfield was particularly gratified by exegetical gains.

50. Warfield, *Shorter Writings*, 2:13.

51. Ibid., 683.

52. *Critical Reviews*, 407.

53. Review of *Foundations. A Statement of Christian Belief in Terms of Modern Thought*, by Seven Oxford Men, *Critical Reviews*, 322.

54. *Critical Reviews*, 173.

55. Ibid.

56. Ibid., 177.

57. Ibid., 177-78.

58. Ibid., 178. I have included a detailed summary of Warfield's review of Bousset to indicate Warfield's careful and extensive treatment of the material and to show how radical Bousset's attack was.

59. "The Question of Miracles," in Warfield, *Shorter Writings*, 2:173. Later in the same essay Warfield evaluated David Hume's classic rebuttal of miracles. Hume's attack on the probability of miracles was based on the naturalistic assumption that our overwhelming experience of the uniformity of nature militates against their probability. But Hume's refutation is worthless as a rational argument. By affirming the absolute uniformity of nature, which renders miracles impossible, Hume is unable to answer the question of probability because probability "is the very thing in dispute" (p. 178).

60. *Critical Reviews*, 238.

61. *Critical Reviews*, 238.

62. *Critical Reviews*, 239.

63. Besides reviews, which are the focus of this paper, he produced numerous topical, exegetical, and historical studies. Cf. his *Christology and Criticism* (New York: Oxford University Press, 1929), and essays in *Shorter Writings*.

64. *Critical Reviews*, 266.

65. Ibid., 267.

66. Ibid., 286.

67. Ibid., 270.

68. Ibid., 273-74.

69. Ibid., 275.

70. Ibid., 294.

71. Warfield, *Shorter Writings*, 2:595.

72. Ibid., 596. Ascertaining the facts was as important in biblical study as it was in apologetics. In his review of Hastings' *Dictionary of the Bible*, Vol. 1, Warfield found it superior to other recently published works because of its greater reliability. But Warfield claimed that we still need a dictionary "which renounces speculation and sets out the facts" (*Critical Reviews*, 67). Warfield's remarks are reminiscent of Charles Hodge's statement on theological method in his *Systematic Theology*, that theologians use the facts of the Bible as a scientist uses the facts of nature. (See Vol. 1, pp. 1-17.)

73. Warfield, *Shorter Writings*, 2:596.

74. See Mark A. Noll's careful assessment of common sense as one of Princeton's "themes" in his excellent introductory chapter in *Princeton Theology*, 30-33, and George Marsden's assessments in *Fundamentalism and American Culture: The Shaping of Twentieth Century Evangelicalism, 1870-1925* (New York: Oxford University Press, 1980), 109-18.

75. Vander Stelt's notes and bibliography contain an extensive listing of scholarly works, including dissertations.

76. J. Vander Stelt, *Philosophy and Scripture: A Study of Old Princeton and Westminster Theology* (Marlburg, NJ: Mack Publishing Company, 1978), 182-83.

77. Ibid.

78. In the second part of his book Vander Stelt examines philosophy and Scripture at Westminster Seminary. He stresses the institutional shift away from Princeton Seminary led by Machen and the repudiation of Princeton's philosophical principles under Van Til's guidance. Perhaps Vander Stelt's sharp contrast between Princeton and Westminster might be seen as an attempt to win a hearing from Westminster for the Dutch tradition that he represents.

79. See Hoffecker, *Piety*, ch. 3. Vander Stelt refers to my work and uses some material on Hodge but does not concede that Warfield's work contained any subjective emphases.

80. D. Hart, "The Princeton Mind in the Modern World and the Common Sense of J. Gresham Machen," *Westminster Theological Journal* 45 (1984): 1-25. See also George Marsden's "J. Gresham Machen, History, and Truth," *Westminster Theological Journal* 42 (1979): 157-75.

81. *Critical Reviews*, 244.

82. *Critical Reviews*, 408.

83. Warfield, *Shorter Writings*, 2:449.

84. Ibid., 450.

85. Ibid., 99.

86. Ibid., 95.

87. Ibid., 96.

88. In "Christian Evidences and Recent Criticism" Warfield responded to Huxley's boast that "extinguished theologians lie about the cradle of every science as the strangled snakes beside that of Hercules." He retorted that "[theologians] keep company there with an interesting body of scientific lights"(!) (ibid., 129). Nevertheless, he continues, criticism such as Huxley's only spurs apologists to refine their arguments so that finally they may stand "easily victor against all modern assaults" (ibid., 131).

89. Ibid., 115. A rather significant historical irony is that while the Princetonians not only did not regain a hearing in American culture but also lost control of their Presbyterian denomination (see Lefferts Loetscher, *The Broadening Church* [Philadelphia: University of Pennsylvania Press, 1954]), the Dutch theologians continued to exercise significant cultural influence in their native Holland. See James Skillen and Stanley Carlson-Thies, "Religious and Political Development in Nineteenth Century Holland," *Publius* 12 (Summer 1982): 43-64.

90. Cf. "Phenomenology," in *Encyclopedia of Philosophy*, Vols. 5, 6 (New York: Macmillan Publishing Company, Inc., 1967), 140-44.

91. Warfield, *Shorter Writings*, 2:230.

92. Ibid., 234.

93. Ibid., 236.

94. Ibid.

4

J. GRESHAM MACHEN

W. STANFORD REID

J. Gresham Machen

J. Gresham Machen wielded a wide and important influence in his day, not only in Christian circles, but also on the entire American scene and beyond it. His fundamental motivation was his view of the Reformed theological position. He believed it was the most consistent and defensible expression of the Christian faith. A scholar, a leader, a powerful preacher, and at the same time a man of great charm, he was able to achieve much in his relatively short life. Caspar Wistar Hodge, who did not always agree with Machen, on hearing of his death stated that evangelical Christianity had lost its most outstanding leader and one of its greatest theologians. To understand Machen's importance on the American scene during the first third of this century we must understand his background, his theological development, and what he accomplished during his very active life.

Machen's Background and Development

In attempting to evaluate Machen's theological position and influence, we cannot avoid taking a quick glance at his background and development. But in so doing we have to keep in mind that the late nineteenth and early twentieth centuries were times of great upheaval in the Christian church, particularly in the Western world, with the rise of such phenomena as Higher Criticism, atheistic evolution, and the Marxist-socialist influences in government. The resulting conflicts in ecclesiastical circles in the Netherlands, the United Kingdom, and other countries spilled over into the American ecclesiastical situation with profound results. Consequently, to understand Machen's theological, apologetic, and social viewpoints we must look briefly at his personal experiences and background.

The home in which he was brought up was a Christian home, in which his ties with his mother were very close, and they remained so until the day of her death on October 13, 1931.[1] Educated first in a private school, he then attended Johns Hopkins University, from which he graduated in 1901 and went on to do a year's graduate work in classics under Basil L. Gildersleeve.[2] On his graduation he took his first of many trips to Europe, which whetted his appetite for further study in Germany. Before going to Europe for more academic work, however, he enrolled at Princeton Theological Seminary, although at this time he was by no means sure that he should enter the ministry. On the other hand, he seemed to feel that studying under such scholars as Francis Patton and Benjamin Breckinridge Warfield would be good training, no matter how he decided to spend his life.[3]

During his time at Princeton he had become very interested in the question of the virgin birth of Christ and had written a thesis on it, which was published in the *Princeton Theological Review* (1905-06). Even before this, however, he had left again for Europe to study at Marburg University, where he came under the influence of such Liberal theologians as Adolf Jülicher, Johannes Weiss, and Wilhelm Herrmann, all of whom caused him to have very serious doubts about the theological position that he had accepted at Princeton. From Marburg he went on to Göttingen where he studied under men such as W. Bousset who were as radically liberal as those at Marburg. Meanwhile some of his former professors had been pressing him to come back to Princeton to teach, an invitation that he finally accepted in 1906. He remained in the New Testament Department at Princeton until 1929.[4] But although he was an instructor in the seminary, he did not accept ordination until 1914. It took him eight years, with the help of W. P. Armstrong, Francis Patton, and others, to recover his faith after the experience in Germany.[5] In 1912 he really began his career as a writer with the publication of his address on "Christianity and Culture," and he followed that in 1915 with one on "History and Faith."[6] In both of these he laid down the foundation for most of his life's work, principles from which he never departed.

As he had gradually recovered his faith, Machen had become increasingly aware of the devastating effects of the Higher Criticism of the Scriptures and of the accompanying efforts to water down, if not to destroy entirely, its teachings.[7] As a result he felt convinced that the only answer to such attacks on the gospel was their refutation by an appeal to the historical sources and a proper "common sense" interpretation of their statements. The outcome of this conviction was a number of addresses dealing with such topics as the virgin birth and the resurrection of Christ, which were later published. In these he took a very definite stand on the historical reliability of the biblical record, and devoted considerable time to criticizing and refuting the modernist position. This, however, brought him into conflict with some of the seminary authorities. Although in 1926 the Directors wanted him to become professor of apologetics, a move to which he was not much inclined, the Trustees, led by the president, J. Ross Stevenson, were opposed. The result was a battle that led to the reorganization of the administration: the Board of Directors was abolished and full control of the school was given to a single Board of Trustees to which two signers of the liberal Auburn Affirmation were appointed. The resulting conflict between Machen and the new administration led to his resignation from the seminary in June 1929, on the ground that Princeton had now left its historic theological position.[8]

With the departure of Machen, some others connected with the seminary felt they too should go. As a result they formed a committee to establish a new seminary, Westminster, which opened in Philadelphia as an independent educational institution in the autumn of 1929. In his address at the opening of the new institution, Machen stressed two articles of its constitution. One was the final authority of the Bible, which he characterized as "a plain book addressed to plain men, and . . . it means exactly what it says." The other was that since Princeton was now "lost to the evangelical cause," the new seminary would stand firmly for the Reformed theological position as expressed in the Westminster Confession of Faith. Added to that, he warned that anyone coming to Westminster would find that being a student would entail hard work![9] Naturally Princeton was not pleased with this development, and when, a few years later, the present writer visited Princeton to see some friends, he was given a detailed diagnosis of "Dossie's" paranoia.

The establishment of Westminster, however, did not bring Machen peace and ease of mind. He was also faced with the problem of what would happen to the graduates of the seminary when they were prepared to seek ordination. Some might, of course, go to denominations other than the Presbyterian Church, U.S.A., but he was most anxious that they should enter his church in the hopes of bringing about a true reformation. About this time the novelist Pearl Buck, serving as a missionary in China for the Presbyterian Church's Board of Missions, published in *The Christian Century* an enthusiastic review of the radically liberal *Rethinking Missions*, and followed that in January 1933 with an article in *Harper's Magazine* on the propriety of Christian missions, in which she virtually ruled out the New Testament message as a mystical concept of Christianity, rejecting even the need for the historic person of Christ. When the Board of Missions, while continuing to support Buck, then turned down a Westminster graduate who applied for appointment, and the General Assembly followed this with a vote of confidence for the board, Machen and others felt that action had to be taken. The result was the formation of the Independent Board for Presbyterian Foreign

Missions.[10] Against this move the Presbyterian Church took vigorous action, ordering that the Independent Board be dissolved. When that was not done, the judicial commission took action to discipline the participants, who either resigned or were defrocked. Among them was Machen.[11] Following this the only answer was the formation of a new Presbyterian church. The Presbyterian Church of America, later the Orthodox Presbyterian Church, was organized in 1936.[12]

Yet even the formation of a new church did not solve all problems. For one thing, some of Machen's supporters in the formation of Westminster Seminary, such as Professor Oswald T. Allis and Clarence Macartney, had not favored the formation of the Independent Board, and when plans were laid for the organization of a new Presbyterian church, they withdrew entirely along with some others. This was a great disappointment to Machen. But even more of a blow came when Carl McIntire and J. O. Buswell withdrew to form the Bible Presbyterian Church because of the new church's refusal, under Machen's guidance, to alter the Westminster Confession to make it more premillennial and to require total abstinence from alcoholic liquors a condition of church membership.[13] Added to all this the members of the Independent Board were now divided, for some were not particularly interested in establishing a new Presbyterian church, but instead favored independency.

At this point Machen was invited to go out to North Dakota for the Christmas holiday, which he did, but sadly while traveling around the state in the intense cold he contracted pneumonia and on January 1, 1937, died.[14] So ended the career of one of America's great defenders of the faith.

Machen's Theology

Machen's methodology is basic to an understanding of both his theology and his defense of it. He was not primarily a philosopher, which explains his reluctance to move from the New Testament department to become professor of apologetics at Princeton, and also his enthusiasm for the appointment of Cornelius Van Til to that position. Nor was he primarily a systematic theologian, although he knew his Reformed theology and was prepared to expound it whenever possible, as we can see from his *What Is Faith?* and the two volumes of his radio addresses delivered just before his death.[15] Unfortunately he died before he could complete the radio series, but despite this misfortune, he clearly indicates his grasp of the system of Reformed theology. The fact is that he was a historian, as he indicated in the opening sentence of his 1915 essay "History and Faith" which stated that "the student of the New

Testament should be primarily an historian. The centre and core of all the Bible is history."[16]

Because of this historical orientation, he sought to prove the reliability of the biblical record by a sound historical investigation and analysis of the evidence provided by the documents. One only has to note the course he established on the introduction to the literature and history of the New Testament to realize this. Or what was even better, if one could attend his lectures on Apostolic History and listen to his enthusiastic presentation of the evidence for single authorship of the Gospel of Luke and the Acts of the Apostles, one would soon realize that he was indeed a sound and well-trained historian. His constant insistence in both his expository and his apologetic works on the validity of his historico-grammatical exegesis of the Bible was further evidence of his point of view. Some, even of his followers, however, have claimed that he followed too completely the Scottish Common Sense Philosophy of Thomas Reid, failing to take into consideration the question of the presuppositions of one's thinking. For this some have even declared him merely nineteenth century in his approach. It must be constantly kept in mind, however, that while he insisted that the validity of the historical analysis could lead one to accept facts as true, it did not then lead automatically to acceptance of the doctrine behind those facts. As he pointed out more than once, while one might acknowledge that history showed that Christ died, more was required for one to confess that he died for our sins. He could even state that a non-Christian might believe in Christ's resurrection, but it was only by the work of the Holy Spirit that that individual would believe that Christ rose victor over death for the sinner's justification. The presuppositions or faith of the Christian led to a very different understanding from that of the unbeliever, who began with very different presuppositions.[17]

As mentioned earlier, Machen had come to this specifically Reformed position only gradually. His home background seems to have been evangelical, but not strongly Reformed. During his time of study in Germany he undoubtedly had faced a large number of problems, particularly in dealing with the attacks of the various theological professors on the historical reliability of the New Testament, and had eventually come to realize that without the basic Christian faith, even historical evidence would not bring conviction of the truth of Christianity. This comes out very clearly in his lectures at the Grove City Bible School in 1925, which later appeared as the volume *What Is Faith?* and his radio addresses over station WIP, Philadelphia, just shortly before his death. True, he did not work out the whole problem of presuppositions as did Cornelius Van Til, but he certainly never ignored them in favor of a positivistic view that held that the facts were all that were needed.

Because of his own presuppositions he followed the Reformed position that the Bible is the Word of God. But by doing so, he did not accept a mechanical type of dictation. He held the view that the writers of the Bible used the ordinary sources of information, that they as individuals had personal freedom but that they recorded the facts and their interpretation guided by the Holy Spirit, so that the Bible is truly infallible, the Word of God in the word of man.[18] Hence in order to gain a true and proper understanding of the divine revelation one must study the Bible by the grammatico-historical method. The trouble with so many of the so-called Liberals, he maintained, was that they refused to employ the proper historical method honestly and so twisted the meaning of the Scriptures.[19] A true evangelical and Reformed exegesis, on the other hand, employed the scientific historical method that is the true foundation and source of a sound Christian theology.

When one turns to a study of Machen's actual theology, one finds at its core a typically Reformed doctrine of God. God is triune: Father, Son, and Holy Spirit. This God is sovereign, a theme of which he never became tired. As one reads his various works, whether those primarily expository or primarily apologetic, the sovereignty of God is a constantly recurring note. But equally important in his thought was the fact that God is a gracious and loving God. As he pointed out in the second chapter of *What Is Faith?*, we can believe in God only as we know him, and this means that we must know him as he reveals himself to us in nature, in our own souls, and in the Scriptures of the Old and New Testaments. When we so know him we believe in him and trust ourselves to his sovereign grace.[20]

Only, however, as one comes to God through Jesus Christ, the incarnate Savior, does one truly know God. And Machen, as a New Testament scholar, was therefore very interested in setting forth evidence and arguments for the reliability of the New Testament's witness to Christ as the incarnate divine Savior. His first major work dealing with this matter appeared in 1921 under the title *The Origin of Paul's Religion*. In 1925 and 1926 he had two articles published on the virgin birth and resurrection of Christ, and another in the following year dealing directly with the apostolic witness to Christ.[21] But probably his most important work in this field was *The Virgin Birth of Christ*, published in 1930. In all of these writings he constantly insisted that the different writers of the New Testament books were united in their testimony to Christ.

This testimory was that he is the Son of God, the Savior of the world. In this testimony there was first the fact that he was conceived miraculously in the womb of Mary and thus was the son of a virgin. Machen also spends considerable time with Christ's divine powers and works. These he cites as witnesses to the fact that he was not merely a great and good mortal, but both God and man in one person. At the same time, Machen stresses Christ's teachings as being very relevant and applicable not only to the church, but also to society in our own day and age. Yet he was not prepared to accept the view that Christ's teachings were merely the setting forth of a moral code. They were far different, for Christ said very clearly and certainly that he was much more than merely a teacher. He was the Savior, the promised Messiah.

This stress on Christ as Savior was the expression of Machen's basic religious faith. Rejecting the view that he was merely a teacher and an example, Machen insisted that it is only as one places one's trust in Christ as his Savior who died on Calvary's cross and who rose the third day and ascended into heaven, that one may obtain the forgiveness of sins. Only then may one be truly called a Christian. In his chapter "Faith in Christ" in *What is Faith?* he constantly attacks and criticizes those who would dilute the New Testament message that Christ is the only Savior of men. And if one listened to his preaching one would very quickly realize that the preacher was in every respect an evangelist as well as a scholar. Machen's wholehearted conviction that Christ was *his* Savior is illustrated by his sending a telegram, one of the last acts before his death, to Professor John Murray, in which he said: "I'm so thankful for the active obedience of Christ. No hope without it."[22]

While Machen did not stress the work of the Holy Spirit as he did that of Christ, nevertheless the presence, power, and work of the Third Person of the Trinity is always taken into account when discussing the works of God. One only has to glance at the subject indices in his various works to see this statement borne out. Although he did not lay great stress upon it, Machen accepted the doctrine of Common Grace as part of the work of the Spirit. But even more important was his constant emphasis upon the work of the Spirit in the incarnation, in the writing of the biblical books, and in the regeneration and sanctification of the elect. In this he was following closely in the footsteps of Calvin. The application of Christ's saving work is the action of the Spirit, who in doing this bears witness to both the Father and the Son. In fact, that witness-bearing is what results in both regeneration and faith.[23]

Basic, however, to Machen's view of divine redemption was his insistence upon the doctrines of creation and providence. He emphasized the necessity of realizing that the triune God had created all things out of nothing and constantly sustained and ruled over them from moment to moment. He rejected all deistic or pantheistic attempts either to separate God from creation or to make him simply the essence of creation itself. And he insisted upon the necessity of recognizing the divine creatorship, because nature was the primary means of divine revelation since it was the "work of God's hand." Hence his great appreciation of the beauties of mountain climbing and natural scenery. But especially important was the necessity of recognizing that the creation of man was central to creation, and it was in creation that the drama of God's redemptive work was enacted.[24]

Machen's stress upon the saving work of Christ and the regenerating and sanctifying work of the Spirit arises out of his acceptance of what the Bible says about man. He accepted the doctrine of the Fall without any question, for he could see the sinfulness of man all around, and within. His introduction to *What is Faith?* as well as the chapter "Faith Born of Need" makes this only too clear. Because of man's sin he is alienated from God and has no desire to be reconciled to God, unless God takes the first step and draws the sinner to himself. This reconciliation is the only way in which man may inherit eternal life. Twelve years after he had stated the Reformed position in *What is Faith?* he dealt in his last radio addresses (published after his death under the title *The Christian View of Man*) with the subjects of the creation of man, the covenant of life, man's fall, and God's gift of grace. There he rings the changes on man's sinfulness, but also on God's sovereign predestination, and his working out of that predestination in history.

It is to be regretted that Machen did not live to present the third of his series of radio talks, which would have dealt with the subject of salvation. But the Lord saw fit to take him before that could happen. From his other writings, however, one can understand quite clearly that what he would have said would have been quite in accord with the Reformed tadition. One could quote many passages from his various writings, but perhaps one from *What is Faith?* brings out his views most clearly.

> Certainly, at bottom, faith is in one sense a very simple thing; it simply means that abandoning the vain effort of earning one's way into God's presence we accept the gift of salvation which Christ offers so full and free. Such is the "doctrine"—let us not be afraid of the word—such is the "doctrine" of justification through faith alone.[25]

"Justification by faith alone"—the words of Martin Luther, John Calvin, and the other Protestant Reformers looking back to the Apostle Paul and to Jesus Christ himself—was central to Machen's own Christian experience and so to his thought. Moreover, he knew that this faith was the gift of God through regeneration by the Holy Spirit.[26]

Faith, however, meant loving obedience. He did not hold, as do some modern theologians who claim to be Reformed, that obedience is part of faith, that one is justified by "obedient faith."[27] Works are the outgrowth, the result of faith, not part of it. This he reiterated repeatedly in his chapter "Faith and Works" in *What is Faith?* That one had faith in Christ as Savior resulted in a love for him and obedience to him. This means that the Christian is to obey Christ in all things, even in the ministry of the church. As he put it in a graduation address to the students of Westminster Seminary in 1934, in the midst of the conflict over the Independent Board:

> If you obtain your message from any other authority than the Word of God, if you obtain it from the pronouncements of presbyteries or General Assemblies, then you may wear the garb of ministers, but you are not ministers in the sight of God. You are disloyal to the Lord Jesus Christ: you have betrayed a precious trust.[28]

From this statement we can see that for Machen the central directory of the Christian life was the Scriptures, enlightened by the Holy Spirit in the hearts and minds of faithful Christians.[29]

Unfortunately Machen did not have much to say about eschatology. "Unfortunately" because a thorough study of New Testament teaching on this subject might have helped quite a number of people who were led to reject him as a teacher and a leader because he was not a premillennialist. That he held the amillennial position he stated on a few occasions. Furthermore, when an attempt was made in the early days of the Presbyterian Church of America to change the Westminster Confession to allow more room for premillennialism, he opposed it. He held strongly, however, to the view that God ruled over history and was leading it on to the consummation of all things. More important, apparently, in his thinking was the Christian hope of eternal life in the presence of God, where all things would be made new.[30] Again turning to *What is Faith?* this comes out very clearly in the last chapter "Faith and Hope." No doubt if he had lived to complete his series of radio addresses he would have dealt with this topic in more detail.[31]

In summing up Machen's theology one can only say that it was the theology of a typically Reformed scholar. He did not produce a systematic theology in the usual form, but sought to present doctrine in a popular manner that the ordinary layperson could understand. As he remarked when criticizing A. C. McGiffert's work *The God of the Early Christians,* although he did not agree with it, "it possesses at least one merit that is rare among contemporary religious literature—it is interesting."[32] Machen sought to write books with a similar popular appeal. At the same time, he was always ready to defend the faith, with the result that much of his work was taken up with apologetics. To this we now turn.

The Defense of the Faith

Although Machen's primary interest was the exposition of Christian doctrine, a very close second was his view that the Christian faith must be set forth as a valid system of thought. He believed that a radical change was needed in both the church and society in general. This would come only if there were a reformation similar to that which took place in the sixteenth century, and it would take place only if Christians were prepared to stand up and present the credentials of their beliefs, showing that they met all the requirements of sound thinking. While he acknowledged that ultimately man could not penetrate the mystery of God and the divine purpose or counsel, yet there was enough evidence in the Scriptures to show that what they said was true and historically verifiable.[33]

He felt the need for apologetics centered around the message of the gospel as set forth primarily in the four Gospels and in the writings of the Apostle Paul. Wherever he turned there seemed to be theologians, preachers, journalists, and others who were prepared to attack the Christian's faith and demonstrate that it had been misinterpreted or twisted to be something that was radically different from the historic doctrines. There were those in his own church, such as the signers of the Auburn Affirmation, who while not rejecting Christianity, at least officially, so undermined all basic doctrine that nothing was left. At the same time there were those who simply rejected the Christian teachings as completely wrong. In this class were people such as H. L. Mencken, Pearl Buck, and Albert C. Dieffenbach, who, while acknowledging Machen's strength of character and his loyalty to his position, yet rejected his ideas out of hand.[34]

In the face of dilutions of and direct attacks on the historic Reformed position Machen sought to put up a strong and effective defense. To do this, he insisted that it was possible to prove that the books of the New Testament were historically trustworthy. He maintained that the grammatico-historical approach to and interpretation of the documents, used with "common sense," would show that what they said was true. In this he was clearly following the line of thought of the Princeton school of apologetics, which in turn looked back to Thomas Reid's Scottish "Common Sense Philosophy." And whenever he had the opportunity he went after the Modernists who were attempting to undermine the Christian faith with their twisted and perverted interpretations. His first extensive work in this area was *Christianity and Liberalism*, first published by Macmillan in 1923, but republished seven times, the last printing being done in 1940, three years after his death.

Machen, however, did not believe that merely historical or rational arguments would convince an unbeliever and bring him to faith in Christ. As he pointed out more than once, while a person might know all the arguments for Christ's virgin birth or his resurrection, that person would come to faith only through the action of the Holy Spirit in regenerating the individual. Being very conscious of the noetic influence of sin, which effectively blocked man's spiritual vision, and also of the perversion of the human will, he recognized that even true "common sense" would ultimately make no sense to an individual unless the Holy Spirit opened that person's eyes and changed his or her will. Only then would the person believe.[35]

Having to depend upon the Holy Spirit to bring conviction to the unbeliever did not mean that Machen held to a kind of quietist position in which he waited passively until the Spirit moved. He maintained that the Christian, particularly the preacher, had the duty of proclaiming the gospel wherever and whenever he had the opportunity. Thus he was always ready to present his theological position and defend it even before quite skeptical audiences or in the secular press such as *The New York Times, Forum,* and *The Annals* of the American Academy of Political and Social Science. He did not doubt that he could prove his case if his critics and opponents would only stick to the facts and not attempt to circumvent them by irrational theories.[36] All this meant that the Christian must have freedom to proclaim the gospel and in so doing to evangelize. The gospel had to be carried to the far corners of the earth and it was not to be merely a gospel of feeling or sentiment, but was to have a sound intellectual basis, founded firmly on the revelation contained in the Scriptures.[37]

To carry out what he considered his God-given mandate to stand for the truth of the gospel necessarily involved Machen in controversy, particularly within the Presbyterian Church, U.S.A. He believed that it was the duty of all orthodox Christians to take their stand within the church against those who would pervert the gospel, thus depriving people of the knowledge of God's grace. He also felt that those who had signed the Westminster Confession and then proceeded to undermine its teachings by preaching and teaching doctrines and theories that were in conflict with it were dishonest and should be exposed for what they actually were doing. Since much of the administration of both Princeton Seminary and of the church as a whole seemed to be in the hands of such individuals, Machen was prepared to speak out no matter how unpopular such action would be, and he was maligned for so doing. He refused to modify his position, however, or give in to pressure.[38]

Machen, however, was no schismatic or secessionist. He did not follow the example of so many Christians who refuse "to get involved," and simply withdraw. He stayed in and fought until forced out. He left Princeton because he felt that the entire institution had given up its basic Reformed position, and helped to found Westminster to carry on the Princeton tradition.[39] But he did not leave the Presbyterian Church. Nor did he leave the church later when he helped to organize the Independent

Board, since the official board was accepting candidates who rejected the church's accepted doctrinal standards. Rather, he felt it necessary to organize a board that would maintain the church's professed theological position. The present writer can well remember a speech he made on "set-up" night to the Westminster Dining Club in 1936. After outlining the situation in the Presbyterian Church, U.S.A. at the time, he said forcefully: "But boys, I am not going to leave. This is my church, and I am staying in and fighting until they either change the Confession or throw me out." And they did the latter.[40]

Thus one may see that Machen's apologetic approach was no merely theoretical, classroom stance. It was a desire to defend and maintain the heart of the gospel. As he put it in his essay "Christianity and Liberty":

> Increasingly the great alternative is becoming clearer; give Jesus up, and confess that His portrait is forever hidden in the mists of legend; or else accept Him as a supernatural Person, as He is presented by all the four Gospels and by Paul.[41]

This was his position, and for it he was prepared to do battle both in the church courts and in the world at large.

The Application of the Faith

As we have endeavored to show, Machen was no ivory-tower scholar. One indication of this is his intense interest in the fortunes of the football teams of the area, and he frequently took interested students to see the Army-Navy game, which seems to have been his favorite sports spectacle. Also contrary to much popular opinion, especially at Princeton, he had a strong sense of humor. One who has attended his classes can vouch for that, for his humor appeared even in his lectures. But even more important was his insistence that a good minister must be a stunt man. As a result there was an annual Westminster stunt night at which he was frequently the star as he recited poetry satirizing the weaknesses and foibles of human nature. He was anything but the paranoid individual that many of his foes insisted upon picturing.

In the social field, Machen's primary interest was in the maintenance of freedom for the individual. He was strongly opposed to the increasing tendency toward collectivism in society that he saw growing on every hand. He felt that the civil government was forever attempting to regulate and control in order to make all citizens of the same pattern and so destroy the individual's wish to be an individual, different from others. He himself was no conformist, and he did not feel that others should be made to conform to the humors of a group of bureaucrats in Washington or in one of the state capitols. Therefore, he was constantly, and on every appropriate occasion, demanding that the individual should have liberty consonant with the liberty of his fellow citizens. Where true Christianity reigns, liberty is the rule. "God is free, and where He is, there is liberty and life."[42]

Some of his opponents objected to his call for liberty at the same time that he demanded the disciplining of heretics within the church. Where was the freedom for which he fought? He pointed out, however, that there is a difference between voluntary and involuntary organizations. The state is an involuntary organization of which one is a member whether he wishes or not. The state that interferes with one's liberty must be restrained. In the case of a voluntary organization such as the church, no one is forced to enter. "Insistence on fundamental agreement within a voluntary organization is therefore not at all inconsistent with insistence upon the widest tolerance in the state."[43] He consequently insisted that the church not only had the right but also the duty to remove those who contravened the fundamental agreement. Thus he was prepared to battle for wide freedom under the state, but at the same time for close adherence to the constitution of voluntary bodies such as the church.

Machen's concept of state tolerance was not just centered on one or two things, but seems to have had a wide-angle lens. For instance, the story went the rounds at Westminster Seminary that at one point the city council of Philadelphia proposed enacting a law that would have forbidden jaywalking. An open session of the council was held to determine whether the people of the city wanted such a rule. Machen, who appeared at the council, voiced strong opposition to the rule as an infringement of the citizens' freedom and was to a considerable extent responsible for the proposal being dropped. Although he did not live to see it, he pointed out that the constant eroding of freedom would lead to national and international disasters throughout the world. He should have lived to 1984!

Liberty of action generally, however, was not the only aspect of Machen's concern. He was particularly interested in the matter of freedom of choice in education and backed the concept of the Christian school. He viewed the education of his own day as falling far short of what true education should be, pointing out that there was a tendency toward theory and not an emphasis upon learning the facts. He stressed the view that merely learning some techniques or methods of approaching facts was not really education. He felt that the whole idea of learning as a discipline involving the entire individual was being disregarded. In addition he insisted that while technical education was important, the study of broader subjects such as the humanities was being neglected, as were all attempts at moral education. "By this purely secular, non-moral and non-religious, training we produce not a real human being but a horrible Frankenstein. . . ." Furthermore, such education seeks to make everyone conform to one pattern or mold and teaches that all religious faiths are of the same value and that character must be built upon human experience, rather than upon the law of God.[44] It was these latter considerations that weighed so heavily in his mind in his opposition to the whole system of compulsory public education. But he also opposed any attempt to introduce Bible reading into the public schools, since that, too, could be dangerous, for without proper direction the Bible message could be distorted and changed. Furthermore, it would conflict with the whole concept of freedom of religion.[45]

The solution to this problem, as far as Machen was concerned, was the Christian school. True, he recognized that not every place had or could afford such a school. If that were the case, then there should be released-time instruction. If on the other hand it would be possible to have a Christian school that could teach from a truly Christian perspective, such a school should be established. However, and this was important to his thought, the parents must be able to determine. He pointed out that certain laws that had been proposed in Congress aimed at taking away the parents' right to determine their children's training, placing it instead in the hands of governmental bureaucrats. This he felt was definitely wrong and should be stopped.

The reason for Machen's preference for the Christian school was twofold. In the first place he believed that released time tended to give schoolchildren the idea that Christianity affected only a part of life, and a not very significant one at that. Most of life was dealt with in the secular-humanistic classrooms of the public school. Second, insisting that Christianity gave a world-and-life view that dealt with all aspects of human existence, he held that the entire curriculum of the Christian school should be taught from that point of view. At the same time, he stressed that the Christian school must do its job effectively so that even those who were not Christians would give it their backing, not only for its teaching but because "they really love freedom and the noble traditions of our people." Even more important was the need for the Christian part of the nation to give its support to the Christian school, not as a competitor of the Christian family, but as a support to what Christian parents were seeking to do in the home.[46]

Although Machen made no claim to be a prophet, nor the son of a prophet, many of the questions that he raised with regard not only to education, but to the whole structure of the Anglo-American cultural patterns seem to be moving toward a fulfillment that he foresaw. He was strongly opposed to the establishment of a federal Department of Education that would so regulate education that everything in that field would become monolithic and at the same time, in order to accommodate everybody, would maintain minimum standards. We are now beginning to see this in innovations such as "Process Writing," which are being introduced into schools, with the result that many college freshmen now have to take remedial English courses in order to be able to do their academic work. And much the same effect may be seen in other fields, even in automobile manufacture where thousands of cars have to be recalled each year in order to remedy mechanical defects of one kind or another. To Machen this would not be in any way surprising.[47]

The only solution to this problem would be a new Reformation. This would not be a harking back to the sixteenth century, but a new Reformation wrought by the Spirit of God in the contemporary Christian church. The result would be a restoration of true liberty to mankind in which "thinking [would] again come to its rights." Theological Modernism, which has led to much of the intellectual degradation of the day, would be pushed aside by those who were characterized by faith in Christ as Savior and Lord, and who, possessed "by an heroic honesty," would take their stand without any consideration of consequences. With such a movement, he believed, would come a new Renaissance that would encourage true originality, independence of mind, and "plain common sense."[48]

Such was the theological position of J. Gresham Machen and his application of it. Theologically he was not significantly different from his teacher B. B. Warfield, nor from John Calvin, nor even from the writers of the New Testament. His, however, was a different situation and set of circumstances from theirs. Faced with a decline in Reformed orthodoxy at Princeton and in the Presbyterian Church, U.S.A., and with the growing influence of godless, materialistic humanism in society as a whole, he was prepared to speak out. Believing in the objectivity of truth and employing a sound critical-historical approach to the Christian faith as set forth in the Bible, the Word of God, he attacked the growth of heresy within the Presbyterian Church, and also sought in very practical ways to offset and circumvent the forces that he believed were carrying it in a direction that would destroy it as a true Christian church. At the same time, he took his stand against the humanistic trends in society, calling for Christians to assert themselves as members of society, in order that they might be salt that has not lost its savor. He hoped and prayed for a new Reformation that would revive the church, and renew and reform the social structures.

In the introduction to this volume, George Marsden has delineated three types of Reformed theology: the doctrinal, the cultural, and the evangelistic. In a very real sense, Machen embraced all three. He represented the first in his strong defense of the doctrines of the faith; the second in his constant emphasis upon the Christian's responsibility to take social action; and the third in his willingness to proclaim the grace of God in Jesus Christ whenever he had an opportunity. For these reasons his influence went far beyond the confines of the Reformed community in America.

But how much influence did he have? This, of course, is hard to estimate. Undoubtedly he influenced many of his students at both Princeton and Westminster, but his sudden decease at a relatively early age appears to have cut back this influence, at least in the eyes of those who see such events only in their space-time context. It may well be, however, that in the purpose and plan of God he succeeded in sowing seed that may be part of the spiritual harvest that will bring to fruition the Reformation for which he longed.

Notes: J. Gresham Machen

1. Ned B. Stonehouse, *J. Gresham Machen: A Biographical Memoir* (Grand Rapids: Wm. B. Eerdmans Publishing Company, 1954), 564.
2. Ibid., 42, 47ff.
3. Ibid., ch. 3.
4. Ibid., chs. 5-6.
5. Ibid., 193ff.
6. Ibid., 205-06; J. G. Machen, *What Is Christianity? and Other Addresses*, ed. Ned B. Stonehouse (Grand Rapids: Wm. B. Eerdmans Publishing Company, 1951), 156-85.
7. D. G. Hart, "The Princeton Mind in the Modern World and the Common Sense of J. Gresham Machen," *Westminster Theological Journal* 45 (1984): 10ff.
8. Stonehouse, *J. Gresham Machen*, 441ff.
9. Machen, "Westminster Seminary: Its Plan and Purpose," in *What Is Christianity?* 224ff.
10. Cf. Machen, "The Christian View of Missions," in *What Is Christianity?* 148ff.; Stonehouse, *J. Gresham Machen*, 472ff.
11. Ibid., 491.
12. Ibid., 495ff.
13. Ibid., 504.
14. Ibid., 437.
15. J. Gresham Machen, *What Is Faith?* (New York: Macmillan Publishing Company, Inc., 1925); *The Christian Faith in the Modern World* (New York: Macmillan Publishing Company, 1936); *The Christian View of Man* (Grand Rapids: Wm. B. Eerdmans Publishing Company, 1937).
16. Machen, *What Is Christianity?* 170.
17. Ibid., 102-03; Machen, *What Is Faith?* 47-48, 127-28, 151. Cf. *The New Testament: An Introduction to Its Literature and History* (Carlisle, PA: Banner of Truth, 1976) and also the discussions of this in Hart, "Princeton Mind"; Syd-

ney E. Ahlstrom, "The Scottish Philosophy and American Theology," *Church History* 24 (1955): 257ff.; George M. Marsden, "J. Gresham Machen, History, and Truth," *Westminster Theological Journal* 42 (1979-80): 157ff.

18. Machen, *Christian Faith in the Modern World*, 33ff.

19. Machen, *What Is Faith?* 23.

20. Ibid., 75ff.; Machen, *Christian Faith in the Modern World*, 117-18.

21. Machen, *What Is Christianity?* 24ff.

22. Stonehouse, *J. Gresham Machen*, 508.

23. Machen, *What Is Faith?* 171, 190ff., 207ff.; *The Christian Faith in the Modern World*, 152, 231ff.; *The Christian View of Man*, 164ff., 215-16, 289, 296.

24. Machen, *What Is Faith?* 59-60, 65-66; *The Christian View of Man*, 84ff.; *What Is Christianity?* 141, 304ff.

25. Ibid., 181, 190-91, 203, 209.

26. Ibid., 135ff., 190-91, 207-08; Machen, *Christian View of Man*, 175-76, 288, 291.

27. Cf. M. Karlberg, "Justification in Redemptive History," *Westminster Theological Journal* 43 (1981): 213-14.

28. Machen, *What Is Christianity?* 240.

29. Machen, *Christianity and Liberalism* (Philadelphia: Presbyterian Guardian, 1940), 136, 146-47.

30. Ibid., 147-48.

31. Machen, *Christian View of Man*, 84ff.

32. Machen, *What Is Faith?* 54.

33. Machen, "Christian Scholarship and the Defence of the Faith," in *What Is Christianity?* 126ff.; *Christianity and Liberalism*, Introduction.

34. Cf. his comments on McGiffert in *What Is Faith?* 54ff.; cf. also 210ff., 234ff., and Stonehouse, *J. Gresham Machen*, 473ff.

35. Cf. n. 23.

36. Cf. Machen, *What Is Christianity?* 126ff., 138ff.

37. Cf. Machen, "The Christian View of Missions," in *What Is Christianity?* 148ff.

38. Machen, *What is Faith?* 103; *Christian View of Man*, 131ff.

39. Machen, *What Is Christianity?* 224ff.; Stonehouse, *J. Gresham Machen*, chs. 22-23.

40. Ibid., chs. 40-41.

41. Machen, *What Is Christianity?* 271.

42. Ibid., 267ff.; Machen, *Christian View of Man*, 227ff.; *What Is Faith?* 181; *Christian View of Man*, 10.

43. Machen, "The Necessity of the Christian School," in *What Is Christianity?* 248ff.

44. Ibid., 296ff.; Machen, *What Is Faith?* 15ff.

45. Ibid., 15ff.

46. Ibid., 18ff., 103ff., 184.

47. Ibid., 15ff.

48. Ibid., 18ff., 103ff., 184.

1

THE DUTCH SCHOOLS

JAMES D. BRATT

Abraham Kuyper

In 1898 a Dutch Reformed minister recently arrived in the United States made his first contribution to that perennial topic of immigrant discussion, the contrast between Old World and New World cultures. For this observer, Foppe Ten Hoor, the difference appeared most clearly in work styles, which in turn reflected geographical constraints. In America, where land and resources existed in nearly absurd abundance, people who could work and move on quickly tended to stay on the surface of things, and regarded all affairs with pragmatic judgment. Netherlanders, however, with their limited terrain, had to be thorough and cautious, paying close heed to distinctions and boundaries, delving to the roots of things. The first group was enamored of results, action, and change; the second, with principle, theory, and tradition. The difference had consequences in all realms, Ten Hoor concluded, but most importantly in the theological.[1]

How his audience should negotiate the conflict that their mixed status (Dutch and American) entailed, Ten Hoor left to later occasions. More important for our purposes here is his delineation, on the verge of the twentieth century, of seminal "Dutch" characteristics; for the body of theological work the group would produce in that century bears out Ten Hoor's profile remarkably well. Most striking, perhaps, is Ten Hoor's very act of addressing such cultural concerns precisely in his role as professor of systematic theology at the Christian Reformed seminary in Grand Rapids. That the post brought with it this license, even mandate, to speak to any and all issues and that no office in the entire community held more prestige attest to the priority of place the Dutch Reformed have given theology.

Some of theology's function for this group is thus evident in Ten Hoor's decree. So is an uneasy duality at the heart of that function. On the one hand, as Ten Hoor insisted in hundreds of subsequent lectures and pages of commentary, Reformed doctrine was God's own truth, eter-

nal, unchanging, fixed in his revelatory Word, the best interpretation of
that Word. On the other hand, Dutch theology bore the stamp of a particular culture and was used by Ten Hoor and many others to differen-
tiate "our people" from the "American world," even from other Reformed
groups in that world. Quite simply, theology could not escape serving
Dutch Americans as the medium of intellectual exchange, for their
churches served as the center of their local communities and their denominations as the national networks binding these together. As all sorts
of social dynamics and cultural issues—churchly or not, intraethnic or
involving the outside world—registered in ecclesiastical terms, theology
became the means of communal debate, confirmation, and resolution.
Hence the theology professorship's broad portfolio and the community's
doctrinal passion. Theology had to be but could not be left an eternal
code of truth beyond the vagaries of interest and perception. Doctrine
and life worked in a close and continuing dialectic, each speaking to the
other as—and sometimes more—fully and directly as the fondest theorists of Calvinism might wish. Ten Hoor worked better than he knew in
that quick, and quite typical, concluding leap from the earth to the
religious.

Our analysis of this theology will move from the more common to
the more particular; that is, first reviewing those elements that the Dutch
share with other American Protestants, especially with evangelicals and
other Reformed camps; then examining the features that have differen-
tiated them from these; and finally tracing the issues of controversy
within the community itself and the separate schools thereby produced.
Put another way, we can describe Dutch-American distinctiveness and
debates as functions of a particular selection and combination of elements from the general Reformed fund, and analyze that selection-com-
bination process according to different trajectories of launch from the
Netherlandic background, shifting patterns of consensus and tension
within the community, and the ongoing dialectic between the community and the surrounding American world.

The Wider Context of Calvinism

The themes of commonality and particularity are prefigured in all
three of Dutch Calvinism's confessional standards. That there were three
suggests the motif of plurality as well. The Belgic Confession (1561),
written in the fires of intense religious strife, gave primordial definition
to the Dutch church, but also showed, in its anti-Catholic and anti-Ana-
baptist strains, how the Dutch could comport well with other Reformed
movements whether on the continent or in America. The Heidelberg
Catechism (1563), on the other hand, was famous for its pastoral, irenic

nature. Written to promote unity between the Reformed and Lutherans in Germany, the document became as well a bridge between the Dutch and German Reformed, again on both sides of the Atlantic. Its practical piety also allowed its readers a way of negotiating the tension between orthodoxy and pietism that proved so disruptive elsewhere. Finally, the Canons of Dort (1619), forged in "a virtual ecumenical council of Reformed churches," buttressed the Dutch in their predestinarian, theocentric identity and in the scholastic methodology they would share for centuries with the descendants of Westminster.[2]

Since the proceedings at Dort coincided with the founding of New Netherland in the Hudson Valley, the Dutch church in North America came into being with this full confessional structure at its disposal. It hardly made distinguished use of this resource or of any other, however, subserving rather the colony's economic purposes and suffering with its demographic, political, and diplomatic misfortunes.[3] The English conquest (1664) cost the Dutch church its preferred status, and for the next century it remained in a mixed state—an enclave for ethnocultural maintenance, yet a base of significant public power, uneasily housing both Jersey farmers and a Manhattan commercial elite. These divisions were to some extent mirrored in the controversy that ensued upon New Jersey pastor Theodore J. Frelinghuysen's use of "awakening" measures in the 1720s.[4] By the 1750s the church had divided into two camps, the "Coetus" (representing the Frelinghuysen line, with a platform of pietism and home rule), and the "Conferentie" (New York-based, holding more to the Amsterdam connection and confessional-liturgical traditions). Each group established connections with the respective "New" and "Old Light" factions in denominations around them. Yet rather than gravitating to these other orbits, the two sides were reunited with each other in the 1770s. The architect of the fusion, John H. Livingston, aptly represented the church's settled character: pious and intellectual, American (Yale) and Amsterdam educated, in contact with outsiders but first attentive to the home front.[5]

Signal features of this process, it should be noted, were no more "distinctively American" than characteristically "Dutch Reformed." The Netherlands was as central in the rise of evangelical pietism as pietism was in that nation's religious history in the century after 1650. Frelinghuysen himself was a child of the movement and brought it with him as an immigrant to America in 1720.[6] Moreover, in the Dutch case pietism generally had confessional orthodoxy as an ally, not—as often happened elsewhere—as an antagonist. This was the result of the long struggle within the Netherlandic church between the followers of Jacobus Arminius (and later, Descartes) and the strict Dortian party, which saw the former gradually gain tolerance, then dominance, so that orthodoxy became a minority view among the church elite. Over the same period, the more devout in hundreds of local congregations had been organizing conventicles to help prosecute a more rigorous type of religion than the established church could enforce. These found the themes of orthodoxy quite more to their taste than liberal esteem of reason and human nature; and the traditionalist theologians found in them a welcome base of support.[7] It was here, then, that pietism and confessionalism were married; that Gijsbert Voetius, champion of orthodoxy, and Willem à Brakel, exemplar of practical divinity, were bound together, to be venerated for generations as chief of "de oude schrijvers," "fathers" of the true faith.[8]

Such loyalties also figured prominently in the two developments of early nineteenth-century Dutch history most germane to our purposes. In the post-Napoleonic restructuring of the Reformed Church, local autonomy seemed threatened by an increasingly centralized administration, which had—even worse—opened the way for liturgical and doctrinal "corruption." The ensuing "secession" (in 1834) and formation of a network of "truly Reformed" churches essentially represented the old conventicle principles and clientele in more radical guise.[9] A decade later, the Seceder network provided key mechanisms of mobilization, transportation, and leadership for a new wave of Dutch emigration to America. Since this precedent was remembered for the whole second phase (1845-1920) of Dutch immigration, and since emigration and Secession appealed to the same strata of Dutch society, the orthodox made up a disproportionately high percentage of the nineteenth-century immigrants—and of the post-World War II migrants to Canada as well.[10] Hence the conservative branches of Dutch Calvinism took a central role in shaping the new ethnic subculture.

A pietist-confessionalist conjunction in the conventicle-Seceder mode thus forms the baseline of Dutch theology in America. It was also the source of the group's several similarities with its new Protestant neighbors. Like every strain in the American revivalist-evangelical tradition, Dutch pietism insisted that faith be deep, personal, and heartfelt, that it proceed from and through a bare confrontation with one's own unworthiness and the exclusive merits of Christ. Postconversion, the believer was to maintain the intimacy of this deliverance through daily introspection and devotions; was to "practice godliness," rejecting the "things of the flesh and the world"; and throughout, was to submit to the appraisal, admonition, and encouragement of the fellow "faithful."[11] Doctrinal comparisons, on the other hand, are more difficult since American evangelicals have hardly been of one mind on theological detail. But the Dutch have shared their characteristic, unifying insistence on a high view of scriptural veracity and authority, on Christianity's finality, and, in face of Enlightenment and Modernist critiques, on the plausibility

and necessity of the supernatural, miraculous, and transcendent in religion and metaphysics. As one of their typical assessments concluded,
the Fundamentalist "is our fellow believer," but the Modernist "is on the
side of the anti-Christ and cannot be recognized as a believer at all."[12]
So were the Dutch placed on the American spectrum.

The full extent of these congruences was best evident in the 1925-1950
era. Both the Dutch and the evangelicals entered the period lashed by
the cultural crisis that had been precipitated by World War I. Both responded with a subcultural strategy—the Dutch reinforcing an inherited
structure, the evangelicals building theirs new. Both took militant anti-
Modernism as their overriding outlook, their prime motive force, for the
entire era; and both moved toward strict, maximal claims as a result. On
the side of ethics, the era began for the Dutch with their largest denomination officially (and unprecedentedly) proscribing three forms of
"worldliness": dancing, gambling, and theater attendance.[13] An evangelical's list might have looked somewhat different (usually including
smoking and drinking, which were still tolerated—if no longer virtually
mandatory—among the Dutch), but the strategy of defensiveness, legalism, and symbolic repudiation of larger cultural trends was the same.
As to theology, this was the clearest era of confessionalist hegemony in
Dutch-American history. Appropriately, Louis Berkhof was its presiding
figure; his *Reformed Dogmatics*, in three volumes, its definitive production. Though it became the best-known Dutch contribution to American
theology, Berkhof's work had first of all an intracommunal intent. It was
to be at once the *summa* of the inherited faith and the touchstone for
measuring all other (read, "outside") opinion, an intellectual fortress
amid "the widespread doctrinal indifference . . . superficiality and confusion . . . [and] insidious errors" of "the present day." Yet virtually any
evangelical of the era, even those put off by Berkhof's Reformed insis-
tencies, could cheer the priority (in logic, deference, and elaboration) he
gave to Scripture, and relish his emphatic reassertion of every doctrinal
construction offensive to liberalism.[14]

Dutch Distinctives

The very degree of similarity, however, prompted demonstrations
of particularity. Not only did Berkhof's anti-Arminian strictures have
this role vis-à-vis most revivalist and holiness movements; so did the
confessional thoroughness and intensity, the systematization and doctrinalism evident in the Dutch tradition. If Berkhof's statement of purpose intended "insidious errors" for Modernists, "widespread doctrinal
indifference, superficiality and confusion" covered large reaches of the
evangelical complex. It was there (to conclude Berkhof's statement) that

"sects . . . are springing up like mushrooms on every side." Nor was this Berkhof's complaint alone. From his predecessor, Foppe Ten Hoor, to his successors in the post-World War II era, from every Dutch-American denomination, from press as well as pulpit, the Dutch mounted a persistent critique of American Protestantism's creedal reductionism, and of the cultural spirit it evidenced. From this perspective, Fundamentalism with its "short list" and Modernism with its "no list" of "essential doctrines" looked oddly similar, and the "Bible alone" claims of small sects only echoed the doctrinal ignorance of big denominations. The phenomenon in general showed that the churches were mirroring all too faithfully the character of the society around them. The individualistic egotism and pragmatism of the second appeared as the characteristic "subjectivism" and "moralism" of the first—that is, the designation of personal experience or feelings on the one hand or practical action on the other as *the* core, and inevitably the extent, of Christianity.[15]

Confessional consciousness, expectably, offered several corrective counterpoints. For Foppe Ten Hoor, it presented a foil against Anglo-American—and not coincidentally, Arminian, subbiblical—ways.[16] For the more optimistic, it opened up the treasures, and the warning lessons, of the centuries of church history.

> To turn one's back on the historic creeds is therefore to turn one's back on what God has given us through the struggle of centuries, and to run the risk of trying to build up once more what has already been tried and found wanting. . . . To preach a creed is one of the very best methods possible . . . of avoiding tangents and vagaries, of securing a balanced and full-orbed presentation of the Bible as a whole. . . .[17]

But for everyone, it forestalled the drift to liberalism on the left and pious self-absorption on the right to which the subjective impulse was particularly prone. The confessions alone had the resources equal to the challenges and temptations of modern culture. Moreover, this seemed the scripturally given psychology. True, one must experience salvation and prove it in action; but without recourse to the full body of biblical truth, to a holistic system mindful of first principles and aware of their logical implications and complications, these would prove fleeting, filled more with the spirit of the age than with that of the Word.[18]

Besides doctrinalism, several specific tenets worked to distinguish the Dutch among conservative Protestants. Persistently, discussions in this vein brought up the ideas of covenant and kingdom. The intertwining of the two and the vision they supported were best articulated by Abraham Kuyper (1837-1920), the eminent Netherlander whose Neo-Calvinistic movement did much to restore the concepts to the heart of Dutch

Reformed concern.[19] Of the dual goals that drove Kuyper throughout his staggeringly multifarious career, success in the first—combatting liberalism—required the second—awakening the devout from their pietistic slumbers. To be *Calvinists* again, Kuyper told his followers, they had to recognize the lordship of Christ over all areas of life, which meant that they could neither dismiss various fields (art, science, politics) as inherently "worldly" nor participate in these simply with and as non-Christians, but must bring into each a distinctively Christian commitment and program. The result would be an "organic church," working outside ecclesiastical institutional walls, but with a coherent plan and mutual discipline, living out the Word of God in "every sphere of life" and so building up the Kingdom of God in the midst of the world. Covenant figured centrally in this conception as the mechanism or ground of divine sovereignty (the "channel through which the waters of election flow"), just as kingdom denoted its scope or end.[20]

One measure of the Kuyperian presence among Dutch-Americans, their perennial efforts at Christian cultural action, has been much noted. It was from Kuyper that they got their early concern with "worldview," their habitual confidence in speaking to every phase of modern culture, from science to social theory, geopolitics to economics, and their determination to uncover philosophical preconceptions in every academic credo, every social program. But the covenant-kingdom conjunction itself played a major role in this project by shaping a Dutch-American church ethos that contrasted markedly, in their eyes, with that of the evangelical world. Put simply, covenant was arrayed against revivalism as a model of Christian initiation and against dispensationalism as a view of history; and kingdom stood over against individualism as the scope of God's purpose, and against mere soul-saving as the end. Against spiritual moods, the pressures of life, and faddish "winds of doctrine," the covenant rooted the believer firmly in social and historical context, and above all in the lasting will of God. He did not exist as a lonely individual but as part of a corporate body that supported him even as he contributed to its vitality. He did not have to extract the full message of faith from the Bible anew, nor alone puzzle out its complicated relationships with daily life, for he stood heir to the whole heritage of Christian history. Nor was the present era a parenthesis in the divine plan, allowing of only "spiritual" ends and means for Christian action. God's ages were an organic whole, as were his people, so a full-bodied, earthly witness to redemption was still the Christian mandate. Drawing off lifelong nurture, not just a single episode (periodically "renewed") of emotional "conversion," the life of faith would not be restricted to Sunday worship and special "spiritual" moments during the week but would involve everyday habits, customs, and work in home, shop, and school. More boldly, placed in the fabric of his peers and the order of generations past and present, believers could transcend the level of personal ethics alone and address collective structures, broad cultural movements, with the redemptive message.[21]

This vision manifests the basic axioms of Dutch Reformed thinking: the will of God, not the whims of man; organic connections, not fragments or individual parts. But the program's usual implementation shows the ethnic-communal factor in the group's life as well. "Kingdom-building" was too readily left at the construction of a cradle-to-grave institutional framework for the mutual association of Dutch-Americans; and the magisterial process of divine election through the corridors of time could devolve to just the baptism and indoctrination of the group's next generation. "God does not save people at random," said one commentator to this point, "but follows a certain order, and perpetuates his covenant from generation to generation through the families of believers"—Dutch-American believers, it turned out.[22] Grand visions and small achievements thus became the besetting paradox of this group. But perhaps that only manifested the dissonance it felt in the new land. With so few sharing their tastes, they worried with considerable realism that their salt liberally sprinkled might only lose its savor.

The "outsiders" with whom the Dutch felt most compatible were the "old Princeton" sector of American Presbyterianism. Confessionalism, theocentricity, and some of the same cultural vision the two shared. Just as important were the personal links between them: Geerhardus Vos, West Michigan's donation to the Princeton Seminary faculty in 1893, who drew a generation of future Dutch Reformed leaders there for graduate training; and J. Gresham Machen, who popularized the conservative Presbyterian cause among the Dutch in the great battles of the 1920s, winning funds and faculty for his new institutions.[23] But even here affinities were crossed by differences, the most obvious being epistemological. First, Princeton theology, deeply beholden to Scottish Common Sense Realism, tended to minimize the effect of sin upon human reason. Second, it posited that Christianity—and Christianity alone—was a rationally demonstrable and coherent system, that any fair-minded person could and would see the same and be brought to faith accordingly, and that apologetics was therefore the theologian's highest labor. Dutch Neo-Calvinism, in contrast, joined continental dialectical Idealism to a radical Augustinian psychology. There simply was no religiously neutral rational faculty or middle ground, Kuyper insisted again and again. Reason, like every other faculty, impulse, or activity, proceeded from and worked to serve one's fundamental commitment—in Kuyperian parlance, one's (necessarily religious) "life-principle." Accordingly, the world could contain any number of relatively coherent worldviews, none of which could finally convince another of its own superiority on strictly rational grounds. Apologetics would therefore be the last concern of the theologian, who should work instead to elaborate the full complex of faith on its own presuppositions for the battle of world systems.[24]

This disagreement hardly broke relations between the two schools. Benjamin B. Warfield, the lion of Princeton, praised Kuyper's work even though this part of it "utterly mystified" him.[25] But especially with J. Gresham Machen, Warfield's successor, further variances were shown that, added to the first, subtly complicated the connection. Machen's reformation of culture aimed at "all areas of thought," Kuyper's at "all areas of life." Machen had an individualistic, contractarian, and laissez-faire view of the state and society (and the first two also for the church), all of which were anathema to Kuyper. Kuyper's approach was intuitive, passionate, and populistic; Machen's intellectualist, controlled, aristocratic.

Though Machen differed with Kuyper in significant ways, he brought to the faculty of Westminster Theological Seminary a disciple of Kuyper's, Cornelius Van Til. Kuyper had discerned an absolute antithesis in all of life (including all scholarly work) between believer and unbeliever. The consequences of the Fall is a radically abnormal world. Only the sovereign regenerating work of the Holy Spirit can overcome the rebellion of unbelief. Van Til used Kuyper's notion of the antithesis to develop his presuppositional apologetics. For Van Til unregenerate man actively suppresses his knowledge of God. Man is not ignorant, he is rebellious. Man is never neutral or objective in his evaluation of evidence. Rather, in every act of interpretation and understanding man acts either as a servant of God or as an unbeliever asserting his autonomy. A key task of apologetics is to show the inadequacies of non-Christian or inconsistently Christian thought. This perspective led Van Til to analyze not only what a theologian or philosopher said, but also what he should have said according to the basic orientation of his views. Van Til pressed people to face the necessary extension of their views. After Machen died, Van Til's apologetic system gained the enthusiastic support of the Westminster faculty.

Machen's orthodox Presbyterians, nonetheless, did not converge as steadily with the Dutch Reformed as might have been expected. The principal theological divergence over time involved the issue of biblical infallibility. The Kuyperian stress on the inner testimony of the Holy Spirit allowed an alternative to the Princetonian inerrancist-propositional model. Only some among the Dutch Reformed (and those the more identifiably Kuyperian, though Van Til was not among them) took that option, however; their opponents (perhaps the more traditionally confessional) preferred the more Princetonian conception. It might have been only appropriate, in turn, that the Presbyterian-based Rogers-McKim proposal showed considerable debts to Dutch Calvinist sources.[26]

Conflict Within Dutch Faith

This hint of intracommunal differences brings us to our third area of concern, the persistent presence of conflict within the Dutch Reformed circle itself. The most striking instance was its early division into two denominational camps: the Reformed Church in America (RCA), descended from the colonial era and attracting the early leadership and much of the rank and file of the post-1845 immigration; and the Christian Reformed Church (CRC), which emerged out of two breaks with that leadership, one in 1857, the other in 1880, and eventually garnered a majority of the later arrivals.[27] The CRC also inherited, therefore, virtually all of the Kuyperian influx into Dutch America and all of the tensions with the Seceder school that Neo-Calvinism induced. Thus, pietist-confessionalist vs. Neo-Calvinist is the second strain persisting throughout the group's history. Finally, both of these parties could divide within themselves as well, and forge coalitions across their earlier opposition. Thus, sometimes Kuyperians stood together against the pietists; other times some Kuyperians and pietists joined together against other kinds of Kuyperians and pietists; and throughout, the two denominations engaged each other variously in open warfare, armed peace, or cool suspicion.

The denominational divide did not simply reflect, as was long surmised, the Seceder–National Church rivalry from the Old World. The immigrant (Western) sector of the RCA and the CRC were equally beholden at their origins to Seceder clergy and clientele. Rather, the schism grew out of a tension within the Secession itself, which allowed two different perceptions of the Reformed heritage and the American situation. The RCA West represented that wing of the movement oriented toward experiential piety and practical morality—the very emphases, of course, of the antebellum American evangelicalism in which the RCA East participated. The affinity was reinforced by the correspondence between evangelicalism's favored-church status in the nineteenth century and the increasingly National Church background of the immigrants the RCA West attracted after 1880.[28] Thus the RCA became fixed on the relatively conservative side of mainstream Protestantism: generally orthodox but not overly concerned with Reformed confessional specifics; convinced of the Protestant character of the United States, and enthusiastic for the various early twentieth-century crusades designed to strengthen that character at home and spread it abroad. That stance persisted even after the crusades had failed. The RCA maintained in the post-Protestant ethos of mid-twentieth-century America the distinguishing marks of a mainstream affiliation: membership in the National and World Councils of Churches, wariness of anti-Modernist crusading, and entertainment of proposals for church union.[29]

That each of these was challenged from within the RCA West shows, however, the persistence there as well of the more cautious, confessionally emphatic Secessionist stream. That tradition was even stronger—we might say predominant—in the CRC, characterizing Ten Hoor and Berkhof on the seminary level and the majority of the denomination's clerical and editorial leaders through at least World War II. To this perspective, modern times constituted not an opportunity but a threat for faith, and the church was called not to move into the world but to attend to the loyal remnant. America's "Christian character" turned out to be a seductive veneer hiding a secular heart; and maximal Reformed consciousness—rather than ecumenical ventures in either the revivalist or social reform mode—seemed the only antidote sufficient to the threat. Yet befitting their common Seceder rootage, this was a defensive, as the RCA optimists' was an outgoing, pietism. Neither countenanced Kuyper's holistic, systemic approaches; both focused their energies within the institutional church, upon individual soul-saving and personal behavioral symbolics—we might say, upon missions and moralism.[30]

Neo-Calvinist discontent with this posture flared both in pointed disputes and in a persistent culturalist concern. The latter was clearly evident, for example, in the 1930-1950 era of Confessionalist hegemony when certain CRC ministers and academics, clustered around Calvin College and Seminary, sponsored conferences and a monthly journal dedicated to providing a comprehensive and distinctively Reformed interpretation of current philosophical, sociopolitical, and international affairs. Only such, this party claimed, was adequate to both the richness of the Christian heritage and the desperate needs of the modern era. Yet this project's anti-Modernist agenda comported well enough with the Confessionalists' to keep peace in the denominational house.[31] Such harmony did not always obtain. In fact, both the earliest and the latest theological battles in the CRC grew from the pietist–Neo-Calvinist tension, and both involved questions arising from that traditional seedbed of Reformed controversy, the doctrine of predestination.

In the first dispute (1890-1905), the timing of election itself opened the issue. The supralapsarians, representing the Neo-Calvinist line, placed election before the fall of man, indeed before creation itself, and correlatively placed regeneration virtually at birth, before baptism and "conversion experiences," which were taken as merely confirming what had already been effected by the will of God. This construction, the supras argued, best fit Calvinism's theocentricity, anchored the individual's salvation in the eternal will of God, and released the pulpit and pew from emotionalism and self-absorption for the comprehensive cultural witness that was the church's true business. The infralapsarians' reversals on all these points bespoke their Seceder heritage. So did their critique of the opposition's clientele. Abstract speculation might please the "dreaming philosophers," the arrogant elite, that comprised Kuyper's movement, Foppe Ten Hoor declared, but the health of the Reformed churches would lie always with the humble, who cherished the vital piety that Scripture and confession had ever mandated. Let "scientific" theologians have their worldly glory; the despised of the earth would inherit the Kingdom of Heaven. Happily for Ten Hoor, the infras' success in this case did not have to wait that long, as the Synod of Utrecht's (1905) decision for their side of the debate was accepted in Dutch America as well.[32]

The most recent controversy in the CRC involved similar hostilities but quickly moved from the nature of the will of God to the nature of his Word. Again the intelligentsia precipitated the conflict (in 1962), only this time arguing that election, as expressed in the Dortian statement on limited atonement, could be read as unduly restrictive. The Confessionalists saw this as an attack upon their hegemony, and the CRC Synod's somewhat tepid resolution of the matter in 1967 proved them right.[33] For the two sides almost immediately (1969-1972) clashed again over a more momentous issue, the nature and authority of Scripture. With this debate, denominational control shifted to the "progressives" who stood, albeit at some remove, in Kuyper's descent. The Confessionalists' inerrant-propositionalist constructs were demoted, though hardly excised, at crucial points. The Bible's authority, the Synod declared, lay not simply in divine inspiration but in its redemptive message; its meaning and veracity involved not so much empirical "facts" in various domains (geological, biological, historical) as its purpose of salvation and its focus in Christ.[34] A more clearly Neo-Calvinist formulation also entered the field at this juncture, reflecting the influence of Herman Dooyeweerd, one of Kuyper's successors at Amsterdam, among post-World War II immigrants to Canada. The Dooyeweerdians, as they became known, articulated a tripartite notion of revelation: besides (and perhaps through and before) the Inscripturated (Bible) and Incarnate (Christ) Word stood God's creation ordinances (the Law Word), by which the Christians' redemptive witness to all areas of society and culture could proceed. The Confessionalists could hardly decide which of these constructions troubled them more, and could draw little comfort from the rivalry between the two.[35] Indeed, one reason for the 1970s change in denominational power was the alliance of the two Neo-Calvinist parties, as opposed to the mutual recrimination and then coalescence, by one side or the other, with the Confessionalists that had occurred at two earlier crises.

That Kuyper spawned two schools instead of one owed largely to a basic ambiguity in his thought. On the one hand, Kuyper preached religious antithesis: the life-principles of Christians and unbelievers were diametrically opposed, the spiritual qualities of their respective actions were inevitably antagonistic, and Christians should therefore pursue their work in society from their own separate organizations. Later in his career, without diminishing this idea, Kuyper resurrected the doctrine of common grace: that God gave to humanity grace which, while not "saving," enabled them to attain much virtue and truth; that achievements in politics and scholarship, art and technology, which were not motivated by faith might still be cherished as gifts of God; and that cooperation between Christians and unbelievers was therefore possible and necessary.[36] Kuyper's American followers, unable to harness this paradox as had their master, diverged into schools that can be designated antithetical and positive. The first saw corruption (in principle and practice) present everywhere in the world, stressed the negative or condemnatory purpose of Christian sociocultural witness, and absolutized the need for separate organization. The second hoped to realize some of the improvements that the Christian critique offered society and sanctioned cooperation with people of different principles to this end.[37] That the Kuyperians thus divided along the same defensive-outgoing lines as had the pietists explains the types of interparty coalitions that were made. That the two fiercest conflicts in CRC history occurred between the two Calvinist factions, and both times in the wake of world wars, demonstrates the group's metaphorical use of theology. Common grace, as the doctrine relating the church to the world, cast in theological terms the question of Dutch America's relation to the outside world, exactly the issue that wartime nationalism had raised most intensely.

The first of these battles, like that of the early 1970s, took rise from the issue of Scripture. Drawing connections with the Modernist-Fundamentalist debate then reaching its zenith, a Confessionalist-Antithetical coalition in the early 1920s accused Roelof Janssen, chief positive Calvinist on the Grand Rapids faculty, of practicing higher criticism in his Old Testament instruction and of thereby partaking dangerously of the rationalistic and naturalistic spirit of the age. Janssen's reply, however appealed to Kuyper, Herman Bavinck, and other Reformed authorities, continental and American, to establish his orthodoxy and to turn the charges back on his critics. It was their denial of common grace, explicit among the Antitheticals, implicit among the Confessionalists, Janssen argued, that forced them to denigrate humanity's residual abilities, to eliminate God's grace from the natural realm, and to misconstrue the nature of miracles, revelation, and science. The debate's increasing focus on the relations between Old Testament Israel and surrounding nations hinted at the cultural issue involved: both sides saw the future of the Dutch "Israel" in America to be at stake. Enough of the community were suspicious of "progressive" adaptation to the nation that had, in World War I, so badly treated them that the tide swung against Janssen. He guaranteed the conclusion by refusing to testify before the 1922

Synod.[38] But then the tide swung against the Antithetical members of his prosecution, the CRC pastors Herman Hoeksema and Henry Danhof. Their absolutizing of the antithesis, and post-facto declaration that common grace had indeed been the root issue in the Janssen case, cost them their Confessionalist allies. These coalesced with positive Calvinists at the 1924 Synod to declare Hoeksema and Danhof in error. Common grace was Reformed orthodoxy, though more useful for evangelism than for cultural cooperation, and Hoeksema and Danhof were ordered to stop saying otherwise. They did not, and joined Janssen in the ranks of the demoted.[39]

The Confessionalist regime that this settlement installed lasted until after World War II. Then the drama was played out again, only with a less conclusive ending. Again, a "progressive" party arose at Calvin Seminary (George Stob and Harry Boer, with James Daane helping from the outside), eager to bear positive witness to the American world. Again, the Confessionalist majority brought accusations of the "heresy" currently in the air, i.e., "Barthianism"; and again they allied with Antithetical voices—Cornelius Van Til and H. Evan Runner—to quash the new school. The battle at the Seminary was dismissed (also the fate of the entire faculty) as a conflict of personalities, however, and the factions settled into uneasy coexistence.[40] Antitheticalism came to lodge chiefly among the Canadians in the CRC, positive Calvinism in the *Reformed Journal* and the denominational bureaucracy, and intelligentsia Confessionalism in *Torch and Trumpet* (later the *Outlook*), northwest Iowa, and assorted clergy who felt increasingly displaced, marginalized, in their own denomination.

Future Prospects

What will be the future course of Dutch-American theology depends much upon the future course of the community it has guided and served. Here signs are ambiguous. As to factional differentiation, each party now has connections with natural allies in the American Protestant world: the Confessionalists with conservative Presbyterians, Lutherans, and other battlers for the Bible; both types of Kuyperians with "progressive" elements in neo-evangelicalism; the RCA West with mainstream sociopolitical missions in the World Council of Churches. But each group has also returned to Netherlandic models for sustenance: Dort, Dooyeweerd, G. C. Berkouwer, and A. A. van Ruler, respectively.[41] As to communal persistence, the group's theological productivity has never been so high; neither, thanks to televised religion, has its rank and file ever been so open to non-Reformed pieties, programs, and personalities of every sort. As to past issues of debate, common grace—

because it was so tied to the question of acculturation—will not likely cause uproar again, although its implications will be detectable. The question of hermeneutics will probably remain central, although less in itself than because of the clashing sociocultural agendas for which it has been both source and legitimation. The outcome of that struggle, finally, lies hidden in the oldest subject of dispute, the will of God, which for these Calvinists must always be the beginning of the matter, and the end.

Notes: The Dutch Schools

1. Foppe M. Ten Hoor, "De Amerikanisatie onzer Kerk," *Gereformeerde Amerikaan* 2 (May-June 1898): 180-87, 206-15. See similarly (all in *Gereformeerde Amerikaan*) his "Het Engelsch Christendom," 5 (October 1901): 457-63; "Is het Christendom in Strijd met de Rede?" 18 (March 1914): 106-20; and a second series on Americanization, 13 (January-March, May, September 1909).

2. For the background of these documents, see Philip Schaff, ed., *The Creeds of Christendom* (New York: Harper, 1877), 1:502-23, 531-54. The quoted phrase is from Sydney E. Ahlstrom, *A Religious History of the American People* (New Haven: Yale University Press, 1972), 203.

3. For a capsule survey, see Ahlstrom, *Religious History*, 200-204; George L. Smith, *Religion and Trade in New Netherland* (Ithaca: Cornell University Press, 1973), is a detailed study.

4. The best biography is James Tanis, *Dutch Calvinistic Pietism in the Middle Colonies: A Study of the Life and Theology of Theodorus Jacobus Frelinghuysen* (The Hague: Martinus Nijhoff, 1967). See also Herman Harmelink III, "Another Look at Frelinghuysen and His 'Awakening,' " *Church History* 55 (1968): 423-38.

5. These events are presented in close detail in John P. Luidens, "The Americanization of the Dutch Reformed Church" (Ph.D. diss., University of Oklahoma, 1969).

6. Tanis, *Dutch Calvinistic Pietism*, 16-41.

7. F. Ernest Stoeffler, *The Rise of Evangelical Pietism* (Leiden: E. J. Brill, 1967), 116-17, 127-48.

8. On Brakel, ibid., 156-57; on Voetius, see Otto de Jong in A. G. Weiler et al., *Geschiedenis van der Kerk in Nederland* (Utrecht: Aula, 1963), 138-40. Dutch parishioners in America were reading these authorities in the pulpit and in private as final arbiters as late as 1900; see Henry Beets, *De Christelijke Gereformeerde Kerk in Noord Amerika* (Grand Rapids: Grand Rapids Printing Company, 1918), 22-27.

9. The best recent treatment of the Secession in Dutch is H. Algra, *Het Wonder van de 19e Eeuw* (Franeker: T. Wever, 1966). See also James D. Bratt, *Dutch Calvinism in Modern America: A History of a Conservative Subculture* (Grand Rapids: Wm. B. Eerdmans Publishing Company, 1984), 5-10.

10. The relevant data and bibliography on this much discussed issue are available in ibid., 7-10, 227-28. Hereafter, "Dutch" and "Dutch Reformed" have reference to the ethnoreligious community in North America, unless otherwise indicated.

11. Stoeffler gives great detail on the Dutch case vis-à-vis general pietist contours in his *Rise of Evangelical Pietism*, 109-79 and 6-23, respectively.

12. Clarence Bouma, "Ecumenism: Spurious and Genuine," *Calvin Forum* 15 (November 1949): 61-62. For the sources and contours of Dutch theological antiliberalism, see Bratt, *Dutch Calvinism*, 20-22, 127-31, 134.

13. See *Agenda of the Synod of the Christian Reformed Church, 1928*, 4-56.

14. Louis Berkhof, *Manual of Reformed Doctrine* (Grand Rapids: Wm. B. Eerdmans Publishing Company, 1933), 5; this was the one-volume distillation of *Reformed Dogmatics* (Grand Rapids: Wm. B. Eerdmans Publishing Company, 1932), intended for more popular use. For Berkhof's treatment of Scripture, see *Reformed Dogmatics*, 1:14-18, 24-30, 138-79. His broader critique of liberalism is evident in *Aspects of Liberalism* (Grand Rapids: Wm. B. Eerdmans Publishing Company, 1951).

15. Pre-World War I analyses of this sort, directed at "Methodism," are covered in Bratt, *Dutch Calvinism*, 58-60, 248-49; and Henry Zwaanstra, *Reformed Thought and Experience in a New World: A Study of the Christian Reformed Church and Its American Environment, 1890-1918* (Kampen: J. H. Kok, 1973), 43-49. For the interwar commentary, see Bratt, *Dutch Calvinism*, 132-34, 273-75.

16. Foppe M. Ten Hoor, "Het Engelsch Christendom," *Gereformeerde Amerikaan* 5 (October 1901): 457-63, and "Is het Christendom in Strijd met de Rede?" *Gereformeerde Amerikaan* 18 (March 1914): 106-20.

17. John E. Kuizenga, "Why We Need a Creed," *Leader*, 22 November 1922, 9.

18. Of very many statements on this point, a few succinct declarations are Clarence Bouma, "How Dead Is Calvinism?" *Calvin Forum* 1 (October 1935): 51-52; Ralph Stob, "Men of Principle," *Banner*, 29 November 1935, 1086; Lewis Smedes, "Evangelicals, What Next?" *Reformed Journal* 19 (November 1969): 4. Exemplary larger works are Bastian Kruithof, *The Christ of the Cosmic Road* (Grand Rapids: Wm. B. Eerdmans Publishing Company, 1937); and Henry Zylstra, *Testament of Vision* (Grand Rapids: Wm. B. Eerdmans Publishing Company, 1956).

19. A fine, brief introduction to Kuyper in English is Dirk Jellema, "Abraham Kuyper's Attack on Liberalism," *Review of Politics* 19 (October 1957): 472-85; see also Bratt, *Dutch Calvinism*, 14-33. An excellent sketch in Dutch is Jan Romein, "Abraham Kuyper: De Klokkenist der Kleine Luyden," in *Erflaters van onze Beschaving* (Amsterdam: Queridos, 1971). Three representative works of Kuyper in English translation are *Lectures on Calvinism* (Grand Rapids: Wm. B. Eerdmans Publishing Company, 1961 [1898]), *Christianity and the Class Struggle* (Grand Rapids: Piet Hein, 1950 [1891]), and *To Be Near Unto God* (Grand Rapids: Wm. B. Eerdmans Publishing Company, 1924).

20. See J. C. Rullman's precis of Kuyper's fullest elaboration of the doctrine of the covenant (*De Leer der Verbonden* [Amsterdam, 1885]), in *Kuyper-Bibliographie* (Kampen: J. H. Kok, 1940), 3:251.

21. This material is more fully elaborated in James D. Bratt, "The Covenant Traditions of Dutch Americans," in Daniel Elazar and John Kincaid, eds., *The Covenant Connection: Federal Theology and the Origins of Modern Politics* (Carolina Academic Press, forthcoming). Primary works from three different eras are John Van Lonkhuyzen, *Heilig Zaad* (Grand Rapids: n.p., 1916), 3; William Hendriksen, *The Covenant of Grace* (Grand Rapids: Wm. B. Eerdmans Publishing Company, 1932), 12-13; and Andrew Kuyvenhoven, *Partnership: A Study of the Covenant* (Grand Rapids: Board of Publications, CRC, 1974). Secondary analyses of these themes are conveniently available in Peter De Klerk and Richard R. De Ridder,

eds., *Perspectives on the Christian Reformed Church* (Grand Rapids: Baker Book House, 1983): Anthony A. Hoekema, "The Christian Reformed Church and the Covenant," 185-201; and Fred H. Klooster, "The Kingdom of God in the History of the Christian Reformed Church," 203-24.

22. Hendriksen, *Covenant of Grace*, 65.

23. Bratt, *Dutch Calvinism*, 107, 128-29. Names and statistics of CRC leaders attending "old Princeton" are available on p. 270, n. 21. Dutch-related members of the Westminster Seminary faculty were R. B. Kuiper, Ned B. Stonehouse, and Cornelius Van Til.

24. George M. Marsden, *Fundamentalism and American Culture: The Shaping of Twentieth Century Evangelicalism, 1870-1925* (New York: Oxford University Press, 1980), 114-16, gives a succinct comparison. Much greater detail, from the Kuyperian point of view, is available in John Vander Stelt, *Philosophy and Scripture: A Study in Old Princeton and Westminster Theology* (Marlton, NJ: Mack Publishing Company, 1978).

25. Marsden, *Fundamentalism and American Culture*, 115.

26. Jack B. Rogers and Donald K. McKim, *The Authority and Interpretation of the Bible: An Historical Approach* (New York: Harper and Row, 1979); the Dutch theologians concerned are Gerrit C. Berkouwer and, through him, Herman Bavinck, Kuyper's contemporary in Amsterdam. A critical assessment of this connection is Richard B. Gaffin, Jr., "Old Amsterdam and Inerrancy?" *Westminster Theological Journal* 44 (1982): 250-89, and 45 (1983): 219-72.

27. A review from the RCA side is William Van Eyck, *Landmarks of the Reformed Fathers* (Grand Rapids: Wm. B. Eerdmans Publishing Company, 1922); from the CRC side, Henry Beets, *De Christelijke Gereformeerde Kerk in Noord Amerika*, 66-120. Valuable statistical and social scientific analyses of the first schism are available in Robert P. Swierenga, "Local-Cosmopolitan Theory and Immigrant Religion: The Social Bases of the Antebellum Dutch Reformed Schism," *Journal of Social History* 14 (Fall 1980): 113-35, esp. 123.

28. Swierenga, "Local-Cosmopolitan Theory," 123, 130.

29. Herman Harmelink III, *Ecumenism and the Reformed Church* (Grand Rapids: Wm. B. Eerdmans Publishing Company, 1968), illustrates, directly and indirectly, all three of these points.

30. This mentality in the CRC is presented in great detail for the 1890-1918 era in Zwaanstra, *Reformed Thought and Experience*, 70-95; over the longer run in Bratt, *Dutch Calvinism*, 47-50, 125-41, 190-95, 207-10. On the RCA side, ibid., 125, 135-37, 197-99, 205-06.

31. The journal was the *Calvin Forum*; for its views, see Bratt, *Dutch Calvinism*, 126, 142-56.

32. Ibid., 46-49. Exemplary statements on the infra side are Foppe M. Ten Hoor, "Principieele Bezwaren," *Gereformeerde Amerikaan* 9 (May and August 1905); Lammert J. Hulst and Gerrit K. Hemkes, *Oud- en Nieuwe-Calvinisme* (Grand Rapids: Eerdmans-Sevensma, 1913). On the supra side, John Van Lonkhuyzen, *Heilig Zaad*, and Richard Gaffin, ed., *Redemptive History and Biblical Interpretation: The Shorter Writings of Geerhardus Vos*, 231ff., 240-47, 263ff.

33. On this, the so-called "Dekker" case (after its protagonist, Harold Dekker, Professor of Missions at Calvin Seminary), see Dekker's articles in the *Reformed Journal*, December 1962-March 1963, and those of James Daane and Harry Boer in the same periodical, October 1964-March 1965. The opposition's case was best made by R. B. Kuiper in *God-Centered Evangelism* (Grand Rapids: Baker

Book House, 1957), and "Professor Dekker on God's Universal Love," *Torch and Trumpet* 13 (March 1963): 4-9. For the Synodical debate, see *Acts of Synod of the CRC, 1967*, 486-607, 727-38.

34. For the final statement, known as "Report 44," see *Acts of Synod of the CRC, 1972*, 493-546.

35. This principle and its implications are dramatically presented in John A. Olthuis et al., *Out of Concern for the Church* (Toronto: Wedge Publishing Company, 1970). The Confessionalist response is John Vander Ploeg, "One 'Word of God' or Three?" *Outlook* 22 (February 1972): 5-8.

36. Bratt, *Dutch Calvinism*, 18-20; Simon J. Ridderbos, *De Theologische-Cultuurbeschouwing van Abraham Kuyper* (Kampen: J. H. Kok, 1947), 30-131, 233-57.

37. Bratt, *Dutch Calvinism*, 50-54; Zwaanstra, *Reformed Thought and Experience*, 95-131.

38. Bratt, *Dutch Calvinism*, 105-10, presents a review of the case and its literature.

39. Ibid., 110-15. Whereas Janssen went into exile as a broker in Chicago, Hoeksema and Danhof started their own denomination, the Protestant Reformed Church.

40. Ibid., 190-96. The principals' major statements on the issue were: Cornelius Van Til, *Common Grace* (Philadelphia: Presbyterian and Reformed Publishing Company, 1947); H. Evan Runner, "Het Roer Om!" *Torch and Trumpet* 3 (April 1953): 1-4, and a series in the same journal, April-October 1955; William Masselink, *General Revelation and Common Grace* (Grand Rapids: Wm. B. Eerdmans Publishing Company, 1953); and James Daane, *A Theology of Grace* (Grand Rapids: Wm. B. Eerdmans Publishing Company, 1954).

To put all these debates in chronological order:

1) RCA-CRC split, 1857 and 1880-1882.
2) Supra-Infra debate, 1890-1905.
3) Common grace I (Janssen and Hoeksema cases), 1918-1924.
4) Common grace II, 1950-1960.
5) "Dekker case" (limited atonement), 1962-1967; leading on to "Report 44" debate (nature and authority of Scripture), 1969-1972.

41. On the role of Dooyeweerd and Berkouwer, see nn. 35 and 26 above, respectively. On the example of Dort, see, e.g., Peter Y. De Jong, ed., *Crisis in the Reformed Churches: Essays in Commemoration of the Great Synod of Dort, 1618-1619* (Grand Rapids: Reformed Fellowship, 1968). On A. A. van Ruler, see the special issue of *Reformed Review* devoted to him: 26 (Winter 1973).

2

LOUIS BERKHOF

HENRY ZWAANSTRA

Louis Berkhof

During the period prior to the First World War, the Christian Reformed Church was self-consciously and openly Dutch-American. As hyphenated Americans, members and leaders in the Christian Reformed Church were preoccupied with Americanization. Being deeply committed to their Dutch Reformed theological and churchly heritage, they strenuously sought to resist the intrusion of American religious ideas and practices that would detract from or otherwise endanger their inherited tradition. Yet they were Americans convinced that they had a special task and calling in America. Louis Berkhof belonged to this generation. He was thoroughly bilingual, capable of expressing himself with equal facility in either Dutch or English. He was also deeply committed to preserving the Dutch Reformed theological tradition in the Christian Reformed Church. This tradition, properly preserved and represented, he believed was relevant for American thought and life.

Early in the twentieth century, the climate of theological opinion in America was not particularly conducive to dogmatic theology nor cordial to historic Reformed theology and Calvinism. The intellectual spirit of the age promoted the rise and progress of liberal theology and the Social Gospel. At the same time it provoked a conservative reaction that took the form of Fundamentalism. Louis Berkhof did his theological reflection and work in this environment. Before he concluded his career, Neoorthodoxy or Crisis Theology appeared on the American scene. He interacted with this theology, too, in its initial stages.

Louis Berkhof's life and work were immersed in the Christian Reformed Church. To it he devoted his time and energy. He served the Christian Reformed Church briefly as a pastor and preacher. For 38 years he was a professor of theology. During the last 13 of these years, he was also the president of Calvin Theological Seminary. He regularly served as an advisor to Christian Reformed Church synods. Being a gifted public speaker, Berkhof frequently addressed convocations and audiences.

It was, however, as a writer that he made his greatest and most enduring contribution to the Christian Reformed Church.

Being a person with broad interests, Berkhof wrote on many subjects. In addition to the theological works for which he is best known, he addressed social issues and problems, modern trends of thought, and such matters as Christian education, evangelism, missions, and the spiritual life. He was a contributor to periodicals widely read within the Christian Reformed Church such as *De Gereformeerde Amerikaan* (The Reformed American) and the *Calvin Forum*. He also regularly wrote series of articles in the denominational weeklies, *The Banner* and *De Wachter*. Berkhof's impact on the American theological world and the theological world at large was an uncalculated and unanticipated result of the favorable reception of his publications in systematic theology.

Formative Years: 1873-1906

Louis Berkhof was born on October 13, 1873, in Emmen, Drenthe, The Netherlands. His parents, Jan and Geesje (ter Poorten) Berkhof, were members of the Christelijke Gereformeerde Kerk (Christian Reformed Church). This church came into existence as a result of a secession from the Nederlands Hervormde Kerk (Netherlands Reformed Church) or state church in 1834. The Berkhofs' religious life, like that of most members of the churches of the Secession of 1834, consisted of deep and simple piety fused with devotion to the Reformed faith articulated in the historic confessions of the Reformed churches in The Netherlands. In 1882, when Louis was 8 years old, the Berkhof family emigrated to the United States, settling in Grand Rapids, Michigan.

At this time the Neo-Calvinist movement in The Netherlands under the leadership of Dr. Abraham Kuyper was already well underway. Kuyper was a man of extraordinary genius and deep personal piety. In addition to leading a second secession from The Netherlands Reformed Church in 1886 called the "Doleantie," Kuyper was the founder of the Free University of Amsterdam (1880) and its first professor in dogmatics. He was instrumental in bringing into existence a Christian school system from the elementary to the university level. He greatly advanced the cause of separate Christian labor organizations and succeeded in making the Anti-Revolutionary political party founded by Groen van Prinsterer into an effective Christian political force. For many years Kuyper served in the Dutch Parliament and was twice elected Prime Minister. The churches of the secessions of 1834 and 1886 united in 1892 to form De Gereformeerde Kerken in Nederland (The Reformed Churches in The Netherlands). The Neo-Calvinist movement, the Kuyperian ideas that inspired it, and the impact it made on social, political, and church life in The Netherlands all exercised considerable formative influence on the Christian Reformed Church in America and on the life and thought of Louis Berkhof.

When Louis was a teenager, he was an active member (secretary) of the first Reformed Young Men's Society organized in Grand Rapids, Michigan.[1] The society's purpose was to study Reformed doctrine and the principles of Calvinism for all areas of human life. Later Berkhof was reported to have said that he owed more to the young men's society than he would ever be able to repay. In that society he learned to study and express himself. There he also began to realize that God had given him some talents for labor in his kingdom. And there, he said, the desire to serve God in the ministry was awakened and began to ripen.[2] Berkhof was one of the first to urge the local society to organize on a denominational scale. The American Federation of Reformed Young Men's Societies soon came into existence. For many years Berkhof's book, *Subjects and Outlines*, specially prepared for the American Federation in 1918, was used as a study guide. The work covered a wide range of subjects: Bible History, Reformed Doctrine, General and American Church History, and various educational, social, and political issues. It concluded with a long list of resolutions for debate. After becoming a theological professor, Berkhof continued to show his loyalty to the organization and to repay the debt he owed to it by serving no less than 15 years on its Executive Board.[3]

Sometime in 1893 Berkhof publicly professed his faith in Christ in the Alpine Avenue Christian Reformed Church. In September of that year at the age of 19, he enrolled in the Theological School of the Christian Reformed Church. At the time the Theological School consisted of two parts, a literary department with a four-year course of study and a theological department with a three-year program of study. The literary department was gradually expanded into Calvin College and the theological department later became Calvin Theological Seminary.

In the spring of 1893 the Theological School sustained a severe loss when the youthful, brilliant, and much-loved professor of dogmatics and exegetical theology, Geerhardus Vos, accepted an appointment to teach biblical theology at Princeton Seminary.[4] Vos did, however, leave his reputation and unpublished lectures in dogmatics behind. Berkhof heard about the former; the latter he undoubtedly used.

Hendericus Beuker was Berkhof's teacher in dogmatics. Beuker was a graduate of the Theological School of the Christelijke Gereformeerde Kerk in Kampen, The Netherlands. After distinguishing himself as a capable pastor and churchman in The Netherlands, he emigrated to America in 1893. The following year he was appointed to teach dogmatics. Beuker's intellectual gifts were certainly adequate to the task. He was a severe critic of the German liberal theology and higher criticism of the day. Although himself an infralapsarian, he respected Kuyper for his scholarly work and appreciated the counterforce Kuyper posed to the "fearfully destructive hurricanes" coming out of the German universities.[5] Beuker was most favorably impressed with the theological thought and erudition of Herman Bavinck. When the first volume of Bavinck's *Gereformeerde Dogmatiek* (Reformed Dogmatics) appeared, Beuker judged it a fundamental contribution to theological science and a great blessing for the Reformed churches.[6] Early in 1900, the same year Berkhof graduated from the Theological School, Beuker died. Foppe M. Ten Hoor began teaching dogmatics in the fall of that year and continued to do so until retirement in 1924.

On September 16, 1900, Louis Berkhof was ordained to the ministry in the Christian Reformed Church in Allendale, Michigan. Less than two years later, his name was included in a list of potential candidates for appointment to a new chair in exegetical theology. The appointment, however, went to Roelof Janssen, a relatively unknown quantity in the Christian Reformed Church except for the fact that he held a Ph.D. degree from the University of Halle in Germany and was studying at Kampen. Janssen's advanced degree, even though it was not in theology, influenced the outcome of the synod's decision.[7] Berkhof decided to seek more formal education.

From 1902 to 1904 Berkhof studied at Princeton Seminary, a bastion of Reformed orthodoxy. There he came under the tutelage of Benjamin Warfield and Geerhardus Vos. Both men were staunch defenders of Reformed confessional orthodoxy and the authority of Holy Scripture, including verbal infallibility and inerrancy. H. Henry Meeter, professor of Bible at Calvin College and for many years a close personal friend of Berkhof, reported that Berkhof frequently said that he owed more to Vos than anyone else for his insights into Reformed theology.[8] Princeton awarded Berkhof the Bachelor of Divinity degree.

In August 1904, Berkhof was installed as minister of the Oakdale Park Christian Reformed Church in Grand Rapids, Michigan. There he quickly established a reputation for his insights into Scripture, carefully crafted sermons, and gifts in public speaking.[9] In addition to his work in the congregation, Berkhof promoted the cause of Christian education in the denomination with a pamphlet published in 1905, *Het Christelijk Onderwijs en Onze Kerkelijke Toekomst* (Christian Education and the Future of Our Church). While at Oakdale Park he also took some courses, chiefly in philosophy, by correspondence through the University of Chicago.

The Board of Trustees did not recommend Janssen for reappointment in 1906. Unresolved conflicts had arisen between him and Ten Hoor regarding the authority of the church in the study of theology. Furthermore, some members of the board were convinced that Janssen's teaching unmistakably leaned toward higher criticism.[10] In the absence of a recommendation from the board, the synod prepared a nomination for exegetical theology. Berkhof, the vice president of the synod, was included in the nomination and later chosen by a large majority to fill the vacant chair.[11]

Professor of Exegetical Theology and New Testament Studies: 1906-1924

On September 5, 1906, in the Commerce Street Christian Reformed Church, Louis Berkhof was installed as professor of exegetical theology. The same evening he delivered an inaugural address in the Dutch language entitled "De Verklaring der Heilige Schrift" (The Exposition of the Holy Scriptures). It was a noteworthy occasion and address. Berkhof argued that the correct interpretation of Scripture was contingent on a proper understanding of the Scriptures' peculiar character as the Word of God. He then proceeded to indicate how Scripture itself was threatened by many dangers such as higher criticism, liberal theology, modern biblical theology, and recent historical and archaeological discoveries. He concluded by emphasizing the great importance of the view of Scripture and its interpretation that he presented for ministers of the Word.[12]

From 1906 to 1914 Berkhof taught all the Old Testament and New Testament courses offered at Calvin Seminary: Hebrew, New Testament Greek, Old Testament and New Testament Exegesis, Introduction to the Old Testament and New Testament, and Old Testament and New Testament History.

In 1911 he published in the Dutch language a textbook on biblical hermeneutics.[13] In comparison with recent hermeneutical studies, Berkhof's treatment was simple and unsophisticated. In a manner that was to become characteristic of Berkhof, he first dealt with the task and history of the science of biblical interpretation, and then elaborated the essentials of the grammatical-historical theological method. In 1937, this work, only slightly edited, was published for the use of English-speaking students under the title *Principles of Biblical Interpretation*. During the time Berkhof taught both Old and New Testament he published only one special study, a pamphlet on the book of Joshua, *Life Under the Law in a Pure Theocracy* (1914).

In spite of his heavy teaching load and the breadth of his assignment, Berkhof did not neglect the pressing social issues and problems agitating the American church world and the Christian Reformed Church. For the benefit of the Dutch-American members of the Christian Reformed Church, Berkhof wrote *Christendom en Level* (Christianity and Life). As the title suggests, the work dealt with a wide range of issues pertaining to Christianity and culture. It also specifically addressed needs confronting Reformed people of Dutch ancestry as they faced the American world. Published in 1912, the book was described in *De Wachter* as one in which lines were drawn, fundamentals laid out, and valuable counsel given.[14]

The following year Berkhof wrote *The Church and Social Problems*. This was his first English-language publication. The pamphlet better than any other single source illustrates the breadth of Berkhof's interests and sympathies, his knowledge of contemporary American theological literature, his capacity for balanced judgment, and his ability to engage discursively and critically in theological issues and problems. In this work Berkhof gives a strikingly different impression from that presented in his textbooks on theology.

Berkhof proceeded on the assumption that the gospel of Jesus Christ was the greatest liberating force in the world, eminently applicable to the pressing social problems of the age. After briefly outlining the nature of the present social problem including quotations without additional critical comment from such works as Walter Rauschenbusch's *Christianity and the Social Crisis* and Josiah Strong's *The Challenge of the City*, Berkhof surveyed the history of the church's role in the existing social crisis. He acknowledged that the church itself contributed to the crisis and that many of the charges being brought against the church for social negligence, such as aiming at the salvation of the individual only while showing little concern for the regeneration of society, and preaching a one-sided "other-worldly" gospel that did not touch the realities of life, were true. The church definitely had social duties and responsibilities that were not being met.[15]

Berkhof thought the church, both as a spiritual fellowship of believers and as an organization, had a task in the movement for social reform. Natural and spiritual life could not be neatly compartmentalized, nor could the responsibilities for human life simply be parceled out so that the church as an institution found its duty only in the spiritual sphere. The church as an organization also had a role to play in social reforms. After emphasizing that the church should be a nursery for true, healthy, and vigorous spiritual life, Berkhof forthrightly asserted that the church should never forget the social message entrusted to it. The church was God's chosen instrument not only to save individuals and to prepare them for eternal life, but also to implement as much as possible the Kingdom of God on earth. The Bible contained many directives for social life, revealed principles that should control social reform, and offered the only final solution to social problems. Ministers of the gospel should fearlessly and clearly proclaim the broad principles underlying social life. The church also should exemplify in its own social life the social principles for which it stood in addition to bringing the gospel to the masses in the great cities of the nation. The church, he said, ought to make a thorough study of the present social problems and of the various movements working for social improvement. In conclusion Berkhof sounded the separatistic note characteristic of many Kuyperian Calvinists calling Christians to organize on a distinctively and positively Christian basis for social and philanthropic action.[16]

In 1914 the synod decided to divide exegetical theology into Old Testament and New Testament departments. Berkhof was given the assignment in New Testament. In spite of previous difficulties with Roelof Janssen, the synod by a sizable majority elected him to teach Old Testament.[17]

A reduced teaching load and a more narrowly circumscribed area of research enabled Berkhof to put his pen to work. In 1915 he wrote *Biblical Archaeology*, a study in the history and cultures of the Ancient Near East, and *Introduction to the New Testament*. *The Christian Laborer in the Industrial Struggle* appeared the following year. Although this pamphlet exhibited the same learned qualities as his earlier address on social issues, its focus was more limited and its purpose more parochial. Berkhof wrote to persuade the Christian Reformed Church of the incompatibility of membership in religiously neutral labor organizations and membership in the church of Christ.[18]

In the midst of the international turmoil and upheavals occasioned by the First World War, Henry Bultema, pastor of the First Christian Reformed Church in Muskegon, Michigan, published *Maranatha*.[19] The central thesis of Bultema's book was that the unfulfilled prophecies in the Bible should be interpreted literally just like those that have already been fulfilled. Bultema also attempted to defend chiliastic and premillennial views. *Maranatha* provoked an immediate response in the Christian Reformed Church. Berkhof was asked to speak on the subject. He did so in English. At the request of friends and because of the urgency of the matter, Berkhof had his address published in edited and expanded form in Dutch.[20] In April 1918 *Premillennialisme: Zijn Schrifttuurlike Basis en Enkele van Zijn Practische Gevolgtrekkingen* (Premillennialism: Its Scriptural Basis and Some of Its Practical Consequences) appeared. Berkhof cordially and judiciously refrained from mentioning Bultema in the text. In the notes Bultema and *Maranatha* appear along with other American premillennialists and their works.

After expressing great respect for the premillennialists' unconditional acceptance of the Bible as the Word of God and for the warmth of their devotion to Scripture, a striking contrast to the "icebergs of higher criticism," Berkhof proceeded to elaborate four objections to their views. Berkhof's first and most fundamental objection was to the premillennialists' mistaken insistence on a strictly literal interpretation of the prophetic writings. According to Berkhof the historic Christian church in its exegesis of prophecy self-consciously accepted and applied a different hermeneutical principle from that of the premillennialists. Those holding premillennial views did not deal adequately with the progressive and historical character of God's revelation. Berkhof insisted that the historical form in which a prophecy was given belonged to the essence of the prophecy and that it was proper to make a distinction between a literal historical explanation of a prophecy and its fulfillment. Berkhof also criticized the premillennialists for not interpreting Scripture according to the analogy of Scripture. In this respect they were following a practice wholly in agreement with modern, liberal exegetes. Berkhof further stated that Revelation 20:4-6 should also be interpreted according to the analogy of the New Testament. The Dutch theologians Kuyper, Bavinck, Greydanus, and Hoekstra so interpreted the text, as did Warfield, Vos, Milligan, and Eckman. And finally Berkhof asserted that by insisting on a literal fulfillment of prophecy the premillennialists got involved in all kinds of contradictions and bound God in fulfilling prophecies to conditions and situations that existed when the predictions were first given.[21]

Berkhof's second objection to premillennialism focused on the thousand-year kingdom of Christ and the doctrine of the second resurrection. After a rather extensive treatment of the texts appealed to in support of the doctrines, Berkhof concluded that the scriptural basis for both was very weak.[22]

Thirdly, Berkhof objected to the premillennialists' absolute separation of Israel and the church. The separation resulted in a denial of the spiritual unity between them. Berkhof argued that this separation and denial destroyed the unity of God's revelation, conflicted with the organic nature of his redemptive work, negated the salvation of humanity in Jesus Christ, and robbed the church of Christ of the blessings of the covenant.[23]

Finally, Berkhof objected to the premillennialists' customary use of the distinction between the Kingdom and the church in the New Testament. Again they separated the two so that Christ's present kingship was denied. Quoting Vos, Berkhof argued that the church is a form that the Kingdom takes after Christ's death and resurrection. He concluded by saying that the Kingdom is a present reality, its subjects are united with Christ in the church, and Christ is now really king.[24]

The synod agreed with Berkhof. Bultema and *Maranatha* were tested strictly by the standards of Reformed confessional orthodoxy and found wanting for separating Israel and the church, and the church and the

Kingdom, thus denying the spiritual unity between Israel and the church and the present kingship of Christ. Bultema was later deposed. He and his followers formed the Berean Church.[25]

In 1919 Louis Berkhof and three of his colleagues, William Heyns, Foppe Ten Hoor, and Samuel Volbeda, sent a letter to the Board of Trustees informing the board that student reactions to Janssen's teaching "irresistibly" raised the question whether or not Janssen was doing an injustice to the authority, infallibility, and trustworthiness of Holy Scripture.[26] The four professors did this without previously talking to Janssen. A bitter and heated controversy resulted. On the basis of student notes the four professors contended that Janssen denied the Mosaic authorship of the Pentateuch, the historicity of miracles recorded in the Bible, and the messianic significance of certain passages of the Old Testament. Janssen's explanation of many other Old Testament passages was also objectionable.[27] In the professors' judgment the Reformed doctrine of the inspiration, authority, infallibility, and trustworthiness of Scripture was threatened.[28] Given the rationalistic principles undergirding Janssen's approach, the professors predicted that his teaching, if allowed to continue, would certainly lead to a surrender of the authority of Scripture to modern critical science and a denial of Scripture as a divine redemptive revelation. It would also rob members of Christian Reformed congregations of their infallible rule for faith and life and the denomination of its Reformed distinctiveness, causing it to sink away into the watered-down Christianity so evident in the American world.[29]

Janssen replied to the four professors. In his reply he stated that all science including theology has for its aim the discovery of truth. In the quest for truth the empirical approach could not be avoided; thus all theological investigation, in the nature of the case, had to be critical. Janssen further affirmed that his scientific work rested on the presupposition that Scripture was God's infallible revelation. Nevertheless, in interpreting Scripture Scripture itself should be allowed to speak. The interpreter should not allow his presuppositions to determine the meaning of the text. Scripture stood above dogmatics and the latter should not be permitted to control the former. The meaning of Scripture, therefore, should not be a foregone conclusion. According to Janssen the Dutch Reformed theologians Kuyper, Bavinck, Aalders, and Grosheide agreed with this position.[30]

Janssen refused to appear at the synod where the matter was to be adjudicated because many of his accusers were also delegated to synod and in his judgment it was unfair for them to operate at the same time as plaintiffs and judges.[31] On the basis of the student notes, the synod found Janssen's point of view and method deficient because he did not give faith the role it deserved in theological science and because he did not allow the Bible as the divinely inspired Word of God to predetermine his conclusions. The synod also criticized him for subjectifying special revelation. Although the synod was careful not to charge Janssen with denying the inspiration of Scripture, it said that elements in his teaching could not be harmonized with the Reformed understanding of inspiration. The synod deposed Janssen from office.[32] Since Janssen had no following in the church, a schism did not result. A few younger ministers did, however, leave the church due to their unhappiness with the synodical procedures and the deposition.[33]

During the years of the Janssen controversy, Louis Berkhof's reputation as a theologian and churchman accelerated both inside and outside the Christian Reformed Church. In 1919 Berkhof was offered the presidency of Calvin College.[34] Three years later he was asked to become the editor of *De Wachter*.[35] Berkhof declined both appointments. During the 1920-21 academic year, Berkhof was invited to give the Stone Lectures at Princeton Seminary. He spoke on "The Kingdom of God in Modern Thought and Life."

In 1924 the Christian Reformed Church was again embroiled in theological controversy. The issue this time was common grace. Two capable and popular ministers, Herman Hoeksema and Henry Danhof, had written and spoken against the doctrine. Berkhof did not get directly involved in the dispute before the meeting of synod. In adjudicating the matter the synod officially declared three points: (1) the existence of a general or common grace of God shown to all men, (2) the restraint of sin by the general work of the Holy Spirit, and (3) the ability of the unregenerate to perform civic righteousness.[36] Disciplinary measures against the ministers who opposed the doctrine of common grace and the synodical decisions led to a schism of some proportion and to the formation of the Protestant Reformed Church. The following year, when protests and appeals were still pending, Berkhof entered the controversy with *De Drie Punten in Alle Deelen Gereformeerd* (The Three Points in All Parts Reformed). In 1926 the synod did not sustain the protests and appeals of the opponents of the three points.

Professor of Systematic Theology and President of Calvin Seminary: 1926-1944

After teaching dogmatics in the Dutch language for 24 years, Foppe Ten Hoor retired in 1924. Although the synod considered shifting Berkhof from New Testament studies to dogmatics, it decided instead to appoint Dr. Clarence Bouma as professor of dogmatics.[37] Two years later, the synod decided to separate apologetics and ethics from dogmatics. Bouma chose the former areas of theology, thus creating a vacancy in the latter. That Berkhof aspired to teach dogmatics was common knowledge in the church.[38] In the judgment of some his work on the "Three Points" clearly demonstrated an ability to do so.[39] Berkhof's interest went beyond a simple personal predilection. He considered biblical studies in some respects preparatory to the science of dogmatics, which made use of the fruits of biblical theology.[40] The synod complied with many interests and desires and appointed Louis Berkhof professor of dogmatic theology.[41]

After 1926 the turbulent storms of theological controversy in the Christian Reformed Church subsided never to return again with the same intensity during Berkhof's lifetime. The church had purged itself of premillennialism, the threat of free scientific inquiry and biblical criticism, and the danger of too narrow a conception of the operation of the Holy Spirit in human cultural life. With the retirement of Ten Hoor, the last vestige of enthusiastic infralapsarianism also disappeared.[42] An amazing theological consensus, basically conservative and deeply rooted in traditional Reformed confessional orthodoxy, resulted. In this general climate of theological opinion, and in harmony with it, Berkhof engaged in theological research, reflection, teaching, and writing.

During the first years that he taught dogmatics, Berkhof concentrated on research and teaching. He produced a special doctrinal study, *The Assurance of Faith*, in 1928. In 1931 the Board of Trustees decided to discontinue the annual rotating Rectorship at Calvin Seminary and to appoint a more permanent administrative head. Berkhof was a logical choice. He had frequently functioned as the spokesman for the faculty and had during the present academic year served very capably as Rector. Moreover, he enjoyed the confidence of the church and the respect of the students. The board elected Louis Berkhof the first President of Calvin Seminary, a position he held concomitantly with his professorship for 13 years.[43]

On September 9, 1931, a celebration was held commemorating Berkhof's 25th anniversary as professor of theology. On the same festive occasion he was installed as president of Calvin Seminary. Berkhof delivered an inaugural address entitled "Our Seminary and the Modern Spirit." The address is noteworthy in that it clearly indicated the content and direction of his thinking. In the speech Berkhof also commented on the specific purpose and task of Calvin Seminary. He began by putting the subject in historical perspective. During the previous century the modern scientific method and the theological thought of Schleiermacher made an impact on theological education. The Social Gospel also produced an increased emphasis on applied Christianity. As a result of these new directions seminaries were now breaking away from church control, and, under the banner of intellectual freedom, were loosing themselves

from the authority of God's Word. A clearly discernible shift from dogmatics to practical theology and from church-centered to social-centered
interests was also evident. Berkhof said that Calvin Seminary had not
adapted itself in the past to these new directions and that it would not
in the future accommodate itself to any changes that would compromise
its stand on the Word of God and on the confessional standards of the
church. Calvin Seminary did not recognize erring human reason as a
source of divine truth and would not permit it to stand in judgment on
the Word of God. The seminary would continue to honor the supernatural and would refuse to submit to present-day liberalism, which was
bound to degenerate into pure naturalism. Speaking in the first person
Berkhof said, "We accept the Reformed system of truth which was handed
down to us by previous generations, attempt to exhibit it in all its com-
prehensiveness and in all its beauty and logical consistency, seek to
defend it against all opposing systems, and endeavor to carry it forward
to still greater perfection in harmony with the structural lines that were
clearly indicated in its past development."[44]

As a professor of systematic theology, Berkhof believed his primary
task was to present scriptural truth comprehensively and in logical order
and to do so in a manner compatible with historical Reformed theology.
He further sought to illuminate Reformed thought by contrasting it with
what he considered aberrant doctrinal positions. In treating a doctrine,
Berkhof ordinarily defined and presented the Reformed view, commented briefly on the history of the doctrine, then indicated the scriptural basis for the Reformed position, and finally discussed and critiqued
alternative views. His basic criticism of Roman Catholic theology was
that it made the hierarchical church the source of and authority for dogma.
His sharpest barbs were, however, directed at modern liberal theology.
This school of thought reduced theology to anthropology or to the mere
study of religion. In Berkhof's judgment the modern psychological, so-
ciological, and philosophical approaches to religion could never satisfy
the demands for genuine theological inquiry and statement. Wherever
appropriate he summarized and commented critically on the theologies
of Schleiermacher and Ritschl. Berkhof's treatment of contemporary
neoorthodoxy and neoorthodox theologians such as Barth, Brunner, and
Niebuhr was brief, but not without penetrating insight. He appreciated
their criticism of modern liberalism, their consciousness of the broken
human condition, and their emphasis on the necessity of special revelation and the grace of God for salvation. He did not, however, agree
with their basic theological position, and the strictures they placed on
Reformation theology. Consequently he sincerely doubted that their
thought represented historic Calvinism.[45]

According to Berkhof the object of investigation in theology was the knowledge of God as he revealed himself in Holy Scripture. Although it is impossible for man to know God as God knows himself, God could be known because and insofar as he revealed himself. In a somewhat Hegelian manner, Berkhof asserted that the knowledge of God formed the content of special revelation. Special revelation itself was an unfolding of the knowledge of God and the redemptive idea in Christ Jesus.[46] Although strictly speaking special revelation was broader than Holy Scripture, practically and concretely special revelation was synonymous with Scripture. Consequently Holy Scripture was the sole source for the subject matter of dogmatic theology. It was also the only authoritative norm or standard for judging the truth formulated and affirmed in theology.[47]

In Berkhof's judgment Reformed systematic theology was a scientific enterprise.[48] Holy Scripture contained truths in the form of facts and ideas, but it did not present a logical system that could simply be copied. The Bible, however, did itself suggest that the truths it presented were interrelated. God also saw truth as a unit and the truth revealed in the Word of God was an organic whole. Moreover, man as a rational creature had an irrepressible urge to comprehend truth in its unity. The peculiar task, therefore, of the systematic theologian was to think God's thoughts after him under the guidance of the Holy Spirit, to assimilate comprehensively the truth revealed in the Word of God, and to reproduce it logically in systematic form. Although Berkhof strenuously rejected the use of speculative reason as a source and norm of theological truth, he affirmed the proper and necessary function of reason for uniting the particular ideas and facts contained in the Word of God and for organizing them into a coherent system of truth. Reason should not, however, be permitted to function independently of faith. In theological science faith corresponded with the revealed knowledge of God and served as the necessary instrument within man for appropriating divine truth. In brief, faith appropriated revealed truth, reason organized and systematized it.[49]

And finally, according to Berkhof, Reformed dogmatic theology was an ecclesiastical affair. The church as a whole under the guidance of the Holy Spirit engages in the reflective activity that produces dogma. When the church collectively reflects on the truth of God's Word, this truth takes definite shape in the consciousness of the church and is formulated in clearly defined doctrines. Although Scripture always remains the source, norm, and final test for all dogmatic truth, the creeds and confessions of the church provide a nucleus of subject matter for dogmatic theology. Berkhof insisted that the theologian is always the theologian of a particular church. He receives the truth in the fellowship of the church, shares the church's convictions regarding it, and promises to teach in harmony with it as long as the church's understanding of the truth is not contrary to the Word of God.[50]

A surprising number of systematic theologians met Berkhof's basic criteria. He approved the works of the American theologians Robert Breckinridge, James H. Thornwell, Robert L. Dabney, Charles Hodge, Archibald A. Hodge, William G. Shedd, Henry B. Smith, Benjamin B. Warfield, and John L. Giradeau. He much preferred, however, the writings of the Dutch Reformed theologians Kuyper and Bavinck.[51]

Berkhof's major writings in systematic theology grew out of his classroom work and as textbooks were intended to meet the needs of students who could no longer read Kuyper and Bavinck. His *magnum opus*, *Systematic Theology*, was first published in two volumes in 1932 with the title *Reformed Dogmatics*. Later the same year the *Introductory Volume to Reformed Dogmatics* appeared in print. A revised and enlarged edition of *Reformed Dogmatics* was published in one volume in 1941 with the title *Systematic Theology*. Again, Berkhof revised the introductory volume and, in order to bring it in line with the major work, he renamed it *Introductory Volume to Systematic Theology*. Berkhof did not make a case for the change in titles except to say that it seemed better in America to use the title "Systematic Theology." He also called attention to the fact that even Warfield had defended the title.[52] To complete the textbook series in systematic theology, Berkhof in 1937 wrote a brief but comprehensive *History of Christian Doctrines*. Berkhof's book indicates that he was acquainted with a large body of literature on the subject including the works of Harnack, Loofs, Seeberg, and Newman. In it he descriptively presented the history of Christian doctrine in an orderly, nonjudgmental way. To assist students in their study of systematic theology, Berkhof's *Textual Aid to Systematic Theology* was published in 1942. In addition to these textbooks Berkhof wrote two special doctrinal studies, *The Vicarious Atonement through Christ* (1936) and *Recent Trends in Theology* (1944), before he retired.

Louis Berkhof was not a creative and imaginative theologian. Although he recognized that the systematic theologian had a critical as well as a constructive and defensive task,[53] he was not reflectively critical of the system he proposed nor aware of serious theological problems yet to be resolved. He believed that Reformed theology since Calvin had through the centuries assumed a more or less definite form.

In the Preface to his *Introductory Volume* published in 1932, Berkhof acknowledged that the general plan of his work was based on the first volume of Bavinck's *Gereformeerde Dogmatiek* and that in a few chapters he followed Bavinck's argumentation as well. In the revised edition, Berkhof included no such admission. Except for later additions, especially comments on neoorthodox theologians whom Bavinck antedated,

Berkhof, however, remained dependent on Bavinck for both the structure and content of his theology. In his *Systematic Theology*, Berkhof was only slightly less dependent on Bavinck. In this work Berkhof often rearranged materials taken from Bavinck's volumes and occasionally introduced a new division of the material. Berkhof's treatment of Barth and Brunner in the 1941 edition was original work. Nevertheless Berkhof's theology was essentially the theology of Herman Bavinck. Berkhof was also dependent on Bavinck for the names of most of the theologians he mentioned and on whose views he commented. The scriptural references Berkhof cited were for the most part taken from Bavinck's volumes. Bavinck, however, usually referred to many more texts than Berkhof, and occasionally Berkhof cited passages not found in Bavinck. Berkhof was, however, pervasively dependent on Bavinck, often to the point of literally reproducing Bavinck's words and phrases.[54]

Louis Berkhof possessed remarkable intellectual and personal gifts for doing systematic theology. A voracious reader and diligent scholar, Berkhof was theologically well informed. He had a unique capacity to assimilate a large body of material, to sort out its essential content, and reproduce it in condensed form. He was especially adept at defining theological terms and making theological distinctions. His clear, concise, coherent, and systematic lectures and writings bore the stamp of his penetrating and orderly mind. As a person he was reserved, dignified, gracious, humble, and thoroughly human. Berkhof was no fighter. He innately disliked controversy. These intellectual gifts and personal qualities combined in Berkhof to produce a theologian who knew how to present Reformed doctrine in a systematic way and who could at the same time accurately represent and fairly judge other theological positions.

Berkhof retired in 1944. At the time he retired, he was still physically and mentally vigorous. He later wrote *Aspects of Liberalism* (1951), *The Kingdom of God* (1951),[55] and *The Second Coming of Christ* (1953). When he died on May 18, 1957, he was still regularly contributing articles in the church periodicals on Christian doctrine.

No theologian or churchman has made a greater impact on the Christian Reformed Church than Professor Berkhof. During the 38 years of his professional career, he was directly involved in the instruction and training of over 300 Christian Reformed Church ministers. His textbooks in systematic theology became virtual standards of Reformed theological orthodoxy in the Christian Reformed Church. For many years candidates for the ministry were examined by the synod before being declared eligible for the ministry. In these examinations each candidate was questioned for twenty minutes on the introduction (prolegomena) to Reformed theology and for another twenty minutes on each of the six loci of systematic theology. After sustaining the synodical examination, a candidate had to submit to a similar examination in systematic theology at the classical level before being ordained to the ministry. In these examinations Berkhof's *Systematic Theology* provided both the basis for the questions and the content for the correct answers.

Reports on the celebrations honoring Berkhof when he became president of Calvin Seminary and when he retired as well as memorial articles that appeared in the church papers when he died indicate that he was greatly esteemed as a person and scholar and much trusted as a teacher and churchman. No one else in the history of the Christian Reformed Church has been so honored and respected.

Berkhof established a theological reputation in America almost exclusively through the publication of *Systematic Theology*. An Eerdmans' advertisement stated that since the death of Warfield, Hodge, Kuyper, and Bavinck, Professor Louis Berkhof occupied a unique place in the world of Reformed dogmatics. His *Systematic Theology* was unequalled by any contemporary treatise in the English language. The advertisement further quoted Samuel G. Craig, who said that Berkhof's work was the most important work on systematic theology from an American source to appear in recent years.[56] In addition to Calvin Seminary many other conservative American theological schools and Bible colleges have used Berkhof's *Systematic Theology* as a textbook for instruction.[57]

Berkhof's *Systematic Theology* brought him international recognition as a Reformed theologian. English editions of his work have been sold in Australia, Canada, South Africa, England, and other European countries. This work has also been translated into Chinese, Japanese, Korean, Spanish, and Portuguese.

Recognizing Berkhof's administrative experience and his international reputation as an orthodox Reformed theologian, the delegates from conservative Reformed churches from many parts of the world chose Louis Berkhof to be the president of the first assembly of the Reformed Ecumenical Synod meeting in June 1946 in Grand Rapids, Michigan.

Notes: Louis Berkhof

1. *Young Calvinist*, October 1931, 3.
2. *Young Calvinist*, July 1957, 4.
3. Ibid.
4. Geerhardus Vos graduated from the Theological School in 1883. The same year Vos enrolled in a postgraduate course of studies at Princeton Seminary. From Princeton he went to the University of Berlin where he studied for one year. In 1888 Vos received a Ph.D. degree from the University of Strassburg. From 1888 to 1893 he taught at the Theological School where his work was highly

esteemed by his colleagues and students. Although no criticism was expressed regarding his teaching in biblical studies, opposition was raised to his dependence on Kuyper, especially Kuyper's supralapsarianism, in dogmatics. Vos's decision to go to Princeton was based on a variety of things, not the least of which was the attractiveness and challenge of the Princeton offer. The new chair of biblical theology at Princeton was very likely specially designed to offset the influence of Dr. Charles A. Briggs, who taught the same subject at Union Seminary in New York. Vos's first love was biblical theology, not dogmatics.

5. Address to the Synod of the Reformed Churches in The Netherlands in 1899, printed in *Acta der Synode, 1900*, 93.

6. *De Wachter*, 11 March 1896, 4. Herman Bavinck was also a son of the churches of the Secession of 1834 in The Netherlands. He first taught dogmatics in the Theological School at Kampen and then accepted an appointment to teach the same subject in 1902 at the Free University of Amsterdam.

7. *Acta der Synode, 1902*, 26; *De Wachter*, 25 July 1902, 1.

8. *De Wachter*, 11 June 1957, 5.

9. Ibid.

10. Cf. G. D. De Jong, "The History of the Development of the Theological School," in *Semi-Centennial Volume* (Grand Rapids: Published for the Semi-Centennial Committee of the Theological School and Calvin College, 1926), 37.

11. *Acta der Synode, 1906*, 34.

12. *The Banner*, 14 September 1906, 233.

13. Louis Berkhof, *Beknopte Bijbelsche Hermeneutiek* (Kampen: J. H. Kok, 1911), 1-209.

14. *De Wachter*, 10 December 1913, 5.

15. Louis Berkhof, *The Church and Social Problems* (Grand Rapids: Eerdmans-Sevensma, 1913), 3, 4, 9-12, 16-20.

16. Ibid., 16-20.

17. *Acta der Synode, 1914*, 27. After not being reappointed in 1906, Janssen studied in Germany, Scotland, and The Netherlands. He also completed a course of studies qualifying him for candidacy for the ministry at the Free University of Amsterdam. According to G. D. De Jong, the synod presumed that Dr. Janssen had "learned a great deal since 1906" (De Jong, "History," 41).

18. The synod did not completely agree with Berkhof. It advised Christian laborers, if they were compelled to join neutral unions in order to provide for themselves, powerfully to witness by word and deed within the unions to the fact that they belonged to Christ and sought his honor. *Acta der Synode, 1916*, 38-39. This was the only major issue in the Christian Reformed Church during Berkhof's life on which Berkhof and the synod differed.

19. Henry Bultema, *Maranatha: Eene Studie Over de Onvervulde Profetie* (Maranatha: A Study Concerning Unfulfilled Prophecy) (Grand Rapids: Eerdmans-Sevensma, 1917).

20. The reason is obvious. The synod was to meet in June and many synodical delegates could read and understand Dutch better than English.

21. Louis Berkhof, *Premillennialisme* (Grand Rapids: Eerdmans-Sevensma, 1918), 18-29.

22. Ibid., 30-40.

23. Ibid., 41-46.

24. Ibid., 52-53.

25. For a more complete history of the controversy, see John H. Krom-

minga, *The Christian Reformed Church: A Study in Orthodoxy* (Grand Rapids: Baker Book House, 1949), 72-74.

26. The letter is reproduced in F. M. Ten Hoor, W. Heyns, L. Berkhof, and S. Volbeda, *Nadere Toelichting omtrent De Zaak Janssen* (A Closer Look Concerning the Janssen Case) (Holland: Holland Printing Company, n.d.), 3.

27. Ibid., 34-63.

28. Ibid., 63-80.

29. Ibid., 82-83.

30. R. Janssen, *Voortzetting Van Den Strijd* (Continuing the Struggle) (Grand Rapids: n.p., 1922), 4-6.

31. Letter of Janssen to the synod, *Acta der Synode, 1922,* 27.

32. *Acta der Synode, 1922,* 270-78. For a more detailed history of the Janssen Case see Kromminga, *Christian Reformed Church,* 75-79.

33. The two most prominent were Quirinus Breen and R. B. Kuiper. Breen later was awarded a Ph.D. degree in church history from the University of Chicago and taught for many years at the University of Oregon. R. B. Kuiper, Janssen's brother-in-law, went to the Reformed Church in America. Without acknowledging he had made a mistake, Kuiper recanted positively and profusely in *As to Being Reformed* (Grand Rapids: Wm. B. Eerdmans Publishing Company, 1926). Kuiper later was appointed president of Calvin College (1930), professor of practical theology at Westminster Seminary (1933), and president of Calvin Seminary (1953).

34. *Minutes of the Board of Trustees,* June 1919.

35. *Acta der Synode, 1922,* 47.

36. *Acta der Synode, 1924,* 145-47. For a brief history of the controversy see Kromminga, *Christian Reformed Church,* 82-86.

37. *Acta der Synode, 1924,* 32.

38. Clarence Bouma, "Retirement," *Calvin Forum,* October 1944, 35.

39. *The Banner,* 23 October 1925, 676.

40. Louis Berkhof, *Introductory Volume to Systematic Theology,* rev. ed. (Grand Rapids: Wm. B. Eerdmans Publishing Company, 1941), 38, 60.

41. *Acta der Synode, 1926,* 107.

42. Ten Hoor was a vigorous proponent of the infralapsarian position and stridently opposed to Kuyper. Berkhof correctly represented the supra- and infralapsarian positions on the question of the logical order of the decrees. He did not consider the two views as absolutely antithetical and rendered the opinion that both were necessarily inconsistent yet compatible with Reformed confessional orthodoxy. He did not, however, indicate that historically the two positions came to represent very different systems of theology touching many doctrinal points. Cf. *Systematic Theology* (Grand Rapids: Wm. B. Eerdmans Publishing Company, 1941), 118-25.

43. Report of the Board of Trustees, *Acts of Synod, 1932,* 207-08.

44. *The Banner,* 11 September 1931, 791-92, 806.

45. Berkhof does not comment on Reinhold Niebuhr in his books on systematic theology. For his evaluation of Niebuhr's theology see his reviews of *The Nature and Destiny of Man,* in *The Banner,* 24 September 1943, 792, and of *Christianity and Power Politics,* in *The Banner,* 23 May 1941, 504.

46. Berkhof, *Introductory Volume,* 35-36, 61, 136, and his *History of Christian Doctrines* (Grand Rapids: Wm. B. Eerdmans Publishing Company, 1937), 25.

47. Berkhof, *Introductory Volume,* 58, 60.

48. Berkhof quite simply considered any systematized body of knowledge a science (ibid., 47).

49. Ibid., 61-62, 67-68, 72, 97, 181.

50. Ibid., 23, 37, 64.

51. Ibid., 89.

52. Ibid., 17. Berkhof's major theological works were published in condensed form for college students with the title *Manual of Reformed Doctrine* (1933). In 1938 the *Manual* was further reduced for use by high-school students. It carried the title *Summary of Christian Doctrine*.

53. Berkhof, *Introductory Volume*, 58-59.

54. For examples of the extent of Berkhof's dependence on Bavinck compare Bavinck's discussion of the nature of special revelation in *Gereformeerde Dogmatiek* (Kampen: J. H. Kok, 1918), 1:362, with Berkhof's treatment of the same subject in his *Introductory Volume*, 139-40, and Bavinck's view on the wisdom of God in 2:195-96 with Berkhof's view (*Systematic Theology*, 68-69).

55. Much of the material from Berkhof's unpublished Stone Lectures was presented in this work. Berkhof was still appreciative of the social conception of the Kingdom of God articulated in the Social Gospel for correcting the older one-sided individualism and one-sided eschatological understanding of the Kingdom. Now, however, he found serious fault with the modern theological underpinnings of the Social Gospel (Louis Berkhof, *The Kingdom of God* [Grand Rapids: Wm. B. Eerdmans Publishing Company, 1951], 73-85).

56. *The Banner*, 22 April 1949, 501.

57. H. Henry Meeter listed the following: Fuller Theological Seminary, Columbia Theological Seminary, Louisville Presbyterian Seminary, Southern Baptist Theological Seminary, Gordon Divinity School, Gordon College of Theology and Missions, Western Theological Seminary, Erskine College and Theological Seminary, Northeastern Bible Institute, Providence-Barrington Bible College, Bob Jones University, and Moody Bible Institute (*De Wachter*, 11 June 1957, 14).

3

HERMAN DOOYEWEERD IN NORTH AMERICA

C. T. McINTIRE

Herman Dooyeweerd

Dooyeweerd and the Institute for Christian Studies

When surveying the Reformed tradition in Christian thought, we quite naturally turn to theologians and theology. And, indeed, all the other thinkers treated in this volume are known for their theology. But, as in the Roman Catholic tradition, there is in Reformed thought a strong and vital tradition of Christian philosophy. It is here that we meet Herman Dooyeweerd (1894-1977) in North America.[1]

In this essay I shall first examine Dooyeweerd's thought as introduced in North America, and then see what happened to his thought in the next generation in North America, especially in a group of philosophers and philosophically minded scholars influenced by Dooyeweerd and associated in one way or another with what is now known as the Institute for Christian Studies in Toronto. Unlike some of the other essays in this volume, our survey will take us right up to the present day.

Dooyeweerd was a legal scholar and philosopher at the Free University of Amsterdam from 1926 until his retirement in 1965. His most significant work was *A New Critique of Theoretical Thought* (4 vols.), published in its definitive form in English in North America between 1953 and 1958.[2]

Immediately after the publication of this work he traveled twice to North America, once in the fall of 1958 and again in the spring of 1959. The 1959 visit included a lecture tour of several universities and colleges, beginning with Harvard, as well as some public lectures for general audiences. The result was the book based on his lectures, *In the Twilight of Western Thought* (1960), written in English. *Twilight* is probably Dooyeweerd's best introduction to his own thought.[3] The 1958 visit included a meeting with the board of the Institute's ancestor organization, then only recently established in Ontario, known as the Association for Re-

157

formed Scientific Studies (ARSS). The result there was Dooyeweerd's suggestion to the ARSS that they write a new creed, an educational creed, that would affirm Christian principles directly germane to scholarship and higher education.[4]

Dooyeweerd's thought had been known in North America before the mid-1950s. Notably, he had published a brief earlier work in English, *Transcendental Problems of Philosophic Thought* (1948),[5] and Cornelius Van Til of Westminster Theological Seminary had spoken of Dooyeweerd's work to his students in the 1930s. Eventually two North American philosophers, David Freeman and William S. Young, working with Dooyeweerd and an English teacher from The Netherlands, collaborated to produce the new English version we know as the *New Critique*.[6] This, together with his two visits, established Dooyeweerd's presence in North America from the 1950s onward.

His thought became a noticeable element in circles associated with the Christian Reformed Church (CRC). At Calvin College, the CRC's official college, Professor H. Evan Runner became the able advocate of Dooyeweerd's thought.[7] Runner had gone to Holland at Van Til's suggestion and studied with Dooyeweerd and his colleague (and brother-in-law), the philosopher D. H. T. Vollenhoven.[8] Runner's channels at Calvin were his lectures to large classes in the Philosophy Department and his charismatic leadership of a student club, the Groen van Prinsterer Society. Runner founded the club in 1953 and attracted mainly students whose families had recently immigrated to Canada from The Netherlands. Dooyeweerd's thought also had strong supporters in two new independent colleges in the CRC orbit, Dordt College in Iowa, established in 1955, and Trinity Christian College in Illinois, founded in 1959.[9] Periodicals associated with the CRC took notice of Dooyeweerd, including the *Calvin Forum* and the *Torch and Trumpet*. The Reformed Fellowship, a CRC laymen's group that published *Torch and Trumpet*, sponsored Dooyeweerd's 1959 lecture tour.

The chief focus of interest in Dooyeweerd's thought, however, was the new Association for Reformed Scientific Studies (ARSS). It had been founded in 1956 by a small group of Dutch immigrants, both lay and clergy, in the CRC for the purpose of establishing in Canada an institution of higher learning on the model of the Free University of Amsterdam. The educational creed that Dooyeweerd had suggested in 1958 appeared in 1961. It was written by Vollenhoven, Dooyeweerd's brother-in-law, together with Professor Runner. The ARSS sponsored student conferences starting in 1959 and published the lectures first in a series known as *Christian Perspectives*, and in later years in books. In 1967 the ARSS changed its name to the Association for the Advancement of Christian Scholarship (AACS) and founded the Institute for Christian Studies in Toronto (ICS). The Institute, modeled on the interdisciplinary Philo-sophical Institute of the Free University, offered seminars, gradually con-structed a curriculum, gathered a small faculty of eight or nine members, named another seven nonresident fellows, and eventually awarded mas-ter's degrees in philosophy. In 1983 ICS received Royal Assent to a Charter from the Parliament of Ontario, and the AACS formally ceased to exist, leaving the ICS to carry on.[10]

Since 1956 scholars associated with the ICS and its antecedents have written a sizable body of books and articles for both scholarly and non-scholarly audiences. No one thinker has emerged as predominant. In-stead, their writings might be called the workings of a community of scholars. These works comprise much of the scholarship of the next gen-eration after Dooyeweerd in North America.[11]

This next generation has passed through three phases.[12] The first phase, during the 1950s and 1960s, consisted chiefly of translating Dutch scholarship into English, bringing Dutch scholars to North America, sending North American students to Amsterdam, and promoting Dooye-weerd's thought with the enthusiasm and aggressiveness that disciples have for their master. The second phase, from the late 1960s to the late 1970s, included converting the Institute into a serious academic com-munity, taking the first important steps of independence from Dooye-weerd's thought yet continuing in the tradition of Dooyeweerd, and opening up differences between conservative and progressive emphases among the broad group of scholars who related to Dooyeweerd's thought. The third phase, since the late 1970s, has featured the production of new scholarship that in general continued the tradition of Christian thought identified with Dooyeweerd, while being fully involved in contemporary scholarship within the academic world at large. Often significant differ-ences continued to appear among those who related to Dooyeweerd's tradition. Through this process of transmutation the scholars in this broad group sought to sift the enduring from the ephemeral.

Dooyeweerd's Thought

Dooyeweerd presented the primary elements of his thought in *A New Critique of Theoretical Thought*.[13] That work itself was a revised edition based on a translation of his three-volume *De Wijsbegeerte der Wetsidee* (*The Philosophy of the Law-Idea*) published in Holland in 1935-36. Altogether Dooyeweerd published more than 200 books and articles in the fields of law, political theory, and philosophy. His thought touched a wide range of areas—ontology, epistemology, social philosophy, phi-losophy of history, aesthetics, philosophy of science, legal theory, polit-ical philosophy, the history of law, theology, and the history of philosophy. He was a comprehensive thinker with an amazing versatility, and his ideas were capable of inspiring thought in almost any field of learning. As a system builder he may be compared with philosophers Jacques Maritain and Bernard Lonergan, theologian Paul Tillich, historian Arnold Toynbee, and social theorists Talcott Parsons and Pitrikim Sorokin. He sought to continue the Christian tradition of the great Dutch thinker and prime minister of the preceding generation, Abraham Kuyper (1901-1905).

Dooyeweerd claimed that he wrote, not theology, but philosophy informed by Christian insights. As such, he wrote not about God but about the general structure of the world and human existence. The characteristic elements of his thought may be grouped under the following themes: 1. religion; 2. creation, fall, and redemption; 3. modal theory; 4. individuality theory; and 5. the opening process of history.

1. *Religion.* [14] Dooyeweerd understood religion to be the supreme motive of human existence. He contended that we are related either to God in the totality of our being or to an idol, an alternative to God whether transcendent or this-worldly. Accordingly, religion is not a distinct department of life or something that we can do without if we so choose. Understood in this way, every human being is religious, and nothing that we do in life is separable from religion. All of life is from God, dependent upon God, and responsive to God.

According to Dooyeweerd, religion is integrative and central to life. Our religion is rooted in our hearts as the manifestation of our unity, what the Scriptures call our soul or spirit. He rejected all notions of a dualism between soul and body, and instead interpreted soul as the unifying totality of our being as related to God or a substitute.

Religion is the basic dynamic, the "ground motive," of our lives. God calls us and we respond, but not always in ways faithful to the will of God. Dooyeweerd, following St. Augustine, believed that there are two great types of this "ground motive"—the Spirit of God and the Spirit of the Evil One. He suggested that these have been translated into four specific ground motives—the Greek-Roman pagan motive of form and matter; the Christian motive of creation, fall, and redemption; the originally medieval motive of grace and nature that seeks a synthesis between pagan and Christian religion; and the secular humanist motive of freedom and nature. Thinkers empowered according to this modern secular motive, such as Immanuel Kant, are certain that "religion" is not relevant to theoretical thought and that reason is autonomous. The basic thesis of Dooyeweerd's "new critique" of theoretical thought is that belief in the autonomy of reason is a pretension that cannot hide the religious character of all thought.

2. *Creation, Fall, and Redemption.* This is the religious ground mo-

tive that is consonant with the Scriptures. Dooyeweerd explained its meaning in this way: *creation* denotes that all of reality is God's, a disclosure of his will, and good; *fall* indicates our radical resistance to the love of God and love of our neighbor, because of which our existence as God's creatures is filled with suffering and evil; *redemption* turns us to Jesus Christ by whom we may be radically restored to God and our neighbors, and the whole creation may become as it ought to be, the re-creation of God.

Dooyeweerd regarded his entire philosophy as an attempt to manifest the dynamic of this Christian religious motive in theoretical terms. He conceived of theory as an explication of the law-structure of creation. He emphasized the conflict among the fruits of the two Spirits—of God and of the Evil One—as the "antithesis" due to the Fall that divided thought from thought and persons from persons, even as it cut through the lives of Christians. He stressed that the structures of creation were norms by which God called us to do what is healthy and to work out by means of human action the redemption that Jesus Christ accomplished.

3. *Modal Theory*.[15] The first of two ways in which Dooyeweerd conceptualized reality was in his modal theory. In this he explicitly sought to expand upon the idea of "sphere sovereignty" put forward by Kuyper. Whereas in religion we tend toward the integration and unity of our lives, in the actual expression of our lives we manifest diversity. As Dooyeweerd depicted it, reality is temporal, and cosmic time, like a prism, refracts the unity of the one light into many diverse modes of existence. The modes are aspects of reality, the many different ways in which an entity exists or an act occurs. The modal aspects are, on one side, structures or laws of creation; on the other, they are the various ways in which we exist historically, no one of which is reducible to any other.

Dooyeweerd provisionally identified fifteen modal aspects of reality, including the numerical, biotic, psychical, lingual, jural, and pistic (faith). Each aspect revealed a law or norm that characterized the aspect. For example, the biotic law is organic growth, the lingual norm is symbolic signification, and the jural norm is justice. Dooyeweerd worked out a very elaborate system by which he explained how each aspect referred by analogy to every other aspect, networking the aspects of reality in a complex but magnificent integration. He showed how each scholarly discipline pertained especially to a unique aspect, such as biology to the biotic, linguistics to the lingual, and theology to the pistic. Philosophy had the task of overall integration, such as by theorizing about the modes and their interrelations as a whole, while each science treated its own aspect within the context of philosophical interrelations.

4. *Individuality Theory*.[16] While his modal theory looked at *aspects* of reality—e.g., biotic, jural, pistic—his individuality theory analyzed

whole phenomena of reality—e.g., trees, states, and churches. Whereas by means of modality analysis he identified specific kinds of aspects of entities, by means of individuality analysis he identified kinds of entities.

The important issue is to apprehend the unique and irreducible character of each modal aspect or each kind of entity. For example, in modal theory faith (pistic) manifests a unique character according to the norm of faith (transcendental certainty) and may not be reduced to the social or psychic aspects of faith. In individuality theory churches are communities properly characterized by faith and may not rightly be treated as merely social or economic in character, although those aspects are also present. Dooyeweerd was thus both a pluralist and an antireductionist; he accepted the diversity of created reality as basic.

His individuality theory enabled him to explain how there could be different kinds of entities, yet how each kind could exhibit every aspect of reality. For example, states such as France and Canada are characteristically jural communities united around the jural norm of justice. At the same time, states exhibit spatial, economic, social, and all the other modal aspects. They do so in ways that belong to a jurally qualified institution. Thus, states do not exist to make a profit or to create friendships, but to maintain justice. In this light, Dooyeweerd regards it as proper for states in the name of justice to redistribute wealth among the citizenry from the richer to the poorer members. Likewise, an industry such as General Motors Corporation rightly exists when it acts according to the characteristic norm of stewardly saving care for the human and natural resources of creation. While GM needs to match income with expenditure, even here the aim should not be to make profit, but act according to that norm of stewardship, in relation to all the other aspects of reality, including the aesthetic quality of the workplace and the equity of the decision-making process.

According to his theory, people express their religion directly by means of their response to the norm appropriate to each different kind of entity.

5. *History.*[17] Dooyeweerd's philosophy of history provided the invisible backbone of his whole system of thought. The elements of his philosophy of history were scattered, however. He regarded his theory of time as the basis of his system. It was an unusual notion of time. He called it cosmic time, and identified it as the pluriform diversity of the modal aspects. He contrasted it with the unity and coherence of reality as centered in the human heart, which he treated as supratemporal (beyond time). As a result there were different sorts of time, for example, linguistic time, astronomic time, or jural time.

What he called the historical aspect was merely one appearance of time as past, present, and future. The historical aspect he supposed was one mode among the fifteen he identified. It had to do with power, control, or mastery, and he sometimes called it the cultural mode. He believed that historical study specialized in analysis of the historical mode of any thing.

This historical mode served as the foundation or starting point for a very complicated process, called "the opening process," that swept through the modes in the actual course of any thing's history. By means of the opening process, static or closed cultures were made to develop by means of differentiation, individualization, and new integration. In this manner Dooyeweerd believed the world could unfold in fulfillment of the cultural mandate of Genesis 1. History would become a process of development initiated by faith. Dooyeweerd's vision of history was sweeping, and he linked it directly to St. Augustine's vision of the two cities in struggle for the course of history.

Many other elements of Dooyeweerd's thought, particularly in epistemology and philosophical anthropology, could be mentioned, but these five are both central and characteristic enough to indicate the thrust of his work.

The Generation after Dooyeweerd

When Dooyeweerd's work appeared in North America in the 1950s, a number of scholars took notice of it in books and articles. William S. Young, one of the translators of the *New Critique*, was the first, and he referred to it in his book *Towards a Reformed Philosophy* (1952). The second translator, David H. Freeman, completed a doctoral dissertation at the University of Pennsylvania, partly on Dooyeweerd (1958), and he published *Recent Studies in Philosophy and Theology* (1962) in which he compared Dooyeweerd with Étienne Gilson, Jacques Maritain, and Paul Tillich. Ronald Nash wrote *Dooyeweerd and the Amsterdam Philosophy* (1962), and Arthur Holmes included Dooyeweerd in *Christian Philosophy in the Twentieth Century* (1969). Rousas John Rushdoony discussed Dooyeweerd in several essays, including his Introduction to Dooyeweerd's *In The Twilight of Western Thought* (1960).[18]

These and many other writings contributed to an awareness of Dooyeweerd's thought. Evan Runner and the Association for Reformed Scientific Studies (ARSS) in Ontario, however, sought to go the next step and act on Dooyeweerd's thought. Runner and his Groen van Prinsterer Society at Calvin College inspired Hendrik Hart, Bernard Zylstra, James Olthuis, and Arnold De Graaff to go to the Free University of Amsterdam for their doctoral studies. Dooyeweerd supervised Zylstra's dissertation on Harold Laski's political theory. Hart went into general philosophy, writing on John Dewey's epistemology. Olthuis wrote on ethics and theology, and De Graaff wrote on psychology and education. Calvin Seerveld, only indirectly influenced by Runner at Calvin, went to Amsterdam earlier on his own to work under Vollenhoven, completing a dissertation on Benedetto Croce's aesthetics.[19] These five became the first members of the faculty of the Institute for Christian Studies after it opened in 1967.

The other avenue of Runner's influence was the series of annual student conferences begun by the ARSS in 1959 in Ontario. Runner's lectures at the first two were published separately by the ARSS in 1960 and 1961 and eventually put together as a book, *The Relation of the Bible to Learning* (1967).[20] Runner's themes were all Dooyeweerd's—religion, the ground-motives and the religious antithesis, sphere sovereignty and the modal theory, and the law of God in creation.

But some recognizably new emphases appeared in Runner's version of some of these themes. Chief of these was his stress on the Word of God, by which he meant the Bible. Dooyeweerd's emphasis, it may be said, was always on Creation-Order as a reality in the context of which the Scriptures were needed as a guide. Runner reversed the emphasis, in keeping with his North American Evangelical and Reformed experience, and made the Bible the centerpiece. Parallel with this, Runner stressed the religious character of everything under the new banner of "life is religion," and, in contrast with Dooyeweerd, put less emphasis on the theoretical analysis of reality. Thirdly, Runner accented the "religious antithesis," the utter opposition in thought and scholarship between the way of God and all other spirits. Dooyeweerd, by contrast, while working with the notion of religious antithesis in the sense of St. Augustine, had stressed creating his own system of thought in debate with other kinds of thought. Fourthly, Runner transformed the notion of working with Dooyeweerd's thought into a mission that Dutch Calvinistic youth in North America should especially undertake. With this he reversed the trend in Dooyeweerd from his accentuated Calvinism in the 1920s and 1930s to his ecumenical Christian thought based on the common scriptural message in the 1950s. (Dooyeweerd desired to change the name of his thought from Calvinistic philosophy to the more general term Christian philosophy.) By means of these four new emphases, Runner helped to create a small movement possessing an élan and a compelling purpose.

The founding of the Institute for Christian Studies in Toronto implemented Dooyeweerd's thought in a most tangible way. His thought was not made official, so to speak, but it did serve as the unwritten basis for interdisciplinary scholarly discourse within the Institute. It offered a model with two applications—first, for the intrinsic integration of Christian insight with scholarly thought, and second, for the identification and interrelation of all fields of scholarly study. The character and curriculum of the Institute reflected both applications at once.[21] The Institute regarded itself from the start as a *philosophical* rather than a theological school. Following Dooyeweerd, it regarded each field of academic study as resting upon a philosophical basis in which fundamental decisions were made about human nature, the purpose of life, and the character of reality. And such matters are the very ones that Christian insights directly illuminated. The Institute adopted Dooyeweerd's theory that philosophy by definition was an integrative endeavor, with respect to which Christian insights concerning the wholeness and integrity of reality were directly relevant.

By the early 1970s the Institute created two core courses—biblical foundations and philosophical foundations. In so doing it stressed that the Scriptures were not the special document of theology students and biblical scholars, but the integrative and directive religious source for the insights basic to any field of study. Thus philosophy, pursued according to biblical insights, served to ground and orient each academic field. For the rest, they added courses in the philosophy of as many fields as they could, given the limits of financial resources and personnel.

In the late 1970s the Institute faculty numbered nine scholars who taught in the areas of philosophy, history of philosophy, theology, philosophical theology, philosophy of history, political theory, economic and social philosophy, psychological theory, and philosophical aesthetics. The course of study was rounded out by a second-year interdisciplinary seminar that involved most fields, and by research on master's theses.

The Institute was founded with two clear mandates: to pursue the religious reformation of various scholarly fields, and to pursue academic research.[22] Both aims—reformation and research—were by definition inclined toward innovation. But both also required a stable institutional format and a stable relation with the supporting constituency. These needs for innovation and stabilization could—and did—often conflict. I have already referred to three phases in the Institute's history—the aggressive, the settling down, and the academically productive phases. These can now be paraphrased as the transition from being a movement to being a scholarly institution. Both founding mandates, actively pursued, were conducive to such a transition.

Included in the transition was a new relation to Dooyeweerd's thought. Whereas at the beginning the Institute depended on Dooyeweerd, by the late 1970s the faculty members had each moved to fresh terrain but always with Dooyeweerd's thought in the background. It is possible to review the five thematic elements of Dooyeweerd's thought surveyed earlier and observe what became of them in the teaching and writings of the Institute's faculty. The most important work for this comparison is a volume of essays entitled *The Legacy of Herman Dooyeweerd: Reflection on Critical Philosophy in the Christian Tradition* (1985).[23] The essays were written by six authors who were faculty members of the Institute. Of the many other writings by Institute scholars, especially notable are Hendrik Hart's *Understanding Our World: An Integral Ontology* (1984) and Calvin Seerveld's *Rainbows for the Fallen World: Aesthetic Life and Artistic Task* (1980).[24]

Two general observations may be made at the outset.[25] First, Dooyeweerd's system as a whole has not been taken over by the next generation. This may mean no more than observing that only Dooyeweerd could maintain Dooyeweerd's system, and that any subsequent thinkers who tried to do so would become scholastic disciples and not a group of scholars with their own contributions to make. Second, what did continue were some general orientations and some general themes and insights of a philosophically relevant kind concerning what was important and how to proceed in philosophy. These observations will become concrete as we review the five themes.

1. *Religion.* Institute members would agree that Dooyeweerd made his point about the religious basis of theoretical thought, indeed of all human activity. All humans are religious and as such their lives are oriented toward God or some substitute. Thus, the relation between religion and scholarship is intrinsic and integral.

They would grant, further, that religion is a motivating power, but it appears that no Institute scholar continues to work with the idea of religious ground-motives in Western civilization. None would carry on Dooyeweerd's extensive analysis of the polar tensions within the ground motives by which he interpreted the history of culture and philosophy. None would regard the heart as distinguishable from the whole of our person and our functioning; some have suggested that Dooyeweerd created a new dualistic view of our human make-up, in spite of his best intentions.

2. *Creation, Fall, and Redemption.* All the Institute scholars would regard this as an insightful summary of the central theme of the Scriptures concerning the world. But they would differ about whether it should be treated as a "ground motive" as did Dooyeweerd in the 1950s, or merely as a theme, or triad of themes, as Dooyeweerd did in the 1920s and 1930s. They all would regard an understanding of reality as creation, structured and good, as basic to Christian philosophizing. Likewise, they would understand the work of Jesus Christ as re-creation and in principle culturally pervasive in overcoming the effects of evil and suffering.

3. *Modal Theory.* All would agree that some sort of modal analysis is useful and valid to account for the constitutional diversity of reality.

Indeed, modal analysis would be taken as the chief means of identifying and interrelating the various distinct academic disciplines. But Institute scholars differ on what the modes may be, what their characterizing norms may be, and to what degree modal analysis is useful.

Some regard modal theory as useful first of all merely as an indicator of ontologically irreducible diversity. Others actively pursue modal analysis. For example, Olthuis stays fairly close to Dooyeweerd's version of the aspect of faith as transcendental certainty, calling it simply certitude. He agrees that theology is a special theoretical discipline focused on the mode of faith (certitude). Seerveld thinks Dooyeweerd is right about an aesthetic mode and aesthetics as a special science, but he rejects Dooyeweerd's understanding of aesthetics as having to do with harmony and beauty. He works instead with notions of allusiveness and imagination. Probably all would reject Dooyeweerd's proposal that there is a historical mode, and would work instead toward a more embracive understanding of history. Hart makes the move of conceiving of the modes, not as aspects, an idea that has static and spatial connotations, but as functions, calling up active and operational suggestions. All would agree that philosophy is best treated as an integrative as well as an analytic discipline, charged with conceptualizing the bases and interrelations of all the scholarly fields.

4. *Individuality Theory.* Probably all would think that theorizing about the structure of individual entities is important. Hart calls such phenomena "functors" and discusses functions (modal) as what functors do. But he does not pursue the theme of functors as fully as he does modal functions. Seerveld distinguishes art works as individual entities that are aesthetic in character from the aesthetic aspect of other non-aesthetic entities (such as someone's home).

On the whole, scholarly attention to individuality theory is slight compared with attention to modal theory. All would, however, stress the importance of a pluralist social theory that honored the distinctive yet interrelated character of each kind of social institution and relationship—churches, governments, colleges, neighborhoods, cities, labor unions, families, and so on.

5. *History.* I have already mentioned that all would reject the notion that history could be accounted for by means of Dooyeweerd's historical mode. All would also reject Dooyeweerd's theory of the heart as supratemporal, above and beyond time and history. They would disagree about whether time should be regarded as synonymous with ordered diversity (as in Dooyeweerd), or more pervasively identified as process and past-present-future relations. And they would disagree about the value of Dooyeweerd's theory of the opening process. The judgment

from the historian's angle has been that Dooyeweerd's theory wrongly elevates development above all other processes of history. What is needed is more theorizing about the great variety of temporal-historical processes, and this in a wide multi-cultural way. Dooyeweerd's relating of history to the cultural mandate of Genesis 1 would seem insightful as a way of identifying human responsibilities in history making, but more subtlety and actual historical analysis would be needed in order to create a more flexible philosophy of history influenced by Christian insights.

Conclusion

No doubt Herman Dooyeweerd has been the most creative philosopher in the Reformed tradition thus far in the twentieth century. However, the barriers to recognizing his creativity and transposing his philosophy to North America have not been small. His categories, special language, and method were shaped in a Dutch and European religious and philosophical milieu very different from that of his North American counterparts. The prevailing North American traditions of Reformed theology and analytic philosophy were unsympathetic to his thought. The Dutch Canadian community, which has been the chief transmitter of Dooyeweerd's thought, was separated from the mainstream of academic discourse like any immigrant group. The early aspirations to build a movement with a unique and exclusive salvific message needlessly impeded normal discourse about Dooyeweerd's thought.

Nonetheless, the presence of Dooyeweerd's thought in North America has been very beneficial. Once the effort is made to become acquainted with Dooyeweerd's work, the character of his creativity is evident.

The generation after Dooyeweerd has successfully made the transition to viable, innovative scholarship in full discourse with the North American academic community as a whole. Institute scholars have meaningfully relativized Dooyeweerd while seeking to distill the more enduring legacy he has to offer.

What may continue and be of value to others is not Dooyeweerd's system or his specific formulations, but a type of approach to scholarship. That approach may perhaps be summarized in this way: the impulse to explore reality empirically and theoretically, so that the irreducible diversity yet the coherent integration of reality is respected, that the insights of the Christian religion are intrinsic to scholarship in full discourse with the academic world, and that the results are of service to God and to all people.

Notes: Herman Dooyeweerd in North America

1. See "Christian Philosophy," *Encyclopedia Britannica* (15th edition, 1974), IV: 555-62; and *Philosophy in the 20th Century: Catholic and Christian,* ed. George F. McLean, 2 vols. (New York: Frederick Unger, 1967).

We should note from the outset that there is another strong tradition of Reformed philosophy in North America that emphasizes philosophy of religion and rational discourse about claims concerning God, and that has associated with the tradition of Anglo-American thought known as analytic philosophy. In spite of differences, there are nonetheless strong affinities between philosophers in that Reformed line of thought and Dooyeweerd, chiefly by way of Dooyeweerd's predecessor Abraham Kuyper. See Hendrik Hart and Johan van der Hoeven, eds., *Rationality in the Calvinian Tradition* (Washington: University Press of America, 1983); and Alvin Plantinga and Nicholas Wolterstorff, eds., *Faith and Rationality: Reason and Belief in God* (Notre Dame: University of Notre Dame Press, 1983).

2. Dooyeweerd, *A New Critique of Theoretical Thought,* 4 vols. (Amsterdam: Paris; Philadelphia: Presbyterian and Reformed Publishing Company, 1953-1958). Hereafter *New Critique.*

3. Dooyeweerd, *In the Twilight of Western Thought* (Philadelphia: Presbyterian and Reformed Publishing Company, 1960). Hereafter *Twilight.*

4. The text of the educational creed is published in the *Academic Bulletin* of the Institute for Christian Studies.

5. Dooyeweerd, *Transcendental Problems of Philosophic Thought* (Grand Rapids: Wm. B. Eerdmans Publishing Company, 1948).

6. Freeman and Young collaborated on Volume 1, while Freeman and H. DeJongste collaborated on Volumes 2 and 3. Dooyeweerd went over the entire English version himself and revised and added sections.

7. On Runner, see John Kraay and Anthony Tol, eds., *Hearing and Doing: Philosophical Essays dedicated to H. Evan Runner* (Toronto: Wedge Publishing Company, 1979); and Henry Vander Goot, ed., *Life Is Religion: Essays in Honor of H. Evan Runner* (St. Catharines: Paideia Press, 1981).

8. On Vollenhoven, see *The Idea of Christian Philosophy: Essays in Honour of D. H. T. Vollenhoven* (Toronto: Wedge Publishing Company, 1973).

9. Two more Reformed colleges in CRC circles were founded in Canada, both with Dooyeweerd's thought as a factor, Redeemer College, Hamilton, Ontario (1982), and The King's College, Edmonton, Alberta (1979).

10. The history of the ARSS, AACS, and ICS has yet to be written. A special issue of the ICS Newsletter, *Perspective,* published in 1981 on the twenty-fifth anniversary of the founding of the ARSS, gives many interesting historical vignettes.

11. A partial list to 1975 is published in L. Kalsbeek, *Contours of a Christian Philosophy: An Introduction to Herman Dooyeweerd's Thought* (Toronto: Wedge Publishing Company, 1975), 313-39.

12. What follows is based on countless documents and personal observations over the years since 1960.

13. This treatment of Dooyeweerd's thought is based chiefly on the *New Critique,* his *magnum opus.* His published works through 1977 are listed in the back of a book that is an excellent scholarly introduction to his thought, Hendrik Van Eikema Hommes, *Inleiding tot de Wijsbegeerte van Herman Dooyeweerd* (The Hague: Martinus Nijhoff, 1982). The book by Kalsbeek, mentioned above, is also good and very readable. Other books to consult are Dooyeweerd's *Twilight,* and

his *Roots of Western Culture: Pagan, Secular, and Christian Options* (Toronto: Wedge Publishing Company, 1979).

14. Dooyeweerd treats religion, and creation, fall, redemption, in *New Critique*, Vol. 1.

15. He discusses modal theory in *New Critique*, Vol. 2.

16. Individuality theory is the subject of *New Critique*, Vol. 3.

17. Most of his philosophy of history is discussed in *New Critique*, Vol. 2, but much is scattered throughout the whole work.

18. Young, *Towards a Reformed Philosophy* (Franeker: T. Wever, 1952); Freeman, *Recent Studies in Philosophy and Theology* (Philadelphia: Presbyterian and Reformed Publishing Company, 1962); Nash, *Dooyeweerd and the Amsterdam Philosophy* (Grand Rapids: Zondervan Publishing House, 1962); Holmes, *Christian Philosophy in the Twentieth Century* (Nutley, NJ: Craig, 1969); Rushdoony, "Introduction," *Twilight*, vii-xvi.

19. Hart, *Communal Certainty and Authorized Truth* (Amsterdam: Swets and Zeitlinger, 1966); Zylstra, *From Pluralism to Collectivism* (Assen: Van Gorcum, 1968; New York: Humanities Press, 1970); Olthuis, *Facts, Values, and Ethics* (Assen: Van Gorcum, 1968; New York: Humanities Press, 1969); De Graaff, *The Educational Ministry of the Church* (Nutley, NJ: Craig, 1968); Seerveld, *Benedetto Croce's Earlier Aesthetic Theories and Literary Criticism* (Kampen: J. H. Kok, 1958).

20. Runner, *The Relation of the Bible to Learning* (Toronto: ARSS, 1967).

21. The Institute's statements of purpose and its curriculum have been presented in its *Academic Bulletin*, issued every year or two since 1967.

22. These mandates are presented in the Preamble and the Educational Creed of the ARSS (now ICS), which are printed in the ICS *Academic Bulletin*.

23. *The Legacy of Herman Dooyeweerd: Reflections on Critical Philosophy in the Christian Tradition* (Washington: University Press of America, 1985).

24. Hart, *Understanding Our World* (Washington: University Press of America, 1984); Seerveld, *Rainbows for the Fallen World* (Toronto: Tuppence Press, 1980). A full listing of publications by members of the Institute's faculty and associates may be obtained from the Institute, 229 College Street, Toronto, Ontario, M5T 1R4.

25. What follows is based on my reading of most of the publications by Institute scholars as well as firsthand knowledge of their teaching.

4

CORNELIUS VAN TIL

WESLEY A. ROBERTS

Cornelius Van Til

REFORMED theologians have been concerned not only with a correct understanding of the Christian faith but also with the rational defense and justification of Christianity's truth claims. The latter activity falls within the discipline of apologetics, long regarded as a branch of theology. Reformed theologians, however, are not agreed on the relation of apologetics to the theological encyclopedia as a whole. B. B. Warfield, for example, argued that apologetics is the discipline that establishes the knowledge of God that theology explicates.[1] Dutch theologians like Abraham Kuyper and Herman Bavinck argued that apologetics should not precede but follow upon the work of systematic theology that determines the content of the Christian faith.

Cornelius Van Til, a student of both the old Princeton school of theologians and the great Dutch Reformed thinkers, sees a mutual dependence of apologetics and systematic theology.[2] Van Til is not a systematician but an apologist with a strong commitment to Reformed theology that permeates all his writings.

Van Til is regarded by many as one of the foremost Christian apologists of our time. He is perhaps the most controversial Reformed thinker of the twentieth century, the man responsible for initiating a new approach to apologetics. At Princeton Theological Seminary, Van Til was introduced to the traditional method of apologetics espoused by giants of the theological world such as Charles Hodge, B. B. Warfield, Francis L. Patton, William Brenton Greene, Jr., and J. Gresham Machen. This method "is to present evidence and arguments from all different lines of thought in an attempt to show that God exists and that the Bible is the Word of God, and that the burden of inferential proof is so great that there is no excuse for an unbeliever to reject Christianity."[3]

During the academic year 1928-1929, while serving as instructor in apologetics at Princeton, Van Til had an opportunity to assess the apologetic methodology he had received as a student and was using as a teacher. He became convinced that this method was not consistent with the teachings of the Reformed faith. It was not, however, until he joined the faculty of the newly founded Westminster Theological Seminary in September of 1929 as Professor of Apologetics that he began to work out his new approach. Van Til's doctoral work in philosophy had made him aware of the insight of post-Kantian metaphysicians that "the given presuppositions of any philosophical position predetermined and governed much of its later outworkings."[4] When he applied this notion to the traditional apologetic method he saw that this method accepted the non-Christian presuppositions of its adversaries rather than challenged them. This led Van Til to his "pioneering insight" that in apologetics the presuppositions and not merely attendant arguments have to be biblical.[5] His reading of the writings of Abraham Kuyper and Herman Bavinck further strengthened his viewpoint that in apologetics one must not begin with human reason or some supposedly neutral position. Rather, one must begin with the presupposition that there is a God and that men are responsible to him. Information about this God is presented in the inspired Scriptures. This was the beginning of presuppositional apologetics with which Van Til's name has been identified for the past half century.

Van Til maintains an uncompromising commitment to Reformed theology. It is the Reformed expression of the Christian faith that he seeks to defend. He admits his indebtedness to the classic Reformed theologians and quotes freely from them. He is willing to go beyond them, however, in areas where he thinks they are weak. He thinks that he can best honor men such as Warfield and Kuyper by building on the main thrust of their thought rather than by carrying on what is inconsistent with their basic position.[6] Bernard Ramm has given a fine summary of Van Til's location within the Reformed faith:

> Van Til has made a sustained effort to have an apologetic system that grows naturally out of the reformed system of theology. The godfather of his system is certainly John Calvin, although he admits that Augustine was the first Christian theologian to try to work out a Christian metaphysics and epistemology. His more immediate apologetic relatives are such great Dutch thinkers as Kuyper and Bavinck and such outstanding Calvinists as Hodge and Warfield. He has had great sympathy with the Calvinistic philosophy as recently developed at the Free University of Amsterdam by Vollenhoven and Dooyeweerd.[7]

It is Van Til's conviction that in Calvinism more than any other form of Protestantism the message of Christianity is clearly presented as a challenge to the wisdom of the world.

Van Til's apologetic writings contain so much exposition of Reformed theology that critics have charged that he confuses apologetics with systematic theology.[8] This is a common misunderstanding of Van Til's position. Van Til does believe that "defense and positive statement go hand in hand" but he makes a distinction between the two.[9] The misunderstanding arises from Van Til's insistence that theology must have an apologetic thrust, and apologetics must expound theology. The difference in practice, as Frame points out, is a difference in emphasis rather than of subject matter.[10] To understand Van Til's apologetic is at the same time to understand his theology. For his epistemology is based on his metaphysics. Fundamental to his system is the Creator-creature distinction, which is kept in focus at all times. Without this basic distinction in mind one cannot grasp the significance of Van Til's position.

Christian Metaphysics

The doctrine of God is of fundamental importance to Van Til's apologetics. Everything in his system is made to turn on the existence of God. To him God is the absolute, self-conscious Being who is the source of all finite being and knowledge. Consequently, the "ontological" Trinity is made the category of interpretation for all things and the final reference point in all human thinking. The most basic fact of all facts is the existence of the triune God. Thus he asserts, "I hold that belief in God is not merely as reasonable as other belief, or even a little or infinitely more probably true than other belief; I hold rather that unless you believe in God you can logically believe in nothing else."[11]

Theologically, Van Til believes that every doctrine is bound to be false if the first and basic doctrine of God is false. "For apologetics it means that the non-Christian forms of metaphysics cannot be challenged in their basic assumptions."[12] The God of whom Van Til speaks is not one whose existence can be proved by philosophical arguments. He is the self-contained and self-sufficient God who has revealed himself in Scripture.

Unlike the old Princeton theologians who accepted the historically formulated theistic proofs, Van Til maintains that these arguments are invalid. If they were valid, he says, Christianity would not be true.[13] Van Til's point is that the non-Christian formulation of these "proofs" does not refer to the God of Scripture but to a finite god who is no God.[14] He does see value, however, in a Christian formulation of these proofs that rests on the ideas of creation and providence. As such, they appeal to what the natural man knows to be true because he is a creature of God.[15] He believes that the objective evidence for the existence of God and of the comprehensive governance of the world is so plain that men cannot get away from it. They see it about them and within them.[16]

God's existence therefore should be presented by the apologist not as "possible" or "probable," but as certain.

It is from his view of God that Van Til develops his view of reality. He believes Christianity is committed to a two-layer theory of reality or being. By this he means that God has one kind of being and the universe another kind, which is produced and sustained by God. God's being is infinite, eternal, and unchangeable; that of the universe is finite, temporal, and changeable.[17] This distinction allows him to address the philosophical problem of the one-and-many, the relation of unity to diversity. He distinguishes between the Eternal One-and-Many and the temporal one-and-many. In God unity and plurality are both ultimate and eternal. Unity is not sacrificed to plurality nor plurality to unity. The temporal one-and-many is the result of God's creation. Therefore the various aspects of created reality are made to sustain relations to one another according to the design of the Creator. He explains it as follows:

> All aspects being equally created, no one aspect of reality may be regarded as more ultimate than another. Thus the created *one and many* may in this respect be said to be *equal* to one another; they are equally derived and equally dependent upon God who sustains them both. The particulars or facts of the universe do and must act in accord with universals and laws. Thus there is order in the created universe. On the other hand, the laws may not and can never reduce the particulars to abstract particulars or reduce their individuality in any manner. The laws are but generalizations of God's method of working with particulars.[18]

Van Til seeks to be true to the Scriptures in his theory of reality. The triune God is placed at the center of his thinking and is brought to bear on every issue of philosophical importance.

Christian Epistemology

Van Til's theory of knowledge is based on his metaphysics. For there to be any validity to man's knowledge, Van Til believes we must presuppose the triune God revealed in the Bible. He believes that if the question of knowledge is made independent of the question of being, we are in effect excluding the Christian answer to the question of knowledge. Once we accept the biblical testimony with regard to God and man our knowledge will be true insofar as it corresponds with God's knowledge. The Christian, therefore, cannot be neutral to the nature of reality when he asks about the nature of knowledge.[19]

Starting with God's knowledge, Van Til argues that God's knowledge of himself and of the created universe is exhaustive. In other words, there can be no new knowledge for God about himself or the universe. God's knowledge is analytic in that he is himself the source of all that can be known. He does not add to his knowledge, which is eternal, analytic, comprehensive, and inexhaustible.[20]

From God's knowledge of himself, Van Til advances to God's knowledge of the universe. God's knowledge of the universe depends on his knowledge of himself.[21] He made the universe in accordance with his eternal plan, so its very existence depends on his knowledge. As a creature made in the image of God man can and does have true knowledge. God's knowledge is the standard of man's knowledge. "The one must be determinative and the other subordinate."[22] Van Til, however, is careful to point out that although man's knowledge of God must be true, it is not and cannot be exhaustive. Creatures cannot have comprehensive knowledge.[23]

Since man can know God truly it follows that he can also know the world truly. Van Til uses the doctrine of creation as the basis for his assertion. Since both the subject (man) and the object (created reality) of human knowledge are created by God, there must be objective knowledge. Subject and object are adapted to one another according to the plan of God. This is seen in the fact that man (subject) was given a mandate to interpret the world of objects under God. Without this interpretation of the universe by man, Van Til believes, the world would be meaningless.[24] The objectivity of knowledge, therefore, rests on the doctrine of creation. If this doctrine is relinquished, the particulars or facts of the universe would be unrelated and could not be in fruitful contact with one another.

Seeing, then, that the objects of knowledge are brought into relation with the human mind according to God's creative purpose, these objects will not be truly interpreted if they are not brought into relation with the divine mind. God being the ultimate category of interpretation, the things in the universe must be interpreted in relation to him.[25]

Van Til also points out that since God is incomprehensible to us, our knowledge, though true, is partial and always finds itself involved in paradox or seeming contradiction. "Our knowledge is analogical and therefore must be paradoxical."[26] To God there is no mystery, no paradox, but to finite man there is. God's comprehensive plan takes in all the facts but we do not need to know this plan; all we need to know is that reality is rationally controlled by God's plan.

The doctrine of revelation is important to Van Til's concept of epistemology. Since it is according to God's plan that finite things are made, Van Til insists that all knowledge that any finite creature would have must rest upon the revelation of God. Thus the knowledge that we have of the simplest objects of the physical universe is based upon the revelational activity of God.[27]

Van Til follows both Kuyper and Bavinck in stressing the fact that Scripture is *the* objective principle of knowledge for the Christian. This means that the truths of the Scriptures must be taken as the light in which all the facts of experience are to be interpreted. It follows necessarily that if Scripture holds such a crucial position its pronouncements about reality cannot be subject to the scrutiny of reason but must be taken on their own authority.[28] Van Til is aware that such a position will be criticized as authoritarian but he maintains that God's revelation is always authoritarian.[29]

> All the objections that are brought against such a position spring, in the last analysis, from the assumption that the human person is ultimate and as such should properly act as judge of all claims to authority that are made by anyone. But if man is not autonomous . . . then man should subordinate his reason to the Scriptures and seek in the light of it to interpret his experience.[30]

Van Til is opposed to both the rationalist and empiricist theories of knowledge. He criticizes Descartes for maintaining that man has knowledge within himself apart from God. Descartes's position does not recognize that all knowledge of man presupposes revelation. This also holds true for the empiricists. "Though they opposed the innate ideas of Descartes, they were no more ready to recognize the true place of revelation than was Descartes. For them the mind was a *tabula rasa*. But the mind of man as created by God cannot be a *tabula rasa*."[31] Van Til, of course, believes in innate knowledge but not in the Cartesian sense since it has no place for revelation. He sees innate knowledge as having a certain thought content, although it is involuntary and appears most clearly at the intuitional level of man's consciousness.[32] This innate knowledge does not work independently of acquired knowledge. They are correlative to one another.[33] Van Til's approach to epistemology, then, is neither inductive nor deductive, *a priori* nor *a posteriori*, as these terms have been historically understood.

Critics of Van Til have charged him with stripping men of sound intelligence. Clark Pinnock, for example, asserts that Van Til cannot escape the charge of fideism, the view that truth in religion is ultimately based on faith rather than on reasoning or evidence.[34] Pinnock, like most of his critics, misunderstands Van Til's view of the role of reason. Van Til does have a lofty concept of reason but he is careful to make reason function in total dependence on God. He believes reason is a gift given by God to man in order that he might order the revelation of God for himself. But it was never meant to function by itself without relationship to authoritative supernatural revelation.[35]

The law of contradiction is, for Van Til, the expression on a created level of the internal coherence of God's nature. He insists that the Christian should never appeal to this law as something capable of deciding what is possible or impossible. Rather,

> Christians should employ the law of contradiction, whether negatively or positively, as a means by which to systematize the facts of revelation; whether these facts are found in the universe at large or in the Scriptures. The law of contradiction cannot be thought of as operating anywhere except against the background of the nature of God.[36]

This position is set in sharp contrast to the position of the non-Christian that assumes that logic is a timeless, impersonal principle. Van Til points out that on the non-Christian assumptions no intelligible assertions can be made about the world of reality, which is really a world of chance. The non-Christian is bound to fall into self-contradictions since no assertions can be made about chance.[37]

In pointing out the dilemma of the natural man, Van Til does not intend to belittle the intellectual ability of the non-Christian. He wants merely to point out that non-Christian philosophy ought to admit that there is a dimension of reality that is beyond its reach and therefore it ought to listen to the voice of authority. Van Til admits that non-Christians often do have brilliant minds.

> We may greatly admire such a mind for what, in spite of its basic principle and because of the fact that God has released its powers in his restraining grace, it has done. For all that it must not be forgotten that this mind is still, be its name Aristotle, a covenant-breaker in Adam.[38]

However skillful the non-Christian may be in his use of logic, Van Til believes that once revelation is excluded he is bound to arrive at a conclusion contrary to the truth. He cites the example of Aristotle, who knew how to use logic. Aristotle, however, came to the conclusion that God is not the creator of man, knows nothing, and is not a person. "His conclusion was consistent with his premise. His logic was involved in his metaphysics as his metaphysics was involved in his logic."[39] It is Van Til's position therefore that revelation should not be presented for the judgment of the natural man, for every logical activity in which any man engages is in the service of his total vision.[40]

Starting Point and Methodology in Apologetics

The question of where one begins in presenting the claims of Christianity has been much debated since Van Til introduced his "new approach" to apologetics. It is Van Til's firm belief that the question of starting point is largely determined by one's theology. Thus he consistently sets the Reformed faith over against Roman Catholicism and Arminianism.

As a presuppositionalist, Van Til starts with the presupposition of the existence of God. His doctrine of God requires that it be made foundational to everything else as a principle of explanation. "If God is self-sufficient then he alone is self-explanatory. And if he alone is self-explanatory then he must be the final reference point in all human predication. He is like the sun from which all lights on earth derive their power of illumination."[41] The alternative to this, according to Van Til, would be to make man the final reference point, in which case he need not subject his mind to the revelation of God as absolutely authoritative for him. All that would be necessary is for man to refer to God as an expert who has had greater experience than he; but he need not make all thoughts captive to the obedience of Christ.[42]

Van Til maintains, therefore, that only on the presupposition of divine self-sufficiency and man's complete dependence can the difference between the Christian and the non-Christian points of view be clearly pointed out. The most basic difference between the two systems is to be found in their presuppositions. On the assumption of the non-Christian (that is, of human ultimacy), his system is one in which he himself occupies the place that God occupies in Christian theology.[43]

If, as Van Til points out, the Christian and non-Christian start from positions that are mutually exclusive, the question as to whether there is a point of contact for the presentation of the gospel to the non-Christian becomes one of tremendous importance. Stated differently, the issue has to do with whether there is a common point of agreement anywhere in the entire range of human discourse on which Christian and non-Christian can agree and argue their respective cases. If there is no common ground then there is no way of presenting the gospel to the mind and heart of man.

Van Til believes it is impossible to find a common area of knowledge between believers and nonbelievers unless there is agreement between them as to the nature of man himself. He bases this view on the fact that the human mind as the knowing subject makes its contribution to the knowledge it obtains. But since there is no agreement on the nature of man there can be no agreement on a common area of knowledge.[44] Therefore, epistemologically believers and nonbelievers are said to have nothing in common even though metaphysically they have all things in common.[45] Van Til admits that there is a sense in which all men have the facts "in common," since both saint and sinner are face to face with God and the universe of God. But because the sinner is like the man who wears colored glasses everything will be seen in a different light.[46]

Because Van Til refuses to compromise with the nonbeliever, he tells us that the only point of contact is that of head-on collision.[47] This does not mean that he has closed the door to the presentation of the gospel. The metaphysical point of contact is still open; it is to be found within the natural man. He tells us:

> With Calvin I find the point of contact for the presentation of the gospel to non-Christians in the fact that they are made in the image of God and as such have the ineradicable sense of deity within them. Their own consciousness is inherently and exclusively revelational of God to themselves. No one can help knowing God for in knowing himself he knows God. His self-consciousness is totally devoid of content, unless as Calvin puts it at the beginning of his *Institutes*, man knows himself as a creature before God. There are no atheistic men because no man can deny the revelational activity of the true God within him. . . . Every human being is by virtue of his being made in the image of God accessible to God. And as such he is accessible to one who without compromise presses upon him the claims of God.[48]

Van Til's position has not been without criticism. By stating in such an emphatic manner that the Christian and the non-Christian have nothing in common epistemologically, he has been accused of being confused on the question of common knowledge.[49] He is also accused of making unregenerate man totally devoid of knowledge.[50] These criticisms, however, are not valid, for Van Til does recognize the fact that the natural man is not always consistent with his antitheistic principle of interpretation. He constantly introduces the term "in principle" to qualify his statements about the natural man. He says very clearly that as long as the natural man *self-consciously* works from his satanic principle he can have no notion in common with the believer because the unbeliever's epistemology is informed by his ethical hostility to God.[51] Van Til, however, tells us that in the course of history the natural man is *not fully* self-conscious of his own position. Like the prodigal he cannot altogether stifle his father's voice. There is a conflict of notions within him of which he is not fully conscious. The principle of autonomy seeks to suppress his knowledge of God, and the restraining power of God's common grace seeks to suppress the principle of autonomy. This internal semiconscious conflict makes it impossible for him to proceed consistently from the one principle or the other.[52]

It is because of this situation, in which the natural man does not self-consciously work from his principles, that Van Til believes cooperation between believer and unbeliever in the field of science is possible.

> Though all of the natural man's interpretations are from an ultimate
> point of view equally unsatisfactory, there is a sense in which he
> knows something about everything, about God as well as the world,
> and that in this sense he knows more about the world than about
> God. *This distinction is not only true, but important to make.* Many
> non-Christians have been great scientists. Often non-Christians
> have a better knowledge of the things of this world than Christians
> have.[53]

Van Til maintains this position on the ground that the world is not what
non-Christians assume that it is, a world of chance, and is what Christians assume that it is, a world run by the counsel of God. It is for this
reason that "even non-Christians have knowledge."[54]

Van Til's method of presenting Christianity is quite simple. Instead
of trying to prove the truth of Christianity to the natural man, he assumes
its truth at the outset and then challenges the presupposition of the
natural man, pointing out that on his principles nothing is true, and
nothing can be accounted for. Some critics view this approach as being
too dogmatic. Van Til accepts this criticism because he believes God
speaks to man in Scripture with absolute authority.

> A Reformed method of apologetics must seek to vindicate the Re-
> formed life and world view as Christianity come to its own. . . .
> This implies a refusal to grant that any area or aspect of reality, any
> fact or any law of nature or of history can be correctly interpreted
> except it be seen in the light of the main doctrines of Christianity.[55]

It is quite evident that Van Til does not present Christianity apol-
ogetically; neither does he admit that the natural man's interpretation of
life is correct up to a point. Appeal to common facts is meaningless as
far as he is concerned. This sets Van Til's approach at odds with the
traditional method. He points out that the Romanist and Arminian views
of Christianity force them to agree with the natural man in his principles
of methodology to see whether or not Christian theism is true. This is
due to the fact that they view the question of methodology, like that of
starting point, as a neutral matter.[56] The Reformed apologist, however,
cannot agree with the methodology of the natural man, which is tied up
with his interpretation of himself as the ultimate reference point. Therefore, rather than utilizing the natural man's erroneous methodology in
order to establish a point of contact with him for the gospel, the Reformed apologist finds his point of contact in the sense of deity that the
natural man seeks to suppress. The point of contact is in the nature of
a head-on collision—system with system.[57]

Van Til's method of reasoning by presupposition is controlled by
his epistemological and metaphysical principles. The "ontological" Trin-

ity is as basic to his methodology as it is to the doctrines of Christianity. Van Til's conclusion is just as fixed as his starting point. If Bertrand Russell could accuse Thomas Aquinas of possessing little of the true philosophic spirit because he knew his conclusion in advance,[58] Van Til, on this score, could be criticized for having none whatsoever. But the claim to neutrality in the investigation of truth by non-Christian thinkers is a delusion. It is this so-called neutrality, Van Til believes, that is used in an *a priori* manner to exclude the truth of Christianity before the outset of the investigation. Not to assume the truth of Christianity as a fundamental axiom in its defense would, for Van Til, be a denial of the very thing one is seeking to establish. Thus he offers no apology for his method of reasoning by presupposition.

This method of reasoning is seen by Van Til as indirect rather than direct.[59] By this he means that the issue between believers and nonbelievers relative to Christianity cannot be settled by a direct appeal to "facts" or "laws" whose nature and significance are already agreed upon by both parties in the debate. Since there is no agreement on the "facts" or "laws," the question must be settled indirectly.[60] That means the apologist is required to place himself on his opponent's position, assuming its correctness for argument's sake, in order to show him that on such a position the "facts" and the "laws" have no meaning. Conversely, the non-Christian will be asked to place himself upon the Christian position for argument's sake in order to be shown that only upon the Christian basis are "facts" and "laws" intelligible.[61] Van Til's aim is to challenge the knowledge of God that the natural man has but suppresses.

In contrast to his Reformed approach, Van Til sees the traditional method as being unable to challenge the presuppositions of the non-Christian at the outset of the argument. The reason is that "the Romanist and the evangelical are in some measure in agreement with the non-Christian on his presuppositions. They too attribute a measure of autonomy to man."[62] Van Til's conclusion is that the Romanist-evangelical method of defending Christianity has to compromise it while defending it. "As it cannot clearly show the difference between the Christian and non-Christian view of things, so it cannot present any clear-cut reason why the non-Christian should forsake his position."[63]

Even though Van Til is convinced that the non-Christian method is self-destructive, he does believe that the Reformed apologist should show interest in it. He believes the apologist should make a critical analysis of it, and even join his non-Christian friend in the use of it. "But he should do so self-consciously with the purpose of showing that its most consistent application not merely leads away from Christian theism but in leading away from Christian theism leads to destruction of reason as well as science."[64] Van Til's hope is that the non-Christian will see that Christianity is the only position that gives human reason a field for successful operation and a method of true progress in knowledge.[65]

From this one may be tempted to conclude that Van Til believes non-Christians cannot discover truth by the methods they employ, but that would be incorrect. He believes that because non-Christians are never able to employ their own methods consistently[66] they can discover truth. However, this is a discovery made

> in terms of principles that are borrowed wittingly or unwittingly from Christianity. The fact of science and its progress is inexplicable except upon the presupposition that the world is made and controlled by God through Christ and that man is made and renewed in the image of God through Christ.[67]

Throughout his career Van Til has been very critical of "the Arminian method" that has more or less characterized Protestant apologetics since the time of Bishop Joseph Butler. He believes Arminianism offers to the natural man a Christian theology with foreign elements in that it sees man as having ultimate ability to accept or reject salvation. "God has to await the election returns to see whether he is chosen as God or set aside."[68] This, Van Til believes, places the Arminian at the mercy of the natural man. For if the natural man is consistent he will tell the Arminian that "a little autonomy involves absolute autonomy, and a little reality set free from the plan of God involves all reality set free from the plan of God. After that the reduction process is simply a matter of time."[69] It should be noted here that what Van Til is criticizing is Arminianism as a system of theology and the method of apologetics employed to fit that system.

In contrast to Arminianism, Van Til believes that only in the Reformed faith can an uncompromising method of apologetics be found. "The Reformed apologist throws down the gauntlet and challenges his opponent to a duel of life and death from the start."[70] He does this because he knows that if the natural man is allowed to interpret any aspect of experience in terms of his principles without destroying the idea of intelligibility, then he has a right to claim that there is no reason why he cannot interpret the whole of experience in terms of his principles.[71] Only through reasoning by presupposition, Van Til believes, can one overcome the self-frustrating situation that the traditional method cannot avoid.

Cornelius Van Til has done a great service to apologetic methodology by seeking to develop a method that is consistent with the great doctrines of the Reformed faith. In his "epistemologically" self-conscious Calvinism he presents a consistent Christianity that effectively challenges any worldview that begins with any presupposition other than the triune God of Scripture. He boldly presents Christianity not as a worldview but as a divine system of truth that alone makes human experience intelligible and meaningful.

Notes: Cornelius Van Til

1. Benjamin B. Warfield, "Apologetics," in *The New Schaff-Herzog Encyclopedia of Religious Knowledge* (Grand Rapids: Baker Book House, 1951), 233.

2. Cornelius Van Til, *Apologetics* (Course syllabus, 1959), 3.

3. Floyd E. Hamilton, *The Basis of Christian Faith* (New York: Harper and Row, 1964), xiv.

4. William White, Jr., *Van Til: Defender of the Faith* (Nashville: Thomas Nelson, 1979), 74.

5. Ibid., 75.

6. Cornelius Van Til, *The Defense of the Faith* (Philadelphia: Presbyterian and Reformed Publishing Company, 1955), 397.

7. Bernard Ramm, *Types of Apologetic Systems* (Wheaton, IL: Van Kampen Press, 1953), 184-85.

8. In E. R. Geehan, ed., *Jerusalem and Athens* (Nutley, NJ: Presbyterian and Reformed Publishing Company, 1971), 349, 391-92.

9. Van Til, *Apologetics*, 3-4.

10. John Frame, *Van Til: The Theologian* (Phillipsburg, NJ: Pilgrim Publishing Company, 1976), 4.

11. Cornelius Van Til, *Why I Believe in God* (Philadelphia: Presbyterian and Reformed Publishing Company, n.d.), 20.

12. Van Til, *Apologetics*, 9.

13. Cornelius Van Til, *Introduction to Systematic Theology* (Course syllabus, 1961), 199.

14. Ibid., 198.

15. Van Til, *The Defense of the Faith*, 197.

16. Ibid., 254.

17. Van Til, *Apologetics*, 8.

18. Van Til, *The Defense of the Faith*, 42-44.

19. Ibid., 50.

20. Ibid., 51-52.

21. Ibid., 56.

22. Ibid.

23. Ibid., 57-58.

24. Ibid., 60.

25. Ibid., 61.

26. Ibid.

27. Ibid., 282-83.

28. Ibid., 125.

29. Ibid.

30. Ibid.

31. Van Til, *An Introduction to Systematic Theology*, 195.

32. Ibid.

33. Ibid., 197.

34. Geehan, ed., *Jerusalem and Athens*, 423.

35. Van Til, *An Introduction to Systematic Theology*, 189.

36. Ibid., 11.

37. Van Til, *The Defense of the Faith*, 143-44.

38. Ibid., 298.

39. Ibid.

40. Cornelius Van Til, *The Case for Calvinism* (Philadelphia: Presbyterian and Reformed Publishing Company, 1955), 137.

41. Cornelius Van Til, *A Christian Theory of Knowledge* (Course syllabus, 1954), 2.

42. Ibid.

43. Ibid., 4.

44. Van Til, *The Defense of the Faith*, 84.

45. Ibid., 260.

46. In B. B. Warfield, *The Inspiration and Authority of the Bible* (Philadelphia: Presbyterian and Reformed Publishing Company, 1948), 20.

47. Cornelius Van Til, *The Intellectual Challenge of the Gospel* (Phillipsburg, NJ: Lewis J. Grotennis, 1963), 19.

48. Van Til, *The Defense of the Faith*, 257.

49. Gordon H. Clark, "Apologetics," in *Contemporary Evangelical Thought*, ed. Carl F. H. Henry (New York: Channel Press, 1957), 155.

50. Ibid., 156.

51. Van Til, *The Defense of the Faith*, 189-90.

52. Ibid., 190.

53. Ibid., 286.

54. Ibid.

55. Ibid., 113.

56. Ibid., 113-14.

57. Ibid., 115-16.

58. Bertrand Russell, *A History of Western Philosophy* (New York: Simon and Schuster, 1945), 463.

59. Van Til, *Defense of the Faith*, 117.

60. Ibid.

61. Ibid., 117-18.

62. Van Til, *A Christian Theory of Knowledge*, 6.

63. Ibid.

64. Van Til, *The Defense of the Faith*, 119.

65. Ibid.

66. Ibid., 120.

67. Van Til, *The Case for Calvinism*, 106-07.

68. Van Til, *The Defense of the Faith*, 128-29.

69. Ibid., 129.

70. Ibid., 130.

71. Ibid., 198.

1

THE SOUTHERN TRADITION

MORTON SMITH

THERE are several distinctively southern developments of Reformed thought in America. The Reformed faith is found primarily in the mainline Presbyterian Church, though it should be recognized that other branches of the Church in the South have held to the Reformed Faith to a greater or lesser degree. The Associate Reformed Presbyterian Church, for example, still maintains the Reformed faith as set forth in the Westminster standards. The Cumberland Presbyterians have rejected the doctrines of full predestination, and thus hold only a corrupted form of them. Various Baptist groups hold to elements of the Reformed faith. Taking Warfield's basic premise, that all true Christians hold to Reformed faith wherever they are true to the Word, one could also say that all evangelical churches in the South hold elements of the Reformed faith.

The South was greatly affected by the revival movements of the past two centuries. One of the results of these revival movements was the development of the common consensus on the Christian religion that marked the "Bible Belt." The basic elements of this consensus are an acceptance of the Bible as God's Holy Word, the recognition of our sinful and lost condition, and the conviction that the only way of salvation is to be found in Christ, who is to be received by faith. Insofar as these are all points that the Reformed faith teaches, it may be said that this much of the faith is held by the vast majority of all evangelical churches in the South. This same revivalism, on the other hand, with its strong emphasis on human ability to respond to gospel invitations, tended to minimize or even deny the Reformed distinctives, such as the doctrines of election, definite atonement, and efficacious grace.

Presbyterianism in the Colonial Period

Because the main developments in Reformed thought occurred in the Presbyterian Church, we shall concentrate on this church. The history of Presbyterianism in the South extends back to the first permanent settlement in Virginia in 1607. Ernest Trice Thompson in his *Presbyterians in the South* indicates that during the Colonial period there was no "South," but three different societies in the southern colonies: the Chesapeake society, based on tobacco; the Carolina society, built on rice and indigo; and finally the Back Country, still in the process of formation at the time of the Revolution.[1]

The Chesapeake society was the oldest. The Virginia Company's charter prescribed that "the word and services of God be preached, planted and used according to the rites and doctrines of the Church of England." The control of the Company was in the hands of the Puritans until the revocation of the charter in 1624. With the assumption of royal control of the colony in 1624, an act of conformity was passed. During the 1640s, despite Puritan control of Parliament in England, Governor William Berkeley continued to enforce conformity to the Church of England. This resulted in the departure of a number of colonists to Maryland at the invitation of Governor William Stone. They settled in Anne Arundel, Charles, and Prince George counties, near the present city of Annapolis. It is of interest that the ancestors of B. B. Warfield, one of America's greatest Presbyterian theologians, came to this region during this time.

During the period of the Commonwealth in England, the Puritans of Virginia were unmolested. A number of Scottish settlers arrived during the seventeenth century and settled along the Elizabeth River, near present-day Norfolk. Others settled along the Rappahannock, James, and Potomac Rivers.

Francis Makemie's main labors were on the eastern shore of Virginia and Maryland. He is sometimes known as the father of American Presbyterianism because of his leadership in organizing the first presbytery in the colonies. This was the Presbytery of Philadelphia, founded in 1705 or 1706. It had a very small beginning. There were four ministers from Maryland, two from Delaware, and one from Philadelphia.

Further South, there was a settlement of Presbyterians around Charleston, South Carolina, which had no relationship with the Presbytery of Philadelphia. The earliest records of Reformed worship in that area are of the French Huguenots. The last will and testament of a certain Caesar Mozé reveals that there must have been a French church in the Charleston area as early as 1687. There were also a goodly number of Scots, Dutch, and New England Puritans in South Carolina. An independent church, sometimes called Presbyterian, was formed in Charleston about 1690. It was composed of various peoples: French, Scots, Scotch-Irish, and New Englanders. A whole colony of New Englanders moved to South Carolina to found a Congregational church at Dorchester in

1696. Between 1752 and 1771 much of this group transplanted itself to Liberty County, Georgia, and established Midway Church there. From this Congregational church a large number of young men were fed into the ministry of various denominations. The Presbyterians received some 30, including Thomas Goulding, first professor at Columbia Seminary, and Daniel Baker, the great Presbyterian evangelist to the old Southwest. An independent Scottish Church was established in Savannah, Georgia, which still exists as the Independent Presbyterian Church of Savannah. Its grant of land from George II states that it is to be used for such "as are or shall be professors of the Doctrines of the Church of Scotland, agreeable to the Confession of Faith. . . ."[2]

An independent presbytery developed in the Charleston area, which George Howe, historian of the Presbyterian Church in South Carolina to 1850, dates from 1728. This presbytery required subscription to the *Westminster Confession of Faith*, as indicated in correspondence regarding the Rev. Josiah Smith, who was excluded in 1730 because of his refusal to subscribe. This presbytery passed out of existence at the time of the Revolution.

The independence of spirit reflected in the Charleston-Savannah area has been characteristic of much southern thought. No doubt it was forced on the early Presbyterians of this southern region simply by their distance from the rest of the American Presbyterians, but it was to leave a mark on the South Carolina Presbyterian mind. The people of this same area disagreed with their brethren in 1837-38 and formed the Independent Presbyterian denomination, which went its own way until the War between the States overshadowed their differences and brought about a union with other Southern Presbyterians.

The mainline Synod of the Presbyterian Church in 1729 adopted the *Westminster Confession* and *Catechisms* as the confession of faith of the Synod. Having thus declared herself, the Church might be assumed to have embarked on smooth sailing, but such was not the case. A controversy arose that was to divide the Church in 1741 between the Old Side Synod of Philadelphia and what later became the New Side Synod of New York. This division occurred in part as a result of the great revivals of George Whitefield and his followers and the development of the "log colleges" and academies for the training of ministers. The New Side, which espoused the revivals and the use of the academies, planted a number of churches in Virginia.

The Blairs maintained an Academy at Fagg's Manor, Chester County, Pennsylvania, at which Samuel Davies was to be educated. Davies may properly be called the "Father of Southern Presbyterianism" since his labors brought about the establishment of the Mother Presbytery of the South, namely, Hanover Presbytery. He labored off and on in Virginia from 1747 to 1759, and convened the first meeting of the Presbytery of Hanover on December 3, 1755, at the direction of the Synod of New York. The effects of his ministry were felt over all of Virginia and North Carolina. He held the *Westminster Confession* and *Catechisms* in the highest esteem. It was his regular practice to teach the *Shorter Catechism* to all of his members, and to have it recited at the worship service on Sunday.

William Henry Foote, writing a century later, in 1850, speaks of John Robinson and Samuel Davies and of their teachers, the Tennents and the Blairs, as laying a foundation that "had a controlling influence over Virginia Presbyterians in creed and practice" to his day. He says:

> From the time of these men, the Virginia ministers and people have believed in awakenings,—in spiritual exercises in religion,—in the power of godliness in men's hearts and lives. From deep conviction they have been believers in the depravity of human nature,—the sovereignty of God,—original sin,—and the absolute necessity of the new birth. Hoping for justification by the righteousness of Christ made theirs by faith, believing it would be safe to appear in it, in the judgment to come, ministers and people rejoiced in the unsearchable riches of Christ, through trials and difficulties that would make ordinary spirits tremble and quit the field. By the help of God they have left us a good report.[3]

In 1746 John Blair organized churches at North Mountain, New Providence, Timber Ridge, and the Fork of the James; these became the nucleus of Lexington Presbytery. It was out of the New Providence and Timber Ridge Churches that Liberty Hall Academy, the predecessor of Washington College (now Washington and Lee University), was to come. William Graham was the first teacher at the academy. He taught Archibald Alexander, the founding professor of Princeton Seminary. Others who came from this school were Moses Hoge, John Holt Rice, and George Addison Baxter. Hoge was the first professor of theology, appointed by the Synod of Virginia. Rice succeeded him, and founded Union Seminary. Baxter was professor of theology there at the time of the Old School–New School division of 1837.

Despite the fact that the Presbyterian Church of the South was marked with the revivalism of the New Side, there was a failure to follow up the gains of the first awakening. One of the major problems lay in the requirement of the Presbyterian Church for a highly educated ministry. There was a dearth of institutions in the South for such preparation. The Baptists and Methodists, on the other hand, had no such requirement. They used the itinerant system and the revivalism of Whitefield to reach the masses, and thus many who otherwise would have been Presbyterians were taken over into these groups. Even as

Presbyterians became established in the Southland and set up schools and academies, they were not able to keep pace with the demand for ministers during this period. It is hard to see how it would have been possible to have met the demands of the day with the limited resources that were available. Whether a plan could have been worked out and executed to meet the needs or not, it must be admitted that the Presbyterians failed to work out such a plan.

Presbyterianism After the Revolution

The period of the Revolution and following was marked by skepticism and widespread immorality. Especially was this true on the frontier. God graciously sent a revival of religion during this era, however. As early as 1787 an awakening began at Hampden-Sydney College in Prince Edward County, Virginia, that was to affect Presbyterianism for future generations because of those brought under its influence. It was a movement that enjoyed the participation of the President of the College, John Blair Smith. It spread to the sister institution of the Presbyterians across the Blue Ridge, Liberty Hall Academy, where William Graham participated in it. Through these two institutions the future leadership of the Presbyterian Church was affected. Archibald Alexander gave his heart to Christ under its influence. This young man was to become one of the country's greatest theologians. He received his theological education from William Graham. In 1812 he was called by the General Assembly to found Princeton Seminary. He was to serve there until his death in 1851. Charles Hodge was one of his students and became his colleague on the faculty. He taught a theology that was to become known as "Princeton Theology." Herman Bavinck described this theology thus: "The so-called Princeton Theology is chiefly a reproduction of the Calvinism of the seventeenth century, as it is formulated in the *Westminster Confession* and the *Consensus Helveticus*, and especially elucidated by F. Turretin in his *Theologia Elenctica*."[4] One may well question whether it should be called "Princeton" since it was taken from Virginia to Princeton by Alexander. Bavinck is correct in identifying this theology with that of Turretin. His work was used as the textbook on theology at both Princeton and Union Seminaries prior to the publication of Hodge's *Systematic Theology* at Princeton and Dabney's *Lectures in Systematic Theology* at Union.

Others to be affected by the revival in Virginia were Moses Hoge, John Holt Rice, George Addison Baxter, and Drury Lacy, all of whom helped to shape the theology of Virginia Presbyterianism. Moses Hoge was the President of Hampden-Sydney and the first officially appointed teacher of theology of the Synod of Virginia. John Holt Rice was to become the founder of Union Theological Seminary, and George Addison Baxter to succeed him there as Professor of Theology. Through these men the following generations received their training in the same sort of Presbyterianism that Alexander had carried to Princeton from Virginia. The affinity of Union and Princeton can be seen in a letter written by Rice to Alexander concerning his own hopes for his newly formed seminary:

> If, however, a Seminary can be established in the South, many will frequent it, who will not go to the North. . . . But my plan is, if we can succeed here, to take Princeton as our model, to hold constant correspondence with that great and most valuable institution, to get the most promising of our young men to finish off at Princeton; and, in a word, as far as possible, make this a sort of branch of that, so as to have your spirit diffused through us, and do all that can be done to bind the different parts of the Church together.[5]

That such a close relationship continued to exist is a matter of historical record. It may be seen in a number of ways. For one thing, both of these institutions were associated with the Old School branch of the Church in 1837 and following. Robert L. Dabney of Union Seminary received a call to Princeton in 1860. Again in 1915 Union Seminary sought to obtain the services of J. Gresham Machen of Princeton in New Testament. As recently as 1930-1940 Union Seminary had a Systematic Theology professor, James Porter Smith, who taught the same theology as that set forth at Princeton. The testimony of Smith's brother-in-law, the Rev. Gaston Boyle, is to this effect: "I am positive that he believed and taught the system of theology taught by Hodge and Dabney, including their beliefs concerning election, predestination and the inspiration of the Scriptures."[6] Thus the same theology that was taken by Alexander from Virginia and planted at Princeton continued to be the theology both of Princeton Seminary and of Union Seminary in Virginia for at least a century.

The Hampden-Sydney revival was to have far-reaching effects on the frontier, for through it James McGready was influenced to enter into evangelistic efforts in North Carolina. Thus the revival spread to Guilford and Orange Counties in 1791. McGready had a number of other ministers associated with him in his revival efforts, and moved into Kentucky. In 1798 McGready drew up a covenant with others to pray for one year for a revival. In answer to their prayer the revival began with the semi-annual sacramental service celebrated in July 1799 at Red River. The following year saw an increase of the revival in Cumberland County. McGready initiated the camp meeting that was to become characteristic of the Great Revival. He invited people to come prepared to camp for a sacramental season at Gasper River.

The Great Revival was a mixed blessing. On the one hand, many were brought to confess Christ as Savior. On the other hand, it led to the excesses for which the Kentucky revivals became known, namely, jerking, rolling, running, dancing, and barking. Not all the ministers countenanced such exercises, though some encouraged them and thus encouraged confusion. A worse side-effect of the revivals was the fact that there arose an uneducated ministry in Kentucky that, because of lack of training in the Scriptures and the standards of the church, began preaching and teaching something less than the full gospel of sovereign grace. A number of young men were licensed or ordained in the newly formed Cumberland Presbytery without having to subscribe to the *Confession of Faith*, except so far as they believed it to agree with the Word of God. Some rejected in particular the "alleged fatalism" of the Confession, which they thought the doctrines of predestination and reprobation implied. When, in response to complaint, the Synod of Kentucky investigated the irregularities and called for those licensed and ordained under such procedure to be reexamined, they refused to obey. The following year the Synod dissolved the Presbytery. Those who were unwilling to submit to the Synod withdrew and established a new and independent Cumberland Presbytery in 1810. Changes were made in the *Westminster Confession* by this group. Schaff summarizes the effect of their change: "The Cumberland Confession teaches on the one hand conditional election and unlimited atonement, and on the other, the final perseverance of the saints. It is an eclectic compromise between Calvinism and Arminianism; it is half Calvinistic and half Arminian, and makes no attempt to harmonize these antagonistic elements."[7]

In addition to the Cumberland Schism of 1810 there was another schism in the Upper Kentucky region led by Barton Stone. This movement was particularly anticonfessional. It arose because of the objection by more orthodox Presbyterians to the Arminianism of some of the revivalists. They in turn assumed that the creedal subscription of Presbyterianism was antievangelistic, and renounced creedal subscription. There was first an attempt to form an independent Presbytery of Springfield, which would be a part of the Presbyterian Church but not under the Synod of Kentucky. This Presbytery lasted just nine months during 1803-04. Some of its members were drawn away into the Shaker groups, while Barton Stone, rejecting all denominationalism, founded the so-called "Christian Church." In 1832 this body was to become associated with the group started by Thomas and Alexander Campbell under the name "Disciples of Christ." This movement continues in the South under the name "The Church of Christ" as well as the Christian Church. Sad to say, the "Church of Christ" has departed from the doctrine of justification by faith alone of the Protestant Reformation. They hold to a faith-plus-works doctrine, including the necessity of water baptism for salvation.

Despite the loss of the Cumberland and Disciples groups and the confusion caused by the excesses of the Great Revival, this movement did greatly affect the moral life of the country. Hays says, "Religion, from being a mere matter of contempt on the part of public men, became an essential and influential part of the general public sentiment of the Country."[8]

Generally speaking, only a few Presbyterian ministers were involved in these reactions to the full Calvinism of the Reformed faith. One of the basic problems in both the Cumberland and Disciples divisions was a lack of proper education of the revivalists and ministers ordained in Kentucky. This serves to confirm the historic position of the Presbyterian Church of insisting on a well-educated ministry, for it is all too easy to deviate from the full counsel of God if one has not been properly trained in handling the Word of Truth.

While the South was faced with the deviations brought on by revivalism, the Presbyterian Church in the North was involved in a plan to settle the newly opened Middle West that allowed New England Congregationalists to enter the Presbyterian Church without subscribing to the Westminster standards. Hopkinsian theology was on the rise in New England at this time. This meant that many of the Congregationalists who joined the Presbyterian Church came with a theology that was not Reformed. This became known as New School Theology.

By and large the Presbyterian Church in the South was not affected by New School Theology. There was a consciousness in the South of the fact that there was a difference between the Church North and South. This gave rise to the concept of "our Southern Zion" as early as the 1820s. The southern mind-set of simple trust in the Bible tended to cause a reaction against theological debate on matters that were not as clear as the basic evangelical tenets. The South remained generally aloof from the Old School–New School controversy. It was only with the clear deviation by the 1836 Assembly from the historic Reformed faith that Southerners became aroused.

Thompson says: "The Southern presbyteries, holding the balance of power in the Assembly, were generally in favor of ecclesiastical boards rather than the independent and co-operative Societies, and were overwhelmingly staunch in their adherence to the Westminster Standards and thus opposed to the New School 'heresies.' "[9]

Only in east Tennessee, where there was a breakdown of church discipline, was a college established where the Hopkinsian errors were taught. It is difficult to understand the failure of the Church to exercise discipline here, except that the founder of Abingdon Presbytery and the president of Greeneville College was the one who introduced these views. There was a natural hesitancy on the part of men more recently come to the presbytery and of some who had been educated under Mr. Balch to bring a charge against him. Also, the seriousness of Hopkinsian views was not fully recognized, especially in the light of the fact that Balch affirmed his belief in the *Confession* whenever brought before a court. A basic lesson to be learned is that personalities or position should not be allowed to prevent the proper exercise of discipline. Had the 1837 division ñot come when it did, a great deal more of the New School theology might have developed in the South than actually did develop.

It is interesting to observe that the few Southern Presbyterians who united with the New School Assembly did so for other than doctrinal reasons. Only in Tennessee, where, as we have already seen, the New School theology had a foothold, was there a majority of New School adherents. Even here it was not really because of theological agreement with the New School that these adhered to the New School Assembly. Rather, this may be accounted for by the influence of Hezekiah Balch, and by the fact that this area had been largely dependent on the American Home Missionary Society and the American Educational Society, both based in New England, for financial support. J. E. Alexander, historian of the Synod, says, "Though doctrinal differences constituted one of the causes of the division, it was evidently only a small portion of the Presbyterian ministers of the New School Body who held the doctrines of the New Divinity, at least in their full extent. The great majority of them were no doubt strictly orthodox and were influenced by the other considerations already mentioned."[10] The record of the Synod states the grounds as "the unconstitutional and unrighteous acts" of the two Reforming Assemblies, without mentioning doctrinal grounds.

In most of the other Synods minorities went independent, as in the case of the minority of the Presbytery of Charleston-Union and the Presbytery of Etowah in Georgia, which joined the New School Church. (The Charleston-Union Presbytery rejoined the Old School in 1852, and the Etowah Presbytery disappeared a few years after its formation.) In general, these defections from the Old School Church were not on theological grounds. The fear that the New School group would eventually denounce slavery as unchristian was appealed to by some as a ground for going with the Old School. On the other hand, the fear of centralization of power as represented by the 1837 exscinding action of the General Assembly was the motivation for some in Mississippi and South Carolina to withdraw from the Old School Assembly. Many felt that the actions of the 1837 Assembly had been unconstitutional, and thus allied themselves with the New School. Thompson concludes that "New School support in the South, with the possible exception of eastern Tennessee, was based overwhelmingly on opposition to what seemed unauthorized and unconstitutional authority exercised by the two Reforming Assemblies."[11]

Distinctive Theological Emphases

The Southern Presbyterian Church was essentially Old School in character. It is well to see what was peculiar to this brand of Presbyterianism. First, it was marked by strict subscription to the Westminster standards as the confession and constitution of the Church. Being thus committed to the Westminster standards, it was a Calvinistic church, embracing all of the tenets that go under that name.

The historic Puritan and Scottish doctrine of the sole headship of Christ over his church was maintained. Out of this came the high view of the church, that it is a positive institution of Christ and must do only what he teaches it to do in his Word. Thornwell of South Carolina was to carry out this principle with the greatest consistency, opposing at points such men as Charles Hodge of Princeton on certain matters of polity. Though Thornwell did not carry the day in the undivided church, his views were to prevail in the Southern Church after 1861.

Thornwell maintained that the church "is a positive institution, and therefore must show a definite warrant for everything that she does. It is not enough that her measures are not condemned, they must be sanctioned, positively sanctioned, by the power which ordains her, or they are null and void."[12] He opposed the use of boards to carry out the work of the church. Rather, the church courts ought to handle this directly. Instead of an independent, or semi-independent, board carrying on the work of missions the General Assembly should carry this work on through committees directly responsible to the Assembly. This position was adopted by the Southern Presbyterian Church, and though it abandoned it in the 1940s, the Presbyterian Church in America, which separated from the Southern Church in 1973, has returned to it.

A distinctively southern view of the office of the ruling elder arose. Following the 1837-38 division the practice of having the ruling elder lay hands on a man being ordained to the office of the ministry began in Kentucky. The General Assembly of 1843 declared that "neither the Constitution nor the practice of our Church authorizes Ruling Elders to impose hands in the ordination of ministers."[13] Drs. R. J. Breckinridge and J. H. Thornwell took issue with this double ruling of the Assembly. They maintained that the New Testament elder included both teaching and ruling elders, that as true elders they were an integral element of a presbytery and thus necessary to its regular constitution, and that they had a right to participate in all of the actions of presbytery including all steps to the ordination of ministers. The Assembly, however, in 1844 followed Hodge in denying the necessity of ruling elders in presbytery, and their right to participate in the ordination of ministers.With the division of 1861 the view of Thornwell became the accepted view of the Southern Presbyterian Church and continues to be one of the distinctives of this Church.[14] This has also been carried over into the Presbyterian Church in America.

Another southern development in church polity was the idea that the office of deacon is to handle all the temporal affairs of the church. This was first enunciated by Thomas Smythe of Charleston, South Carolina. The idea of systematic benevolences was also developed during this period, and had the support of such Southerners as Stuart Robinson and J. H. Thornwell. Generally speaking, the southern leaders of this period opposed instrumental music and liturgical elements in the worship service. This, of course, grows out of the *jure divino* view of church polity and worship that was held in the South.

This same view of the church was applied to the burning social issue of slavery:

> The Church of Christ is a spiritual body, whose jurisdiction extends only to the religious faith and moral conduct of her members. She cannot legislate where Christ has not legislated, nor make terms of membership which He has not made. . . .
>
> Since Christ and his inspired Apostles did not make the holding of slaves a bar to communion, we, as a court of Christ, have no authority to do so; since they did not attempt to remove it from the Church by legislation, we have no authority to legislate on the subject.[15]

This view of the church, which prevented the Assembly from legislating on the issue of slavery, kept the Old School body intact until 1861. Only then, under the heat of the circumstances of war, did the Assembly break with this principle and pass the Gardiner Spring Resolution. This resolution in effect decided the political issue between the North and South, and virtually exscinded all Southern Presbyterians from the Church. It said:

> Resolved, . . . that this General Assembly . . . do hereby acknowledge and declare our obligations to promote and perpetuate, so far as in us lies, the integrity of these United States, and to strengthen, uphold, and encourage the Federal Government in the exercise of all its functions under our noble Constitution; and to this Constitution in all its provisions, requirements, and principles, we profess our unabated loyalty. . . .[16]

Charles Hodge of Princeton, with 57 others, protested this action of the Assembly. This protest states in part: "The General Assembly in thus deciding a political question, and in making that decision practically a condition of membership to the Church, has, in our judgment, violated the Constitution of the Church, and usurped the prerogative of its Divine Master."[17]

B. M. Palmer, first Moderator of the Southern Assembly, declared:

This question, lying wholly within the domain of politics, the General Assembly assumed the right to determine; so that, even if not ejected by what was equivalent to an act of expulsion, the Southern Presbyteries were compelled to separate themselves, in order to preserve the crown rights of the Redeemer and the spiritual independence of His kingdom and the Church. . . .[18]

The Presbyteries of the South dissolved their connection with the General Assembly of the Presbyterian Church in the United States of America. A total of 47 Presbyteries, making up 10 Synods, thus withdrew. On the 4th of December, 1861, at the First Presbyterian Church of Augusta, Georgia, the commissioners from these Presbyteries met and constituted the first General Assembly of the Presbyterian Church in the Confederate States of America. This meeting was opened with a stirring sermon on the Kingship of Christ over His Church by B. M. Palmer, pastor of the First Presbyterian Church of New Orleans. After adopting its official name, the Assembly then formally adopted the Westminster standards as its constitution, thus continuing the American Presbyterian tradition of commitment to these doctrinal standards. That the Southern Presbyterian Church saw itself as a distinctively Old School Presbyterian Church may be seen in the fact that she spoke out most clearly against the way in which the Old and New School branches of the Northern church reunited in 1869, which she judged to be a total abandonment of the Old School heritage.[19]

The Southern Presbyterian Church was marked by certain distinctive characteristics during the first 75 years of its life. They were a commitment to the Bible as the inspired and infallible Word of God; a thoroughgoing and enthusiastic Calvinism, regarded as a part of the gospel that was to be preached to the people; and a view of the mission of the church as spiritual, which was maintained both in theory and in practice. She developed an ecclesiastical polity that was distinguished for its constitutionality, particularly as seen in the complete parity of the ruling elders with the teaching elders, the carefully defined spheres and rights of the several courts, and its opposition to centralism. She stood for a strict construction of and adherence to the Westminster standards both in theory and in practice.

The newborn Church was especially interested in missions as the supreme work of the church. Among the resolutions of that first Assembly regarding missions is this classic statement regarding the place of missionary work in the life of the church:

> Finally, the General Assembly desires distinctly and deliberately to inscribe on our church's banner, as she now unfurls it to the world, in immediate connection with the headship of our Lord, his last command: "Go ye into all the world and preach the gospel to every creature"; regarding this as the great end of her organization, and obedience to it as the indispensable condition of her Lord's promised presence, and as one great comprehensive object, a proper conception of whose vast magnitude and grandeur is the only thing which, in connection with the love of Christ, can ever sufficiently arouse her energies and develop her resources so as to cause her to carry on, with the vigor and efficiency which true fealty to her Lord demands, those other agencies necessary to her internal growth and home prosperity.[20]

A particular development in Southern Presbyterian theological thought should be noted. It was the development of the doctrine of adoption as a separate *locus* in the Columbia Seminary school of thought. Hodge and Dabney had followed Turretin and dealt with adoption in connection with justification. The Columbia theologians followed the *Confession* and *Catechisms,* and thus developed the doctrine of adoption as a separate *locus.* This line of thinking began with John L. Girardeau of Columbia, and was continued by R. A. Webb, his son-in-law, who taught at Louisville Seminary. He produced a work entitled *The Reformed Doctrine of Adoption,* which was printed after his death.

Prior to the War between the States, the southern way of life allowed time for the development of a deep scholarship. Men such as Alexander, Thornwell, Dabney, Warfield, and Machen were all products of the South. They are among the most distinguished theologians America has produced. After the War, and during the long course of the slow recovery of the South from the cultural upheaval that her defeat brought, relatively few scholars arose from the South. The result is that though the seminaries of the South remained essentially sound up to the 1930s and 1940s, they were not really producing deep thinkers. Orthodoxy began to be looked upon as unscholarly. In the meantime Presbyterians of the North drifted into liberalism. Thus, when Southerners went north for theological training they were exposed to liberalism, even at Princeton after Machen's departure in 1929. These men came back to teach at the southern seminaries. Their appeal to the rising young generation was that scholarship was on the liberal side. The result was a rapid decline of the Southern Presbyterian Church into liberalism. The last

General Assembly controlled by the conservative element in the Southern Presbyterian Church was in 1939. Since that time the orthodox Christian has had a constant struggle to maintain his position in the Southern Presbyterian Church.

Recent Developments

There was a group that saw the necessity of reforming their Church. They developed several different means of reform. First, the *Southern Presbyterian Journal* (now the *Presbyterian Journal*) became a rallying point for conservatives in the Church. The *Journal* had its beginnings in the late 1940s. Unsuccessful efforts were launched by students of Columbia Theological Seminary during the early 1950s to have a liberal professor removed. A number of these men are now in the leadership of the Presbyterian Church in America. Successful efforts were launched to keep some of the presbyteries and synods of the deep South conservative. Belhaven College became a coeducational institution in 1954, and soon began training a stream of pre-ministerial students who became convinced of the Reformed faith and maintained their convictions even though many attended the liberal seminaries of the denomination. A number of these men now constitute a significant element of the ministers of the Presbyterian Church in America. In addition to this, the Pensacola Theological Institute began to bring in Reformed scholars and preachers from all over the world. They trained not only theological students, but also a large number of laymen from across the South.

One of the most encouraging occurrences was the increasing number of conservative young men who were getting advanced degrees and returning to the South as strongly committed and well-trained defenders of the historic faith. Though committed to the basic Reformed faith that they had learned in the South, they brought with them insights from their various schools of study, thus enriching the theological thought of the South.

The outside institution that had the greatest influence on the conservative Southern Presbyterians was Westminster Theological Seminary. There are several reasons for this. One that has already been noted is the affinity that the Southern Presbyterians had with the Old Princeton theology. Westminster was, of course, the successor of Old Princeton. Second, a fair number of Southern Presbyterian ministers were educated at Westminster. The influence of these became particularly evident in the movement toward a new Church, since a number of these individuals became teachers.

In 1964 the foundations of the Reformed Theological Seminary of Jackson, Mississippi, were laid, and this seminary opened its doors in

1966. Though there was no actual formal relationship between Reformed Seminary and Westminster, the original faculty of Reformed Seminary, of which the present writer was a member, viewed it as something of a daughter seminary to Westminster. Several members of that faculty had been trained at Westminster. They certainly felt that the theology they were teaching was the same as that of Westminster, and thus they looked to Westminster for encouragement and aid. Several of the Westminster faculty, including Dr. Cornelius Van Til, visited Reformed Seminary and gave special lectures. The relation seems to have been similar to that which Union Seminary of Virginia had with Princeton in its early history.

Reformed Seminary became one of the primary sources for conservative ministers serving Presbyterianism in the South. At the beginning most of the graduates of the Seminary were placed in the more conservative presbyteries of the Presbyterian Church in the United States. Many of these were to identify with the Presbyterian Church in America when it was founded in 1973. Others remained in the Presbyterian Church in the United States (now merged with the Northern Church to form the PCUSA). Since the founding of the Presbyterian Church in America, the majority of the graduates of the Seminary have entered its ranks as ministers.

Since its founding, Reformed Theological Seminary has become the primary source of Reformed theological developments in the South. In what follows we shall review some of these developments. The Seminary has witnessed an interesting melding of a number of streams of Reformed thought. The majority of the faculty have been drawn out of the Southern Presbyterian background. These have stood largely in the tradition of Thornwell and Dabney. They have sought to maintain the historic Reformed faith as developed in Southern Presbyterianism, coupling a warmhearted evangelism with full commitment to the Reformed faith. One of the early areas of discussion at the Seminary was the question of how evangelism is to be carried out. Many of the students came to the Seminary with evangelistic methods that reflected an Arminian approach to man and not the Reformed view. Efforts were made to encourage men to think through more consistently the implications of the Reformed faith in the area of evangelism. Generally speaking, the Seminary encouraged the Evangelism Explosion methods developed at the Coral Ridge Presbyterian Church, Fort Lauderdale, Florida, to get people involved in personal evangelism. The present writer has written a pamphlet entitled "Reformed Evangelism" that has had a good reception.

A particular area where the influence of Westminster is seen is in the field of apologetics. Westminster Seminary departed from the Old Princeton theology in the study of apologetics as developed under the tutelage of Cornelius Van Til. Had Westminster Seminary not been formed

in 1929 under the leadership of J. Gresham Machen, Dr. Van Til no doubt
would have developed his thinking at Princeton, since he was already
on the faculty there before Westminster began. The apologetics of Dr.
Van Til has come to be known as presuppositional apologetics, as opposed to the traditional evidential apologetics of Old Princeton. American
Presbyterianism in general had uncritically accepted the evidential approach to apologetics in its conflict with the deism of the eighteenth
century. The present writer, who had some of his theological training at
Westminster Seminary, taught both Systematic Theology and Apologetics at Reformed Seminary during its first decade. In theology, he followed the exegetical, biblical theological method of Professor John Murray.
In apologetics he taught the presuppositional approach. A large number
of Reformed graduates are thus committed to this view of theology and
apologetics.

One of the interesting developments that took place at Reformed
Seminary during this period was the brief professorship of Dr. Gregg
Bahnsen in the field of apologetics and ethics. It was during this time
that he published his book *Theonomy in Christian Ethics.* A number of
his students became committed to reconstructionist postmillennialism
and to theonomy. Though Dr. Bahnsen is no longer at Reformed Seminary, the impact of his instruction there is still felt in the South in that
a small number of his followers are now in the ministry of the Presbyterian Church in America. Though the question of whether theonomy
is acceptable in the Presbyterian Church in America has been raised, the
Church has declined to get into this matter. It has indicated that theonomy should not become a test of orthodoxy. Not all have been pleased
with this position, but they have permitted the coexistence in the Presbyterian Church in America of theonomists and nontheonomists.

Two groups of theonomists have left the PCA in order to have what
they consider greater freedom in the propagation of their views. The
first of these is the Westminster Presbyterian Church of Tyler, Texas. This
Church operates a small theological school called Geneva, and produces
a number of publications. Some of this Tyler group have renounced the
time-honored "regulative principle" of worship of the Westminster Catechism of the Presbyterian Church, which states that we are to include
in worship only what the Bible teaches. This group also espouses paedo-
communion.

The other group that left the PCA over theonomy is a small group
of churches headed by the Chalcedon Presbyterian Church of the Atlanta
area. These churches have formed a small Presbyterian denomination
known as the Reformed Presbyterian Church in the United States. This
group has not displayed the same kinds of deviations from historic Pres-

byterianism that the Tyler group has shown. Both groups hold to recon-structionist postmillennialism.

A revival of postmillennialism as an acceptable eschatological view has occurred in Southern Presbyterianism during the past two decades. Though the majority of the ministers in the South hold to amillennialism, there are a large number of pre- and postmillennialists. Not all of the postmillennialists hold to the reconstructionist view of R. J. Rushdoony, but many hold to a more traditional postmillennialism.

Still another stream of thought that has entered Southern Presby-terian circles, largely through Westminster and Reformed Theological Seminaries, is the concept of a Christian world-and-life view. Abraham Kuyper's Stone Lectures on *Calvinism*, delivered at Princeton Theological Seminary in 1898, introduced this broad concept to the American Pres-byterian world. Earlier American Presbyterians had practiced the idea of living their faith out in various areas of life, as may be seen from the fact that many of them were influential in early American political life. In the South, however, there had been something of a drawing back from it, due to a misapplication of Thornwell's doctrine of the spirituality of the church. Many Southern Presbyterians applied this to their per-sonal lives as well as to the church. With the carefully thought-out ideas of Kuyper and his development of "sphere sovereignty" a more balanced view of how we are to view the application of Christian principles to every area of life, and not just to the church, was found. The theonomists, of course, embrace this concept, but so do many others who are not fully identified with theonomy. For example, the Christian Studies Center of Memphis, Tennessee, has been seeking to propagate the Kuyperian world-and-life view for a number of years through publications and lectures. This organization has been established and kept alive through the un-tiring labors of Robert Metcalf, a ruling elder of the Second Presbyterian Church of Memphis. The Christian Studies Center has not met with great success, but is cited here as an illustration of the breadth of Re-formed thought that now exists in the South.

With the recognition of the stranglehold that the liberals had on all of the institutions and agencies of the Presbyterian Church in the United States, and with the beginning of groups departing from that Church, the leadership of the conservatives in the PCUS determined that there should be a separation from that Church in 1973. Generally speaking, an effort was put forth to make this as peaceable as possible. Churches and individuals simply notified their presbyteries of their intention to leave. The first General Assembly of the Presbyterian Church in America was held at Birmingham on December 4, 1973.

This body saw itself as continuing the historic Presbyterian faith that the Southern Presbyterian Church had held during its early years, and which it had in turn received from the Old School Presbyterian Church prior to that. The PCA may be called an Old School Presbyterian Church, holding to the inerrancy of the Scripture in the original autographs, strict subscription to the *Westminster Confession* and *Catechisms*, and to Southern Presbyterian Church polity.

This Church has from its beginning seen as its mission to reach across the whole nation, and not to remain a regional church as the Southern Presbyterian Church had done. In 1982 the Reformed Presbyterian Church, Evangelical Synod joined the PCA, accepting its Southern Presbyterian polity. Thus, this polity is now being practiced across the entire nation in this new and growing Church. The roots of the RPCES went back largely to the Old School segment of the Northern Church. It held to the Old Princeton theology. Thus in this "joining and receiving" the streams of "Southern" and "Princeton" theology again merged.

The Southern Presbyterian Church (PCUS) has united with the Northern Church (UPCUSA) to form the Presbyterian Church in the United States of America. There remain those who are sound in the faith in this Church, but by and large the denomination must be characterized as liberal in persuasion and direction. The distinctives of the earlier Southern Presbyterians have been lost in this body. These distinctives are now carried on in the Presbyterian Church in America, which encompasses both Canada and the United States.

In this essay we have traced some of the distinctive developments of Southern Presbyterian thought on the American church scene. We have seen that there has been a separate development in the past, but we have also noted that in this century a good deal of broadening has taken place. This seems to be in accord with what is presently happening to the South. Increasingly the South is becoming amalgamated with the rest of the country in its thought and culture. One wonders whether there will continue to be a distinctively Southern Presbyterian strand of theology, or whether it will not eventually be merged into the broad stream of Reformed thought found both in America and abroad. Should the Southern distinctives gradually be lost, some of the South's contributions will no doubt become a part of the larger whole, while the South itself will benefit from the many advances in Reformed thought that are taking place in other parts of the Lord's vineyard.

Notes: The Southern Tradition

1. Ernest Trice Thompson, *Presbyterians in the South,* vol. 1, *1607-1861* (Richmond, VA: John Knox Press, 1963), 629.

2. *History of the Independent Church and Sunday School, Savannah, Ga.* (Savannah: George N. Nichols, 1882).

3. William Henry Foote, *Sketches of Virginia: Historical and Biographical* (Philadelphia: n.p., 1850), 1:146.

4. Herman Bavinck, *Gereformeerde Dogmatiek*, 4th ed. (Kampen, J. H. Kok, 1928), 1:177.

5. John Holt Rice, Letter to Archibald Alexander, dated Richmond, March 5th, 1823, in William Maxwell, *A Memoir of the Rev. John H. Rice, D.D.* (Philadelphia and Richmond, VA: n.p., 1835), 233.

6. Letter from Gaston Boyle to Morton H. Smith, November 1961, in Morton Howison Smith, *Studies in Southern Presbyterian Theology* (Amsterdam: Van Campen, 1962), 320.

7. Philip Schaff, *Creeds of Christendom*, 4th ed. (New York: Harper and Brothers, 1919), 1:815. Cf. 3:771-76 for the Cumberland Confession.

8. George P. Hays, *Presbyterians, a Popular Narrative of Their Origin, Progress, and Achievements* (New York: J. A. Hill and Company, 1892), 151.

9. Ibid., 384.

10. *A Brief History of the Synod of Tennessee from 1817 to 1887* (Philadelphia: MacCalla & Company, 1890), 32-33, cited by Thompson, *Presbyterians*, 409.

11. Ibid., 412.

12. James Henry Thornwell, *Collected Writings* (Richmond: Presbyterian Committee of Publication, 1881), 4:210.

13. Cited from *Minutes of the General Assembly (O.S.) 1843*, 183.

14. See Thornwell, *Collected Writings*.

15. *Minutes of the General Assembly (O.S.) 1845*, 16-17.

16. *Minutes of the General Assembly (O.S.) 1861*, 16-17.

17. Ibid., 340.

18. Thomas Carey Johnson, *The Life and Letters of Benjamin Morgan Palmer* (Richmond, VA: n.p., 1906), 502.

19. *Minutes, PCUS, 1870*, 529; also in *Alexander's Digest, 1888*, 451, and in *Digest 1861-1965*, 342.

20. *Minutes PCCSA, 1861*, 17.

2

ROBERT LEWIS DABNEY

DOUGLAS FLOYD KELLY

Robert Lewis Dabney

ROBERT Lewis Dabney was perhaps the greatest, and certainly the most prolific, Southern Presbyterian theologian of nineteenth-century America. Reformed theologians of Europe such as Lecerf, Bavinck, and Barth spoke of Dabney with appreciation and respect. The great Charles Hodge of Princeton so highly regarded Dabney that he repeatedly urged him to join the Princeton faculty in 1860. In later years, A. A. Hodge and W. G. T. Shedd considered Dabney to be the greatest teacher of theology in the United States. B. B. Warfield said: ". . . Dr. Dabney was not only an influential statesman and a powerful ecclesiastical force, not only an acute philosophiser and a profound theologian, but also a devoted Christian—which is best of all."[1]

Yet for all his massive abilities, voluminous writings, and widespread personal prestige, Dabney lived to see his own theological and ecclesiastical influence drastically wane, so that near the end of his life he could sadly say: "I have no audience."[2] From his death in 1898 until the early 1960s, Dabney's work was largely eclipsed in his own denomination, not to mention the wider church. The reasons for his rise to prominence and then his rather drastic decline are found primarily in his theological stance and secondarily in the events and attitudes of his own eventful life and times.

Dabney's Life

While much of Dabney's *Systematic Theology*, for instance, is in the standard Reformed idiom and thus speaks for itself, it would be very difficult—if not impossible—to understand his social, economic, and political philosophy as well as many of his more directly religious essays unless we took into account the cultural and historical context of his life in the Old South. Unlike many theologians who pass their lives in sequestered libraries and classrooms, Dabney, like Abraham Kuyper of Holland, lived much of his life in public positions during tumultuous times.

His biographer, Thomas Cary Johnson, wrote:

> The lives even of most great preachers pass in such quiet that the historian finds little to dwell upon. What he says of one day's labor and achievements may be said of almost every other day. Such was not the life of Dr. Dabney. His life touched so many points in the common history of church and state and touched them in a way so unusual that it is impossible to give an adequate sketch in a few pages.[3]

Dabney was born March 5, 1820, on South Anna River in Louisa County, Virginia, the fourth of six children. His parents, Charles and Elizabeth Dabney, were typical Virginia country gentry. Charles was Colonel of the county militia, as well as a magistrate and member of the county court. He owned a tobacco and grain plantation, two mills, and several slaves, and was an elder in the Presbyterian Church. The older Dabneys had been brought up during times of revival in Virginia (the latter years of the "Second Great Awakening"), and maintained a strict but warmly evangelical household. In this Calvinist home not only were the Bible and Westminster Shorter Catechism taught, but the children "caught" the principles of conservative, decentralized republican forms of government from frequent conversations between their parents and visitors. The Virginia of Washington, Madison, Jefferson, Henry, and Marshall had never ceased to be politically minded and intensely committed to the liberties guaranteed (to the property-holding classes) by constitutional, representative civil government.

In the Dabney home there was a mingling of Calvinist simplicity and Puritan hard work with an element of aristocratic leisure based on the "peculiarly southern" institution of domestic slavery. Dabney grew up deeply loving the life and institutions of his native Virginia and of the larger antebellum South. It was to him the ideal blending of plainness and modesty with the richness of genuine Christian culture. Dabney once wrote an entire letter describing the surprised reaction of a "proud New Yorker" to the unexpected gentility and culture of Richmond society.[4]

Life became much harder for the Dabney family when the father, Charles, died in early middle age in 1833. Robert, then age 13, had to take on a good deal of responsibility for the management of the plantation and the well-being of his brothers and sisters. His letters show that strong cords of mutual affection bound this family together to the last.

In the midst of all his responsibilities, young Robert Dabney received a very competent education for his time and place:

> He received his preparatory training in country schools taught by his brother and other able men. The schedule of studies did not cover many lines, but very thorough work was done in Latin, Greek, Algebra, and Geometry. His zeal led him to ride once a week to get Dr. Thomas Wharey, his mother's pastor, to drill him in Mathematics.
>
> He spent a short time at Hampden-Sydney College; it covered three sessions, as the course then ran . . . (in 1836 and 1837). . . . He finished Mathematics, Physics, Latin and Greek. When he left the college the faculty sent his mother a report and assigned him the most distinguished rank in behavior, and the most distinguished rank in industry. He was the only one of his class so highly ranked.[5]

Toward the end of his time at Hampden-Sydney "the college was visited by a powerful and genuine awakening." Dabney was converted during this revival in September of 1837, and many years later commented that "The most important event of this period to me was my profession of faith in Christ."[6]

Dabney left Hampden-Sydney without completing his course in order to come home and help his mother improve the precarious financial position of their plantation. For about two years Robert, though a slaveholder, worked with his hands quarrying stone, rebuilt one of the family mills, managed the fields, and in addition opened and taught a neighborhood school—all of this at age 18!

Dabney's education was not finished, however,

> . . . because he found a way to enter the University of Virginia at Charlottesville. His uncle, Reuben Lewis, living near the University, had offered to give him board for himself and horse. The University offered fuller courses of study under more distinguished professors. . . . On July 5, 1842, he received his degree of Master of Arts. His study had made him a thinker.[7]

Robert returned to his mother's plantation for two more years of physical work, teaching of classes, and newspaper writing. He did so well as a writer that he was offered a job with one of the largest papers in the state—a forerunner of greater things to come. During this time he managed to save a few hundred dollars; this he was to spend on his subsequent education for the Presbyterian ministry.

> In November, 1844, he entered Union Seminary at Hampden-Sydney, Va. This institution was under a cloud of depression. There were only three professors: Dr. Samuel B. Wilson was Professor of Systematic and Polemic Theology, Dr. Samuel L. Graham of Eccle-

siastical History, Dr. Francis R. Sampson of Oriental Literature.
There were only eighteen students. Some from Virginia and North
Carolina were at Columbia and Princeton. Mr. Dabney chose the
smaller Seminary, for he believed in building up home institutions.[8]

By this time American Presbyterianism had divided into two major
streams: New School and Old School. New School Presbyterianism,
largely—though not entirely—in the North, was more open to the spirit
of the age, and accommodated itself theologically to some aspects of
Arminianism and other elements of post-Enlightenment thought. The
Old School, which comprised a slight majority in the North and a vast
majority in the South, cordially and strictly held to the robust Calvinism
of the Westminster standards, and consciously saw itself as challenging
the errors of the age. The Presbyterian Church in America had split over
this very issue in 1837. Union Seminary, like its more illustrious northern
sister, Princeton Seminary, was solidly in the Old School camp.

Perhaps the greatest single influence on young Dabney at Union
was the fine scholar and pious saint, Dr. Francis R. Sampson. One of
Dabney's first major writings was to be the biography of Sampson in
1854. "In mature old age Dr. Dabney wrote: 'If I ever had any intellectual
growth and vigor, I owed it to three things—first, the Master of Arts'
Course in the University of Virginia; second, to Dr. F. R. Sampson, and
third, to my subsequent mastery of Turretin.' "[9]

In the summer of 1846 Dabney finished his studies at Union and
was licensed by West Hanover Presbytery. His Latin thesis was "Quo-
modo Homo Justificatus Sit?" and his Greek exegesis on Hebrews 6:4-6.
Although Dabney was a tall, large-framed man, his health at this stage
was rather poor and his life was not expected to be a long one. Thus the
Presbytery assigned him to three small, remote congregations as a home
missionary in his native Louisa County. In spite of his poor health, his
ministrations here were very faithful and warmly appreciated.

In 1847 Dabney was called to be pastor of the Tinkling Spring
Church in Augusta County, near Staunton, Virginia. He had an effective
ministry here among the (at times) headstrong Scotch-Irish for over six
years. During this time of hard study, continual pastoral work, and diligent exegetical preaching attended by deep and agonizing prayer, many
blessings entered into the life of pastor and congregation. Dabney was
the architect for a new church building (which still stands); he met Miss
Lavinia Morrison, daughter of a neighboring minister, whom he loved
at first sight and soon married; and to crown it all a revival broke out
in the church in 1850, during which over 30 persons were brought to
Christ.

Dabney demonstrated his practical bent and many-sided abilities by building his own house out of stone that he himself had cut. "He was a good practical farmer, a good teacher, a good pastor, a capital member of a military staff. He was a skillful mechanic and furniture maker. . . . He bound books well, drew maps and plans for buildings."[10]

In 1853, at the age of 33, Dabney was called to the Chair of Ecclesiastical History and Polity at Union Seminary in Hampden-Sydney. For the next thirty years this was to be the scene of his major life's work as teacher, writer, churchman, statesman, soldier, and—above all—theologian.

> With characteristic energy he prepared a course of study that made young men master the facts and principles of history. He impressed the importance of acquiring good habits of study, as a preparation for life. He made such a reputation that in a few years he was invited to teach at Princeton, but he declined it.
>
> He spent his vacations in traveling through Virginia and North Carolina seeking students, funds and the support of presbyteries and congregations. By 1859 the number of students had increased to fifty-nine, new professors had been secured. . . . Never again was the Seminary considered as a liability, but a great asset.
>
> He was called to the presidency of Hampden-Sydney College in 1858, to the Fifth Avenue Church of New York in 1860, and also to Princeton in 1860, but he remained at Union.[11]

In 1859 Dabney was transferred to the Chair of Theology, which he undertook with enthusiasm, immense competence, and fresh vitality. Dabney believed that Systematic Theology must be based fairly and squarely upon an exegesis of the Scriptures. In an article in 1856, Dabney described the work of both professors and students at Union Seminary:

> . . . each professor shall be required to expound some portion of the original Scriptures. This is important to the teacher himself, that he may be brought into immediate contact with the Word of God. . . . Exegetical study is the great means for cultivating a right literary spirit in the theologian.[12]
>
> The student begins with the great fact that the Word of God (in the originals) is the grand repository of all the *data* of the science of divinity. . . . the Professor of Systematic and Pastoral Theology . . . teaches him, with the Bible still in his hand to methodize and understand the mutual relations of the Scripture facts and doctrines that they may assume in his mind the strength of *a system*.[13]

Dabney taught by means of dialogue. Two days before he lectured on a subject he wrote on the board a series of questions for his students. (Many of these questions are preserved at the beginning of each of the chapters in his *Systematic Theology*.) Along with the questions Dabney gave the students specific readings in various theologians—especially

Turretin in Latin and Dick in English. The class had to answer the questions in writing, which Dabney corrected; then he lectured on the subject.

During these years Dabney also served as copastor of the College Church, and was beginning to turn out a good deal of writing, especially in church periodicals. The pleasant though demanding routine of his scholarly life was soon to be interrupted by a momentous event that would change not only his own life, but that of the entire nation: the bitter and devastating War Between the States from 1861-1865.

The causes of this War are highly complex, but perhaps primarily revolved around the question of states' rights versus centralized national authority. Many in the South believed that the northern states were taking unfair advantage of the Union to advance their own economic interests (through tariffs, for instance), and that the various states had the constitutional right to withdraw from the Union; whereas many in the North felt that the states had no such rights, and that the power of the central government should be used to abolish southern slavery.

At first, Dabney—like most Virginians (and unlike most South Carolinians)—was a moderate on the question of both slavery and withdrawal.[14] Just before the outbreak of hostilities he joined with other evangelical ministers of both North and South in pleading with Christians in all parts of America to pray and do all they could to avoid fratricidal conflict.[15] In his earlier years he certainly favored the gradual emancipation of all slaves.[16] When the War did break out, however, Dabney committed himself wholeheartedly to the southern cause. His thinking became increasingly partisan and colored by all the emotion and vehemence of the "underdog" in this painful and deathly struggle. For the rest of his life he would believe that the southern cause was totally righteous and that "Yankeedom" was totally wicked.

Dabney firmly believed that the War was caused by the French Revolution "Jacobin" principles of New England Unitarian abolitionists and their liberal congressional "hacks," who wished to turn the original constitutional republic with its emphasis on state and local power into a secularized, centralized democratic power.[17] While a recent work by historian Otto Scott[18] indicates that there was at least an element of truth in this assessment, nonetheless Dabney's attitude was a gross oversimplification and in a sense ignored—or treated with contempt—the vital question of how the rest of the world felt about the morality of slavery.[19]

Not only was Dabney a literary apologist for the South and preacher to the troops, but for a while he served on the front lines as Chief of Staff to the famous Confederate general and pious Presbyterian deacon, Thomas J. "Stonewall" Jackson. Jackson said that Dabney was the most efficient officer he ever had.[20] Before the War ended, Dabney wrote a large and popular biography of Jackson. Not long after, he wrote *A De-*

fense of Virginia and Through Her of the South, which showed that slavery was not explicitly condemned by the Scriptures as sinful, and argued that it had been the most beneficial economic and moral system for all concerned in the South.

From a strictly exegetical viewpoint, Dabney was right that the Scriptures never specifically condemned slavery, and yet in retrospect it seems strange and sad that he and the other southern defenders of slavery totally failed to come to terms with the implications of the biblical Jubilee—that a slave who became a brother in the faith must be given his freedom after seven years since he is now in the covenant[21]—and with the equally important fact that Christianity established new moral and social conditions that would render personal bondage unacceptable. Unlike Professor Frank Bell Lewis, who felt that Dabney's major failure at this point was his identification with the conservative Bibliocentrism of nineteenth-century Virginia rather than with the more liberal Jeffersonian tradition of eighteenth-century Virginia, we would suggest that Dabney was not overly biblical on this subject; on the contrary, he did not go as far as his Bible should have taken him.[22] Like all other fallen men, including theologians, he had blind spots where his devotion to the culture made it difficult for him to interpret the will of God.

After the bitter defeat of the South in 1865 and then the agony and humiliation of impoverishing Reconstruction, much of Dabney's life seemed to be lived under deepening shadows. He seriously considered emigrating from the United States, but decided to stay. As his biographer says, for the rest of his life "he was at war with much in his age."[23]

The eighteenth-century secularist Enlightenment and its nineteenth-century European developments were bringing vast changes in the Western world, and it seems clear that the War between the States hastened the breakdown of the relative isolation and conservative Christian consensus of the American South. "French" political radicalism, "German" Higher Criticism of the Scriptures, and "British" evolutionism were all influencing the intellectual classes of America, while a broad, basically Arminian type of evangelicalism with new methodologies (developed by evangelists Finney and Moody) was deeply influencing the popular classes. In the philosophical world, the very possibility of objective knowledge of reality—and specifically of any true knowledge of a personal God—was being radically questioned and excluded from consideration. Dabney waged vigorous and vehement war against all of these powerful, secularizing trends of the century.

Almost never an obscurantist, Dabney carefully read the works of the enemies of biblical Calvinism, and traced their errors down to their poisonous roots. He had a wide interest and a mind that could successfully grapple with complex issues in philosophy, logic, sociology, and economics. He brought vigorous, and at times caustic and scathing criticism to bear on humanistic and Arminian trends. He offered uncompromising, and sometimes painful, solutions from the Word of God to a remarkably broad variety of questions.

While his analysis and solutions were generally well grounded biblically, and not infrequently manifested a radically brilliant insight, nevertheless his stringent tone, inflexibility, and on occasion lack of proper tact alienated many who otherwise might have fought on his side. On the other hand, a careful reading of his life and times will indicate that the basic reason for his increasing lack of popularity (even among his own Southern Presbyterians) was not his all too real failures of tone and tact, but his uncompromising, public insistence on total loyalty to the traditional biblical Calvinism that was becoming an embarrassment to the post-Enlightenment, broadening Evangelical mainstream that was inundating all of America's churches, the Reformed included.

Although he had had the honor of serving the (Southern) Presbyterian Church in the United States as Moderator in 1870, and had continued to publish widely read articles and significant books, still he was swimming against the mainstream as he opposed any sort of union with the Northern Presbyterian Church; as he opposed public education (as inherently secularist); as he opposed Moody/Sankey type "revivals"; and as he continued to oppose social and business accommodation of Southerners with the increasingly dominant "Yankee" capitalistic economy and culture.[24] By 1883 Dabney keenly felt "his loss of influence at the Seminary."[25] According to Frank B. Lewis, the Seminary authorities "had refused to accept his proposals for the future of that institution"; Dabney "felt himself isolated from the main currents of the life of the Southern Church," and "his long list of controversies had won him the reputation of being cantankerous."[26] In addition to this, his health was bad and his doctors advised a drier climate.

Thus (we can imagine with much sadness and frustration) he accepted a call to teach at the University of Texas in Austin, in the Chair of Moral and Mental Philosophy. While there in the final stage of his ever active life, he organized the Theological Seminary of Austin and wrote very widely in the fields of sociology, politics, philosophy, and economics.[27] In 1889 he became completely blind, but was able to continue teaching, preaching, and writing. As Dabney remained thoroughly conservative and Calvinist, however, the University of Texas was moving in a more liberal direction.[28] Because of this, in what was undoubtedly a parable of his life, Dabney was asked to resign in 1894. He continued to lecture and write, and two significant books came from his pen within a year of his death in 1898: *The Atonement* and *The Practical Philosophy*.

Dabney as a Theologian and Philosopher

Dabney's theological approach and methodology is remarkably similar to that of the Westminster standards: it is biblical (and to a degree exegetical), it is moderate and nonspeculative, and it faces the hardest questions while attempting to avoid harshness. If Dabney made extreme statements (and he did), these were made in the realm of politics and social philosophy, but almost never in theology. He wrote his theology the way standard church confessions are written—with the larger Reformed and Christian community in mind. Dabney certainly followed the advice of the Scottish Commissioner Henderson to the Westminster Assembly of the 1640s: "Let us avoid all scholastical disputes and unnecessary distinctions."

Dabney nobly exemplifies in his own theology what he says about the enduring quality of the Westminster standards:

> . . . The second marked trait of the Confession (is) its doctrinal moderation. . . . The Assembly . . . was too wise to attempt the conciliating of opposites by the surrendering of any essential member of the system of revealed truth. They present us the Pauline, Augustinian or Calvinist creed in its integrity. But on the other hand, they avoid every excess and every extreme statement. They refrained with a wise moderation from committing the Church of God on either side of those *"isms"* which agitated and perplexed the professors of the Reformed Theology.

Then Dabney illustrates the moderation of the Westminster Confession on the disputed questions of the Being and providence of God, supra- and infralapsarianism, mediate and immediate imputation, and general eschatology, which avoids commitment to either post- or premillennial theories.[29]

Dabney's lifelong insistence on balance, nonspeculation, and moderation in theological statement seems to come in part from his old Seminary predecessor, Baxter, in part from the Scottish theologian whose work he continually used, John Dick, and also from the Westminster standards themselves. Based on an analysis of his *Systematic Theology*, Lewis shows that of the more than 150 authors referred to by Dabney, those most frequently appealed to were—in this order—Turretin, Dick, Hill, Hodge, Knapp, Watson, Ridgeley, Calvin, Thornwell, and Witsius.[30] We note an absence of reference to his contemporary Dutch theologians, and very little direct interaction with any of the Fathers of the Greek or Latin Church (and in this, he and most other nineteenth-century American Reformed theologians were unlike Calvin). He does, however, make use of both Anselm and Thomas Aquinas in the original. Certainly Dabney did not mind differing from Calvin, Edwards, Dick, Hodge, and other respected Reformed scholars, although he did not seem to delight in differing, for instance, from Hodge in the way Thornwell appeared at times to do.

Another constituent element of Dabney's theological method was his adherence to the Scottish Common Sense Philosophy of Realism. He comments on this commitment extensively in his *Sensualistic Philosophy of the Nineteenth Century*, where he opposes the skeptical conclusions of the various forms of empirical and associational psychology and philosophy by means of the assumption of the original powers of the mind to form valid judgments that penetrate reality on the basis of data presented to the mind through the senses. Dabney saw the crux of the question as whether the mind can know objective truth:

> It is related that when the plan of Locke's Essay was first reported to his great contemporary, Leibniz, before the book had yet appeared in Germany, and the narrator stated that all was founded on a literal acceptance of the old scholastic law, *Nihil in intellectu quod non prius in sensu*, the great German replied, *Etiam, nisi intellectus ipse*. These words contain the key to the whole discussion. . . . In attempting to enumerate the affections of the mind, it overlooked the mind itself. . . .
>
> The *Ego* is a real existence. If our cognitions have any regular method, then it must be by virtue of some primary principles of cognition which are subjective to the mind. While we claim no "innate ideas", yet it is evident that the intelligence has some innate norms, which determine the nature of its processes, whenever the objective world presents the occasion of them. To deny this, we must not only believe the absurdity of regular series of effects without any regulative cause in their subject; but we must also deny totally the spontaneity of the mind.[31]

Thus, following Reid, Dabney presupposed the reality and validity of the mind, and the reality of cause and effect. Rather like Cornelius Van Til (who was born the decade Dabney died), Dabney showed that even to argue against these premises, one had to use them, and thus: "None but theists can consistently use induction."[32] Also like the later theologian Van Til, Dabney demonstrated that nontheists, too, reasoned on the basis of unproven, faith assumptions: "He who declares that science cannot have any *a priori* truths, virtually adopts as his *a priori* truth the ground maxim of that psychology. . . ."[33]

> These recent unbelievers admit the established facts; but, having approached them with the foregone conclusion that there can be no supernatural cause, they are reduced, for a pretended explanation, to a set of unproved hypotheses and fantastic guesses, which they offer us for verities, in most ludicrous contradiction to the very spirit of their "positive philosophy."[34]

Again he is like Van Til and Kuyper in showing the inevitable bias of the human mind against God's truth because of its commitment to a self-serving conceptual framework:

> . . . all who reason can see that no moral conclusion can be a pure intellection, but that some voluntary element must enter for good or for evil into the sources of every such judgment. No man on earth reasons towards objects which he either likes or dislikes strongly, with the same complete intellectual impartiality with which he reasons about pure mathematics. . . . All people, while agreeing perfectly upon the truths of mathematics and numbers, differ more or less upon questions of property rights, law-suits, character, politics, medicine, and religion. It is because all these objects of thought involve elements which appeal to the feelings and the will.[35]

If Dabney had affinities with the presuppositional school of Kuyper and Van Til on the analysis of human reasoning, his views of natural theology and apologetics were certainly unlike theirs, and followed in the general line of Aquinas, Butler, Alexander, Chalmers, and Hodge. He followed the traditional Catholic and Reformed approach of first studying natural, and then revealed theology. It is perhaps here that his reliance upon Scottish Realism most shows through, when for example he establishes the traditional proofs for God's existence on the basis of cause and effect in the line of Thomas Reid against the arguments of Hume. Interestingly, Dabney, like Aquinas, did not favor the ontological argument for God's existence.

In his natural theology Dabney has very little, if anything, original or fresh to say, and like most natural theologians quietly imports a good deal of content from Scripture as to the Being and ways of God (which would be exceedingly difficult to see in nature unless one already knew the Scriptures). There are two areas, however, which stand on the border of natural and revealed theology, where he had some bright insights (which he did not develop systematically). These areas would later be developed in the twentieth century by thinkers such as Van Til and Francis Schaeffer on the one hand and Thomas F. Torrance on the other.[36]

As though he were anticipating Van Til, Schaeffer, and others, Dabney deals in a helpful way with the question of how a finite human mind can think and know the Infinite. This question was occasioned by Dabney's reaction to the Scottish philosopher Sir William Hamilton, who on this matter was influenced more by Kant than by Reid, and held that the limited mind cannot think "unconditioned" or infinite Being.[37] Dabney makes it clear that we can know truly that which is infinite without knowing completely or exhaustively.

> The finite mind would need to become infinite, in order to contain a complete and exhaustive conception of any infinite being. But we

do not claim such a conception. The finite mind may remain finite, and yet contain an incomplete, yet valid, apprehension of infinite being.[38]

The use of the word "apprehension" shows the deep insight of Dabney into the roots of this question (as opposed to the word "comprehension"). In his *Systematic Theology* Dabney explores in greater detail the important epistemological difference between apprehension (which finite minds can do of the infinite) and comprehension (which they cannot).[39] But even if the human mind only claims to apprehend God (rather than comprehend him), on what basis can one claim that even *that* is possible (as someone like Mansel, the follower of Hamilton and Kant, would have argued)?

Dabney clearly sees that the answer lies in the direction of man's creation in the image of God. God is infinite and personal, and man is finite but, because created in God's image, also personal. Thus, in spite of the difference between infinity and finitude, the personal can know the personal.[40] This would be developed more clearly in the next century by scholars such as Van Til and Schaeffer, but this insight was already an important element in the epistemology of Dabney.

Dabney also manifested penetrating insight into a second boundary area between natural and revealed theology, into what Thomas F. Torrance has called the necessary and irreducible "triadic structure of revelation" (i.e., God, man, *and* nature).[41] That is, Dabney clearly pointed out that any objectively valid revelation from God to man always involves the structures of created nature. Thus nature, far from being an embarrassment and hindrance to revelation, is its medium. Dabney deals with this important epistemological matter when he comments on the widespread biblical phenomenon of anthropomorphism, which was such an offense to the nineteenth-century idealism that depreciated nature as well as history ("the eternal truths of reason can never be expressed in the accidental facts of history"). The cutting off of Jesus and the church from their roots in Judaism, the desupernaturalizing of Christ and the Scriptures, and then the ultimate loss of "the historical Jesus" and consequent denial of the Incarnation were all part and parcel of the idealistic assumption that eternal reality and truth cannot be validly expressed and apprehended in the structures of nature and history.

In the course of his argumentation against Hume, Mill, and Spencer (on their denial of causation as a theistic proof), Dabney goes to the root of the matter of anthropomorphism and the very possibility of divine revelation in the created order:

> . . . if God has made the human mind "after His image, in His likeness," this would effectually guarantee all our legitimately ra-

tional processes of thought against vice from *anthropomorphism*. For, in thinking according to the natural laws of our minds, we would be thinking precisely as God bids us think. . . . The unreasonableness of the demand, that we shall reject any conception of the divine working, though reached by normal (human) inference, merely because it may be anthropomorphic, appears thus. It would equally forbid us to think or learn at all, either concerning God, or any other Being or concept different from man: for, if we are not allowed to think in the forms of thought natural and normal for us, we are forbidden to think at all. All man's cognition must be anthropomorphic, or nothing.[42]

He makes the same point, in a more directly theological way, in his *Systematic Theology:*

But when the inspired witness, the Bible, comes to us, with attestation, (by miracles, prophecies, &c.,) exactly suited to the forms of the human understanding, and assures us that our spirits are made in the likeness of God's, all fear of our theology, as made invalid by anthropomorphism, is removed. And especially when we are shown the Messiah, as the image of the invisible God, and hear Him reason, we have a complete verification.[43]

Dabney does not deal with some of the related philosophical problems involved in this concept of the essential triadic structure of revelation. Moreover, he does not even begin to develop in a systematic manner the epistemological and theological ramifications of it as T. F. Torrance does a century later, but his profound theological discernment certainly pointed him in the right direction.

In his voluminous work in the area of revealed theology, Dabney's approach may be consistently characterized as thoroughly conservative and displaying contempt for all innovation and speculation. Dabney adhered so closely in both letter and spirit to the Westminster standards that in a speech before the Southern Presbyterian General Assembly the last year of his life, he could seriously make this very strong assertion: ". . . the Confession will need no amendment until the Bible needs to be amended."[44] On the other hand, Dabney saw himself as above all a biblical and exegetical theologian. While he was not like a Geerhardus Vos, for example, who took into profound consideration the reality of progressive, historical development of revelation within the Scriptures themselves, he was in some respects a forerunner of great exegetical theologians such as B. B. Warfield and John Murray, who were prepared to question received Reformed terminology and concepts in light of careful word study and contextual opening of a passage. That is, on many occasions (though far from always) Dabney can be looked on as something of a bridge between the earlier traditional prooftexting of a Turretin and the later contextual, exegetical research of Warfield and Vos.[45] Many examples of the sort of faithful grappling with a text that yields sound exegetical theology can be pointed out in Dabney.[46] A model of his exegetical openness is his treatment of John 3:16, in which he differs with the traditional interpretation of such great Reformed theologians as John Owen in refusing to restrict the meaning of "world" to "all the elect."[47] Because of his careful exegetical study of some aspects of Bible covenants, Dabney in a certain sense seems to have anticipated the work of John Murray and others in stressing the very close relationship between the Mosaic and Abrahamic Covenants.[48] Granted Dabney's own consistent exegetical emphasis in theology, it is not surprising that he preferred, as Frank B. Lewis has pointed out, scriptural rather than speculative theologians.[49]

Closely related to Dabney's submission to the plain text of Scripture and his commitment to the sober and moderate Calvinism of the Westminster standards is his continual disavowal of all types of theological speculation—Reformed speculation included! Many are the places where Dabney says (over against the distinctions between infra- and supralapsarianism, mediate and immediate imputation, creationism and traducianism, etc.), ". . . this is a question which never ought to have been raised."[50] Here he follows the spirit of Calvin rather than of Beza and Gomarus.

In accordance with his moderate, non–"hyper"-Calvinism, and unlike the stringent spirit of some of his political and social statements, Dabney labors very hard to avoid all harshness as he faces the hard questions of theology. For instance, he definitely wishes to leave the door open to the possibility of the universal salvation of all who die in infancy.[51] He does not like the thought involved in the term "Limited" Atonement, and while he clearly affirms the "particular redemption" of the elect, still he prefers (against Dr. William Cunningham of Scotland) to hold to a certain "general design" in the atonement, a "sincere offer of mercy," and "a sense in which Christ 'died for' all those ends, and for the persons affected by them."[52]

Following John Dick of Scotland, Dabney attempts to describe the decree of reprobation in the mildest terms possible, omitting condemnation from the decree.[53] He criticizes his great contemporary, Charles Hodge of Princeton, for the undue harshness implied in his scheme of immediate imputation of the sin of Adam to his offspring.[54] Dabney dislikes any viewpoint of election that underrates or turns into a fiction the genuine pity and mercy of God for lost sinners.[55] Likewise he repudiates all "hyper-" systems that refrain from urging lost sinners to seek the face of God and pray.[56]

Apparently with no trepidation, Dabney enters the lists of the traditional argument (which ran through such varied schools as Plato, the New England Puritans, A. E. Taylor, and Van Til) over whether something is morally right because God commands it, or does he command it because it is right? Unlike most of the Puritans, and more in the line of Plato, Dabney thinks it sounds too harshly arbitrary to say that right is right because God wills it.[57] Of course he carefully states that he does not mean that there is a standard outside or above God. Still, Dabney seems to be lacking his usual penetration of the issues here, and out of fear of harsh overtones does not seem able to appreciate the important point being raised by the Puritans. Certainly his disagreement with the Puritans is merely terminological and not substantial, but he has not grasped, or simply dissents from, the propriety of their terminological concern.

As we would expect in a noninnovator, most of Dabney's work in the various topics of revealed theology is not notably different from the position of his scholastic Calvinist predecessors and his great conservative Reformed contemporaries. Some parts of his thought, nevertheless, do deserve comment. There are at least two areas of the theological curriculum where Dabney appears to have made some real contributions, especially in the sense of stating in a fresh, clear, and generally attractive way complex and difficult truths, and there is a third area where, in terms of the contribution of Calvin himself, Dabney's thought seems to miss the mark.

The late Professor John Murray of Westminster reportedly considered his own major contribution to Reformed theology to have been in the area of anthropology: especially the question of the Adamic Administration.[58] A careful reading of Dabney's *Systematic Theology*, *Sensualistic Philosophy of the Nineteenth Century*, and *Practical Philosophy* would seem to indicate that Dabney's fullest contribution to the development of the traditional Reformed theological curriculum also lies in the area of anthropology: particularly in his description of the *habitus* of the personality and also in his minute work on the place of the feelings in the human makeup.

Dabney's work on the *habitus* is usually in the context of such questions as free will, natural inability and moral responsibility, divine providence and human spontaneity, the influence of regeneration on the intellect and will, and the general causative effects of the character on human thought and action. In the course of these discussions, Dabney at times finds himself disagreeing with and correcting fellow Reformed scholars such as Hodge, Thornwell, and Dick.

By *habitus* Dabney essentially meant the basic dispositional and motivational complex at the roots of the human personality that determines what one's character is and thus what one's choices and actions are.[59] Dabney felt that he was being more consistently clear than Dick, Thornwell, or Hodge in showing that the entire soul is a unity (or "monad") both in its unregenerate and regenerate states,[60] and that if this unity is not kept in the forefront of a Christian anthropology, then confusion will result in several areas. Therefore, Dabney clarifies or corrects confused thinking in some areas of the theology of Dick (on the inability of the natural man to understand Scripture), of Thornwell (on the will's natural inability and the righteousness of God), of Hodge (on the illumination of the mind and depravity of the whole soul), and of the controversial southern minister and writer Bledsoe in dialogue with Jonathan Edwards (on the freedom and spontaneity of the will).[61] Dabney's writings on the effects of regeneration on the whole character (based on the change of dispositional *habitus*) are marked by a lucidity and pungency in the line of the old Scottish divine, Thomas Boston.[62]

Given Dabney's interest in and study of human psychology (especially in his *Practical Philosophy* and *Sensualistic Philosophy*), it comes as no surprise that he has much clarity and several insights to contribute to Reformed theological anthropology in the area of the feelings. Unlike those forms of rationalistic theology (whether of the liberal or fundamentalist variety) that tend to treat the human mind as though it were in neutral abstraction from the complex motivations and feelings of the moral character, Dabney perceives the immense moral, epistemological, and theological importance and influence of man's subjective emotions. Dabney knew that feelings were important and required careful analysis and consideration as a part of the theological curriculum because:

> Essentially, feelings are man's motive power. Intellect is the cold and latent magnetism which directs the ship's compass. . . . Feeling is that elastic energy which throbs within the machinery, and gives propulsion to its wheels. . . . The vigor of the functions of cognition itself depends, in every man, more on the force of the incentive energizing the faculty, than on the native strength or clearness of the intellect. . . . It is chiefly the feelings which make the man.[63]

Dabney carefully examines and categorizes the feelings and judges them to be expressions of man's basic character disposition (or *habitus*).[64] These basic motivational expressions are then related to man's moral obligation or conscience. The relationships and inner workings of basic character, feelings, and conscience are made central to Dabney's system of ethics, and his insights into these interconnections seem often to enable him to "get inside" the motivations, problems, and responsibilities of human beings individually and socially.[65]

Dabney's close study of the feelings, for instance, enables him to give a penetrating analysis of "spurious religious feelings" in which he sheds burning light on carnal, selfish feelings in religion.[66] Dabney's work at this point should be studied by all who have to deal with the "prosperity teaching" of some segments of the "Electronic Church" in America. He offers interesting thoughts on how immersion in emotional novels (today we might substitute "soap operas") can degenerate genuine sentiment into cheap sentimentality, which weakens the vigor of the moral resolve when one goes back into the real world.[67]

In addition to his contribution in the realm of Reformed anthropology, Dabney also clarifies, and in that sense develops, another topic of classical theology: providence. His basic area of concern is the *concursus* between God's sovereign, primary control of all things, and the reality and validity of human and natural secondary causation. In his *Systematic Theology* he deals with the question "How God's effective providence can intervene consistently with the uniformity of natural laws"[68] in a way that he believes is clearer than the expositions of Dick, Hodge, and McCosh.[69] He also corrects what he feels are defects in the doctrine of the physical *concursus* of God in evil as well as in good acts and physical causes, which was held by his great mentor Turretin of seventeenth-century Geneva, and by the Dutch Calvinist Witsius (who followed a false lead from Aquinas at this point).[70]

As we see from his *Sensualistic Philosophy*, Dabney wishes to avoid a hypersupernaturalism that short-circuits moral effort and responsibility, while at the same time strongly affirming the traditional Calvinist doctrine of God's total sovereign control.[71] Dabney prefers not to speak of providence as "the supernatural violating of natural laws," but rather as God's perpetual superintendence of the "regular" law of nature.[72]

A third area of Dabney's work in the traditional theological curriculum deserves comment: his view of the sacraments. Here, in terms of Calvin's sacramental understanding, Dabney seems to take a step backward, giving future generations of Southern Presbyterians a generally weak or low view of the sacraments. Dabney finds Calvin's profound teaching on the powerful and gracious reality of the Holy Spirit's work in effectuating a sacramental union between the physical elements in the sacrament and the blessings of union with Christ's glorified human nature to be ". . . not only incomprehensible, but impossible."[73] Here, perhaps, his commitment to the categories of Scottish Common Sense Realism has restricted the usual depth and richness of his theological discernment. In his own day, a contemporary theologian from South Carolina, John B. Adger, answered this critique of Calvin's view of the sacraments, but still Dabney's viewpoint has predominated in the church.[74]

Dabney as Prophet and Social Critic

Dabney manifests a wider and deeper cultural, social, and political interest than any other theologian of nineteenth-century America. He was in a sense ahead of his time in spanning the fields of both sociology and religion. His penetrating theological critique of culture is at times like that of E. Rosenstock-Huessy and R. J. Rushdoony. While Thornwell and Shedd were more eloquent than Dabney, Hodge more influential, and B. M. Palmer a greater preacher, Dabney excels them all as a prophet. In a very limited yet real sense, Dabney was like Ezekiel and Jeremiah in that the development of his prophetic gift was very costly to himself: he passed through the fires of experiencing the bitter defeat of his homeland and the resultant breakup of the southern culture that was the pride and joy of his heart. This was both his strength and his weakness: the defeat of the South served to give him uncanny insight into the future problems of American culture, and at the same time tended so to wrench his emotions that his thought became prejudiced and his moral vision blinded in some very important areas of human life and endeavor.

Dabney's open hatred of the post-Civil War industrialization of American society made him an outsider to the developing cultural consensus, and strengthened the vision of his ever keen moral eye to penetrate the weaknesses of America's increasingly secularist materialism and industrialism. Dabney utilizes a strong, largely correct, and far from comforting critique of the evils of debt capitalism,[75] of the immoral use of the civil government by the industrial plutocracy to enforce monopolies that crushed smaller competitors,[76] of the dishonesty of monetary inflation,[77] of the treatment of man as a machine,[78] and of the certainty of the eventual de-Christianization and secularization of public school education.[79] Most sobering of all, he foresaw the coming, twentieth-century struggle in America for religious and civil liberties between a powerful centralized state with totalitarian temptations and a broad and shallow church that had forgotten the theological and constitutional basis of liberty.[80]

Dabney also had valid insights into the general weakening of Reformed theology and practice in the Calvinist churches of late nineteenth-century America. He foresaw impending problems with the weakening of Christian intellectual resistance to evolutionary speculation[81] and to higher criticism of the Scriptures,[82] the decline toward liberalism in the theological seminaries,[83] the decline of serious church discipline,[84] the growth of human inventions and the loss of real unction in worship,[85] and the bitter harvest to be reaped from humanly induced methods of more rapid and successful evangelism,[86] and he even discussed the development of the false split between Christ as Savior and Christ as Lord.[87] Dabney apparently offended many as he deplored the growing tendency of Christians to indulge themselves in luxury and to be forgetful of the poor.[88]

Much less happy in biblical insight was the deeply jaundiced viewpoint that Dabney turned upon the situation of the black people. In addition to supporting slavery before the War, he vehemently protested the ecclesiastical equality of black people as potential officers in white churches and presbyteries after the War.[89] He opposed tax-paid education for blacks in Virginia (but he opposed it for poor whites as well).[90] He held that the blacks were culturally inferior[91] (he seems to leave the question of whether they were personally inferior an open one), and hence he theorized that it would take untold generations before blacks could be raised to cultural equality with whites. This sort of attitude of course helped drive the black freedmen from white churches to the detriment of the unity of the body of Christ and healing of the nation.

In retrospect, it seems sadly shortsighted that Dabney could offer the people of the Reconstruction South such a clear solution from degeneracy in times of oppression, and yet fail to see that the very same solution should hold true of the blacks, who were also created in the image of God. In "The Duty of the Hour" Dabney advises:

> The correlated duty is that of anxiously preserving our integrity and self-respect. . . . The victims of unrighteous oppression, are usually degraded by their unavenged wrongs. . . . The man who has ceased to feel moral indignation for wrong has ceased to feel the claims of virtue. Nor is there a valid reason for your insensibility to evil, in the fact that you yourself are the object of it.[92]

Undoubtedly Dabney's greatest blind spot in this whole matter was, as Terry Johnson has pointed out, his underestimation of the power of the gospel in the life and culture of blacks (which can make saints, leaders, and heroes of them as well as of any other people).[93]

Dabney's prophecy, then, was both remarkably right and grievously wrong. As his close friend and biographer, T. C. Johnson, has pointed out, Dabney was often too pessimistic about the future of the church.[94] And as Charles R. Wilson has noted, Dabney failed to see that "a separate southern religion [would] survive in the postwar South, as a foundation for a distinctive southern culture."[95]

We whose unperceived blind spots will be deplored by future Christian generations will not speak too harshly of Dabney, who was marked by the fallenness of his own time and culture, as we are by ours. The way forward is to see beyond him by standing on his shoulders— and on those of all the saints and doctors of the church in all ages.

It is interesting to note that Dabney, who said "I have no audience" and described himself as "the Cassandra of Yankeedom,"[96] now, in the 1980s, has a larger audience than any time during his life. Indeed, since the mid-1960s nearly all of his works have been reprinted (in some cases, several times) on both sides of the Atlantic. Perhaps T. C. Johnson was right when he wrote some eighty years ago:

Dr. Dabney was a great man. We cannot tell just how great yet. One cannot see how great Mt. Blanc is while standing at its foot. One hundred years from now men will be able to see him better.[97]

Notes: Robert Lewis Dabney

1. B. B. Warfield in *The Princeton Theological Review* (1905).
2. R. L. Dabney, *Discussions: Evangelical and Theological*, 2 vols. (London: The Banner of Truth Trust, 1962), 2:558.
3. Thomas Cary Johnson, *In Memoriam: R. L. Dabney* (Knoxville: University of Tennessee Press, 1898), 7.
4. Thomas Cary Johnson, *The Life and Letters of Robert Lewis Dabney* (Edinburgh: The Banner of Truth Trust, 1977 [1903]), 192.
5. C. T. Thompson, "Robert Lewis Dabney—The Conservative," *The Union Seminary Review* 35 (January 1924), 155-56.
6. Johnson, *Life and Letters*, 42-43.
7. Thompson, "R. L. Dabney," 156.
8. Ibid., 157.
9. Ibid.
10. Johnson, *Life and Letters*, 551.
11. Thompson, "R. L. Dabney," 159-60.
12. Johnson, *Life and Letters*, 153.
13. Ibid., 151-52.
14. Ibid., 210-34.
15. See "Christians, Pray for Your Country," in R. L. Dabney, *Discussions*, 2:393-400.
16. James H. Smylie, "The Burden of Southern Church Historians: World Mission, Regional Captivity, Reconciliation," *Journal of Presbyterian History* 46 (December 1968), 295.
17. Dabney regularly criticizes "Jacobinism," e.g., in *Discussions by Robert L. Dabney*, 4 vols. (Harrisonburg: Sprinkle Publications, 1979-1980), 4:542; 3:498ff.; *A Defence of Virginia and through Her the South* (Harrisonburg: Sprinkle Publications, 1977), 254; *Life and Campaigns of Lieut.-Gen. Thomas J. Jackson* (Harrisonburg: Sprinkle Publications, 1976), 162-69, 159-61; *The Sensualistic Philosophy of the Nineteenth Century* (Anson D. F. Randolph, 1887), 58.
18. Otto J. Scott, *The Secret Six: John Brown and the Abolitionist Movement* (New York: Times Books, 1979). Of course, some in the North saw the War as a southern, slaveholders' conspiracy; see William A. Clebsch, *Christian Interpretations of the Civil War* (Philadelphia: Fortress Press, 1969), 2, 6.
19. This is not to imply that Dabney does not deal openly and boldly with slavery, for he does in *Defence of Virginia* and elsewhere, but rather that he could not take seriously the moral challenge raised by nearly all other Christians throughout the Western world. Instead, he tended to discount the challenge as motivated by "Jacobinism" (or as we would say, "radical secular humanism").
20. Johnson, *Life and Letters*, 272.
21. Lev. 25:39-55. See also Exod. 21:2.
22. Frank Bell Lewis, *Robert Lewis Dabney: Southern Presbyterian Apologist* (Ph.D. diss., Duke University, 1946), 213-14.

23. Johnson, *Life and Letters*, 568.

24. See "The New South," in Dabney, *Discussions*, 4:1-24.

25. Smylie, "The Burden of Southern Church Historians," 292.

26. Lewis, *Robert Lewis Dabney*, 30.

27. See Dabney, *Discussions*, Vols. 3 and 4, and *Practical Philosophy*.

28. David H. Overy, *Robert Lewis Dabney: Apostle of the Old South* (Ph.D. diss., University of Wisconsin, 1967), 292-98.

29. Dabney, "The Doctrinal Contents of the Confession of Faith," in *Memorial Volume of the Westminster Assembly, 1647-1897* (Richmond, VA: The Presbyterian Committee of Publication, 1897), 95.

30. Lewis, *Robert Lewis Dabney*, 161.

31. Dabney, *Sensualistic Philosophy*, 248-49.

32. Ibid., 412.

33. Ibid., 97; see also p. 54 on J. S. Mill's circular reasoning.

34. Ibid., 100.

35. Dabney, *Discussions*, 4:512-13.

36. There is no line of direct thought from Dabney to these scholars. Their insights were not developed in dialogue with his writings.

37. See Dabney, *Sensualistic Philosophy*, ch. 10, esp. 216-17.

38. Ibid., 223.

39. Dabney, *Systematic Theology*, 149, also 138-39. Saint Hilary works with this distinction as early as the fourth century in the first two books of his *De Trinitate*, but it is highly unlikely that Dabney had read this. Hilary of course influenced Calvin, whom Dabney had read.

40. Dabney, *Sensualistic Philosophy*, 138-39, 230-31, 237-38, etc.

41. See, e.g., Thomas F. Torrance, *Reality and Evangelical Theology* (Philadelphia: The Westminster Press, 1982) and *God and Rationality* (London: Oxford University Press, 1971), ch. 4.

42. Dabney, *Sensualistic Philosophy*, 405-06. Again, early fathers such as Novatian of Rome in the third century had dealt very clearly with anthropomorphisms in terms of God's accommodation to man's littleness, and this had influenced Calvin, whom Dabney knew, if not Novatian.

43. Dabney, *Systematic Theology*, 295; see also his *Discussions*, 1:297.

44. Dabney, "Doctrinal Contents of the Confession of Faith," 94.

45. Probably Joseph Addison Alexander of Princeton, had he lived longer, would have been even more of a bridge in this direction than Dabney; but of course Alexander was not primarily a systematic theologian.

46. See, e.g., Dabney, *Discussions*, 1:238 (on repentance); ibid., 262-63 (on Rom. 5); ibid., 271 (on "sinned in Adam"); ibid., 312 (on John 3:16); ibid., 555ff. (an exposition of I Cor. 3:10-15); *Systematic Theology*, 34 (original sin); ibid., 35 (imputation of Adam's guilt); ibid., 207-08 (on the eternal generation of the Son); ibid., 386 (on Col. 2:16-17); ibid., 573-77 (on the "understanding" and the "heart"); ibid., 619ff. (good exegetical work on justification).

47. Dabney, *Systematic Theology*, 527-28, 535; *Discussions*, 1:311-13.

48. *Systematic Theology*, 454-55. Cf. John Murray, *The Covenant of Grace* (London: The Tyndale Press, 1956).

49. Lewis, *Robert Lewis Dabney*, 164.

50. *Systematic Theology*, 233 (on the order of the decrees). Note also his refusal to speculate in other areas of theology: ibid., 317, 320, 338-39, 340-41; *Discussions*, 1:290. Dabney explains well why he dislikes theological speculation in his critique of Hodge and Turretin on "immediate imputation" in ibid., 1:165-66:

Nearly all Dr. Hodge's positions may be found in the ninth chapter of Turretin's Locus on Original Sin. The true verdict on this history of opinion seems to us this: that a few of the more acute and forward of the Calvinistic divines were tempted, by their love of system and symmetry of statement and over-confidence in their own logic, to excogitate the ill-starred distinction of the antecedent and gratuitous imputation. Their error here was exactly like that of the supralapsarians, who thought they could throw light and symmetry on the doctrine of the decree by assigning what they thought was the logical order of sequence to its parts. But they became "wise above that which was written." They added no light to the mystery of the decree, but they misrepresented the moral attributes of God, and provoked a crowd of natural cavils and objections. The distinction of supralapsarians and infralapsarians ought never to have been heard of. . . . So, say we, this distinction of the antecedent imputation ought never to have been drawn. . . . But the difference with Dr. Hodge seems to have been this: his love of systematizing enticed him to adopt the extreme points of his great teacher, Turretin.

51. See Dabney, *Discussions*, 3:193-94, 200-05; also his *Review of Theodosia Ernest; Or, the Heroine of Faith* (Richmond: Shepperson and Graves, 1869).

52. *Systematic Theology*, 529.

53. Ibid., 239. Dr. Morton Smith suggests with insight that Dabney's refusal to parallel the decrees of election and reprobation is like that of G. C. Berkouwer, who says, "The Gospel can be understood and preached only if balance, symmetry, and parallelism are excluded" (*Divine Election*, 202); quoted in Morton Smith, *Studies in Southern Presbyterian Theology* (Amsterdam: Jacob Van Campen, 1962), 214.

54. Dabney, *Discussions*, 1:144-45, 166-67; *Systematic Theology*, 342.

55. See Dabney, *Discussions*, 1:285-86, 307; *Systematic Theology*, 532-33, 559.

56. Ibid., 609.

57. Ibid., 163-64; also *Sensualistic Philosophy*, 324. Terrill Elniff explains the significance of this debate among the New England Puritans in *The Guise of Every Graceless Heart* (Vallectio, CA: Ross House Books, 1981).

58. Ian H. Murray, "Preface," in *Collected Writings of John Murray* (Edinburgh: The Banner of Truth Trust, 1977), 2:vii-viii.

59. See Dabney, *Discussions*, 3:240-41, where Dabney says:
> . . . this law of free volitions is the soul's own rational and appetitive nature—its *habitus*. Hence the rational free volition is not an uncaused phenomenon in the world of mind; it only arises by reason of its regular efficient, which is the subjective motive. By subjective motive is meant that complex of mental judgment as to the preferable, and subjective appetency for the object which arise together in the mind, on presentation of the object, according to the mind's own native disposition. In a word, the free volition will arise according to and because of the soul's own strongest motive; and that is the reason why it is a rational, a free, and a responsible volition. Hence we believe that such volitions are attended with full certainty—which is what we mean by moral necessity—and also with full freedom.

See also Dabney, *Systematic Theology*, 578:
> The will has its own *habitus*, regulative of all its fundamental acts, which is not a mere modification of the intelligence, but its own co-ordinate, original character; a simple, ultimate fact of the moral constitution. Hence an interaction of will and intellect. On moral and spiritual subjects the practical generalisations of the intellect are founded on the dictates of the disposition of the will.

60. See ibid., 323:
> But when we thus discriminate the faculties, we must not forget the unity and simplicity of the spirit of man. It is a monad. And, as we do not conceive of it as regenerated or sanctified by patches; so neither do we regard it as specifically

depraved by patches. Original corruption is not, specifically, the perversion of a faculty in the soul, but of the soul itself.

61. On Dick see Dabney, *Systematic Theology*, 578; on Thornwell, ibid., 298; on Hodge, ibid., 570-71 and *Discussions*, 1:232-34; on Bledsoe, *Discussions*, 3:181ff. and 211ff.

62. See *Systematic Theology*, Lecture XLVII, esp. 561-62. Cf. Thomas Boston, *Human Nature in its Fourfold State* (London: The Banner of Truth Trust, 1964), part III, "Regeneration."

63. Dabney, *Discussions*, 3:274-75.

64. In his *Practical Philosophy*, Dabney arranged the feelings in terms of pairs under nine "sensibilities." Each pair is bounded at opposite ends by desire and aversion. In light of subsequent developments in psychology before and after, pro and con Freud, Dabney's work is somewhat dated and limited in scope. Yet as ethics it still deserves a serious reading.

65. His "Love of Applause" and "Duties of the Family" are models of penetrating ethical insight, and his "Civic Duties" raises many of the most difficult critical questions that face Christians today who live under hostile regimes (see his *Practical Philosophy*).

66. See Dabney, *Discussions*, 3:456-61.

67. See ibid., 2:161-62.

68. Dabney, *Systematic Theology*, 281.

69. Ibid., 279-80.

70. Ibid., 286-91.

71. See Dabney, *Sensualistic Philosophy*, 352-69.

72. Cf. ibid., 353, 359-60. By this superintendence, God "guides with His skillful but invisible hand to just those combinations which release the powers of the second causes He needs for His purpose, and reduce to potentiality those whose tasks are for the time completed" (359-60).

73. *Systematic Theology*, 811. See also on the question of the nature of our union with Christ, 616-17, 730. Dabney wishes to refute Calvin's *Institutes*, IV, ch. 17 (*Institutes of the Christian Religion*, 2 vols., ed. John T. McNeill, trans. Ford Lewis Battles [Philadelphia: The Westminster Press, 1977]). Ronald S. Wallace's important study *Calvin's Doctrine of Word and Sacrament* (Tyler, TX: Geneva Divinity School Press, 1982, rpt.).

74. See John B. Adger, *My Life and Times, 1810-1899* (Richmond, VA: The Presbyterian Committee of Publication, 1899), 310-26.

75. See esp. David H. Overy, "When the Wicked Beareth Rule: A Southern Critique of Industrial America," *Journal of Presbyterian History* (Summer 1970), esp. 132, 135. See also David H. Overy, *Dabney: Apostle*, 290; also Dabney, *Discussions*, 4:1-24.

76. See Smylie, "The Burden of Southern Church Historians," 291; also Dabney, *The Practical Philosophy*, 476; *Discussions*, 4:53-70 and 321-40; and David H. Overy, *Dabney: Apostle*, 285-88.

77. Dabney, *Discussions*, 4:341-53.

78. Dabney, *Defence of Virginia*, 15; also Overy, "When the Wicked Beareth Rule," 135.

79. See his various articles against the Virginia state school system in *Discussions*, 4:176-247, 260-80. See also E. T. Thompson, *Presbyterians in the South*, 3 vols. (Richmond: John Knox Press, 1963-73), 2:341-49.

80. Dabney predicts in his *Practical Philosophy*, 394:
The history of human rights is, that their intelligent assertors usually learn the true grounds of them "in the furnace of affliction"; that the posterity who inherit

these rights hold them for a while, in pride and ignorant prescription; that after a while, when the true logic of the rights has been forgotten, and when some plausible temptation presses them to do so, the next generation discards the precious rights bodily, and goes back to the practice of the old tyranny. . . .

You may deem it a strange prophecy, but I predict that the time will come in this once free America when the battle for religious liberty will have to be fought over again, and will probably be lost, because the people are already ignorant of its true basis and conditions.

See also his *Discussions*, 3:321, 503.

81. See, e.g., his controversy with Professor Woodrow of Columbia Seminary, who came to accept organic evolution, in *Discussions*, 3:91-181; also *Sensualistic Philosophy*, ch. 6.

82. See Dabney, *Discussions*, 1:350-439.

83. T. C. Johnson, *Life and Letters*, 532.

84. Dabney, *Discussions*, 4:545, 3:564. In an undated letter to the Rev. R. H. Fleming of Woodstock, Virginia, Dabney speaks of the refusal of the Presbyterian General Assembly to speak against current sins, which undercuts sessional discipline, which in turn—Dabney feared—would lead "to the death of the church." This letter is in the collection of the Presbyterian Historical Foundation, Montreat, North Carolina.

85. See R. L. Dabney, *Sacred Rhetoric* (Carlisle, PA: The Banner of Truth Trust, 1979), 115-17 on unction; and Thompson, *Presbyterians in the South*, 2:429-35 on changes in worship.

86. See Dabney, *Discussions*, 2:76-95 and 551-74.

87. Dabney, *Systematic Theology*, 601.

88. See Dabney, *Discussions*, 1:1-28, 4:528; T. C. Johnson, *Life and Letters*, 408.

89. See Dabney, *Discussions*, 2:199-217; Johnson, *Life and Letters*, 319-22.

90. See Dabney, *Discussions*, 4:176-90.

91. See ibid., 25-45.

92. Ibid., 109-12.

93. Terry Johnson, "Gone with the Wind: R. L. Dabney and the Evangelical Defense of Slavery" (Paper written at Gordon-Conwell Theological Seminary), 38.

94. Johnson, *Life and Letters*, 325-26.

95. Charles R. Wilson, "Robert Lewis Dabney: Religion and the Southern Holocaust," *The Virginia Magazine of History and Biography*, 89 (January 1981), 89.

96. Overy, "When the Wicked Beareth Rule," 131.

97. Johnson, *Life and Letters*, p. 569.

3

JAMES HENLEY THORNWELL

LUDER G. WHITLOCK, JR.

James Henley Thornwell

James Henley Thornwell once expressed a desire "to be regarded as the greatest scholar and most talented man that ever lived."[1] Although he failed to achieve that distinction, Thornwell did become one of the outstanding Presbyterian leaders of the nineteenth century, rising rapidly in the esteem of his colleagues, so that in 1847 at the age of 35 he became the youngest moderator of the General Assembly in the history of the Presbyterian Church in the United States. This son of a plantation overseer, as a result of a discussion about Aristotle at a dinner party in New York in 1856, received a copy of Aristotle from Harvard professor George Bancroft, who was sufficiently impressed to inscribe on the flyleaf the following words: "A testimonial of regard to the Rev. Dr. J. H. Thornwell, the most learned of the learned."[2] Daniel Webster, after hearing Thornwell speak at a South Carolina college, was reported to have remarked that he was the greatest pulpit orator he had ever heard.[3] And Henry Ward Beecher referred to him as the most brilliant minister in the Old School Presbyterian Church and the most brilliant debater in the General Assembly.[4] He was selected by the Board of Commissioners on World Missions to preach the anniversary sermon at the General Assembly in New York City in 1856. It is said that Thornwell would have been the first man pointed out to a stranger arriving at his first General Assembly. Moreover, the stranger probably would have been surprised to discover that this small, stooped gentleman so unimpressive in physical appearance was the acclaimed J. H. Thornwell.

In 1837 he was elected to the professorship of Logic and Belles Lettres at South Carolina College where he had graduated first in his class in 1831. He spent the greater part of his professional years at the college, remaining there until 1855 except for one year, 1840-41, during which period he served as the pastor of the First Presbyterian Church in Columbia, South Carolina. Thornwell had a significant influence on the college as professor, chaplain, and president. As the sixth president, he was perhaps the most important person connected with the college until that time, for in him the institution possessed the outstanding religious personality in the state and perhaps the outstanding Presbyterian in the South.[5] In 1855 his tenure as president of the college was terminated in order for him to become Professor of Didactic and Polemic Theology in the theological seminary at Columbia. This he did for the benefit of the seminary, which was at this time in a precarious position insofar as the strength of its faculty was concerned. His presence assured confidence and support for the seminary from the church.

It is not surprising to discover that when the Southern Presbyterian churches withdrew from the Presbyterian Church in the USA in 1861, Thornwell became the principal spokesman for the Presbyterian Church in the Confederate States of America. His "Address to All the Churches of Jesus Christ Throughout the Earth" was unanimously adopted by that body at its initial General Assembly at Augusta, Georgia, in December 1861.[6] It was in the Presbyterian churches of the southern states that he left his lasting mark, and that influence was strongest in the area of ecclesiology.[7] His views essentially became the position of the Presbyterian Church, U.S. for about a century and are to a large degree embodied in the recently formed Presbyterian Church in America.[8]

Ecclesiastical Debate

Thornwell's contribution must be evaluated in the light of the period in which he lived. During the first half of the nineteenth century American Presbyterians became embroiled in heated debate and serious reflection regarding their theology and church government. A primary cause of this intensive discussion was the Plan of Union of 1801, designed to bring Presbyterians and Congregationalists into close cooperation. Their common Calvinistic heritage and regular correspondence dating back to 1766 made the arrangement seem most reasonable.[9] The Plan of Union allowed new congregations to choose a minister from either denomination, to rule themselves according to Presbyterian or Congregational government, and to send official representatives to meetings of either denomination. In addition, voluntary benevolent societies were formed as a joint venture by individuals from both denominations.[10]

This period of cooperation was halted abruptly by the rupture of Presbyterians into Old and New Schools in 1837. The Old School Presbyterians had become convinced that the New England theology was diluting the confessional stance of the Westminster Confession of Faith and that the future of Presbyterianism was in jeopardy. They were evidently even more upset by their inability to control the situation.[11] Therefore, when the Old School Presbyterians found themselves holding the majority of commissioners at the 1837 General Assembly they proceeded to excise the New School Presbyterians, including all churches, presbyteries, and synods received during the period in which the Plan of Union had been in effect.[12] The same General Assembly passed a resolution declaring that the American Home Missionary Society and the American Education Society were exceedingly injurious to the peace and purity of the Presbyterian Church and urged that they no longer be allowed to operate within any of the churches in the denomination.[13]

The aftermath of the division found Old School Presbyterians seeking to identify themselves as Presbyterians in contrast to Congregationalists and other denominations. Consequently, in the year subsequent to the division and until 1860, there were prolonged, often heated, debates regarding the nature of Presbyterian polity. These debates revealed that significant matters of polity had not been thoroughly worked out by the denomination previously. While revolving around topics such as church boards, the status of the ruling elder, and related matters, these debates all centered on the location and exercise of power as that related to the genius of Presbyterianism. They should probably be seen as an expression of a desire to perpetuate the Presbyterian form of government.

Exactly what was the nature and mission of the church and what would that mean for the structure of the church?[14] If various tasks such as evangelism and ministries of mercy were eventually assumed by the voluntary societies, would this mean that the church would ultimately be left with very few functions, perhaps only worship and the administration of the sacraments? Apparently concerns of this nature troubled many Presbyterians, including Charles Hodge, who argued that Thornwell's position would compel the church to divest itself not only of boards, but seminaries, colleges, and similar institutions.[15] On the other hand, if the church were to assume responsibility for the various tasks being addressed at that time by the voluntary Christian organizations, then what organizational changes would be required in order to accomplish that effectively? That question bothered Thornwell and many of his colleagues.

Thornwell harbored intense convictions regarding the distinctiveness of Presbyterian doctrine and polity. He was convinced that the principles involved in the discussions affected the heart and soul of Presbyterianism. For these reasons he entered vigorously into the debates—debates that stretched across a span of more than twenty years and culminated with his famous encounter with Charles Hodge on the issue of the administration of missions at the 1860 General Assembly in Rochester, New York.[16]

The real issue of that debate, as Hodge himself observed, was not merely the propriety of church boards, but "what is Presbyterianism?"[17]

Thornwell claimed that the central question was the organization of the church itself.[18] He insisted that "God gave us our church government, as truly as he gave us our doctrines; and we have no more right to add to the church government, than to add to the doctrine."[19] He visualized the alternatives in this way:

> Thus, one party amongst us holds that Christ gave us the materials and principles of church-government, and has left us to shape them pretty much as we please. But the other holds that God gave us *a Church*, a constitution, laws, Presbyterys, Assemblies, Presbyters, and all the functionaries necessary to a complete organization of his kingdom upon the earth and to its effective operation; that he has revealed an order as well as a *faith*, and that as our attitude in the one case is to hear and *believe*, in the other it is hear and obey. Of one of these parties the motto is, "you may do all that the Scriptures do not forbid"; of the other, "you can do only what the Scriptures command."[20]

The Presbyterianism that Thornwell espoused reserved all power for the church courts. That power belonged to the elders or presbyters who were the rulers of the church. It was not to be vested in voluntary societies or boards that could act independently of the church in its ecclesiastical capacity. If committees or boards existed, they must be directly accountable to the General Assembly of the church.[21]

Another matter of great importance to Thornwell in regard to church government was the status of the ruling elder. Some controversy had occurred during the General Assemblies of 1842-1844 regarding whether or not ruling elders had the right to lay on hands at the ordination of ministers. The 1843 General Assembly concluded that ruling elders did not have that right.[22] The 1843 General Assembly also dealt with another pertinent matter when it ruled that a presbytery meeting could be convened and a quorum could be declared present without the presence of a ruling elder.[23]

Thornwell was convinced that if the rights of the ruling elder were slighted a "sacred hierarchy" would result in the church, and the concentration of power in the hands of the clergy occurring thereby would spell doom for Presbyterianism. He was convinced that the delicate balance of power effected through two classes of presbyters, teaching and ruling elders, could not be dispensed with without serious results for Presbyterianism as a system of government. Moreover, presbyters could not be limited to the clergy, for that would be prelacy. Rather, presbyters were both ruling elders and teaching elders, that is, both laymen and clergy. "Presbyterianism stands or falls with a distinction between ruling and teaching elders," he maintained.[24] In this way the balance of power was maintained within the church courts, and this power was representative, not by proxy, which would be Congregationalism. So power was reserved for the church "in its ecclesiastical capacity," and yet that power was carefully distributed between clergy and laity acting in a representative capacity. In that way he distinguished Presbyterianism from every other form of church government:

> The government of the Church by parliamentary assemblies, composed of two classes of Elders, and of Elders only and so arranged to realize the visible unity of the whole church—this is Presbyterianism.[25]

Since differing views on theology and church government were the principal issues leading to the division of 1837 and, with the slavery issue, continued to dominate the attention of Presbyterians during the remainder of Thornwell's life, it is not surprising that a major portion of his energies was directed to these matters.[26]

Invariably, his immediate recourse for the resolution of the matter was to the authoritative Scriptures. In this respect he found company with Old School Presbyterians and other evangelical Christians of his era. His basic assumption in developing his arguments was the hermeneutical principle that whatever is not commanded in the Bible is forbidden. There would have been a consensus among many of his colleagues in regard to this principle as well. Thornwell is open to criticism, however, for his failure to justify this hermeneutical principle so crucial to the development of his argument. Thornwell's difficulty lay not in the persuasive power of his vigorous logical mind, but rather in a failure to plumb carefully and vigorously the assumptions on which he built his telling arguments.

Another question that comes to mind as one assesses his involvement in the discussions on church government is the degree to which the secular political situation may have influenced Thornwell and his contemporaries in the divergent approaches toward the polity that they adopted. For example, the states'-rights principles that became important factors in southern sectionalism appear to be reflected somewhat in the Thornwellian polity. Perhaps this is the explanation for Thornwell's desire to retain as much authority as possible for presbyteries, especially if it is kept in mind that Thornwell was from South Carolina where southern sentiments were most pronounced and which was also the home state of John C. Calhoun, formulator of the doctrine of nullification. This might also partially explain the keen interest of Southern Presbyterians to maintain a balance of power though the parity of elders since Southerners were sensitive to such matters because of their efforts to maintain a balance of power in Congress as more states were added, both slave and free, and as the population of the northern states swelled more rapidly, yielding them an edge in the House of Representatives. The question is not one of Thornwell's theological integrity, nor that of Southern Presbyterians in general; rather, it is the question to what degree one remains captive to his culture while attempting to understand and apply the truth of the Bible.

Similar questions may be raised regarding Thornwell's position on slavery. He was well aware of the magnitude and pervasiveness of this issue. In his opinion, the Bible did not condemn slavery and so the church should not do so either. Actually, Thronwell concluded,

> The Scriptures not only fail to condemn slavery, they as distinctly sanction it as any other social condition of man. The Church was formally organized in the family of a slaveholder; the relation was divinely regulated among the chosen people of God; and the peculiar duties of the parties are inculcated under the Christian economy. These are facts which cannot be denied.[27]

If that was the case, then Christians needed to the fullest extent possible to bring biblical principles to bear on all aspects of the current practice of slavery. So Thornwell developed a position for a Christian doctrine of slavery that included a careful delineation of the status of the slave as a person made in the image of God and therefore as one who should be regarded as a brother.[28] The master did not have a right to unlimited control, but only a right to his labor.[29] On the other hand, Thornwell argued that if a master should emancipate his slave, then operating on the same benevolent principle a rich man should share all of his estate with his poor neighbors. If such ideas were implemented it would, he warned, bring disaster to all institutions of civilized society.[30]

Scripture and Philosophy

A more reasonable explanation for Thornwell's positions than the influence of the political situation seems to be the influence of Scottish Common Sense Philosophy, resulting in a cultural and social conservativism that typified the views of James Henley Thornwell and Old School Presbyterians.[31] Scottish Common Sense Philosophy dominated Princetonian thought from Witherspoon on and Old School Presbyterianism throughout the first half of the nineteenth century. Princeton was by far the most influential of the northern colleges on southern education.[32] Therefore, it is relatively easy to see how Common Sense Philosophy would have become pervasive in the South. Southern colleges offered courses in moral philosophy, required of all students, introducing Scottish Common Sense Philosophy to them in this manner.[33] This school of philosophy not only became dominant in Old School Presbyterianism, but became "The Reliable Handmaiden of Southern Theology,"[34] and Thornwell was no exception to the rule. There is the specific reason that Robert Henry, Professor of Logic and Ethics at South Carolina College, had studied at Edinburgh. It was said of him that he was the man who had taught South Carolinians to think. Henry, Thornwell's professor, introduced him to Dugald Stuart's writings, and Thornwell read them before moving on to the study of William Hamilton.[35]

Thornwell warmly embraced this mode of thinking, as can be seen from his writings.[36] In his inaugural address as professor at Columbia Theological Seminary, he noted that the task of theological scholarship was to show the complete harmony of sound philosophy and theology.[37] He saw the truth of nature and Scripture in harmony, and he saw them as one system of truth. Since grace presupposed nature, there was a need to lay the natural foundation for an examination of the Scriptures. To begin abruptly with the doctrine of redemption with no connection to natural religion did not appeal to him at all.[38] Thornwell saw moral philosophy as a form of natural theology and the ground of moral obligation to be through philosophical description. Although ethics was based on biblical precept, actually the Scriptures were a validation of the conclusions of Common Sense Philosophy.[39]

That this should be the case seems incongruous with Thornwell's insistence on the final, determinative authority of the Scriptures for faith and practice. His statements regarding this matter are unequivocal:

> Christianity in its living principles and its outward forms is purely a matter of Divine revelation. The great error of the Church in all ages, the fruitful source of her apostasy and crime, has been a presumptuous reliance upon her own understanding. Her own inventions have seduced her from her loyalty to God, and filled her sanctuary with idols and the hearts of her children with vain imaginations. The Bible cuts at the very root of this evil by affording us a perfect and infallible rule of faith and practice. The absolute perfection of the Scriptures as a directory to man was a cardinal principle of the Reformation, and whatever could not be traced to them either directly or by necessary inference was denounced as a human invention—as mere will-worship, which God abhors so deeply that an inspired Apostle has connected it with idolatry or the worshipping of angels.[40]

Of course, there is no question about his desire to be faithful to the Scriptures and for them to serve as his ultimate authority. The question is rather to what degree he was able to achieve this objective as a theologian. In answering this question, the influence of Common Sense Philosophy on his theology must be measured carefully. An evaluation

of Old School Presbyterianism and Princeton theology appears to be
equally applicable to Thornwell:

> In short, what is praiseworthy in this Presbyterian theology is its
> eagerness to be confessionally scriptural, scientifically respectable,
> and culturally relevant. It made a valiant attempt to retain its theo-
> logical orthodoxy while it was constantly surrounded, and at times
> subtly tempted, by formidable philosophical movements that
> seemed, outwardly, at least, to be congenial to a biblical stance.
>
> This desire to be fully biblical was so strong that these Presby-
> terian theologians soon developed the conviction that all their ideas,
> including the philosophical, were of a thoroughly scriptural char-
> acter, as well as the belief that their reading and understanding of
> Scripture was not in any way blurred by superimposed philosoph-
> ical constructs.
>
> It could be maintained that the scriptural intent of Presbyterian
> theology has actually been undermined by the attempts of this the-
> ology, particularly during the nineteenth century, to adapt itself to
> certain philosophical thought-patterns that were then culturally in
> vogue. In fact, these philosophical ideas were generally neither ex-
> pressive of, nor congenial to, a full-orbed, scriptural ontology, an-
> thropology, and epistemology.[41]

Thornwell's affirmation of Common Sense Philosophy invariably
led him to a particular view of the sinful world in which he lived and
how that world could best be brought into conformity to the Bible. In
the first place, he accepted society with all its imperfections as the consequence of God's providential ordering of things.[42] He viewed society
and nature as joint aspects of a whole—one unified scheme. Society
involved a system of relationships rooted in natural law. Therefore, just
as growth and development were slow, gradual processes in nature, in
similar fashion one would anticipate that that would be the case with
God's design for progress and reform in society; one would not expect
it to involve "sudden changes or violent revolutions."[43] The influence of
believing individuals would be an appropriate catalyst for salutary change.

This attitude toward social change sounds somewhat similar to but
is different from Thornwell's view of the "spirituality of the church."[44]
Attributed to Thornwell, this position was a distinctive of Southern Presbyterianism for many years. Essentially, he delineated two separate
spheres of authority and function: the church and the state were "as
planets moving in different orbits."[45] The church, he said,

> is exclusively a spiritual organization, . . . she has nothing to do
> with the voluntary associations of men for various social and civic
> purposes. . . . Her mission is to bring men to the cross, to reconcile
> them to God . . . imbue them with the spirit of the Divine Master

and then send them forth to perform their social duties, to manage society, and perform the functions that pertain to their social and civic relations.[46]

The church was limited in the scope of its activity. It was not to interfere with the state and its decisions. But the individual Christian experienced no such restriction. He was expected to be active, and the more Christians who participated in government, the more Thornwell would have been pleased. He was active himself, drafting a paper on slavery, advocating support of public schools and the inclusion of religious instruction in the curriculum, and shaping a General Assembly statement regarding peace in Mexico. Occasionally the relationships appear to be blurred as, for example, when he joined the Synod of South Carolina in urging the people of South Carolina "to imitate their revolutionary forefathers and stand up for their rights."[47] In holding this position regarding church and state, Thornwell placed himself in the tradition of the Westminster Confession of Faith.

Conclusion

Thornwell must be viewed as a champion of his Old School Presbyterian theological heritage. His forceful, eloquent leadership contributed substantially toward assuring a legacy of orthodoxy for later generations of Southern Presbyterians. His desire to understand the Scriptures and to seek obedient conformity to them in church and society is the essence of what it means to be Reformed. His weakness lay in assuming that his understanding of the Scriptures was not distorted by his philosophical frame of reference, which was weak in regard to the relationship between natural and revealed theology. Thus his remarkable contribution bears the theological and philosophical marks of the nineteenth-century Old School Presbyterian mold in which it was cast.

James Henley Thornwell still casts a long shadow in Southern Presbyterianism, particularly in the nascent Presbyterian Church in America and in the Reformed Theological Seminary in Jackson, Mississippi.

Notes: James Henley Thornwell

1. Benjamin Morgan Palmer, *Life and Letters of James Henley Thornwell* (Richmond: Whittet and Shepperson, 1875), 397.
2. Ibid., 537.
3. Paul L. Garber, "James Henley Thornwell: Presbyterian Defender of the Old South," *Union Seminary Review* 54 (February 1943): 99.
4. Ibid.

5. Daniel W. Hollis, *The University of South Carolina*, 2 vols. (Columbia, SC: University of South Carolina Press, 1951), 1:161.

6. The address provided the rationale for the establishment of the Presbyterian Church in the Confederate States of America.

7. Thomas Peck, a contemporary, thought Thornwell's great contribution was in ecclesiology (Thomas E. Peck, *Miscellanies of Rev. Thomas E. Peck*, ed. T. C. Johnson, 3 vols. [Richmond: The Presbyterian Committee of Publication, 1895], 1:434). Garber, "In whatever manner the Southern Presbyterian church may have departed from the ideals he defined for its establishment in 1861, that denomination remains to an extent the lengthened shadow of James Henley Thornwell as the Scottish church is of John Knox" (Garber, "Thornwell," 99). H. Sheldon Smith concluded that Thornwell's theological thought dominated most of the history of Southern Presbyterianism ("The Church and the Social Order in the Old South as Interpreted by James H. Thornwell," *Church History* 7 [June 1938]: 115ff.).

8. The First General Assembly of the Presbyterian Church in America met in Birmingham, Alabama, on December 4, 1973. The name National Presbyterian Church was selected at this initial assembly, but changed at the 1974 General Assembly.

9. William O. Bracket, Jr., "The Rise and Development of the New School in the Presbyterian Church in the USA to the Reunion of 1869," *The Journal of the Presbyterian Historical Society* 13:121.

10. The American Home Missionary Society and the American Board of Commissioners for Foreign Missions were two of the societies that functioned under the Plan of Union. Tension soon began to rise, however, because of increasing denominational interests in the official boards and agencies of the Presbyterian Church. Cf. Clifford S. Griffin, "Cooperation in Conflict: The Schism in the American Home Missionary Society, 1837-1861," *Journal of the Presbyterian Historical Society* 28 (1960): 213-233.

11. George M. Marsden, *The Evangelical Mind and the New School Presbyterian Experience* (New Haven: Yale University Press, 1970), 59.

12. Approximately half of the denomination was ejected by this action, which eliminated about 100,000 members.

13. This development was not peculiar to Presbyterians alone. Similar efforts emphasizing denominational distinctives were occurring in several major ecclesiastical bodies during the first half of the nineteenth century. This would be expected in the light of the numerical and geographical expansion that was occurring.

14. For samples of recent literature that has grappled with the relationship of church and parachurch groups as well as the structure of the church itself, see Richard G. Hutchenson, Jr., *Mainline Churches and the Evangelicals: A Challenging Crisis* (Atlanta: John Knox Press, 1981); also Hutchenson, *Wheel Within the Wheel: Confronting the Management Crisis of the Pluralistic Church* (Atlanta: John Knox Press, 1979); Howard A. Snyder, *The Problem of Wineskins: Church Structure in a Technological Age* (Downers Grove: InterVarsity Press, 1975); Ralph D. Winter, "The Two Structures of God's Redemptive Mission," in *American Society of Missiology* (1974).

15. *The Collected Writings of James Henley Thornwell* ed. John B. Adger and John L. Girardeau, 4 vols. (Richmond, VA: Presbyterian Committee of Publication, 1871-1881), 1:230-31.

16. For a more detailed account of Thornwell's views on this subject see

Kenneth J. Foreman, Jr., "The Debate on the Administration of Missions by James Henley Thornwell in the Presbyterian Church 1839-1861" (Ph.D. diss., Princeton University, 1977). For a more comprehensive analysis of Thornwell's views see Morton H. Smith, *Studies in Southern Presbyterian Theology* (Jackson, MS: Presbyterian Reformation Society, 1962), 121-82.

17. Charles Hodge, "Presbyterianism," *Biblical Repertory and Princeton Review* 32 (October 8, 1860): 546.

18. Adger and Girardeau, eds., *Collected Writings*, 4:218.

19. Ibid.

20. Ibid.

21. Ibid., 230.

22. *Minutes of a General Assembly of the Presbyterian Church in the USA, 1838-1847* (Philadelphia: Presbyterian Board of Publication and Sabbath School work, n.d.), 276-77.

23. Ibid.

24. Adger and Girardeau, eds., *Collected Writings*, 125.

25. Ibid., 267. It is interesting to note that in the infant Presbyterian Church in the Confederate States of America, Thornwell's position was adopted and the parity of ruling elders and teaching elders was closely guarded. See Ernest T. Thompson, *Presbyterians in the South*, 3 vols. (Richmond: John Knox Press, 1963), 1:516. For an analysis of Thornwell's position on the parity of elders see Luder G. Whitlock, Jr., "Elders and Ecclesiology in the Thought of James Henley Thornwell," *Westminster Theological Journal* 38 (Fall 1974): 44.

26. Lefferts Loetscher, *The Broadening Church* (Philadelphia: University of Pennsylvania Press, 1957), 5; Marsden, *The Evangelical Mind and the New School Presbyterian Experience*, 67.

27. Adger and Girardeau, eds., *Collected Writings*, 4:386-87.

28. Ibid., 403.

29. Thornwell, "The State of the Country," *Southern Presbyterian Review* 13:874.

30. Ibid., 391, 432. Also see H. Shelton Smith, "The Church and the Social Order in the Old South as Interpreted by James H. Thornwell," *Church History* 7 (June 1938): 115-24.

31. An excellent presentation of this point of view is found in Theodore Dwight Bozeman, "Science, Nature, and Society: A New Approach to James Henley Thornwell," *Journal of Presbyterian History* 50 (1972): 307-25; see also Bozeman, *Protestants in an Age of Science: The Baconian Ideal and Antebellum American Religious Thought* (Chapel Hill, NC: University of North Carolina Press, 1977); Loetscher, *The Broadening Church*, 6; V. L. Parrington, *Main Currents in American Thought*, 2 (New York: Harcourt Brace Jovanovich, 1955); D. H. Meyer, *The Instructed Conscience: The Shaping of the American National Ethic* (Philadelphia: University of Pennsylvania Press, 1972); E. Brooks Holifield, *The Gentleman Theologians: American Theology and Southern Culture, 1795-1860* (Durham, NC: Duke University Press, 1978), 110-54.

32. Donald R. Come, "The Influence of Princeton on Higher Education in the South before 1825," *William and Mary Quarterly*, third series, 2 (1945).

33. Holifield, *Gentleman Theologians*, 119.

34. Ibid., 126.

35. Dugald Stuart was a disciple of Thomas Reid at Edinburgh. This phil-

osophical frame of reference was Thornwell's heritage and milieu. Thornwell became, as might be expected, an enthusiastic advocate of the Common Sense Philosophy.

36. For a good synopsis see Bozeman, "Science, Nature, and Society"; also Holifield, *Gentleman Theologians*, 110, 126.

37. Adger and Girardeau, eds., *Collected Writings*, 1:580.

38. Ibid.

39. Holifield, *Gentleman Theologians*, 127.

40. Adger and Girardeau, eds., *Collected Writings*, 4:163-64.

41. John C. Vander Stelt, *Philosophy and Scripture: A Study in Old Princeton and Westminster Theology* (Marlton, NJ: Mack Publishing Company, 1978), 304-05, provides a very helpful survey and extensive critique.

42. Adger and Girardeau, eds., *Collected Writings*, 4:404, 421, 430.

43. Ibid., 428, 431-32.

44. See Ernest Trice Thompson, *The Spirituality of the Church* (Richmond: John Knox Press, 1961); also his *Presbyterians in the South*, Vol. 1; Bozeman, in "Science, Nature, and Society," explains his view in the light of Common Sense Philosophy, which would have disdained meddling with God's providentially ordered affairs. Adam Smith developed his *laissez-faire* economic policy out of similar philosophical principles, Bozeman notes. Is it possible that Thornwell has developed a theological equivalent? Bozeman observes that McCosh in his *Divine Government* adopts a similar pattern of reasoning. Challenging these points of view is Jack P. Maddex, "From Theocracy to Spirituality: The Southern Presbyterian Reversal on Church and State," *Journal of Presbyterian History* 54 (Winter 1976): 438-57. Maddex contends that antebellum Southern Presbyterians did not teach absolute separation of church and state.

45. Adger and Girardeau, eds., *Collected Writings*, 4:177.

46. Ibid., 473.

47. Thompson, *Presbyterians in the South*, 1:558. Thompson notes that the synod, after careful study by some of its members, concluded that a sacred inheritance of rights, as in their case, could not be surrendered without sinning against God. Therefore, this particular action must be evaluated in that light.

BIBLIOGRAPHY

1. Bibliographies and Indexes

It should be noted that many of the works listed in Section 4 contain extensive bibliographical material on the Princetonians as well.

Armstrong, William P. "Index of *The Presbyterian and Reformed Review* XI (1900)–XIII (1902) and *The Princeton Theological Review* I (1903)–XXVII (1929)." *Princeton Theological Review* 27 (July 1929): 487–587.

Biblical Repertory and Princeton Review. Index Volume from 1825 to 1868. Philadelphia: Peter Walker, 1870–1871.

Burr, Nelson R. "The Princeton Theology." In *A Critical Bibliography of Religion in America,* vol. IV, parts 3, 4, and 5, pp. 999–1003 of *Religion in American Life,* edited by James Ward Smith and A. Leland Jamison. Princeton: Princeton University Press, 1961.

Dulles, Joseph H. "Index to Volumes I–X, 1890–1899." *Presbyterian and Reformed Review* 10 (October 1899): 727–98.

Gapp, Kenneth S. "The *Princeton Review* Series and the Contribution of Princeton Theological Seminary to Presbyterian Quarterly Magazines." Typescript, Speer Library, Princeton Theological Seminary, 1960.

Kennedy, Earl William. "Authors of Articles in the *Biblical Repertory and Princeton Review.*" Typescript, Speer Library, Princeton Theological Seminary, 1963.

_____. "Writings about Charles Hodge and His Works. Principally as Found in Periodicals Contained in the Speer Library of Princeton Theological Seminary for the Years 1830–1880." Typescript, Speer Library, Princeton Theological Seminary, 1963.

Meeter, John E., and Nicole, Roger. *A Bibliography of Benjamin Breckinridge Warfield 1851–1921.* Nutley, NJ: Presbyterian and Reformed, 1974.

2. Major Books of the Major Princeton Theologians

This partial list of published books also contains information on where these various volumes are still in print (as of 1981–1982 catalogs). For each author, books are listed in chronological order by date of first publication. Many of these works went through several editions in their authors' own lifetimes.

Archibald Alexander

A Brief Outline of the Evidence of the Christian Religion. Princeton: D.A. Borrenstein, 1825.

The Canon of the Old and New Testaments Ascertained; or, The Bible Complete Without the Apocrypha and Unwritten Traditions. New York: D.A. Borrenstein for G. & C. Carvill, 1826.

Evidences of the Authenticity, Inspiration, and Canonical Authority of the Holy Scriptures. Philadelphia: Presbyterian Board of Publication, 1826. In print, Arno and New York Times, New York.

A Selection of Hymns, Adapted to the Devotions of the Closet, the Family and the Social Circle. New York: Leavitt, 1831.

Counsels of the Aged to the Young. Philadelphia: Key and Biddle, 1833.

History of the Patriarchs. Philadelphia: American Sunday School Union, 1833.

History of the Israelites, from the Death of Joseph to the Death of Moses. Philadelphia: Perkins, 1834.

Thoughts on Religious Experience. Philadelphia: Presbyterian Board of Publication, 1841. In print, Banner of Truth, London.

Biographical Sketches of the Founder and Principal Alumni of the Log College. Princeton: J. T. Robenson, 1845. In print, Banner of Truth, London.

A Brief Compend of Bible Truth. Philadelphia: Presbyterian Board of Publication, 1846.

A History of Colonization on the Western Coast of Africa. Philadelphia: Martien, 1846. In print, Arno and New York Times, New York; Greenwood, Westport, CT.

Theological Essays. New York and London, 1846.

Practical Sermons: To Be Read in Families and Social Meetings. Philadelphia: Presbyterian Board of Publication, 1850.

Outlines of Moral Science. New York: Charles Scribner's Sons, 1852.

A History of the Israelitish Nation, from Their Origin to Their Dispersion at the Destruction of Jerusalem by the Romans. Philadelphia: Martien, 1853.

Practical Truths. New York: American Tract Society, 1857.

Charles Hodge

A Commentary on the Epistle to the Romans. Philadelphia: Grigg & Elliot, 1835. In print, Eerdmans, Grand Rapids; Banner of Truth, London.

The Constitutional History of the Presbyterian Church in the United States of America. Philadelphia: Presbyterian Board of Education, 1840.

The Way of Life. Philadelphia: American Sunday School Union, 1841. In print, Baker, Grand Rapids; Banner of Truth, London. New edition, edited by Mark A. Noll. Mahwah, NJ: Paulist, 1987.

A Commentary on the Epistle to the Ephesians. New York: Carter & Bros., 1856. In print, Baker, Grand Rapids.

Essays and Reviews: Selected from the Princeton Review. New York: Carter & Bros. 1857. In print, Garland, New York.

An Exposition of the First Epistle to the Corinthians. New York: Carter & Bros., 1857. In print, Eerdmans, Grand Rapids; Baker, Grand Rapids; Banner of Truth, London.

An Exposition of the Second Epistle to the Corinthians. New York: Carter & Bros., 1857. In print, Baker, Grand Rapids; Banner of Truth, London.

Systematic Theology. New York: Charles Scribner's Sons, 1872–1873. In print, Eerdmans, Grand Rapids; J. Clarke, Cambridge, England.

What Is Darwinism? New York: Scribners, Armstrong and Company, 1874.

Conference Papers. New York: Charles Scribner's Sons, 1879. In print, as *Princeton Sermons*, Banner of Truth, London.

A. A. Hodge

Outlines of Theology. New York: Carter & Bros., 1860. Rev. and enlarged ed., 1878. In print, Zondervan, Grand Rapids.

The Atonement. Philadelphia: Presbyterian Board of Publication, 1867.

A Commentary on the Confession of Faith. Philadelphia: Presbyterian Board of Publication, 1889. In print, Banner of Truth, London.

The Life of Charles Hodge. New York: Charles Scribner's Sons, 1880. In print, Arno and New York Times, New York.

Inspiration, with B.B. Warfield. Philadelphia: Presbyterian Board of Publication, 1881. In print, Baker, Grand Rapids, with notes, introduction, and bibliographies by Roger R. Nicole.

Popular Lectures on Theological Themes. Philadelphia: Presbyterian Board of Publication, 1887. In print as *Evangelical Theology,* Banner of Truth, London.

B. B. Warfield

An Introduction to the Textual Criticism of the New Testament. London: Hodder and Stoughton, 1886.

The Power of God Unto Salvation. Philadelphia: Presbyterian Board of Publication, 1903.

The Lord of Glory. New York: American Tract Society, 1907.

The Saviour of the World. New York: Hodder and Stoughton, 1914.

The Plan of Salvation. Philadelphia: Presbyterian Board of Publication, 1915. In print, Eerdmans, Grand Rapids.

Faith and Life. "Conferences" in the Oratory of Princeton Seminary. New York: Longmans, Green, 1916. In print, Banner of Truth, London.

Counterfeit Miracles. New York: Charles Scribner's Sons, 1918. In print, Banner of Truth, London.

Revelation and Inspiration, Works: Vol. I. New York: Oxford University Press, 1927. In print, Baker, Grand Rapids.

Biblical Doctrines, Works: Vol. II. New York: Oxford University Press, 1929. In print, Baker, Grand Rapids.

Christology and Criticism, Works: Vol. III. New York: Oxford University Press, 1931. In print, Baker, Grand Rapids.

Studies in Tertullian and Augustine, Works: Vol. IV. New York: Oxford University Press, 1930. In print, Baker, Grand Rapids; Greenwood, Westport, CT.

Calvin and Calvinism, Works: Vol. V. New York: Oxford University Press, 1931. In print, Baker, Grand Rapids.

The Westminster Assembly and Its Work, Works: Vol. VI. New York: Oxford University Press, 1931. In print, Baker, Grand Rapids.

Perfectionism Part One, Works: Vol. VII. New York: Oxford University Press, 1931. In print, Baker, Grand Rapids.

Perfectionism Part Two, Works: Vol. VIII. New York: Oxford University Press, 1931. In print, Baker, Grand Rapids.

Studies in Theology, Works: Vol. IX. New York: Oxford University Press, 1932. In print, Baker, Grand Rapids.

Critical Reviews, Works: Vol. X. New York: Oxford University Press, 1932. In print, Baker, Grand Rapids.

The Inspiration and Authority of the Bible [selected mostly from *Works, Vol. I*]. Philadelphia: Presbyterian and Reformed, 1948.

The Person and Work of Christ [selected mostly from *Works, Vol. III*]. Philadelphia: Presbyterian and Reformed, 1950.

Biblical and Theological Studies [selected mostly from *Works, Vol. II*]. Philadelphia: Presbyterian and Reformed, 1952.

Calvin and Augustine [selected from *Works, Vols. IV* and *V*]. Philadelphia: Presbyterian and Reformed, 1956.

Perfectionism [selected from *Works, Vols. VII* and *VIII*]. Philadelphia: Presbyterian and Reformed, 1958.

Selected Shorter Writings of Benjamin B. Warfield, Vols. I and *II*. Edited by John E. Meeter. Nutley, NJ: Presbyterian and Reformed, 1970 and 1973.

3. Secondary Works

Princeton Seminary and General Studies on the Princeton Theology

Balmer, Randall H. "The Princetonians and Scripture: A Reconsideration." *Westminster Theological Journal* 44 (1982): 352–65.

_____. "The Princetonians, Scripture, and Recent Scholarship." *Journal of Presbyterian History* 60 (Fall 1982): 267–70.

Biographical Catalogue of the Princeton Theological Seminary, 1815–1932, compiled by Edward Howell Roberts. Princeton: Trustees of the Theological Seminary of the Presbyterian Church, 1933.

The Centennial Celebration of the Theological Seminary of the Presbyterian Church in the United States of America at Princeton, New Jersey. Princeton: Princeton Theological Seminary, 1912.

Hart, John W. "Princeton Theological Seminary: The Reorganization of 1929." *Journal of Presbyterian History* 58 (Summer 1980): 124–40.

Hodge, Charles. "Retrospect of the History of the Princeton Review." *Biblical Repertory and Princeton Review. Index Volume,* no. 1 (January 1870): 1–39.

Hoffecker, W. Andrew. "The Devotional Life of Archibald Alexander, Charles Hodge, and Benjamin B. Warfield." *Westminster Theological Journal* 42 (Fall 1979): 111–29.

_____. *Piety and the Princeton Theologians: Archibald Alexander, Charles Hodge, and Benjamin Warfield.* Phillipsburg, NJ: Presbyterian and Reformed; and Grand Rapids: Baker, 1981.

Illick, Joseph E., III. "The Reception of Darwinism at the Theological Seminary and the College at Princeton, New Jersey." *Journal of the Presbyterian Historical Society* 38 (September 1960): 152–65; (December 1960): 234–43.

Linsay, Thomas M. "The Doctrine of Scripture: The Reformers and the Princeton School," In *The Expositor,* Fifth Series, edited by W. Robertson Nicoll, 1:278–93. London: Hodder and Stoughton, 1895.

Noll, Mark A. "The Founding of Princeton Seminary." *Westminster Theological Journal* 42 (Fall 1979): 72–110.

Sandeen, Ernest R. "The Princeton Theology: One Source of Biblical Literalism in American Protestantism." *Church History* 31 (September 1962): 307–21.

Vander Stelt, John C. *Philosophy and Scripture: A Study in Old Princeton and Westminster Theology.* Marlton, NJ.: Mack, 1978.

Woodbridge, John D., and Balmer, Randy. "The Princetonians' Viewpoint of Biblical Authority: An Evaluation of Ernest Sandeen." In *Scripture and Truth,* edited by John D. Woodbridge and D.A. Carson. Grand Rapids: Zondervan, 1983.

Archibald Alexander

Alexander, James Waddel. *The Life of Archibald Alexander.* New York: Charles Scribner's Sons, 1854.

"Archibald Alexander." *Biblical Repertory and Princeton Review. Index Volume,* no. 1 (January 1870): 42–67.

De Witt, John. "Archibald Alexander's Preparation for His Professorship." *Princeton Theological Review* 3 (October 1905): 573–94.

Hodge, Charles. "Memoir of Archibald Alexander." *Biblical Repertory and Princeton Review* 27 (January 1855): 133–59.

Jackson, Gordon E. "Archibald Alexander's *Thoughts on Religious Experience,* a Critical Revisiting." *Journal of Presbyterian History* 51 (Summer 1973): 141–54.

Loetscher, Lefferts A. *Facing the Enlightenment and Pietism: Archibald Alexander and the Founding of Princeton Theological Seminary* (Westport, CT: Greenwood, 1983).

Mackay, John A. "Archibald Alexander (1772–1851): Founding Father." In *Sons of the Prophets*, edited by Hugh T. Kerr. Princeton: Princeton University Press, 1963.

McKim, Donald K. "Archibald Alexander and the Doctrine of Scripture." *Journal of Presbyterian History* 54 (Fall 1976): 355–75.

Nelson, John Oliver. "Archibald Alexander, Winsome Conservative." *Journal of the Presbyterian Historical Society* 35 (March 1957): 15–33.

Okholm, Dennis. "Biblical Inspiration and Infallibility in the Writings of Archibald Alexander." *Trinity Journal* [Trinty Evangelical Divinity School] 5 (Spring 1976): 79–89.

Charles Hodge

Barker, William S. "The Social Views of Charles Hodge (1797–1878): A Study in Nineteenth-Century Calvinism and Conservatism." *Presbyterion: Covenant Seminary Review* 1 (Spring 1975): 1–22.

Cashdollar, Charles D. "The Pursuit of Piety: Charles Hodge's Diary, 1819–1820." *Journal of Presbyterian History* 55 (Fall 1977): 267–74.

"Charles Hodge." *Biblical Repertory and Princeton Review. Index Volume*, no. 2 (1870): 200–11.

Danhof, Ralph J. *Charles Hodge as Dogmatician*. Goes, The Netherlands: Oosterbaan and le Cointre, 1929.

Discourses Commemorative of the Life and Work of Charles Hodge. Philadelphia: Henry B. Ashmead, 1879.

Hodge, Archibald Alexander. *The Life of Charles Hodge*. New York: Charles Scribner's Sons, 1880.

Hogeland, Ronald W. "Charles Hodge, The Association of Gentlemen and Ornamental Womanhood: A Study of Male Conventional Wisdom, 1825–1855." *Journal of Presbyterian History* 53 (Fall 1975): 239–55.

Holifield, E. Brooks. "Mercersburg, Princeton, and the South: The Sacramental Controversy in the Nineteenth Century." *Journal of Presbyterian History* 54 (Summer 1976): 238–57.

Nelson, John Oliver. "Charles Hodge (1797–1878): Nestor of Orthodoxy." In *The Lives of Eighteen from Princeton*, edited by Willard Thorp. Princeton: Princeton University Press, 1946.

Olbricht, Thomas H. "Charles Hodge as an American New Testament Interpreter." *Journal of Presbyterian History* 57 (Summer 1979): 117–33.

Patton, Francis Landey. "Charles Hodge." *Presbyterian Review* 2 (January 1881): 349–77.

Proceedings Connected with the Semi-Centennial Commemorative of the Professorship of Rev. Charles Hodge, D.D., LL.D., April 24, 1872. New York: Anson D.F. Randolph, 1872.

Shriver, George H. "Passages in Friendship: John W. Nevin to Charles Hodge, 1872." *Journal of Presbyterian History* 58 (Summer 1980): 116–22.

Stein, Stephen J. "Stuart and Hodge on Romans 5:12–21: An Exegetical Controversy about Original Sin." *Journal of Presbyterian History* 47 (December 1969): 340–58.

Wells, David F. "The Stout and Persistent 'Theology' of Charles Hodge." *Christianity Today*, August 30, 1974, pp. 10–15.

A. A. Hodge

Patton, Francis Landey. *A Discourse in Memory of Archibald Alexander Hodge.* Philadelphia: Times, 1887.

Paxton, William M. *Address Delivered at the Funeral of Archibald Alexander Hodge.* New York: Anson D. F. Randolph, 1886.

Salmond, C.A. *Princetonian. Charles & A. A. Hodge: With Class and Table Talk of Hodge the Younger.* Edinburgh: Oliphant, Anderson & Ferrier, 1888.

B. B. Warfield

Allis, O.T. "Personal Impressions of Dr. Warfield." *Banner of Truth* 89 (Fall 1971): 10–14.

Craig, Samuel G. "Benjamin B. Warfield." In *Biblical and Theological Studies,* pp. xi–xlviii. Philadelphia: Presbyterian and Reformed, 1952.

Fuller, Daniel P. "Benjamin B. Warfield"s View of Faith and History." *Journal of the Evangelical Theological Society* 11 (Spring 1968): 75–83.

Gerstner, John H. "Warfield's Case for Biblical Inerrancy." In *God's Inerrant Word,* edited by John Warwick Montgomery. Minneapolis: Bethany, 1974.

Grier, W.J. "Benjamin Breckinridge Warfield." *Banner of Truth* 89 (Fall 1971): 3–9.

Krabbendam, Hendrick. "B. B. Warfield vs. G.C. Berkouwer on Scripture." In *Inerrancy: The Extent of Biblical Authority,* edited by Norman L. Geisler. Grand Rapids: Zondervan, 1980.

Murray, Iain et al., eds. "Warfield Commemorative Issue, 1921–1971." *Banner of Truth* 89 (Fall 1971).

Nicole, Roger. "The Inspiration of Scripture: B.B. Warfield and Dr. Dewey M. Beegle." *Gordon Review* 8 (Winter 1964–65): 93–109.

Parsons, Mike. "Warfield and Scripture." *The Churchman* (London) 91 (July 1977): 198–220.

Patton, Francis L. "Benjamin Breckinridge Warfield—A Memorial Address." *Princeton Theological Review* 19 (July 1921): 369–91.

Peter, J.F. "Warfield on the Scriptures." *Reformed Theological Review* 16 (October 19, 1957): 76–84.

Rogers, Jack B. "Van Til and Warfield on Scripture in the Westminister Confession." In *Jerusalem and Athens,* edited by E.R. Geehan. Nutley, NJ: Presbyterian and Reformed, 1971.

Swanton, Robert. "Warfield and Progressive Orthodoxy." *Reformed Theological Review* 23 (October 1964): 74–87.

Torrance, T.F. Review of Warfield's *Inspiration and Authority of the Bible. Scottish Journal of Theology* 7 (March 1854): 104–8.

Wallis, Wilbut B. "Benjamin B. Warfield: Didactic and Polemical Theologian." *Presbyterion: Covenant Seminary Review* 3 (April 1977): 73–94.

Westblade, Donald. "Benjamin B. Warfield on Inspiration and Inerrancy." *Studia Biblica et Theologica* 10 (April 1980): 27–43.

4. Theological, Intellectual, Cultural, Denominational Background

The following are works which place the Princeton theologians in their historical and theological contexts. Many of them contain extensive material on the Princeton theology and the relationship of that theology to wider spheres of Christian and American life.

Ahlstrom, Sydney E. *A Religious History of the American People.* New Haven: Yale University Press, 1972.

_____. "Theology in America: A Historical Survey." In *The Shaping of American Religion,* edited by James Ward Smith and A. Leland Jamison. Princeton: Princeton University Press, 1961.

_____. *Theology in America: The Major Protestant Voices from Puritanism to Neo-Orthodoxy.* Indianapolis: Bobbs-Merrill, 1967.

_____. "The Scottish Philosophy and American Theology." *Church History* 24 (1955): 257–72.

Armstrong, Maurice W. et al., eds. *The Presbyterian Experience: Sources of American Presbyterian History.* Philadelphia: Westminster, 1956.

Baird, Robert. *Religion in the United States of America.* Reprint. New York: Arno and New York Times, 1969 [1844].

Barker, William S. "Inerrancy and the Role of the Bible's Authority: A Review Article." *Presbyterion: Covenant Seminary Review* 6 (Fall 1980): 96–107.

Beardslee, John W., III, ed. and trans. *Reformed Dogmatics: Seventeenth-Century Theology Through the Writings of Wollebius, Voetius, and Turretin.* New York: Oxford University Press, 1965. Reprint. Grand Rapids: Baker, 1977.

Berkhof, Louis. *Introduction to Systematic Theology.* Grand Rapids: Eerdmans, 1932. Reprint. Grand Rapids: Baker, 1979.

Bowden, Henry Warner. *Church History in the Age of Science: Historiographical Patterns in the United States 1876–1918.* Chapel Hill: University of North Carolina Press, 1971.

Bozeman, Theodore Dwight. *Protestants in an Age of Science: The Baconian Ideal and Antebellum American Religious Thought.* Chapel Hill: University of North Carolina Press, 1977.

Brown, Ira V. "The Higher Criticism Comes to America, 1880–1900." *Journal of the Presbyterian Historical Society* 38 (December 1960): 193–212.

Brown, Jerry Wayne. *The Rise of Biblical Criticism in America, 1800–1870: The New England Scholars.* Middletown, CT: Wesleyan University Press, 1969.

Cecil, Anthony C. *The Theological Development of Edwards Amasa Park, Last of the Consistent Calvinists.* Missoula, MT: Scholars Press, 1974.

Collins, Varnum Lansing. *President Witherspoon*. New York: Arno and New York Times, 1968 [1925].

Conforti, Joseph A. *Samuel Hopkins and the New Divinity Movement*. Washington and Grand Rapids: Eerdmans (for the Christian University Press), 1981.

Cross, Barbara M. *Horace Bushnell: Minister to a Changing America*. Chicago: University of Chicago Press, 1958.

Dillenberger, John. *Protestant Thought and Natural Science: A Historical Study*. Nashville: Abingdon, 1960.

Dollar, George W. *A History of Fundamentalism in America*. Greenville, SC: Bob Jones University Press, 1973.

Finney, Charles G. *Memoirs of Rev. Charles G. Finney, Written by Himself*. Reprint. New York: AMS Press, 1973 [1876].

Foster, Frank H. *A Genetic History of the New England Theology*. Chicago: University of Chicago Press, 1907.

Geehan, E.R., ed. *Jerusalem and Athens: Critical Discussions on the Philosophy and Apologetics of Cornelius Van Til*. Nutley, NJ: Presbyterian and Reformed, 1971.

General Catalogue of Princeton University 1746–1906.Princeton: Princeton University Press, 1908.

Grave, S.A. *The Scottish Philosophy of Common Sense*. Oxford: Clarendon Press, 1960.

Haroutunian, Joseph. *Piety Versus Moralism: The Passing of the New England Theology*. New York: Holt, 1932.

Hatch, Nathan O., and Noll, Mark A., eds. *The Bible in America: Essays in Cultural History*. New York: Oxford University Press, 1982.

Hoeveler, J. David, Jr. *James McCosh and the Scottish Intellectual Tradition*. Princeton: Princeton University Press, 1981.

Hofstadter, Richard. "The Revolution in Higher Education." In *Paths of American Thought*, edited by A.M. Schlesinger, Jr., and Morton White. Boston: Houghton Mifflin, 1963.

Holifield, E. Brooks. *The Gentlemen Theologians: American Theology in Southern Culture, 1795–1860*. Durham, NC: Duke University Press, 1978.

Hood, Fred J. *Reformed America: The Middle and Southern States, 1783–1837*. University, AL: University of Alabama Press, 1980.

Hovenkamp, Herbert. *Science and Religion in America, 1800–1860*. Philadelphia: University of Pennsylvania Press, 1978.

Howe, Daniel Walker. *The Unitarian Conscience: Harvard Moral Philosophy, 1805–1861*. Cambridge: Harvard University Press, 1970.

_____, ed. *Victorian America*. Philadelphia: University of Pennsylvania Press, 1976.

Hudson, Winthrop S. *Religion in America*. 3d ed., New York: Charles Scribner's Sons, 1981.

Hutchison, George P. *The History Behind the Reformed Presbyterian Church, Evangelical Synod*. Cherry Hill, NJ: Mack, 1974.

_____. *The Problem of Original Sin in American Presbyterian Theology*. Nutley, NJ: Presbyterian and Reformed, 1972.

Hutchison, William R. *The Modernist Impulse in American Protestantism.* Cambridge: Harvard University Press, 1976.

Kelsey, David H. *The Uses of Scripture in Recent Theology.* Philadelphia: Fortress, 1975.

Kuyper, Abraham. *Principles of Sacred Theology.* Translated by J. Hendrik De Vries. Introduction by B.B. Warfield. Reprint. Grand Rapids: Baker, 1980 [1898].

Loetscher, Lefferts. *The Broadening Church: A Study of Theological Issues in the Presbyterian Church Since 1869.* Philadelphia: University of Pennsylvania Press, 1957.

McLachlan, James, and Harrison, Richard A., eds. *Princetonians: A Biographical Dictionary.* Princeton: Princeton University Press, 1976.

Marsden, George M. "The Collapse of American Evangelical Academia." In *Faith and Rationality,* edited by Nicholas Wolterstorff. Notre Dame, IN: University of Notre Dame Press, 1983.

_____. *The Evangelical Mind and the New School Presbyterian Experience.* New Haven: Yale University Press, 1970.

_____. *Fundamentalism and American Culture: The Shaping of Twentieth-Century American Evangelicalism.* New York: Oxford University Press, 1980.

_____. "On Being Reformed: Our Present Tasks in the American Setting." *Reformed Journal* (September 1981): 14–17.

May, Henry F. *The Enlightenment in America.* New York: Oxford University Press, 1976.

Meyer, D.H. *The Instructed Conscience: The Shaping of the American National Ethic.* Philadelphia: University of Pennsylvania Press, 1972.

Miller, Perry. *The Life of the Mind in America from the Revolution to the Civil War.* New York: Harcourt, Brace and World, 1965.

Moore, James R. *The Post-Darwinian Controversies: A Study of the Protestant Struggle to Come to Terms with Darwin in Great Britain and America, 1870–1900.* Cambridge: Cambridge University Press, 1979.

Nichols, James Hastings, ed. *The Mercersburg Theology.* New York: Oxford University Press 1966.

_____. *Romanticism in American Theology: Nevin and Schaff at Mercersburg.* Chicago: University of Chicago Press, 1961.

Noll, Mark A. "Christian Thinking and the Rise of the American University." *Christian Scholar's Review* 9 (1979): 3–16.

_____. "Who Sets the Stage for Understanding Scripture? Philosophies of Science Often Provide the Logic for Our Hermeneutics." *Christianity Today,* May 23, 1980, pp. 14–18.

Numbers, Ronald L. *Creation by Natural Law: Laplace's Nebular Hypothesis in American Thought.* Seattle: University of Washington Press, 1977.

Oleson, Alexandra, and Brown, Sanborn C., eds. *The Pursuit of Knowledge in the Early American Republic: American Scientific and Learned Societies from Colonial Times to the Civil War.* Baltimore: Johns Hopkins University Press, 1976.

Oleson, Alexandra, and Voss, John, eds. *The Organization of Knowledge in Modern America, 1860–1920.* Baltimore: Johns Hopkins University Press, 1979.

Rennie, Ian. "Mixed Metaphors, Misunderstood Models, and Puzzling Paradigms: A Contemporary Effort to Correct Some Current Misunderstandings Regarding the Authority and Interpretation of the Bible. An Historical Response." Typescript, Institute for Christian Studies, Toronto, 1981.

Reynolds, David S. *Faith in Fiction: The Emergence of Religious Literature in America.* Cambridge: Harvard University Press, 1981.

Rogers, Jack Bartlett. *Scripture in the Westminster Confession: A Problem of Historical Interpretation for American Presbyterianism.* Grand Rapids: Eerdmans, 1967.

Rogers, Jack Bartlett, and McKim, Donald K. *The Authority and Interpretation of the Bible: An Historical Approach.* San Francisco: Harper & Row, 1979.

Sandeen, Ernest R. *The Roots of Fundamentalism: British and American Millenarianism 1800–1930.* Chicago: University of Chicago Press, 1970.

Saum, Lewis O. *The Popular Mood of Pre-Civil War America.* Westport, CT: Greenwood, 1980.

Sloan, Douglas. *The Scottish Enlightenment and the American College Ideal.* New York: Teacher's College Press, 1961.

Smith, Elwyn. *The Presbyterian Minstry in American Culture.* Philadelphia: Westminster, 1962.

Smith, Gary S. "The Spirit of Capitalism Revisited: Calvinists in the Industrial Revolution." *Journal of Presbyterian History* 59 (Winter 1981): 481–97.

Smith, Hilrie Shelton. *Changing Conceptions of Original Sin: A Study in American Theology Since 1750.* New York: Charles Scribner's Sons, 1953.

_____, ed. *Horace Bushnell.* New York: Oxford University Press, 1965.

Smith, Timothy L. *Revivalism and Social Reform in Mid-Nineteenth-Century America.* Nashville: Abingdon, 1957.

Turretin, Francis. *The Doctrine of Scripture.* Edited and translated by John W. Beardslee III. Grand Rapids: Baker, 1981.

Van Til, Cornelius. *The Defense of the Faith.* 2d ed. Philadelphia: Presbyterian and Reformed, 1955.

Veysey, Laurence R. *The Emergence of the American University.* Chicago: University of Chicago Press, 1965.

Wells, David F. "Aftermath and Hindsight of the Atonement Debate." *Bibliotheca Sacra* 145 (1988): 3–14.

_____. "American Society as Seen from the Nineteenth-Century Pulpit." *Bibliotheca Sacra* 144 (1987): 123–43.

_____. "The Collision of Views on the Atonement." *Bibliotheca Sacra* 144 (1987): 363–76.

_____. "Nathaniel William Taylor: Theologian of Revival." Typescript, July 1978.

_____. "The Shaping of the Nineteenth-Century Debate over the Atonement." *Bibliotheca Sacra* 144 (1987): 243–53.

Welter, Rush. *The Mind of America 1820–1860*. New York: Columbia University Press, 1975.

Wertenbaker, Thomas Jefferson. *Princeton 1746–1896*. Princeton: Princeton University Press, 1946.

Willis, E. David. "The Material Assumptions of Integrative Theology: The Conditions of Experiential Church Dogmatics." *Princeton Seminary Bulletin*, n.s. 2 (1979): 232–50.

Woodbridge, John D. "Biblical Authority: Towards an Evaluation of the Rogers and McKim Proposal." *Trinity Journal*, n.s. 1 (Fall 1980): 165–236; expanded as *Biblical Authority: A Critique of the Rogers/McKim Proposal* (Grand Rapids: Zondervan, 1982).

Wright, Conrad. *The Beginnings of Unitarianism in America*. Boston: Starr King, 1955.

Dutch Reformed Theology

1. Historical Background

Balmer, Randall H. *A Perfect Babel of Confusion: Dutch Religion and English Culture in the Middle Colonies*. New York: Oxford University Press, 1989.

Bratt, James D. *Dutch Calvinism in Modern America: A History of a Conservative Subculture*. Grand Rapids: Eerdmans, 1984.

De Jong, Gerald F. *The Dutch in America, 1609–1974*. Boston: Twayne, 1975.

De Klerk, Peter, and De Ridder, Richard, eds. *Perspectives on the Christian Reformed Church: Studies in Its History, Theology, and Ecumenicity*. Grand Rapids: Baker, 1983.

Hageman, Howard G. *Two Centuries Plus: The Story of New Brunswick Seminary*. Grand Rapids: Eerdmans, 1984.

Harmelink, Herman, III. *Ecumenism and the Reformed Church*. Grand Rapids: Eerdmans, 1968.

Kromminga, Dietrich H. *The Christian Reformed Tradition: From the Reformation to the Present*. Grand Rapids: Eerdmans, 1943.

Kromminga, John H. *The Christian Reformed Church: A Study in Orthodoxy*. Grand Rapids: Baker, 1949.

Tanis, James. *Dutch Calvinistic Pietism in the Middle Colonies*. The Hague: Martinus Nijhoff, 1968.

Van Hoeven, James W., ed. *Piety and Patriotism: Bicentennial Studies of the Reformed Church in America, 1776–1976*. Grand Rapids: Eerdmans, 1976.

Zwaanstra, Henry. *Reformed Thought and Experience in a New World: A Study of the Christian Reformed Church and Its American Environment, 1890–1918*. Kampen: J. H. Kok, 1973.

2. Netherlandic Figures

Bavinck, Herman. *Christelijke Wereldbeschouwing*. Kampen: J.H. Bos, 1904.

_____. *Gereformeerde Dogmatiek*. 4 vols. 3d ed. Kampen: Kok, 1918. (English translation of vol.2: *The Doctrine of God*. Grand Rapids: Eerdmans, 1951).

_____. *The Philosophy of Revelation*. New York: Longmans, Green, and Co., 1909.

_____. *Magnalia Dei: Onderwijzing in de Christelijke Religie naar Gereformeerde Belijdenis*. Kampen: J. H. Kok, 1909. (English translation: *Our Reasonable Faith*. Grand Rapids: Eerdmans, 1956).

Berkhof, Hendrikus. *Christ the Meaning of History*. Richmond: John Knox, 1966.

_____. *Christian Faith: An Introduction to the Study of the Faith*. Grand Rapids: Eerdmans, 1986.

Berkouwer, Gerrit C. *Studies in Dogmatics*. 18 vols. Grand Rapids: Eerdmans, 1952–1976.

_____. *The Second Vatican Council and the New Catholicism*. Grand Rapids: Eerdmans, 1965.

_____. *A Half Century of Theology*. Grand Rapids: Eerdmans, 1977.

_____. *The Triumph of Grace in the Theology of Karl Barth*. Grand Rapids: Eerdmans, 1956.

Dooyeweerd, Herman. *In the Twilight of Western Thought: Studies in the Pretended Autonomy of Philosophical Thought*. Philadelphia: Presbyterian and Reformed, 1960.

_____. *A New Critique of Theoretical Thought*. 4 vols. Amsterdam: H. J. Paris; Philadelphia: Presbyterian and Reformed, 1953–1958.

_____. *Roots of Western Culture: Pagan, Secular, and Christian Options*. Toronto: Wedge, 1979.

Kuyper, Abraham. *Encyclopedia of Sacred Theology*. New York: Charles Scribner's Sons, 1898.

_____. *De Gemeene Gratie*. 3 vols. Amsterdam: Hoveker & Wormser, 1902–1904.

_____. *Lectures on Calvinism*. Grand Rapids: Eerdmans, 1961.

_____. *The Practice of Godliness*. Grand Rapids: Eerdmans, 1945.

_____. *Pro Rege, of Het Koningschap van Christus*. 3 vols. Kampen: J. H. Kok, 1911–1912.

_____. *Souvereiniteit in Eigen Kring*. Amsterdam: J. H. Kruyt, 1880.

_____. *To Be Near unto God*. Grand Rapids: Eerdmans, 1924.

_____. *The Work of the Holy Spirit*. New York: Funk & Wagnalls, 1900.

3. 1890–1915

Berkhof, Louis. *The Church and Social Problems*. Grand Rapids: Eerdmans-Sevensma, 1913.

Gaffin, Richard B., Jr., ed. *Redemptive History and Biblical Interpretation: The Shorter Writings of Geerhardus Vos*. Philipsburg, NJ: Presbyterian and Reformed, 1980.

Hulst, Lammert J., and Hemkes, Gerrit K. *Oud- en Nieuw-Calvinisme: Tweeledige inlichting voor ons Hollandische Volk.* . . . Grand Rapids: Eerdmans-Sevensma, 1913.

Kuiper, Barend Klaas. *Ons Opmaken en Bouwen.* Grand Rapids: Eerdmans-Sevensma, 1918.

_____. *The Proposed Calvinistic College at Grand Rapids.* Grand Rapids: Sevensma, 1903.

Semi-Centennial Committee of the Christian Reformed Church. *Gedenkboek van het Vijftigjarig Jubileum der Christelijke Gereformeerde Kerk: A. D. 1857–1907.* Grand Rapids: Hulst-Sevensma, 1907.

Steffens, Nicholas M. "Calvinism and the Theological Crisis." *Presbyterian and Reformed Review* 12 (April 1901): 211–25.

Ten Hoor, Foppe M. Series on Americanization. *Gereformeerde Amerikaan* 2 (May-August 1898) and 13 (January-March, May, September 1909).

_____. Series Contra Supralapsarian/Neo-Calvinism. *Gereformeerde Amerikaan* 9 (May-September 1905) and 20 (February, May, July, September, October 1916).

_____. "De Moderne Positieve Theologie." *Gereformeerde Amerikaan* 12/13 (October 1908-January 1909).

_____. On Mysticism. *Gereformeerde Amerikaan* 1 (March-August 1897).

Van Lonkhuyzen, John. *Billy Sunday: Een Beeld uit het Tegenwoordige Amerikaansche Godsdienstige Leven.* Grand Rapids: Eerdmans-Sevensma, 1916.

4. 1915–1930

Berkhof, Louis. *De Drie Punten in Alle Deelen Gereformeerd.* Grand Rapids: Eerdmans, 1925.

_____. *Premillennialisme: Zijn Schriftuurlijke Basis en Enkele van zijn Practische Gevolgtrekkingen.* Grand Rapids: Eerdmans-Sevensma, 1918.

Berkhof, Louis et al. *Waar Het in de Zaak Janssen Om Gaat.* n.p. , 1922.

Bultema, Harry. *Maranatha! Eene Studie over de Onvervulde Profetie.* Grand Rapids: Eerdmans-Sevensma, 1917.

Christian Reformed Church. *Reports and Decisions in the Case of Dr. R. Janssen.* Synod of Orange City, 1922.

De Jong, Ymen P. *Daden des Heeren: Drie Leerredenen Gehouden in verband met den Wereld Oorlog 1914–1919.* Grand Rapids: n.p., 1919.

_____. *De Komende Christus: Eene Studie ter Weerlegging van de Grondstellingen van het Pre-Millennialisme.* Grand Rapids: Van Noord, 1920.

Dosker, Henry E. *The Dutch Anabaptists.* Philadelphia: Judson, 1921.

Hoeksema, Gertrude. *Therefore Have I Spoken: A Biography of Herman Hoeksema.* Grand Rapids: Reformed Free Publishing Association, 1969.

Hoeksema, Herman. *The Protestant Reformed Churches in America: Their Origin, Early History, and Doctrine.* Grand Rapids: First Protestant Reformed Church, 1936.

_____. *Van Zonde en Genade.* Kalamazoo, MI: n.p. 1923.

Hoeksema, Herman, and Danhof, Henry. *Niet Doopersch Maar Gereformeerd.* n.p., 1922.

Hospers, Gerrit H. *The Reformed Principle of Authority.* Grand Rapids: Eerdmans, 1924.

Janssen, Ralph. *De Crisis in de Christelijke Gereformeerde Kerk in Amerika: Een Strijdschrift.* Grand Rapids: n.p., 1922.

_____. *De Synodale Conclusies.* Grand Rapids: n.p., 1923.

Kuiper, Barend K. *De Vier Paarden uit Openbaring.* Grand Rapids: Eerdmans-Sevensma, 1918.

Kuiper, Herman. *Calvin on Common Grace.* Goes: Oosterbaan & Le Cointre, 1928.

Kuiper, Rienck B. *"Not of the World": Discourses on the Christian's Relation to the World.* Grand Rapids: Eerdmans, 1929.

_____. *While the Bridegroom Tarries: Ten After-the-War Sermons on the Signs of the Times.* Grand Rapids: Van Noord, 1919.

Ten Hoor, Foppe M. et al. *Nadere Toelichting omtrent de Zaak Janssen.* Holland, MI: Holland Printing, 1920.

Van Baalen, Jan Karel. *De Loochening der Gemeene Gratie: Gereformeerd of Doopersch?* Grand Rapids: Eerdmans-Sevensma, 1922.

_____. *Nieuwigheid en Dwaling: De Loochening der Gemeene Gratie Nogmaals Gewogen en te Licht Bevonden.* Grand Rapids: Eerdmans-Sevensma, 1923.

Van Eyck, William O. *Landmarks of the Reformed Fathers: Or, What Van Raalte's People Really Believed.* Grand Rapids: Reformed Press, 1922.

Vos, Geerhardus. *The Self-Disclosure of Jesus.* New York: Doran, 1926.

5. 1930–1950

Beets, Henry. *The Man of Sorrows: A Series of Lenten Sermons.* Grand Rapids: Eerdmans, 1935.

Berkhof, Louis. *Aspects of Liberalism.* Grand Rapids: Eerdmans, 1951.

_____. *The Kingdom of God: The Development of the Idea of the Kingdom, Especially Since the Eighteenth Century.* Grand Rapids: Eerdmans, 1951.

_____. *Manual of Reformed Doctrine.* Grand Rapids: Eerdmans, 1933.

_____. *Reformed Dogmatics.* 3 vols. Grand Rapids: Eerdmans, 1932.

_____. *Riches of Divine Grace: Ten Expository Sermons.* Grand Rapids: Eerdmans, 1948.

_____. *Vicarious Atonement Through Christ.* Grand Rapids: Eerdmans, 1936.

Blekkink, Evert J. *The Fatherhood of God.* Grand Rapids: Eerdmans, 1942.

Blocker, Simon. *When Christ Takes Over.* Grand Rapids: Eerdmans, 1945.

Bouma, Clarence. "Calvinism in American Theology Today." *Journal of Religion* 27 (1947): 34–45.

_____. "Christianity's Finality and New Testament Teaching." *Princeton Theological Review* 26 (1928): 337-58.

_____. "War, Peace, and the Christian." *Calvin Forum* 1 (1935): 99–102.

DeBoer, Cecil. *The If's and Ought's of Ethics: A Preface to Moral Philosophy.* Grand Rapids: Eerdmans, 1936.

DeJong, Peter Y. *The Covenant Idea in New England Theology, 1620–1847.* Grand Rapids: Eerdmans, 1945.

DeVries, John. *Beyond the Atom: An Appraisal of Our Christian Faith in This Age of Atomic Science.* Grand Rapids: Eerdmans, 1948.

Hendriksen, William. *The Covenant of Grace.* Grand Rapids: Eerdmans, 1932.

_____. *More Than Conquerors: An Interpretation of the Book of Revelation.* Grand Rapids: Baker, 1940.

Kromminga, Dietrich H. *The Millennium in the Church: Studies in the History of Christian Chiliasm.* Grand Rapids: Eerdmans, 1945.

Kruithof, Bastian. *The Christ of the Cosmic Road: The Significance of the Incarnation.* Grand Rapids: Eerdmans, 1937.

_____. *The High Points of Calvinism.* Grand Rapids: Baker, 1949.

Kuizenga, John E. *Relevancy of the Pivot Points of the Reformed Faith.* Grand Rapids: Society for Reformed Publications, 1951.

Meeter, H. Henry. *Calvinism: An Interpretation of Its Basic Ideas.* Grand Rapids: Zondervan, 1939.

Pieters, Albertus. *The Facts and Mysteries of the Christian Faith.* Grand Rapids: Eerdmans, 1926.

_____. *Studies in the Revelation of St. John.* Grand Rapids: Eerdmans, 1954.

Tanis, Edward J. *Calvinism and Social Problems.* Grand Rapids: Zondervan, 1936.

Van Baalen, Jan Karel. *The Heritage of the Fathers.* Grand Rapids: Eerdmans, 1948.

Vos, Geerhardus. *Biblical Theology.* Grand Rapids: Eerdmans, 1948.

_____. *The Pauline Eschatology.* Princeton: Princeton University Press, 1930.

Wyngaarden, Martin J. *The Future of the Kingdom in Prophecy and Fulfillment: A Study of the Scope of "Spiritualization" in Scripture.* Grand Rapids: Zondervan, 1934.

6. 1950–1965

Boer, Harry R. *Pentecost and Missions.* Grand Rapids: Eerdmans, 1961.

Bruggink, Donald, ed. *Guilt, Grace, and Gratitude: A Commentary on the Heidelberg Catechism.* New York: Half Moon, 1963.

Buis, Harry. *The Doctrine of Eternal Punishment.* Philadelphia: Presbyterian and Reformed, 1957.

Daane, James. *A Theology of Grace.* Grand Rapids: Eerdmans, 1954.

_____. *The Freedom of God: A Study of Election and Pulpit.* Grand Rapids: Eerdmans, 1973.

De Boer, Cecil. *Responsible Protestantism.* Grand Rapids: Eerdmans, 1957.

DeJong, Alexander C. *The Well-Meant Gospel Offer: The Views of K. Schilder and H. Hoeksema.* Franeker: Wever, 1954.

DeJong, Peter Y. *The Church's Witness to the World.* Grand Rapids: Baker, 1960.

Dekker, Harold. "On the Doctrine of Limited Atonement." *Reformed Journal* 12–14 (December 1962–March 1963; January–March, May, September 1964).

DeKoster, Lester. *All Ye That Labor: An Essay on Christianity, Communism, and the Problem of Evil.* Grand Rapids: Eerdmans, 1956.

Girod, Gordon. *The Deeper Faith.* Grand Rapids: Reformed Publications, 1958.

Hageman, Howard. *Pulpit and Table: Some Chapters in the History of Worship in the Reformed Churches.* Richmond: John Knox, 1962.

Klooster, Fred. *The Significance of Barth's Theology: An Appraisal.* Grand Rapids: Baker, 1961.

Kuiper, Rienck Bouke. *God-Centered Evangelism.* Grand Rapids: Baker, 1961.

———. *For Whom Did Christ Die?* Grand Rapids: Eerdmans, 1959.

———. *To Be or Not to Be Reformed: Whither the Christian Reformed Church?* Grand Rapids: Zondervan, 1959.

Masselink, William. *General Revelation and Common Grace.* Grand Rapids: Eerdmans, 1953.

Stob, Henry. *The Christian Conception of Freedom.* Grand Rapids: Grand Rapids International Publications, 1957.

Van Til, Cornelius. *Common Grace.* Philadelphia: Presbyterian and Reformed, 1947.

Van Til, Henry R. *The Calvinistic Concept of Culture.* Grand Rapids: Baker, 1959.

Verduin, Leonard. *The Reformers and Their Stepchildren.* Grand Rapids: Eerdmans, 1964.

Zylstra, Henry. *Testament of Vision.* Grand Rapids: Eerdmans, 1958.

7. Since 1965

Bril, K. A., Hart, Hendrik, and Klapwijk, Jacob, eds. *The Idea of a Christian Philosophy: Essays in Honor of H. Th. Vollenhoven.* Toronto: Wedge, 1973.

Boer, Harry R. *Above the Battle? The Bible and Its Critics.* Grand Rapids: Eerdmans, 1977.

———. *The Doctrine of Reprobation in the Christian Reformed Church.* Grand Rapids: Eerdmans, 1983.

Bruggink, Donald. *When Faith Takes Form.* Grand Rapids: Eerdmans, 1971.

Christian Reformed Church. *The Nature and Extent of Biblical Authority.* Grand Rapids: Board of Publications of the CRC, 1972.

De Jong, Peter Y., ed. *Crisis in the Reformed Churches: Essays in Commemoration of the Great Synod of Dort, 1618-1619.* Grand Rapids: Reformed Fellowship, 1968.

Hart, Hendrik. *The Challenge of Our Age.* Toronto: Wedge, 1974.

———. *Understanding Our World: An Integrated Ontology.* Lanham, MD: University Press of America, 1984.

Hart, Hendrik, van der Hoeven, Johan, and Wolterstorff, Nicholas, eds. *Rationality in the Calvinian Tradition.* Lanham, MD: University Press of America, 1983.

Heideman, Eugene P. *Our Song of Hope: A Provisional Confession of Faith of the Reformed Churches in America.* Grand Rapids: Eerdmans, 1975.

Hoekema, Anthony. *The Christian Looks at Himself.* Grand Rapids: Eerdmans, 1975.

_____. *Holy Spirit Baptism.* Grand Rapids: Eerdmans, 1972.

Kalsbeek, L. *Contours of a Christian Philosophy.* Toronto: Wedge, 1975.

Kistemaker, Simon. *Interpreting God's Word Today.* Grand Rapids: Baker, 1970.

Kraay, John, and Tol, Anthony, eds. *Hearing and Doing: Philosophical Essays Dedicated to H. Evan Runner.* Toronto: Wedge, 1979.

Kuyper, Lester. *The Scripture Unbroken.* Grand Rapids: Eerdmans, 1978.

McIntire, C. Thomas, ed. *The Legacy of Herman Dooyeweerd.* Lanham, MD: University Press of America, 1985.

Mouw, Richard J. *Called to Holy Worldliness.* Philadelphia: Fortress, 1980.

_____. *Political Evangelism.* Grand Rapids: Eerdmans, 1974.

_____. *Politics and the Biblical Drama.* Grand Rapids: Eerdmans, 1976.

Olthuis, John A. et al. *Out of Concern for the Church.* Toronto: Wedge, 1970.

Osterhaven, M. Eugene. *The Faith of the Church.* Grand Rapids: Eerdmans, 1971.

_____. *The Spirit of the Reformed Tradition.* Grand Rapids: Eerdmans, 1982.

Plantinga, Alvin. *God and Other Minds: A Study of the Rational Justification of Belief in God.* Ithaca: Cornell University Press, 1967.

_____. *God, Freedom, and Evil.* New York: Harper & Row, 1974.

_____, ed. *Faith and Philosophy.* Grand Rapids: Eerdmans, 1964.

Plantinga, Alvin, and Wolterstorff, Nicholas, eds. *Faith and Rationality: Reason and Belief in God.* Notre Dame: University of Notre Dame Press, 1983.

Plantinga, Cornelius. *A Place to Stand: A Reformed Study of Creeds and Confessions.* Grand Rapids: Board of Publications of the CRC, 1979.

Runner, H. Evan. *The Relation of the Bible to Learning.* 3d ed. Toronto: Wedge, 1970.

_____. *Scriptural Religion and the Political Task.* 3d ed. Toronto: Wedge, 1974.

Smedes, Lewis B. *All Things Made New: A Theology of Man's Union with Christ.* Grand Rapids: Eerdmans, 1970.

_____. *Love Within Limits: A Realist's View of 1 Corinthians 13.* Grand Rapids: Eerdmans, 1978.

_____. *Mere Morality: What God Expects from Ordinary People.* Grand Rapids: Eerdmans, 1983.

Stob, Henry. *Ethical Reflections.* Grand Rapids: Eerdmans, 1978.

Vander Goot, Henry, ed. *Life Is Religion: Essays in Honor of H. Evan Runner.* St. Catharines, Ontario: Paideia, 1981.

Vander Stelt, John. *Philosophy and Scripture: A Study in Old Princeton and Westminster Theology.* Marlton, NJ: Mack, 1978.

Van Til, Howard J. *The Fourth Day: What the Bible and the Heavens Are Telling Us about the Creation.* Grand Rapids: Eerdmans, 1986.

Wolterstorff, Nicholas. *Art in Action.* Grand Rapids: Eerdmans, 1980.

_____. *Reason Within the Bounds of Religion.* Grand Rapids: Eerdmans, 1976.

_____. *Until Justice and Peace Embrace.* Grand Rapids: Eerdmans, 1983.

Southern Reformed Theology

1. Theologians of Southern Presbyterianism

Archibald Alexander (1772–1851)

Alexander, Archibald. *Biographical Sketches of the Founder, and Principal Alumni of the Log College.* Princeton, NJ: J. T. Robinson, 1845.

_____. *A Brief Compendium of Bible Truth.* Philadelphia: Presbyterian Board of Publication, 1846.

_____. *Christ's Gracious Invitation to the Labouring and Heavy Laden.* Philadelphia: Presbyterian Board of Publication, 1837.

_____. *Evidences of the Authenticity, Inspiration, and Canonical Authority of the Holy Scriptures.* New York: Arno, 1972.

_____. *A History of the Israelite Nation, From Their Origin to Their Dispersion at the Destruction of Jerusalem by the Romans.* Philadelphia: Martien, 1853.

_____. *Outlines of Moral Science.* New York: Charles Scribner's Sons, 1852.

_____. *Practical Sermons: To Be Read in Families and Social Meetings.* Philadelphia: Presbyterian Board of Publication, 1850?

_____. *Practical Truths. By the Rev. Archibald Alexander . . . Consisting of His Various Writings for the American Tract Society, and Correspondence from the Society's Formation in 1825, to His Death in 1851.* New York: American Tract Society, 1857.

_____. "'The Rev. William Graham,' An Address Delivered Before the Alumni Association of Washington College, VA, June 29, 1843." *Watchman of the South* VII (January 4, 1844): 78.

_____. *Suggestions in Vindication of Sunday Schools: But More Especially for the Improvement of Sunday School Books and the Enlargement of the Plan of Instruction.* Philadelphia, 1829.

_____. *Theories of the Will in the History of Philosophy.* New York: Charles Scribner's Sons, 1898.

_____. *Thoughts on Religious Experience. To Which Is Added an Appendix, Containing "Letters to the Aged."* Philadelphia: Presbyterian Board of Publication, 1841. Reprint. Banner of Truth, 1978.

_____. *A Treatise on Justification by Faith.* Philadelphia: Presbyterian Tract and Sunday School Society, 1837.

Daniel Baker (1791–1857)

Baker, Daniel. *Revival Sermons.* Introduction by William M. Baker. Philadelphia: Martien, 1878.

Robert Lewis Breckinridge (1800–1871)

Breckinridge, Robert Lewis. *Addresses Delivered at the Inauguration of the Professors, in the Danville Theological Seminary.* Pamphlet, October 13, 1853.

_____. *Discussion on American Slavery Between George Thompson, Esq., Agent of the British and Foreign Society for the Abolition of Slavery Throughout the World and Rev. R. J. Breckinridge*. Boston, 1836.

_____. *Fidelity in Our Lot*. Pamphlet, 1855.

_____. *Knowledge of God, Objectively Considered, Being the First Part of Theology Considered as a Science of Positive Truth, Both Inductive and Deductive. . . .* New York: Carter and Brothers, 1858.

_____. *Knowledge of God, Subjectively Considered, Being the Second Part of Theology Considered as a Science of Positive Truth, Both Inductive and Deductive. . . .* New York: Carter and Brothers, 1859.

Robert Lewis Dabney (1820–1898)

Dabney, Robert Lewis. *Christ Our Penal Substitute*. Richmond, VA: Presbyterian Committee of Publication, 1898. Reprint. Harrisonburg, VA: Sprinkle, 1985.

_____. *The Christian Sabbath: Its Nature, Design and Proper Observance by the Rev. R. L. Dabney. . . .* Philadelphia: Presbyterian Board of Publication, 1882.

_____. *Discussions, Evangelical and Theological*. Richmond, VA: Presbyterian Committee of Publication, 1890–1892. Reprint. London: Banner of Truth Trust, 1967–1982.

_____. *The Doctrinal Contents of the Confession: Its Fundamental and Regulative Ideas, and the Necessity and Value of Creeds*. Richmond, VA: Presbyterian Committee of Publication, 1897. Reprint. *The Westminster Confession and Creeds*. Dallas: Presbyterian Heritage, 1983.

_____. *The Five Points of Calvinism*. Richmond, VA: Presbyterian Committee of Publication, 1895.

_____. *The Practical Philosophy, Being the Philosophy of the Feelings, of the Will, and of the Conscience, with the Ascertainment of Particular Rights and Duties*. Kansas City, MO: Hudson, Kimberly, 1897.

_____. *Sacred Rhetoric; or a Course of Lectures on Preaching. Delivered in the Union Theological Seminary of the General Assembly of the Presbyterian Church in the U.S., in Prince Edward, VA*. Richmond, VA: Presbyterian Committee of Publication, 1870.

_____. *The Sensualistic Philosophy of the Nineteenth Century, Considered*. New York: Randolph, 1875.

_____. *Syllabus and Notes of the Course of Systematic and Polemic Theology Taught in Union Theological Seminary, Virginia*. Richmond, VA: Presbyterian Committee of Publication, 1871. Reprint. *Lectures in Systematic Theology*. Grand Rapids: Zondervan, 1972.

Samuel Davies (1723–1761)

Davies, Samuel. *Charity and Truth United; or, the Way of the Multitude Exposed in Six Letters to the Rev. Mr. William Stith, A. M. President of William and Mary College*. Edited by Thomas Clinton Pears, Jr. Philadelphia: General Assembly of the Presbyterian Church in the USA, 1941.

_____. *Collected Poems.* Edited, with an introduction and notes, by Richard Beale Davis. Gainesville, FL: Scholars Facsimiles and Reprints, 1968.

_____. *The Curse of Cowardice: A Sermon Preached to the Militia of Hanover County, Virginia, at a General Muster, May 8, 1758. With a View to Raise a Company for Captain Samuel Meredith.* London: Woodbridge, 1759.

_____. *The Duty of Christians to Propagate Their Religion Among Heathens, Earnestly Recommended to the Masters of Negro Slaves in Virginia. A Sermon Preached in Hanover, January 8, 1757.* London, 1758.

_____. *Letters from the Rev. Samuel Davies, Showing the State of Religion (Particularly Among the Negroes) in Virginia. Likewise an Extract of a Letter from a Gentleman in London to His Friend in the Country, Being Some Observations of the Foregoing.* London, 1759.

_____. *Religion and Patriotism: The Constituents of a Good Soldier. A Sermon Preached to Captain Overton's Independent Company of Volunteers, Raised in Hanover County, Virginia, Aug. 17, 1755.* Philadelphia: James Chattin, 1755.

_____. *Religion and the Public Spirit. A Valedictory Address to the Senior Class, Delivered in Nassau-Hall, September 21, 1760, the Sunday Before Commencement.* New York: William Bradford, 1761.

_____. *The Reverend Samuel Davies Abroad; the Diary of a Journey to England and Scotland, 1753-55.* Edited, with an introduction, by George William Pilcher. Urbana, IL: University of Illinois Press, 1967.

_____. *A Sermon Delivered at Nassau-Hall, January 14, 1761, On the Death of His Late Majesty King George II.* New York: William Bradford, 1761.

_____. *Sermons on Important Subjects, By the Late Reverend and Pious Samuel Davies . . . 5th ed. . . . To Which Are Now Added, Three Occasional Sermons, Not Included in the Former Editions, Memoirs and Character of the Author, and Two Sermons on Occasion of His Death, by the Rev. Drs. Gibbons and Finley. . . .* Edited by Albert Barnes. New York: Carter and Brothers, 1853.

_____. *The State of Religion Among the Protestant Dissenters in Virginia.* Boston: Kneeland, 1951.

_____. *Virginia's Danger and Remedy: Two Discourses Occasioned by the Severe Drought in Sundry Parts of the Country; and the Defeat of General Braddock.* Williamsburg, VA: Hunter, 1956.

John Lafayette Girardeau (1825–1898)

Girardeau, John Lafayette. *Calvinism and Evangelical Arminianism: Compared as to Election, Reprobation, Justification, and Related Doctrines.* Columbia, SC: Duffie; New York: Baker and Taylor, 1890.

_____. *Discussions of Philosophical Questions.* Edited by George A. Blackburn. Richmond, VA: Presbyterian Committee of Publication, 1900.

_____. *Discussions of Theological Questions.* Edited by George A. Blackburn. Richmond, VA: Presbyterian Committee of Publication, 1905.

_____. *Instrumental Music in the Public Worship of the Church*. Richmond, VA: Whittet and Shepperson, 1888.

_____. *Sermons*. Edited by George A. Blackburn under the auspices of the synods of South Carolina, Georgia, Alabama, and Florida. Columbia, SC: State Company, 1907.

_____. *Theology as Science Involving an Inaugural Address*. Columbia, SC: Presbyterian Publication House, 1876. Reproduced in microform, Chicago: American Theological Library Association, 1985.

_____. *The Will in Its Theological Relations*. Columbia, SC: Duffie; New York: Baker and Taylor, 1891.

Moses Drury Hoge (1819–1899)

Hoge, Moses Drury. "The Day of Adversity." *Sermons Selected from the Manuscripts*. Richmond, VA: Pollard, 1821.

_____. *The Perfection of Beauty, and Other Sermons by the Rev. Moses D. Hoge . . . with a Lecture on "The Success of Christianity an Evidence of Its Divine Origin," Delivered at the University of Virginia*. Richmond, VA: Presbyterian Committee of Publication, 1904.

_____. *Sermons Selected from the Manuscripts of the Late Moses Hoge, D.D.* Richmond, VA: Pollard, 1821.

_____. "The Sofists Unmasked; in a Series of Letters, Addressed to Thomas Paine, Author of a Book, Entitled *The Age of Reason*." In R. Watson, *Christian Panoply; Containing an Apology for the Bible*. Richmond: Union Theological Seminary in Virginia, 1797.

_____. *Strictures upon a Pamphlet Lately Published by Jeremiah Walker: Titled "The Fourfold Foundation of Calvinism Examined and Shaken."* Philadelphia: Young, 1792.

George Howe (1802–1883)

Howe, George. *An Appeal to the Young Men of the Presbyterian Church in the Synod of South Carolina and Georgia*. Columbia, SC: Theological Seminary, 1836.

_____. *A Discourse on Theological Education; Delivered on the Bicentenary of the Westminster Assembly of Divines, July, 1843. To Which Is Added, Advice to a Student Preparing for the Ministry*. New York: Leavitt, Trow and Co., 1844.

_____. *History of the Presbyterian Church in South Carolina*. Columbia: Duffie and Chapman, 1870–83.

Charles Colcock Jones (1804–1863)

Jones, Charles Colcock. *A Catechism of Scripture Doctrine and Practice for Families and Sabbath Schools Designed also for the Oral Instruction of Colored Persons*. Charleston: Harrison, 1845.

_____. *A Georgian at Princeton*. Edited by Robert Manson Myers. New York: Harcourt Brace Jovanovich, 1976.

_____. *The Children of Pride: Selected Letters of the Family of the Rev. Dr. Charles Colcock*

Jones for the Years 1860–1868, with the Addition of Several Previously Unpublished Letters. Edited by Robert Manson Myers. New Haven: Yale University Press, 1984.

_____. *The Religious Instruction of the Negroes in the United States.* Savannah: Purse, 1842.

John Leland (1754–1841)

Leland, John. *The Writings of the Late Elder John Leland, Including Some Events in His Life, Written by Himself.* Edited by L.F. Green. New York, 1845.

Benjamin Morgan Palmer (1818–1902)

Palmer, Benjamin Morgan. *The Broken Home; or, Lessons in Sorrow.* 2d ed. New Orleans: Upton, 1891.

_____. *The Family in Its Civil and Churchly Aspects: An Essay in Two Parts.* Harrisonburg, VA: Sprinkle, 1981.

_____. *Formation of Character. Twelve Lectures Delivered in the First Presbyterian Church, New Orleans, LA.* New Orleans: Religious Book Depository, 1889.

_____. "Life, Character, and Genius of the Late Rev. James Henley Thornwell, D.D., LL.D." *Southern Presbyterian Review* 15 (October 1862): 255–309.

_____. *The Life and Letters of James Henley Thornwell: Ex-president of the South Carolina College, Late Professor of Theology in the Theological Seminary at Columbia, South Carolina.* Richmond, VA: Whittet and Shepperson, 1875. Reprint. London: Banner of Truth Trust, 1974.

_____. *The Pious Physician; or, The Claims of Religion upon the Medical Profession.* Richmond, VA: Presbyterian Committee on Publication, 1871.

_____. "The Proposed Plan of Union Between the General Assembly of the Presbyterian Church in the Confederate States of America and the United Synod of the South." *Southern Presbyterian Review* 16 (April 1864): 264–307.

_____. *The South: Her Peril, and Her Duty: A Discourse, Delivered in the First Presbyterian Church, New Orleans, on Thursday, November 29, 1860.* New Orleans: Office of the True Witness and Sentinel, 1860.

_____. *Theology of Prayer: as Viewed in the Religion of Nature and in the System of Grace.* Richmond, VA: Presbyterian Committee of Publication, 1894. Reprint. Harrisonburg, VA: Sprinkle, 1980.

_____. "Thornwell's Writings." *Southern Presbyterian Review* 29 (July 1878): 413–48.

_____. *The Threfold Fellowship and the Threefold Assurance: An Essay in Two Parts.* Richmond, VA: Presbyterian Committee of Publication, 1902.

_____. *A Weekly Publication Containing Sermons by Rev. B. M. Palmer.* 2 vols. Reported by C.W. Colton. New Orleans: Clark and Hofeline, 1875–1876.

Thomas Ephraim Peck, D.D., LL.D. (1822–1893)

Peck, T. E. *Miscellanies of Rev. Thomas E. Peck, D.D., LL.D., Professor of Theology in the Union Theological Seminary in Virginia.* 2 vols. Edited by Rev. T. C. Johnson.

Richmond, VA: Presbyterian Committee of Publication, 1895.

_____. *Notes on Ecclesiology.* Richmond, VA: Presbyterian Committee of Publication, 1892.

David Rice (1733–1816)

Rice, David. *A Lecture on the Divine Decrees, to Which Is Annexed a Few Observations on a Piece Lately Printed in Lexington, Entitled "the Principles of the Methodists, or the Scripture Doctrine of Pre-Destination, Election and Reprobation."* Lexington, KY: John Bradford, 1791.

_____. *A Sermon on the Present Revival of Religion, etc., in This Country; Preached at the Opening of the Kentucky Synod.* Lexington, KY: Joseph Charles, 1803.

_____. *Slavery Inconsistent with Justice and Good Policy, Proved by a Speech, Delivered in the Convention Held at Danville, Kentucky.* Philadelphia, 1804.

John Holt Rice (1818–1878)

Rice, John Holt. *Discourse Delivered Before the General Assembly of the Presbyterian Church in the United States of America on the Opening of Their Session, in 1820.* Philadelphia: Thomas and William Bradford, 1820.

Samuel Stanhope Smith (1750–1819)

Smith, Samuel Stanhope. *An Essay on the Causes of the Variety of Complexion and Figure in the Human Species.* 2d ed., 1810. Reprint. Edited, with an introduction, by Winthrop D. Jordan. Cambridge: Belknap, 1965.

_____. *The Lectures, Corrected and Improved, Which Have Been Delivered for a Series of Years, in the College of New Jersey; on the Subjects of Moral and Political Philosophy.* Trenton, 1812.

Thomas Smyth (1808–1873)

Smyth, Thomas. *Complete Works of Rev. Thomas Smyth, D.D.* Edited by J. William Flinn. 10 vols. Columbia, SC: Bryan, 1908.

James Henley Thornwell (1812–1862)

Thornwell, James Henley. *The Collected Writings of James Henley Thornwell, D.D., LL.D.: Late Professor of Theology in the Theological Seminary at Columbia, South Carolina.* Edited by John B. Adger. Richmond, VA: Presbyterian Committee of Publication, 1871.

_____. *Discourses on Truth: Delivered in the Chapel of the South Carolina College.* New York: Carter, 1854.

_____. *Election and Reprobation.* Jackson, MS: Presbyterian Reformation Society, 1961.

_____. "Slavery and the Religious Instruction of the Colored Population." *Southern Presbyterian Review* 4 (1850): 126–28.

Robert Alexander Webb (1856–1919)

Webb, Robert Alexander. *Christian Salvation, Its Doctrine and Experience, by Robert Alexander Webb.* . . . Richmond, VA: Presbyterian Committee of Publication, 1921. Reprint. Harrisonburg, VA: Sprinkle, 1985.

_____. *The Reformed Doctrine of Adoption.* Grand Rapids: Eerdmans, 1947.

_____. *The Theology of Infant Salvation.* Richmond, VA: Presbyterian Committee of Publication, 1907. Reprint. Harrisonburg, VA: Sprinkle, 1981.

Collected Works

Memorial Volume of the Semi-Centennial of the Theological Seminary at Columbia, South Carolina. Columbia, SC: Presbyterian Publishing House, 1884.

Southern Presbyterian Pulpit: A Collection of Sermons by Ministers of the Southern Presbyterian Church. Richmond, VA: Presbyterian Committee of Publication, 1896.

2. Presbyterian Church in the United States: History and Theology

Adger, John B. "James Henley Thornwell, D.D., LL.D." *Memorial Volume of the Semi-Centennial of the Theological Seminary at Columbia, South Carolina.* Columbia, SC: Presbyterian Publishing House, 1884.

Adger, John B., and Girardeau, John L., eds. *The Collected Writings of James Henley Thornwell, D.D. LL.D.* 4 vols. Richmond, VA: Presbyterian Committee of Publication, 1871–1873.

Alexander, James W. *The Life of Archibald Alexander, C.C., First Professor in the Theological Seminary, at Princeton, New Jersey.* New York: Charles Scribner's Sons, 1854.

_____. "The Rev. Jas. Waddel, D.D." *Watchman of the South* 7 (March 28, 1844): 126, 134, 138.

Alley, Robert S. *The Reverend Mr. Samuel Davies: A Study in Religion and Politics, 1747–1759.* Ph.D. diss., Princeton University, 1962.

Baldwin, Alice M. "Sowers of Sedition: The Political Theories of Some of the New Light Presbyterian Clergy of Virginia and North Carolina." *William and Mary Quarterly* 3d series, 5 (January 1948): 52–76.

Baker, William M. *The Life and Labours of the Rev. Daniel Baker, D.D. Pastor and Evangelist.* Philadelphia: Martien, 1858.

Blackburn, George A., ed. *The Life Work of John L. Girardeau, D.D., LL.D., Late Professor of the Presbyterian Theological Seminary, Columbia, S.C.* Columbia, SC: State Company, 1916.

Bost, George H. *"Samuel Davies" Colonial Revivalist and Champion of Religious Toleration.* Ph.D. diss., University of Chicago, 1959.

Bozeman, Theodore Dwight. *A Nineteenth-Century Baconian Theology: James Henley Thornwell as Enlightenment Theologian.* Th.M. thesis, Union Theological Seminary in Virginia, 1970.

_____. "Science, Nature, and Society: A New Approach to James Henley Thornwell." *Journal of Presbyterian History* 50 (Fall 1972): 306–25.

Brandon, Betty Jane. *Alexander Jeffrey McKelway: Statesman of the New Order.* Ph.D. diss., University of North Carolina at Chapel Hill, 1969.

Burhans, David. *A Study and Evaluation of John Leland's Contribution to American Religious Liberty.* M.A. thesis, Southern Baptist Theological Seminary, Louisville, KY, 1966.

Clarke, Thomas Erskine. *Thomas Smith: Moderate of the Old South.* Th.D. thesis, Union Theological Seminary, 1970.

_____. *Wrestlin' Jacob: A Portrait of Religion in the Old South.* Atlanta: John Knox, 1979.

Deschamps, Margaret Burr. *The Presbyterian Church in the South Atlantic States, 1801–1861.* Atlanta: N.p., 1952.

Dewitt, John. "Princeton College Administrations in the Eighteenth Century." *Presbyterian and Reformed Review* 8 (1897): 387–417.

Farmer, James Oscar. *The Metaphysical Confederacy: James Henley Thornwell and the Synthesis of Southern Values.* Macon: Mercer University Press, 1986.

Fraser, A.M. *Dr. Thornwell as an Ecclesiologist, Centennial Addresses Delivered Before the Synod of South Carolina in the First Presbyterian Church, Columbia, October 23–24, 1912 Commemorating the Birth of the Rev. James Henley Thornwell.* Spartanburg, SC: Band and White, 1913.

Garber, Paul Leslie. "A Centennial Appraisal of James Henley Thornwell." *A Miscellany of American Christianity.* Edited by Stuart C. Henry. Durham: Duke University Press, 1963.

_____. *The Religious Thought of James Henley Thornwell.* Ph.D. diss., Duke University, 1939.

Garth, David Kinney. *The Influence of Scottish Common Sense Philosophy on the Theology of James Henley Thornwell and Robert Lewis Dabney.* Ph.D. diss., Union Theological Seminary, 1979.

Hartness, Robert Worley. *The Educational Work of Robert Jefferson Breckinridge.* Ph.D. diss., Yale University, 1936.

Hickey, Doralyn J. *Benjamin Morgan Palmer: Churchman of the Old South.* Ph.D. diss., Duke University, 1962.

Hill, William. *Autobiographical Sketches of Dr. William Hill, Together with His Account of the Revival of Religion in Prince Edward County and Biographical Sketches of the Life and Character of the Reverend Dr. Moses Hoge of Virginia.* Historical Transcript, no. 4. Richmond, VA: Union Theological Seminary in Virginia, 1968.

Hoge, John Blair. *The Life of Moses Hoge.* Historical Transcript, no. 2. Richmond, VA: Union Theological Seminary in Virginia, 1964.

Hollifield, E. Brooks. *The Gentlemen Theologians: American Theology in Southern Culture, 1795–1860.* Durham: Duke University Press, 1978.

Hood, Fred J. *Reformed America: The Middle and Southern States, 1783–1837.* University, AL: University of Alabama Press, 1980.

Hudson, William Emmit. *"The Least of These": The Beneficences of the Synod of Vir-

ginia. Edited by William E. Hudson. Richmond, VA: Presbyterian Committee of Publication, 1926.

Hurley, James F., and Eagan, Julia Goode. *The Prophet of Zion-Parnassus: Samuel Eusebius McCorkle*. Richmond, VA: Presbyterian Committee of Publication, 1934.

Johnson, Thomas Cary. "The Alleged Differences Between the Northern and Southern Presbyterian Churches." Southern Presbyterian, 1894.

_____. *A History of the Southern Presbyterian Church*. New York: Christian Literature, 1894.

_____. *The Life and Letters of Benjamin Morgan Palmer*. Richmond, VA: Presbyterian Committee of Publication, 1906.

_____. *The Life and Letters of Robert Lewis Dabney*. Richmond, VA: Presbyterian Committee of Publication, 1903.

Kay, Martha W. *The Literary Contributions of the Faculty of Union Theological Seminary, 1807–1941*. M.R.E. thesis, General Assembly's Training School for Lay Workers, 1942.

La Motte, Louis C. *Colored Light, the Story of the Influence of Columbia Theological Seminary, 1828–1936*. Richmond, VA: Presbyterian Committee of Publication, 1937.

Lacy, Benjamin Rice, Jr. *Revivals in the Midst of the Years*. Richmond, VA: John Knox, 1943. Reprint. Hopewell, VA: Royal, 1968.

Law, Thomas H. *Dr. Thornwell as a Teacher and a Preacher, Centennial Addresses Delivered Before the Synod of South Carolina in the First Presbyterian Church, Columbia, October 23–24, 1912, Commemorating the Birth of the Rev. James Henley Thornwell*. Spartanburg, SC: Band and White, 1913.

Lewis, Frank Bell. *Robert Lewis Dabney: Southern Presbyterian Apologist*. Ph.D. diss., Duke University, 1946.

Lingle, Walter L. *Presbyterians, Their History and Beliefs*. Richmond, VA: John Knox, 1945.

Liston, R. T. L. *The Neglected Educational Heritage of Southern Presbyterians: The Smyth Lectures*. Bristol, TN: Liston, n.d.

McAllister, J. Gray. "James Smith, A Memorial by the Faculty of Union Theological Seminary." *Union Seminary Record* LII (January 1941): 103–7.

Macartney, Clarence Edward Noble. "James Waddell: The Blind Preacher of Virginia." *Princeton Theological Review* 19 (October 1921): 621–29.

McElroy, Isaac Stuart. *The Louisville Presbyterian Theological Seminary*. Charlotte, NC: Presbyterian Standard Publishing, 1929.

McIlwaine, Richard. *Hampden-Sidney College: Its Relation and Services to the Presbyterian Church, and to the Cause of Education and Religion; a Discourse, Preached at the Second Presbyterian Church, (M.D. Hoge, D.D., Pastor,) Richmond, Virginia, February 5, 1888*. Richmond, VA: Whittet and Shepperson, 1888.

Macleod, James Lewis. *The Presbyterian Tradition in the South*. Oakwood, GA: Educational Enterprises, 1977.

Maddex, Jack P. "From Theocracy to Spirituality: The Southern Presbyterian Reversal on Church and State." *Journal of Presbyterian History* 54 (1976): 438–57.

Matthews, Donald. *Religion in the Old South.* Chicago: University of Chicago Press, 1974.

Maxwell, William. *A Memoir of the Rev. John H. Rice, D.D.* Philadelphia: Whetham; Richmond, VA: Smith, 1835.

_____. "Memoir of Rev. William Graham." *Virginia Evangelical and Literary Magazine* 4 (1821): 75–79, 150–52, 253–63.

Morrison, Alfred J. *The College of Hampden-Sidney: Calendar of Board Minutes, 1776–1876.* Richmond, VA: Hermitage, 1912.

Mulder, John M. "Joseph Ruggles Wilson: Southern Presbyterian Patriarch." *Journal of Presbyterian History* 52 (1974): 245–71.

Nall, J. H. "Benjamin Morgan Palmer, D.D., LL.D." *Presbyterian Quarterly* 16 (July 1902): 77–92.

Opie, John. "The Melancholy Career of 'Father' David Rice." *Journal of Presbyterian History* 47 (December 1969): 295–319.

Overy, David Henry. *Robert Lewis Dabney: Apostle of the Old South.* Ph.D. diss., University of Wisconsin, 1967.

Parker, Harold M. *Studies in Southern Presbyterian History.* Gunnison, CO: B and B Printers, 1979.

_____. *The United Synod of the South: The Southern New School Presbyterian Church.* Westport, CT: Greenwood, 1988.

Pilcher, George William. "Samuel Davies and the Instruction of Negroes in Virginia." *Virginia Magazine of History and Biography* 74 (July 1966): 293–300.

_____. *Samuel Davies: Apostle of Dissent in Colonial Virginia.* Knoxville, TN: University of Tennessee Press, 1971.

"Presbyterians of the Revolution." *Watchman of the South* 3 (February 20, 1840): 104.

Price, Philip Barbour. *The Life of the Reverend John Holt Rice, D.D.* Richmond, VA: Library of Union Theological Seminary in Virginia, 1963.

Rankin, W. Duncan. *James Henley Thornwell and the Westminster Confession of Faith.* Greenville, SC: A Press, 1986.

Reed, R. C. "A Historical Sketch." *Bulletin Columbia Theological Seminary* (Columbia, SC) 18 (October 1925): 5–15.

Robinson, William Childs. *Columbia Theological Seminary and the Southern Presbyterian Church; a Study in Church History, Presbyterian Policy, Missionary Enterprise, and Religious Thought.* Decatur: Lindsey, 1931.

Rogers, Tommy. "James Henry Thornwell." *Journal of Christian Reconstruction* 7 (1980): 175–205.

Smith, H. Shelton. "The Church and the Social Order in the Old South as Interpreted by James H. Thornwell." *Church History* (June 1938): 115–24.

_____. *Studies in Southern Presbyterian Theology.* Amsterdam: Drukkerij En Uitgeverij Jacob Van Campen, 1862. Reprint. Phillipsburg, NJ: Presbyterian and Reformed, 1987.

_____. *Reformed Evangelism*. Clinton, MS: Multi-Communication Ministries, 1975.

Smylie, James H. *A Cloud of Witnesses: A History of the Presbyterian Church in the United States*. Richmond, VA: CLC Press, 1965.

_____. "Presbyterians and the American Revolution." *Journal of Presbyterian History* 52 (1974): 299–488.

Squires, W. H. T. "John Thomson: Presbyterian Pioneer." *Union Seminary Review* 32 (1920–1921): 149–61.

Thompson, Ernest Trice. *Changing Emphasis in American Preaching*. Philadelphia: Westminster, 1943.

_____. *The Changing South and the Presbyterian Church in the United States*. Richmond, VA: John Knox, 1950.

_____. *Presbyterian Missions in the Southern United States*. Texarkana, AR: Presbyterian Committee of Publication, 1934.

_____. *Presbyterians in the South*. 3 vols. Richmond, VA: John Knox, 1963–1973.

_____. *The Spirituality of the Church: A Distinctive Doctrine of the Presbyterian Church in the United States*. Richmond, VA: John Knox, 1961.

Thompson, Robert Ellis. *A History of the Presbyterian Churches in the United States*. New York: Christian Literature, 1895.

Thomson, C.T. "Robert Lewis Dabnew—The Conservative." *Union Seminary Review* 35 (January 1924): 155–70.

Tyler, James Hoge. *The Family of Hoge: A Genealogy*. Greensboro, NC: Hoge, 1927.

Waddel, John N. *Memorials of Academic Life Being an Historical Sketch of the Waddel Family, Identified Through Three Generations with the History of the Higher Education in the South and Southwest*. Richmond, VA: Presbyterian Committee of Publication, 1891.

Waddel, Joseph A. *Annals of Augusta County, Virginia: From 1726–1871*. 2d ed. Bridgewater, VA: Carrier, 1902.

_____. *The Waddells*. Pamphlet. Richmond, VA: Union Theological Seminary in Virginia, 1901.

Webster, Richard. *A History of the Presbyterian Church in America from Its Origin Until the Year 1760, with Biographical Sketches of Its Early Ministers . . . with a Memoir of the Author, by the Rev. C. Van Rensselaer . . . and an Historical Introduction by the Rev. William Blackwood*. Philadelphia: Wilson, 1857.

Wells, John Miller. *Southern Presbyterian Worthies*. Richmond, VA: Presbyterian Committee of Publication, 1936.

Whaling, Thornton. *Dr. Thornwell as a Theologian, Memorial Addresses Delivered before the General Assembly of 1886 on the Occasion of the Quarter-Centennial of the Organization of the Southern Assembly in 1861*. Presbyterian Committee of Publication, 1886.

White, Henry Alexander. *Southern Presbyterian Leaders, by Henry Alexander White . . . with Portrait Illustrations*. New York: Neale, 1911.

Whitlock, Luder G., Jr. "Elders and Ecclesiology in the Thought of James Henley Thornwell." *Westminster Theological Journal* 37 (1974): 44–56.

3. Histories of the Presbyterian Church in the Southern States

Batchelor, Alexander Ramsay. *Jacob's Ladder: Negro Work of the Presbyterian Church in the United States.* Atlanta: Presbyterian Church in the United States, 1953.

Beard, Delamo L. *Origin and Early History of Presbyterianism in Virginia.* Ph.D. diss., University of Edinburgh, Scotland, 1932.

Brown, Katharine Lowe. *The Role of Presbyterian Dissent in Colonial and Revolutionary Virginia, 1740–1785.* Ph.D. diss., The Johns Hopkins University, 1969.

Bullock, James R. *Heritage and Hope: A Story of Presbyterians in Florida.* Edited by Jerrold Lee Brooks. Orlando: Synod of Florida Presbyterian Church in the United States of America, 1987.

Davidson, Robert. *History of the Presbyterian Church in the State of Kentucky: With a Preliminary Sketch of the Churches in the Valley of Virginia.* New York: Carter; Lexington, KY: Marshall, 1847.

Davis, Robert Pickens. *Maryland Presbyterian History.* Th.D. diss., Union Theological Seminary in Virginia, 1958.

_____. *Virginia Presbyterians in American Life: Hanover Presbytery (1755–1980).* Edited by Patricia Aldridge. Richmond, VA: Hanover Presbytery, 1982.

Ellis, Dorsey Daniel. *Look unto the Rock: A History of the Presbyterian Church, U.S., in West Virginia, 1719–1974.* Parsons, WV: McClain, 1982.

Foote, William Henry. *Sketches of North Carolina, Historical and Biographical.* 3d ed. Synod of North Carolina, Presbyterian Church in the United States, 1965.

_____. *Sketches of Virginia Historical and Biographical.* Philadelphia: Martien, 1850.

Garth, John Goodall. *Sixty Years of Home Missions in the Presbyterian Synod of North Carolina.* Charlotte? 1948?

"History of the Presbytery of Hanover." *Evangelical and Literary Magazine* 11 (1828): 531–38, 657–58.

Hoge, Moses D. *Memorial Discourse on the Planting of Presbyterianism in Kentucky One Hundred Years Ago.* Louisville, KY: Courier-Journal, n.d.

Johnson, Thomas Cary. *Virginia Presbyterianism and Religious Liberty in Colonial and Revolutionary Times.* Richmond, VA: Presbyterian Committee of Publication, 1907.

The King's Business in the Synod of Alabama. Birmingham, AL: Birmingham Publishing, n.d.

Kirk, Cooper. *A History of the Southern Presbyterian Church in Florida 1821–1891.* Ph.D. diss., Florida State University, 1966.

Lodge, Martin Ellsworth. *The Great Awakening in the Middle Colonies.* Ph.D. diss., Berkeley, 1964.

Lowrey, Priscilla M. *The Introduction of Presbyterianism into Mississippi: From the*

Entrance of Early Presbyterian Settlers to the Formation of the Synod of Mississippi in 1835. M.A. thesis, Trinity Evangelical Divinity School, 1974.

McGeachy, Neill Roderick. *Confronted by Challenge: A History of the Presbytery of Concord, 1795–1973, Including the Former Presbytery of King's Mountain and Presbytery of Winston-Salem*. Delmar, 1955.

McIlwaine, Richard. *Hampden-Sidney College: Its Relation and Services to the Presbyterian Church, and to the Cause of Education and Religion; a Discourse, Preached at the Second Presbyterian Church, (M.D. Hoge, D.D., Pastor,) Richmond, Virginia, February 5, 1888*. Richmond, VA: Whittet and Shepperson, 1888.

McIlwain, William E. *The Early Planting of Presbyterianism in West Florida*. Pensacola, FL: McIlwain, 1926.

Mahler, Henry Richard, Jr. *The Contribution of Liberty Hall and Washington College to Presbyterianism in Virginia, 1749–1870*. Th.D. diss., Union Theological Seminary in Virginia, 1952.

Marshall, James Williams. *Presbyterian Churches in Alabama 1811–1936: Part I, Sketches of Churches, Outposts, and Preaching Points in the Synod of Alabama Abbeville, Butler, and Megargel*. Edited by Kenneth J. Foreman, Jr. Foreword by William H. C. Frend. Montreat, NC: Cooling Spring, 1985.

Parker, Harold M. *Bibliography of Published Articles on American Presbyterianism, 1901–1980*. Westport, CT: Greenwood, 1985.

_____. *Studies in Southern Presbyterian History*. Gunnison, CO: B and B Printers, 1979.

_____. *The Synod of Kentucky: From Old School Assembly to the Southern Church*. 1975?

Presbyterian Church in the U.S. Executive Committee of Foreign Missions. *Foundations of World Order: The Foreign Service of the Presbyterian Church, U.S.* Richmond, VA: John Knox, 1941.

Presbyterian Church in the US, Synod of Georgia. Executive Committee of Education. *The Task of the Presbyterian Church in Georgia*. Edited by the Synod's Executive Committee of Education. Executive Committee of Education, 1926?

Rice, David. *An Outline of the History of the Church in the State of Kentucky, During a Period of Forty Years: Containing the Memoirs of Rev. David Rice, and Sketches of the Origin and Present State of Particular Churches, and of the Lives and Labours of a Number of Men Who Were Eminent and Useful in Their Day*. Arranged by Robert H. Bishop. Lexington, KY: Skillman, 1824.

Rumple, Jethro. *The History of Presbyterianism in North Carolina*. Historical Transcript, no. 3. Richmond, VA: Union Theological Seminary in Virginia, 1966.

Stacy, James. *A History of the Presbyterian Church in Georgia*. Completed and edited by C. I. Stacy. Atlanta: Westminster, 1912.

Tenney, Levi. *History of the Presbytery of Central Texas*. Austin: Von Boeckmann, 1895.

Terman, William Jennings, Jr. *The American Revolution and the Baptist and Presbyterian Clergy of Virginia: A Study of Dissenter Opinion and Action*. Ph.D. diss., Michigan State University, 1974.

Wilson, Howard McKnight. "The Story of Synod Presbyterians." *Yesterday and Tomorrow in the Synod of Virginia*. Edited by Henry M. Brimm and William M.E.

Rachal. Richmond, VA: Synod of Virginia, Presbyterian Church in the United States, 1962.

Wright, Louis B. "Pious Reading in Colonial Virginia." *Journal of Southern History* 6 (1940): 383–92.

4. Southern Presbyterians and Slavery

Alvis, Joel Lawrence, Jr. *"The Bounds of Their Habitations": The Southern Presbyterian Church, Racial Ideology and the Civil Rights Movement, 1946–1972.* Ph.D. diss., Auburn University, 1985.

Bailey, Kenneth K. "Protestantism and Afro-Americans in the Old South: Another Look." *Journal of Southern History* 41 (November 1975): 451–72.

_____. *Southern White Protestantism in the Twentieth Century.* New York: Evanston, 1964.

Berlin, Ira. *Slaves Without Masters: The Free Negro in the Antebellum South.* New York, 1976.

Blassingame, John. *The Slave Community: Plantation Life in the Antebellum South.* New York, 1979.

Christie, John W., and Dumont, Dwight L., eds. *George Bourne and The Book and Slavery Irreconcilable.* Philadelphia, 1969.

Daniel, W. Harrison. "Southern Protestantism and the Negro, 1860–1865." In *Time on the Cross: The Economics of American Negro Slavery.* Edited by Robert W. Fogel and Stanley L. Engerman. Boston and Toronto, 1974.

Eaton, Clement. *The Growth of Southern Civilization, 1790–1860.* New York, 1961.

Green, John C. "The American Debate on the Negro's Place in Nature, 1780–1815." *Journal of the History of Ideas* 15 (June 1954): 384–96.

Jenkins, William Sumner. *Pro-Slavery Thought in the Old South.* Chapel Hill, NC: University of North Carolina Press, 1935.

Jordan, Winthrop D. *White Over Black: American Attitudes Toward the Negro, 1550–1812.* Baltimore, 1969.

Kull, Irving Stoddard. "Presbyterian Attitudes Toward Slavery." *Church History* 7 (1938): 101–24.

MacLeod, Duncan J. *Slavery, Race and the American Revolution.* London: Cambridge University Press, 1974.

Martin, Asa Earl. *The Anti-Slavery Movement in Kentucky Prior to 1850.* Louisville: Standard, 1918.

Murray, Andrew E. *Presbyterians and the Negro—A History.* Philadelphia, 1966.

Norton, L. Wesley. *The Religious Press and the Compromise of 1850: A Study of the Relationship of the Methodist, Baptist, and Presbyterian Press to the Slavery Controversy.* Ph.D. diss., University of Illinois, 1959.

Sherer, Lester B. *Slavery and the Churches in Early America 1619–1819.* Grand Rapids, 1975.

Smith, H. Shelton. *In His Image, But . . . : Racism in Southern Religion, 1780–1910.* Durham, 1972.

Stampp, Kenneth. *The Peculiar Institution: Slavery in the Ante-Bellum South.* New York: Knopf, 1956.

Thompson, Ernest Trice. "Black Presbyterians, Education and Evangelism After the Civil War." *Journal of Presbyterian History* 51 (Summer 1973): 174–98.

Thompson, J. Earl. "Slavery and Presbyterianism in the Revolutionary Era." In *The American Presbyterian Reformed Historical Sites Registry*, no. 41.

Wade, Richard C. *Slavery in the Cities: The South 1820–1860.* New York: Oxford University Press, 1968.

5. General Histories of the Presbyterian Church

Baird, Samuel J. *Assembly's Digest, A Collection of the Acts, Deliverances, and Testimonies of the Supreme Judicatory of the Presbyterian Church from Its Origin in America to the Present Time.* Philadelphia, 1855.

Cheeseman, Lewis. *Differences Between Old and New School Presbyterians.* Rochester: Darrow, 1848.

Crocker, Zebulon. *The Catastrophe of the Presbyterian Church in 1837.* New Haven: Noyes, 1837.

Gillette, E. H. *History of the Presbyterian Church in the United States.* Rev. ed. Vol 1. Philadelphia: Presbyterian Board of Publication, 1873.

Hays, George P. *Presbyterians: A Popular Narrative of Their Origin, Progress, Doctrines, and Achievements.* New York: Hill, 1892.

Hodge, Charles. *The Constitutional History of the Presbyterian Church in the United States of America.* Philadelphia: Martien, 1839.

McGill, Alexander T., Hopkins, Samuel M., and Wilson, Samuel J. *A Short History of American Presbyterianism.* Philadelphia: Presbyterian Board of Publication and Sabbath-School Work, 1903.

Smith, Egbert Watson. *The Creed of Presbyterians.* New York: Baker and Taylor, 1901.

Smith, Elwyn Allen. *The Presbyterian Ministry in American Culture: A Study in Changing Concepts, 1700–1900.* Philadelphia: Presbyterian Historical Society, 1962.

Smith, H. Shelton, Handy, Robert T., and Loetscher, Lefferts A. *American Christianity: An Historical Interpretation with Representative Documents.* Vol. 1. New York: Charles Scribner's Sons, 1960.

Sweet, William Warren. *Religion on the American Frontier,* Vol. II, *The Presbyterians 1783–1840, A Collection of Source Materials.* New York: Holt, 1936.

Thompson, Robert Ellis. *A History of the Presbyterian Churches in the United States.* Vol. 6 of *The American Church History Series.* New York: Christian Literature, 1895.

Trinterud, Leonard J. *The Forming of an American Tradition: A Re-examination of Colonial Presbyterianism.* Philadelphia: Westminster, 1949.

Vander Veld, L. G. *The Presbyterian Churches and the Federal Union.* Cambridge: Harvard University Press, 1932.

Webster, Richard. *A History of the Presbyterian Church in America, from Its Origin until the Year 1760, with Biographical Sketches of Its Early Ministers.* Philadelphia: Wilson, 1857.

Wood, James. *Old and New Theology: or, The Doctrinal Differences Which Have Agitated and Divided the Presbyterian Church.* Philadelphia: Presbyterian Board of Publication, 1855.

Zenos, Andrew. C. *Presbyterianism in America: Past, Present and Perspective.* New York: Thomas Nelson and Sons, 1937.

6. Reference Resources

Albaugh, Gaylord P. "American Presbyterian Periodicals and Newspapers, 1752–1830." *Journal of Presbyterian History* 31: 3, 4; 42: 1, 2.

Blackburn, John C. *A Southern Presbyterian Bibliography.* Manuscript. Reformed Theological Seminary Archives.

Beecher, Willis J., comp. *Index of Presbyterian Ministers Containing the Names of All the Ministers of the Presbyterian Church in the United States of America, 1706–1881.* Philadelphia: Presbyterian Board of Publication, 1883.

Bowden, Henry Warner. *Dictionary of American Religious Biography.* Westport, CT: Greenwood, 1977.

Hill, Samuel S. *Encyclopedia of Religion in the South.* Macon: Mercer University Press, 1984.

Lippy, Charles H. *Bibliography of Religion in the South.* Macon: Mercer University Press, 1985.

Morrison, Alfred J. *College of Hampden-Sidney: Dictionary of Biography, 1776–1825.* Hampden-Sidney College, 1920.

Nevin, Alfred, ed. *Encyclopedia of the Presbyterian Church in the United States of America.* Philadelphia: Presbyterian Encyclopedia Publishing, 1884.

Parker, Harold M., Jr. *Bibliography of Published Articles on American Presbyterianism, 1901–1980.* Westport, CT: Greenwood, n.d.

Prince, Harold B., ed. *A Presbyterian Bibliography.* ATLA Bibliography, no. 8. Metuchen, NJ: Scarecrow, 1983.

Scott, E.C. *Ministerial Directory of the Presbyterian Church, U.S. 1861–1941.* Austin: Von Boeckmann-Jones, 1942.

Shulman, Albert M. *The Religious Heritage of America.* New York: Barnes and Company, 1981.

Spence, Thomas Hugh. *The Historical Foundation and Its Treasures.* Montreat, NC: Historical Foundation Publications, 1960.

Sprague, William B. *Annals of the American Pulpit.* Vols. 3 and 4, *The Presbyterians 1783–1840, A Collection of Source Materials.* New York: Holt, 1936.

INDEX

Graham, William, 16, 21, 192, 193
Great Awakening, 4, 41
Great Revival, 194–95
Green, Ashbel, 22, 24, 67
Green, William Henry, 17
Greene, William Brenton, Jr., 173
Groen van Prinsterer Society, 158, 163
Grotius, 57

Hamilton, William, 221, 243
Hampden-Sydney College, 193, 213
Harnack, Adolf, 57, 75
Hart, Hendrik, 163, 166, 167
Harvard Divinity School, 29
Heidelberg Catechism, 116–17
Henry, Carl F. H., 9, 10
Henry, Robert, 243
Hermann, Wilhelm, 96
Heyns, William, 143
Higher Criticism, 20, 96
History of Christian Doctrines (Berkhof), 148
"History and Faith" (Machen), 96, 98–99
history-of-religion school, 77–78
Hodge, A. A., 17, 20, 22, 65, 71, 211
Hodge, Caspar Wistar, 95
Hodge, Charles, 16, 18, 20, 21–22, 23–24, 25, 31, 39–58, 65, 66, 75, 173, 200, 211, 224, 226, 239
Hoeksema, Herman, 128, 144
Hoge, Moses, 192, 193
Holmes, Arthur, 163
Hume, David, 21, 81, 90n
Hutcheson, Francis, 21

In the Twilight of Western Thought (Dooyeweerd), 157
"Inspiration" (Warfield), 19, 20
Institute for Christian Studies (ICS), 157–59, 164–68. *See also* Association for the Advancement of Christian Scholarship; Association for Reformed Scientific Studies
International Council on Biblical Inerrancy, 30
Inter-Varsity Christian Fellowship, 9
InterVarsity Press, 9
Introduction to the New Testament (Berkhof), 141

Janssen, Roelof, 127–28, 138, 143–44, 151n
Jülicher, Adolf, 96

Kant, Immanuel, 83, 160
Kingdom of God, The (Berkhof), 149
Kuiper, R. B., 152n
Kuyper, Abraham, 9, 84, 120–21, 123, 126–27, 136–37, 160, 161, 173, 174
Kuyperianism, 9–10

Lathrop, Joseph, 41–42
Legacy of Herman Dooyeweerd, The, 166
Liberty Hall Academy, 192, 193
Life Under the Law in a Pure Theocracy (Berkhof), 139
Lindsley, Philip, 58–59n
Livingston, John H., 117
Locke, John, 21
Lonergan, Bernard, 160
Luther, Martin, 72

Macartney, Clarence, 98
Machen, J. Gresham, 8, 17, 82, 95–110, 122, 123, 173, 194
McCosh, James, 22
McGiffert, A. C., 103
McGready, James, 194–95
McIntire, Carl, 9, 98
Mackintosh, William, 78
Makemie, Francis, 190
Maranatha (Bultema), 141–43
Maritain, Jacques, 160, 163
Meeter, H. Henry, 138
Mencken, H. L., 104
Metcalf, Robert, 205
Miller, Samuel, 24, 43
Moral Majority, 10
Morse, Jedediah, 43
Murray, John, 204, 223, 224, 225

Nash, Ronald, 163
Neo-Calvinism, 120–23, 125–28, 136–37
Nevin, J. W., 28
New Critique of Theoretical Thought, A (Dooyeweerd), 157, 158, 159
"new evangelicalism," 9
New Haven Theology, 18
"New Measures," 5, 49
"New Scheme of Divinity," 45

Sabatier, Auguste, 57
Sampson, Francis R., 214
Sandeen, Ernest, 30
Schaeffer, Francis, 9, 10
Schliermacher, Friedrich, 75, 83
Seceder network, 118
Second Coming of Christ, The (Berkhof), 149
Second Great Awakening, 48–49
Seeberg, Reinhold, 78–79
Seerveld, Calvin, 164, 166, 167
*Sensualistic Philosophy of the Nineteenth
    Century* (Dabney), 220, 225, 226, 227
Shedd, W. G. T., 211
Smith, James Porter, 194
Smith, John Blair, 193
Smith, Josiah, 191
Smythe, Thomas, 199
social gospel, 8, 145
Sorokin, Pitrikim, 160
*Southern Presbyterian Journal. See
    Presbyterian Journal*
"sphere sovereignty," 205
"Spiritual Culture in the Seminary"
    (Warfield), 69–71
Stevenson, J. Ross, 97
Stob, George, 128
Stone, Barton, 195–96
Strong, Josiah, 140
Subjects and Outlines (Berkhof), 137
Stuart, Dugald, 243
Stuart, Moses, 42, 53
Synod of Utrecht, 126
Systematic Theology (Berkhof). *See Reformed
    Dogmatics*
Systematic Theology (Dabney), 211, 215, 222,
    223, 225, 227
Systematic Theology (C. Hodge), 18, 20, 22,
    25, 39–40

Taylor, Nathaniel W., 18, 23, 27, 40, 43, 44,
    45–48, 50, 56–57
Ten Hoor, Foppe, 115–16, 120, 138, 143, 144
Textual Aid to Systematic Theology (Berkhof),
    148
theonomist movement, 10
Theonomy in Christian Ethics (Bahnsen), 204
Thornwell, James H., 30, 198–99, 226,
    237–45
Tillich, Paul, 160, 163

Torch and Trumpet, 128, 158
Towards a Reformed Theology (Young), 163
Toynbee, Arnold, 160
*Transcendental Problems of Philosophic
    Thought* (Dooyeweerd), 158
Troeltsch, Ernst, 80
Tübingen School, 75
Turretin, Francis, 19, 39, 193, 227

Understanding Our World (Hart), 166
Unitarianism, 42–44
United States Moral and Philosophical
    Society, 42

Van Til, Cornelius, 30, 98, 99, 123, 128, 158,
    173–85, 203, 204, 220
Vicarious Atonement through Christ, The
    (Berkhof), 148
Virgin Birth of Christ, The (Machen), 100
Voetius, Gijsbert, 118
Volbeda, Samuel, 143
Vollenhoven, D. H. T., 158
Vos, Geerhardus, 122, 137, 138, 223

Ware, Henry, 42, 43
Warfield, Benjamin B., 16–17, 18, 19–20, 22,
    65–87, 123, 138, 173, 190, 223
Way of Life (C. Hodge), 25
Webb, R. A., 201
Webster, Daniel, 237
Weiss, Johannes, 79–80, 96
Westminster Presbyterian Church (Tyler,
    Texas), 204
Westminster Theological Seminary, 8, 9, 30,
    90n, 97, 202, 203–4
What Is Faith? (Machen), 98, 99, 100, 101,
    102, 103
Whitefield, George, 191
Witherspoon, John, 16, 21, 81
Woods, Leonard, 42
Worcester, Noah, 43

Young, William S., 158, 163

Zylstra, Bernard, 163

287

David F. Wells is Andrew Mutch Distinguished Professor of Historical and Systematic Theology at Gordon-Conwell Theological Seminary. He has written and edited numerous books including *No Place for Truth* and *God in the Wasteland*.